THE COVENANT KITCHEN

For Carmel,

Eat, drink ....be merry!

Best wishes,

JH & Jodie

THE  Covenant KITCHEN

Food and Wine for the
New Jewish Table

JEFF and JODIE MORGAN

Photographs by Ed Anderson

SCHOCKEN   OUPRESS

All rights reserved. Published in the United States by Schocken Books,
a division of Random House LLC, New York, and distributed in Canada by
Random House of Canada Limited, Toronto, Penguin Random House companies.

Schocken Books and colophon are registered trademarks of Random House LLC.

Library of Congress Cataloging-in-Publication Data
Morgan, Jeff (Winemaker), author.
The covenant kitchen : food and wine for the new Jewish table / Jeff and Jodie Morgan.
pages cm   Includes index.
ISBN 978-0-8052-4325-3 (hardcover).   ISBN 978-0-8052-4326-0 (eBook)
1. Jewish cooking.   2. Food and wine pairing.   1. Morgan, Jodie, author.   11. Title.
TX724.M665   2015   641.5'676—dc23 2014025769

www.schocken.com

Cover photography by Ed Anderson
Cover design by Janet Hansen

Printed in the United States of America
First Edition
2   4   6   8   9   7   5   3   1

*This book is dedicated to our extended Jewish family around the globe—
from Israel, London, Paris, Toronto, and New York to Chicago,
Los Angeles, Berkeley, San Francisco, and the California wine country.
Their love and support has helped us rediscover our rich heritage
and share it through food and wine.*

Contents

Preface

I grew up in a Jewish home in Kansas, where the only kosher wines we knew were very sweet ones made from Concord grapes. But times have changed, and there are a growing number of fine kosher wines made from European grape varieties cultivated in many of the world's finest wine regions.

In 2002, I challenged my friend and colleague Jeff Morgan to make a kosher wine from the Napa Valley that would be as good as the finest non-kosher wines made from the region. Although we are both Jewish, neither Jeff nor I had grown up in a religious community. But for various reasons, we felt compelled to raise the bar for kosher wine.

That decision changed our lives in more ways than we thought it would. I don't have a completely clear understanding of why, in Jewish tradition, wine is a holy beverage, but there's no doubt that wine has the power to inspire. More specifically, kosher wine has inspired both Jeff and me to rediscover and explore our Jewish heritage. And because our peripatetic lives as vintners revolve around food and wine, we have been able to share our own Jewish California wine-country lifestyle with the Jewish community worldwide.

This book offers readers a blueprint for exploring a cornucopia of food and wine while maintaining Jewish tradition and identity. Whatever your background, you will enjoy the recipes featured here. And those who do keep kosher can rest assured that all the recipes are appropriate for a kosher kitchen.

I've known Jeff and Jodie Morgan for fifteen years. On a daily basis, they serve up a wonderfully homegrown sense of hospitality and good taste in their dining room. It's a pleasure to follow their lifestyle perspective and personal Jewish journey through these pages. *The Covenant Kitchen* will enhance mealtime for anyone with a sense of culinary adventure and a taste for tradition.

—LESLIE RUDD
Co-proprietor, Covenant Winery
Vintner, Napa Valley

Foreword

One of my fondest and most vivid childhood memories is of watching my mother lovingly prepare food for our family. Although I certainly enjoyed the result, it was my awareness of her efforts in the preparation that made my mother's food so special. This love and affection in the Jewish home and its role in transmitting traditions from one generation to the next have nurtured the Jewish experience throughout the centuries.

The special quality of the Jewish home is, in fact, highlighted by our Sages, for whom it resonated with sanctity. As far back as the tent of our matriarch, Sarah, our tradition expresses the idea of the home's sanctity. Sarah's tent, the Midrash tells us, was endowed with three wondrous qualities: The Shabbat candles miraculously remained lit from one Shabbat to the next; the challah she prepared expanded far out of proportion to the ingredients she used to make it; and a cloud of purity continuously hovered above the tent in which she lived with Abraham. The wondrous qualities of Sarah's home mirrored the sanctity of the Tabernacle: The flames of the menorah remained lit continuously; the *lechem hapanim*—loaves of show bread used in the Tabernacle service—stayed warm long after they would have been expected to cool; and the Divine Presence itself, expressed in the form of a protective cloud, constantly rested above.

The distinguishing features of Sarah's home reflected the fact that the Jewish home—and particularly the Jewish kitchen—is anything but mundane. On the contrary, when we bake challah, prepare meals, or say a blessing over wine, we are bringing forth a spiritual component latent in our physical world; and in the process we are sanctifying it.

Food has always brought Jewish communities and families together. From our unique religious legacy many culinary customs and cultural delicacies have emerged, creating a veritable smorgasbord of Jewish experiences. The traditional gastronomic delights associated with Shabbat and each of the holidays have served in their own way to bind the Jewish community together and to preserve our heritage. The traditions of Ashkenazic and Sephardic Jewry yield a rich cuisine, which is itself a repository of Jewish culture.

Jeff and Jodie Morgan are intuitively aware of Judaism's remarkable capacity to bring out the spiritual component in food and thereby imbue the physical world with a sense of sanctity. *The Covenant Kitchen* is a labor of love that, in a pleasant and engaging way, reflects this profound understanding.

The book is more than that, however. The Morgans, so experienced and knowledgeable in their fields, have been on a path of discovery of the laws and traditions of kosher, or *kashrut*. Integrating this information into a contemporary cookbook is not an easy task, and *The Covenant Kitchen* is a masterful expression of how one can create modern recipes without sacrificing the standards of a kosher home. *The Covenant Kitchen* is a perfect partnership for OU Press, the publishing division of the Union of Orthodox Jewish Congregations of America, more commonly known as the OU. The OU, founded in 1898, has been the leader in expanding *kashrut* supervision worldwide, and we are proud to join with the Morgans and with Schocken Books in presenting this wonderful synthesis of culinary art and Jewish tradition.

Both the Morgans and the OU are on a journey. Jeff and Jodie have embarked, in a very personal way, on a journey in search of spirituality and meaning. The OU, as well, is on a spiritual quest. Its mission is to bring the message of Judaism and its rich heritage to Jews throughout the world. The light of *kashrut* can be a beacon illuminating this journey. *Kashrut* brings us back to our roots and tradition. *Kashrut* brings us back to Sarah's tent.

—RABBI MENACHEM GENACK
Chief Executive Officer
OU Kosher

A Jewish Culinary Journey

We are in the midst of a renaissance in Jewish dining. The signs are everywhere: a blossoming of upscale kosher restaurants and artisanal delis; the coming of age of the modern Jewish home kitchen, inspired by a new focus on international Jewish cuisines; and the availability of seriously good kosher wines.

The Covenant Kitchen offers a contemporary approach to eating and drinking in the Jewish tradition. The book illustrates our life here in Northern California, where—after growing up in assimilated, secular families—we have rediscovered our Jewish heritage while making kosher wines. It has been a wonderful awakening.

Before moving to California two decades ago, we had lived mostly in New York and France. Jeff, who spent six years as a young musician in Nice and Monte Carlo, would say that his culinary foundation springs from those early days. Indeed, southern France is where Jeff began his ongoing love affair with food and wine, which is now shared by Jodie.

In California, we've been introduced to Asian and Mexican foods, which have also become part of our repertoire. And as we've connected more strongly with our Jewish roots, we've been spending time in Israel, where we have been introduced to the fruits, vegetables, and spices of the ubiquitous *shouk*. These Middle Eastern flavors have found a place at our table as well.

Every recipe in this book is designed with a kosher kitchen in mind (see page 15). Next to each recipe title, you'll see indicated that the dish is either "meat," "dairy," or "pareve" (which means that it contains neither meat nor dairy products). But you don't have to keep kosher to make and enjoy the dishes featured here. They can be prepared by anyone in any kitchen. Most of the ingredients are commonly found in well-provisioned grocery stores, and the great majority of the recipes are straightforward and easy to prepare.

The Mediterranean Diet

With some modifications to accommodate the laws of *kashrut,* the Jews of antiquity adhered to a diet similar to that enjoyed by most Mediterranean people at the time. It was based on olives and olive oil, fresh vegetables, fruit, grains, fish, small quantities of meat and dairy products, and wine.

In recent years, this traditional diet has been proved repeatedly by modern-day science to be a particularly healthy way to eat. In 2013, *The New York Times,* reporting on a Spanish study written up in the *New England Journal of Medicine,* proclaimed "Mediterranean Diet Shown to Halt Heart Disease." The study recommended seven glasses of wine per week (i.e., a glass per day) for most adults. We are neither scientists nor doctors, but it has always seemed to us that a diet based on fresh, seasonal fruit and vegetables, grains, and fish, with moderate amounts of meat and dairy, and accompanied by wine in moderation, is both a sensible and delicious way to maintain a healthy lifestyle. In our home, most of our meals are variations on the Mediterranean diet.

We've organized the book to reflect the rhythm of a typical meal. We begin with an appetizer, salad, or soup, followed by a main course, and then dessert. Special occasions involve an increased number of dishes, and you will find some specific suggestions for Jewish holidays, as well as ideas for holiday menus. Sidebars highlight kitchen or entertaining techniques and information on key ingredients.

By and large, however, the recipes and advice offered here are meant for everyday living. We believe that eating and drinking well on a daily basis not only improves our quality of life but also makes each day special.

It's no accident that we've included the word *wine* in the book's title. Wine is fundamentally connected to Jewish spiritual and culinary traditions. But it is also part of our daily diet at home, just as we believe it was for our ancestors in ancient Israel.

Our goal is to nourish our bodies with fresh, good-tasting, healthful ingredients. And in the pages that follow, we look forward to sharing our story and lifestyle with you.

The Covenant Story

In 2002, a group of loosely affiliated Jewish winemakers in Napa Valley invited Eli Ben Zaken, an Israeli winemaker who was visiting San Francisco, to come pour his well-respected Domaine du Castel red wine. The event occurred at Rudd Oakville Estate, a prestigious vineyard owned by Leslie Rudd. Among those present was Leslie's friend *Covenant Kitchen* co-author Jeff Morgan.

As Jeff tells it: At the time, I was making a non-kosher rosé, and neither Leslie nor I was even remotely observant. After tasting the wine from Israel, Leslie turned to me and said, "That wine tasted a lot better than any kosher wine I grew up drinking at Passover."

Then, in what can only be called a "chutzpa moment," I said to Leslie, "We can make the greatest kosher wine in five thousand years if you let me have ten tons of Rudd Vineyard Cabernet grapes."

Leslie was skeptical. "I don't think so," he replied. "What if you screw it up? We'll have made the worst kosher wine in five thousand years, and it will have come from my vineyard!" But then he thought about it for a bit and said, "Why don't you find another vineyard to experiment with, and I'll partner with you on this project."

A Divine Plan?

My chutzpa moment would never have happened had I not been introduced to modern-day kosher wine a decade earlier. In 1992 I had left a job at a Long Island winery to see if I could establish a new career as a wine writer. For my first freelance assignment, *Wine Spectator* asked me to write a piece on kosher wine for Passover.

"Kosher wine?" I exclaimed. "I don't know anything about kosher wine or kosher food. Yes, I'm Jewish, but I wasn't even bar mitzvahed!"

It soon became apparent that this might be my only chance to write for *Wine Spectator,* so I accepted the job. A crash course in producing kosher wine was provided by the Herzog family, whose eponymous kosher winery is located in Southern California. I then sampled a selection of kosher wines—some of which were quite good—and ate at a few high-end kosher restaurants in New York City. Clearly there was more to kosher wine and fine dining than I had suspected. And that's what I wrote.

Wine Spectator liked the article and hired me to write about a variety of topics. In 1995, the magazine named me West Coast editor, and moved my family and me from New York to San Francisco. I wrote for *Wine Spectator* for eight years, during which time I wrote many articles about kosher wine, usually timed to coincide with Passover. In the process, I became close to the Herzog family and to other kosher winemakers. They made their kosher wine essentially the same way that non-kosher wine was made—except for the requirement that the entire process be in Sabbath-observant hands. (See "Kosher Wine: The Basics," page 22.)

The Dream Becomes Reality

When I first suggested to Leslie that we make kosher wine, I knew that to obtain rabbinical certification we would need a Jewish, Sabbath-observant cellar crew to help make the wine. I thought about the Herzog family and their kosher winery in Southern California, not far from Los Angeles. Would the Herzogs allow me, a potential competitor, to make wine at Herzog Wine Cellars? It was a delicate situation. I decided to fly to New York for a meeting with Nathan Herzog, executive vice president of Herzog's parent company, Royal Wine Corporation, over dinner at a well-known kosher restaurant.

By the time we tucked into our entrees, I had summoned the courage to tell Nathan about our wine project and to ask for his help. "Nathan," I said earnestly, "I want to make the greatest kosher wine in five thousand years." Then, overwhelmed by emotion, I burst into tears. Obviously, there was something else going on inside me—something more profound than a simple plan to make a new wine. But it wasn't until that moment that I realized I was on a quest for something that was about to change my life.

Nathan was touched by my tears and offered to share the winemaking team at the Herzog winery. I then struck a deal with the historic Larkmead Vineyard in Napa Valley to source Cabernet Sauvignon grapes. In the fall of 2003, I transported the first harvest of Napa Valley grapes down to Herzog's Southern California winery in a refrigerated truck. With the help of the Herzog winemaking crew—and critical advice from supportive winemaker friends—Covenant, the dream, became Covenant, the wine.

The first vintage received high praise from two of the nation's premier wine publications—*Robert Parker's Wine Advocate* and *Wine Spectator*. The reviews helped Covenant capture the attention of many Jews with an interest in fine kosher wine.

In 2008, after five successful years making wine at Herzog Wine Cellars, Covenant moved its winemaking operations to Northern California—first to Napa Valley and then, in 2014, to Berkeley. This was made possible by a move to Northern California by Jonathan Hajdu, a strictly Sabbath-observant winemaker who had worked in the cellar at Herzog. Jonathan had participated in all but one of Covenant's vintages and was very familiar with Covenant's winemaking methods. In June 2008, Jonathan signed up as Covenant's associate winemaker.

It was also around this time that Jodie began working full-time for Covenant. Prior to this, she had pursued a career in social work and, like me, was raised in a secular Jewish family in New York. Jodie had been involved in the food and wine industry as well, working as executive director for the American Institute of Wine and Food (AIWF), an organization founded by Robert Mondavi and Julia Child. And she had always been the lead recipe tester in our kitchen! When Jodie took over the responsibility for managing Covenant's business, it freed me to focus more on winemaking, which was exactly what I wanted to do. It was quite a blessing!

With winemaking operations now located in Northern California, we were no longer obliged to truck our grapes for hundreds of miles down to Southern California. We were able to work locally with an increasing number of growers up north. This enabled Covenant to produce a wider variety of wines, including (finally!) a superpremium Cabernet Sauvignon sourced from Leslie Rudd's estate vineyard in Napa Valley. We called that wine Solomon Lot 70, which is derived from Leslie's Hebrew name, Shlomo, or Solomon.

A New Horizon

A change of winemaking venue wasn't the only change in the works. Beginning with the first vintage in 2003, making kosher wine had brought us into close contact with the Orthodox Jewish community. I spent a lot of time working with the Sabbath-observant

Covenant and the Orthodox Union (OU)

Covenant's official status as a kosher winery began in 2003 with its certification by the Union of Orthodox Jewish Congregations of America—or the OU, as it is often called. Its presence in our professional lives has also played an integral and ongoing role in rekindling our interest in our Jewish heritage. The OU has worked closely with us on this book, so our readers may be assured that the highest standards of *kashrut* are maintained throughout its pages. (Of course, for the food created from these recipes to be kosher, only kosher ingredients—with proper *kashrut* certification where necessary—should be used.)

Founded in New York in 1898, the OU originally consisted of a group of fifty Orthodox Jewish synagogues. Its mission was to assist early generations of Jewish immigrants on multiple levels as they embarked on a new life in the New World. Recognizing a need to establish a professional standard for kosher food production, the OU began its kosher food certification program in 1923. It was the first nonprofit, communally sponsored program of its kind. Today, nearly a century later, the OU certifies the *kashrut* of more than five hundred thousand products produced in eighty-three countries.

With time, the OU's activities and service to the Jewish community have expanded beyond food certification. The organization now provides services for the disabled, job placement, youth activities, and public advocacy. Its publishing arm, the OU Press, is a partner in this book. Through its diverse activities, the OU today remains committed to its original goals of unifying, representing, and strengthening Orthodox Jewish life.

cellar crew at Herzog Wine Cellars, which included Joseph Herzog, Nathan's cousin, who managed the California operation.

At the Herzog winery, prayers were said daily and the connection to Jewish life was visceral. But my thoroughly nonreligious New York upbringing as a bagels-and-lox Jew had left me without any religious foundation. Now, through winemaking, I felt a connection that inspired me to learn to read Hebrew and some of the prayers. And in 2008, at age fifty-four, I finally celebrated the bar mitzvah that I had missed out on when I was thirteen.

In 2006, Chabad Rabbi Elchonon Tenenbaum moved from Crown Heights, Brooklyn, to the Napa Valley and opened a new Jewish portal for us. Rabbi Tenenbaum drew us closer to Jewish tradition, and through him Leslie and I eventually each acquired a set of *tefillin*. Covenant now collaborates with Rabbi Tenenbaum to produce a much-loved wine called Cuvée Chabad.

Perhaps the most dramatic manifestation of Covenant's effect on us has been our growing bond with Israel. We began to visit Israel together in 2011, after decades of absence, eventually rediscovering Jeff's family there and also spending time with our daughter, Zoë, who was studying at the University of Haifa. These visits gave birth to a winemaking project called Covenant Israel. The fruits of our labor in Israel will soon be available in our first Israeli vintage.

It can hardly be said that any of us—Jodie, Leslie, or I—has become strictly Sabbath-observant. But making Covenant Wine has rekindled an interest in our heritage, which we think speaks volumes about the spiritual power of producing kosher wine and the enduring traditions of the Jewish people.

From the Wine Country to the City

A Return to Urban Roots

Until recently, we lived in a veritable Garden of Eden called Napa Valley. Just a few minutes' walk from our old Victorian farmhouse were the valley's renowned vineyards, which extended for miles. And surrounding our home were the gardens where Jodie grew much of the produce and herbs used to feed our family and friends. Jodie's backyard chickens laid the freshest eggs imaginable, with deep-orange yolks that enhanced everything from omelets to aioli.

Then, in 2014, after fifteen years spent raising a family in this bucolic setting, we decided to build an urban, kosher winery in the city of Berkeley. Berkeley is actually only a half-hour's drive from the southern edge of Napa Valley (where we continue to source many of our grapes), but there it was much easier to find the larger building we needed to expand our wine production facilities. Not surprisingly, there are a growing number of wineries in the San Francisco Bay Area. Covenant is the first kosher winery to appear on the scene. And along with the new winery, we have also moved our home to Berkeley, because we wanted to be closer to a larger Jewish community than the one in Napa Valley and because our associate winemaker, Jonathan Hajdu, already lived in nearby Oakland. It was time for Jonathan to have a shorter winery commute. Finally, our kids had grown up and moved on, and we were just ready for a change. So we packed our bags and brought our wine-country lifestyle with us to Berkeley.

Today, our kitchen is a blend of Jewish tradition and contemporary California style. Extra virgin olive oil and herbs such as thyme, rosemary, sage, and basil are core ingredients in the pantry. So are garlic and spices such as cumin, cinnamon, and cardamom. Chiles—both hot and fruity—find their way into many favorite dishes as well. And from

Asia, tamari, toasted sesame oil, fresh ginger, and panko add character to select preparations. In truth, the food scene in Berkeley is more diverse than it is in Napa Valley. Dare we say we've found a new kind of Eden?

Kosher Food: The Basics

Observing kosher dietary laws is often associated in people's minds with a healthy lifestyle. While this may be true to a certain extent, the rationale underlying kosher practice is to follow the laws of food preparation and consumption as set down in the Torah and as expounded upon in the Mishnah, Talmud, and codes of Jewish law. For more than two thousand years, rabbis have interpreted and applied these guidelines to contemporary Jewish life.

Those who already keep kosher will probably be aware of the basics outlined on the following pages. For those who do not keep kosher, this section of the book can serve as an introduction or a basic reference. Much of the following information has been pro-

vided by the Union of Orthodox Jewish Congregations of America (OU), our partnering authority on questions regarding *kashrut* for both *The Covenant Kitchen* and Covenant Winery.

In Hebrew, the word *kosher* means "fit" or "proper," as it relates to dietary law and tradition. The basic laws of *kashrut* are laid out in the Bible in the books of Leviticus and Deuteronomy. They include well-known prohibitions against mixing meat and dairy products, consuming fish that do not have fins or scales, and consuming animals that do not have split hooves and do not chew their cuds, such as pigs, camels, and rabbits. The Bible also lists which birds are not kosher. The more we learn about kosher dietary laws, the more we realize how much more there is to learn. It keeps things interesting!

A Word About Margarine

Many kosher cooks substitute margarine for butter when cooking meals that include meat. It will produce a satisfactory result, but be aware that not all margarine is dairy-free, or even kosher. Look for a reputable kosher certification on the packaging, which will also specify whether the margarine is dairy or pareve.

Margarine has traditionally been made from partially hydrogenated vegetable oils, a chemical process that produces trans fats that, like butter and other animal fat, remain solid at room temperature but also resist spoilage. But trans fats have been linked to coronary artery disease and are being phased out of processed food in America. Margarine manufacturers are now producing trans-fat–free products, which are an improvement on the past but are still chemically processed and not without controversy.

In general, we prefer to cook with ingredients that have been minimally processed or, better yet, not processed at all. The Jews of antiquity dined well for thousands of years without margarine and other processed foods. We tend to follow their lead.

Many types of vegetable oil can be used for some recipes that traditionally call for butter. You'll find them throughout this book; we've already made the substitution for you. But if you wish to make a pareve version of one of the recipes here that contains butter, you have the option to substitute margarine for the butter. Use the same quantity of margarine as you would butter.

Meat, Dairy, or Pareve?

All foods (and, by extension, all prepared dishes) fall under one of three categories: meat, dairy, or pareve. Meat products (which includes poultry) cannot be cooked, mixed, or even consumed at the same meal with dairy products. Pareve foods contain neither meat nor dairy and may be cooked, mixed, and consumed with either of them. Fruit, vegetables, and eggs are pareve. So is fish, but there are laws for how fish is to be consumed at a meat meal (see "Fish," page 14).

Every recipe in this book can be made in a kosher kitchen. You will see that each recipe has been designated either meat, dairy, or pareve. For recipes where it's simply the inclusion of butter that renders a recipe dairy, you can substitute a pareve ingredient such as olive oil, canola oil, or margarine, so that the dish can be consumed at a meat meal. (See "A Word About Margarine," above.)

Meat and Poultry

If kosher animals and fowl are not slaughtered according to Jewish law, by a *shochet* , or certified kosher slaughterer (see "Shechita," page 16), they lose their kosher status. Cows, sheep, goats, bison, and deer are some of the more commonly recognized kosher animals.

The Torah lists twenty-four species of forbidden fowl; unlike animals or fish, no particular characteristics are given that determine the kosher status of birds. (They are, however, discussed in the Talmud.) Birds considered to be kosher today are those that Jews have traditionally eaten throughout the millennia, such as chicken, duck, goose, partridge, pheasant, and quail. The turkey, native to the Americas, was not part of this ancient tradition, but contemporary rabbinic authorities have ruled that because turkeys fit the criteria mentioned in the Talmud, they are kosher birds.

Fish

Because they do not have fins and scales, all shellfish—shrimp, crabs, clams, lobster, etc.—are prohibited. Unlike meat and poultry, fish does not have to be slaughtered by a *shochet*. But purchasing kosher fish in a store that also sells non-kosher fish can be problematic because the knives used for cleaning and filleting non-kosher fish cannot be used on kosher fish. The cutting surfaces are a problem, too. It's best to consult a rabbi for possible options. Rabbinic law also prohibits the consumption of fish and meat together, using the same utensils. But a fish course followed by a meat course, with different utensils and a bit of something to eat or drink in between courses, is perfectly acceptable. In fact, Jewish tradition specifically encourages eating both fish and meat at Shabbat meals.

Maintaining a Kosher Kitchen at Home

To keep kosher at home, you'll need a kosher kitchen, which means a kitchen that is set up in such a way that meat and dairy food products are kept completely separate during food preparation and cooking. You will need to have two sets of pots, pans, cutting boards, dishes, storage containers, cutlery, sink racks, and dish towels—one for meat and one for dairy. Color-coding everything (blue for dairy, red for meat works well for most people) is quite helpful in keeping things straight and preventing accidental mix-ups. (Vegetarians have it easy. With no meat in the kitchen, there is no need to have more than one set of anything.) If you want food that has been prepared pareve to remain so, so that it can be eaten with either meat or dairy dishes, you'll also need a set of cookware and utensils that have been designated pareve.

One sink can be used for both meat and dairy, you just have to remember to use the proper sink rack and cleaning pad, and to wash the sink thoroughly between uses. Stovetops can be used for cooking both meat and dairy—just not at the same time. And a single oven—either convection or microwave—can be used for both meat and dairy dishes. But you'll need a rabbi to explain the details of how to do it properly. (This is why many kosher kitchens contain two sinks, two stoves, and two microwave ovens.) A dishwasher can be used only for either meat or dairy. But it's fine to put meat and dairy products in a single refrigerator. Just keep them separate.

CONSUMING MEAT AND DAIRY

Not only is preparing and consuming meat and dairy together prohibited, but dairy products cannot be eaten immediately after consuming meat products. How long one waits depends on local custom, as different Jewish communities throughout the world have established different wait times. The most prevalent custom is to wait six hours after eating meat before consuming dairy. If, however, you want to eat a meat product immediately after having eaten a dairy product, either eat or drink a small amount of something pareve, or thoroughly rinse your mouth. The only exception to this is hard cheese, which is usually, but not exclusively, defined as cheese that has been aged six months or more. After eating that, you have to wait the same amount of time to eat a meat product as you do between eating meat and then dairy. (And, needless to say, you should always wash your hands between handling meat and dairy products.)

IT'S NOT AS DIFFICULT AS IT SEEMS

Yes, it sounds complicated if you've never had a kosher kitchen. For most of our lives, we didn't have one, either. But if a kosher kitchen is something you aspire to, you'll discover that with a little practice, it comes naturally.

Shechita

In *shechita,* ritual kosher slaughtering, the animal's throat is cut at a specific point with a *chalaf,* a specially prepared, razor-sharp, perfectly smooth blade that causes instantaneous death. It is a procedure for which a *shochet* has been rigorously trained and certified. After an animal has been properly slaughtered, its internal organs are inspected for any physiological abnormalities that may render the animal non-kosher, or *treif,* and certain parts of the animal that are not permitted to be eaten are removed. If, upon inspection, the lungs are found to be perfectly smooth, with no adhesions, the meat from that animal is designated "Glatt Kosher" (*glatt* is Yiddish for smooth). If there are adhesions but the *shochet* determines that they are not of a type that renders the animal *treif,* the meat is designated as simply "Kosher."

Because consuming the blood of an animal is forbidden, the blood in meat and poultry must be removed either by soaking and salting or by broiling with an open flame. In days gone by, this was traditionally done by the Jewish homemaker. But today, packaged, certified kosher meat has already been soaked and salted and is ready to be cooked upon purchase. If you're interested in learning about the soaking-and-salting process or the broiling process (chiefly used to *kasher* liver), the Orthodox Union's website explains these processes in great detail.

Eggs

Eggs laid by kosher birds are kosher and pareve. But eggs that are being cracked open (i.e., not boiled in their shells) need to be checked for blood spots and should be discarded if such spots are found. Fish eggs are kosher only if they come from kosher fish. Sturgeon (which has fins as a young fish but eventually loses them) is not considered kosher, so kosher-certified caviar comes from such kosher fish as salmon and whitefish.

Wine

Wine makes good food taste even better. It also promotes conversation and collegiality around the table. Lately, we've learned that wine might also be good for our health! (See "Wine, Tradition, and Health," page 32.)

For Jews, wine has long been linked to religious practice. Sabbath meals and Jewish holiday meals begin with the recitation of *kiddush*—an expanded blessing over wine that, according to many rabbinic opinions, extends back to biblical times and is mentioned in the Mishnah and in later rabbinic writings as well. (*Kiddush* is a derivative of the word *kadosh*, which means sacred.) And wine is a part of the *havdalah* service that marks the conclusion of the Sabbath and of certain holidays. As far back as the biblical era, Jewish families have sanctified the Sabbath and the festivals in this manner. We also know that the Jews of antiquity drank wine regularly, as did their Mediterranean neighbors, for non-sacramental reasons. Grapes are one of the seven agricultural products mentioned in the book of Deuteronomy as being native to the Land of Israel.

Today, wine is becoming an increasingly integral part of contemporary American and Jewish-American dining. In fact, the last two decades have witnessed a sea change in kosher winemaking worldwide. With access to modern techniques and classic European wine grapes, kosher winemakers have embarked on what can only be called a New Age in contemporary kosher wine. These new-generation wines are crafted with such grape varieties as Cabernet Sauvignon, Pinot Noir, Syrah, Chardonnay, and Sauvignon Blanc, which are grown in Europe, the Americas, and Israel. Today's finest kosher wines are on a par with the best non-kosher wines. And sacramental wine can be enjoyed for its gustatory as well as its spiritual qualities.

Kosher wine obviously plays a significant role in our lives. Our Covenant Winery is one of only a handful of kosher wineries operating in California. In this chapter, you'll learn how wine is made at Covenant. We'll also provide you with tips for serving and storing wine as well as pairing wine with food. And we'll explain what makes wine kosher and how wine and Jewish history are interconnected. We hope you'll find answers to many commonly asked wine questions and discover a world of wine that will enhance your dining pleasure for years to come. *L'chaim!*

Jews, Wine, and History

Beginning with Noah in the book of Genesis, Jews have one of the oldest codified relationships to wine of any people on Earth. But truth be told, we are also renowned for producing some famously bad wine. Perhaps that's part of the reason many American Jews don't

drink wine regularly with meals, despite a long-standing cultural connection with the fruit of the vine.

In America, the wine renaissance we are currently witnessing began only about twenty-five years ago. In fact, America as a whole has never really had a wine culture. But both Jews and non-Jews are now making up for lost time. It still surprises us when friends and customers tell us that they have been hoarding a bottle or two of Covenant for years, waiting for the "right moment" to open it. "The right moment?" we ask. "How about tonight?" A good bottle of wine with dinner creates a special occasion!

Wine in Ancient Israel

Winepresses dating back thousands of years can still be found throughout modern-day Israel. Carved deftly into rock outcroppings, they offer us a window into the world of early winemaking. Standing at the edge of one of these old winepresses, it's easy to see that ancient winemaking wasn't so different from winemaking today. Grape juice was squeezed from harvested grapes and allowed to ferment with native, indigenous yeast—which is pretty much the same way we do it at Covenant.

Wine for the Jews of antiquity was both an important component in religious rituals and a fundamental and enjoyable part of the daily diet—if consumed in moderation, of course. In the book of Genesis, Noah and Lot were both punished by God for drunkenness, and the book of Proverbs and the book of Isaiah warn against the consequences of excessive wine consumption. In Genesis, on the other hand, Isaac and Jacob included wine in their blessings to their children, and the book of Psalms and the book of Ecclesiastes associate temperate wine consumption with a God-given joyful experience. Wine was also featured in offerings by the priests in the Temple in Jerusalem more than 2,500 years ago.

With the destruction of the Temple by the Romans in 70 CE and the exile of the Jews from their land, their winemaking skills accompanied them into the Diaspora. According to some sources, the legendary medieval biblical and talmudic commentator Rashi (Rabbi Shlomo ben Yitzchak) owned a vineyard in Troyes, in northern France. His talmudic writings on wine and winemaking make for fascinating reading. Some parts of Europe and the Near East were not as hospitable to wine growing as were others, but wherever there were Jews, there was kosher wine production.

When we recite the *kiddush* over the wine we have produced, we elevate the consumption of food at our Sabbath and holiday meals from a biological function to a sacred experience. It enhances our enjoyment of these meals and helps us in our appreciation of the Sabbath and festival days as holy times of the year.

Kosher Wine: The Basics

While there is basic consensus regarding the fundamentals of the *kashrut* of wine, there is some debate over the details. The information below is based on the guidance of our friends at the OU.

1. What makes wine kosher? The fact is, there is nothing inherent in wine that renders it non-kosher. But to keep it kosher, it can be handled only by Sabbath-observant Jews.

2. Does kosher wine need to be blessed by a rabbi? No. This is a popular misconception. But if a winery wishes to have its wine certified kosher, that certification will have to be provided by a recognized certifying organization (such as the OU) that employs rabbis charged with making sure all *kashrut* requirements are honored.

3. What techniques distinguish kosher winemaking from non-kosher winemaking? There is no such thing as a kosher winemaking technique. Kosher wines can be made exactly the same way as non-kosher wines; the only difference is that no work—from crushing the grapes to bottling the wine—may be done on the Sabbath or on certain other holidays and, as noted above, the wine may be handled only by Sabbath-observant Jews. However, ingredients used in the winemaking process by some (but not all) winemakers, such as clarifying agents or commercial yeasts, will need to have kosher certification. The simple truth is that there is no "best" way to make any wine, and both kosher and non-kosher winemakers are constantly exploring new methods in the cellar.

4. Is there a kosher wine style? No. Kosher wines come in all styles, varieties, and colors. They can be full-bodied or light-bodied; dry or sweet; red, white, or rosé. In America, Concord grapes, developed from native American grapevine seeds in nineteenth-century Concord, Massachusetts, were perceived as the variety that grew best in New England and the Middle Atlantic states (where most American Jews lived back then). However, when fermented, Concord grapes produce a wine with a distinctly "foxy" flavor that is not necessarily appealing. A sweetened version proved more palatable, and so heavily sugared Concord grape wine became the foundation for something mistakenly referred to in America as "traditional" kosher wine. As far as we know, Concord grapes were not found in ancient Israel; hence the word *traditional* is a misnomer. More suited for jams and jellies than for wine, Concord grapes *(Vitis labrusca)* are a different species of grape from that which has traditionally been used for winemaking in Europe and the Middle East *(Vitis vinifera)*. For those of us who make or enjoy drinking such classic varietals as Cabernet Sauvignon or Chardonnay, Concord grape wine remains an odd chapter in the history of kosher winemaking.

5. Are kosher wines boiled? Not anymore. However, some kosher wines may be flash-pasteurized at a temperature that hovers around 180°F. These flash-pasteurized wines are called *mevushal*, which means "cooked" in Hebrew. What's this all about? It's a question that inspires much debate. Some say that heating wine helped sterilize it in ancient times. Others say that heating wine would have discouraged its use by Gentiles in pagan idol-worshipping ceremonies, which would have rendered it unsuitable for use in Jewish religious rituals. Before flash-pasteurization, *mevushal* wine really *was* boiled. It probably didn't taste very good, to Jews or to idol worshippers. In any case, *mevushal* wine may be handled or poured by non-Jews or non-Sabbath–observant Jews, which nowadays facilitates service in kosher restaurants or catering halls that may hire non-Jewish or non-observant waitstaff. In the United States, serving *mevushal* wine in kosher restaurants and catering halls has become the norm. In Europe and Israel, *mevushal* wine is seen less often. If a non-*mevushal* wine is served in a kosher restaurant, a *mashgiach* (a designated on-site *kashrut* supervisor) typically attends to wine service. Ultimately, *mevushal* wines are neither more nor less kosher than non-*mevushal* wines.

It's important to note that some winemakers—and not just kosher winemakers—believe that flash-heating can actually *improve* aromatics and flavor in wine. At Covenant, we don't necessarily subscribe to that belief, and most of our wines are not *mevushal*. But we still have enjoyed many fine *mevushal* wines. In 2013, we created our own *mevushal* wine program at Covenant with two new labels: The Tribe and Mensch. Both wines are put through a relatively new heating process called *flash détente*, which we find to be most in sync with our winemaking methodology, and which meets with the approval of the OU.

Making Wine at Covenant Winery

One time, while visiting Israel's Judean Hills, we hiked up to an old *gat*, or winepress, that had been carved from a great stone outcropping several thousand years ago. It sat at the edge of an ancient village now reduced to an archeological ruin. Oddly enough, the stone wine reservoir was well preserved, with its still-tiled stairway descending to the bottom. For a brief moment, we could feel the life of this vanished community, as the winemakers carried their grapes to the press and made wine in a way not so different from the way we do today.

Of course, we now have temperature-controlled, stainless steel wine tanks, oak barrels, and other modern-day tools for producing wine. But the basic concept remains the same: Grapes are grown and harvested and then pressed and/or de-stemmed. The grape juice is collected in some kind of vat, tank, or barrel. Left alone, this grape juice begins to ferment due to the action of native yeast that live, most probably, in the vineyards or around the winery. The yeast convert the sugar in the juice into alcohol, transforming the sweet juice into dry wine.

Grape quality and wine quality are closely linked. We source our grapes from vineyards in the Napa Valley and other important California wine regions. Some of these vineyards belong to Covenant partner Leslie Rudd. They are planted at his estate winery in Napa Valley's Oakville district and also in another Rudd vineyard high atop Mt. Veeder, also in Napa Valley. Both vineyards consistently produce wines that are among our finest.

The grapes for most of our other wines are purchased from growers with whom we work closely to ensure maximum ripeness and quality. Meticulous attention to detail is the watchword in every vineyard. Vine canopies are trellised to provide adequate sunshine for the leaves and grapes. Grape clusters are regularly thinned to reduce crop-load and increase flavor concentration. And picking decisions are based on achieving a degree of ripeness that will yield the kind of quality wine we hope to make each year.

Not only do we typically ferment our wines with natural, indigenous yeast (like our winemaker ancestors of yore), but we also generally bottle our wines unfiltered. We believe that a less intrusive approach to winemaking often yields the best results in your glass.

Invariably, Rosh Hashanah, Yom Kippur, Sukkot, Shmini Atzeret, and Simchat Torah fall during the grape harvest. Because our wines are kosher, we cannot work on these days or on the Sabbath. It's a special challenge that we embrace in the spirit of tradition!

Wine Varietals

In California and in much of North and South America, wines are generally labeled with the name of the predominant grape variety found in the bottle. Chardonnay, Cabernet Sauvignon, and Pinot Noir, for example, are the names of grapes traditionally grown in Europe and have now been adopted by most of the world's winegrowing regions. They belong to the grape family known as *Vitis vinifera*.

In California, a wine must contain at least 75 percent of the grape varietal that appears on the label. Despite the fact that we rarely see more than a dozen or so varietals on the shelves in wine shops, it's interesting to note that more than one hundred varieties of grapes are grown in California's vineyards. And many more exist throughout the world! Most of these are blended without varietal designation. This is common in Europe, where winemakers traditionally distinguish their wines by the region in which the grapes are grown—like Bordeaux or Burgundy—and not the predominant grape variety in the wine.

In Bordeaux, France, for example, red wines are blends of up to five different classic red grape varieties, which include Cabernet Sauvignon, Merlot, Cabernet Franc, Malbec, and Petite Verdot. (This is sometimes known as a "Bordeaux blend.") But on the wine label you will simply see "Bordeaux" or a subregion—also called an appellation. Aficionados may know that the blend includes some or all of the traditional red Bordeaux grape varieties. But what that blend is, exactly, generally remains a mystery to the consumer.

France's other best-known wine region—Burgundy—doesn't rely on blending as much. With some exceptions, red Burgundy is typically produced only with Pinot Noir grapes; white Burgundy is usually made exclusively from Chardonnay. Spain, Italy, Germany, and Portugal also have their classic grape varieties and blending traditions. German winemakers will often use varietal designations, but the majority of Spanish, Italian, and Portuguese winemakers do not.

Does it matter if you know what blend is in a wine bottle? Not necessarily. It's more important to be able to decide whether or not you like the wine (see "Assessing Wine Quality: What Makes a Wine Taste Good?," page 35). It does help to understand what styles of wine come from which regions. But even if you do know this, there is no substitute for tasting. Just because a wine is made in Bordeaux, for example, doesn't mean you will know what it will taste like. At best, you can make an educated guess. Perhaps that's part of what makes drinking and discovering new wines so interesting. Every vintage—and every bottle—can herald a new discovery.

New World winemakers—and that includes winemakers from just about anywhere outside of Europe—are not as constrained by tradition as their Old World counterparts. The labeling rules are not as strict in the New World, which offers more varied blending opportunities. Is a wine made from a blend of grape varieties better than a wine made from a single variety? Not necessarily. Wine quality depends on the skill of the winemaker and the quality of the grapes. Blending may be an element that affects quality, but it doesn't dictate quality. Those winemakers who wish to break away from varietal designation or tradition can simply give their wines fanciful names, or call them by their color. At Covenant, we do this with our RED C Napa Valley Red Wine—a blend of Cabernet Sauvignon and Petite Sirah—and The Tribe Proprietary Red Wine, a blend of Syrah, Petite Sirah, and Zinfandel.

But the vast majority of New World wines are still labeled varietally. And because we are located in the New World, most of the wine recommendations in this book feature varietal designates.

It's important to note that variations within varietals are quite common, and that not all Chardonnays or Cabernets are created equal. Chardonnay that grows in a dry, hot climate will probably taste different than Chardonnay that grows in a cool climate with more rainfall. The cool-climate Chardonnay may be lower in alcohol and lighter bodied than a full-bodied, richly textured Chardonnay made from grapes grown in a warmer area.

The winemaker's touch also influences a wine's taste; technique can even trump climate. The much-repeated phrase "wine is made in the vineyards" is actually a simplistic platitude. What happens in the vineyard and what happens in the winery are equally important. For example, barrel fermentation in white wines may add richness; tank fermentation may do just the opposite. What kind of oak barrels are used (French or American) and how long a wine remains in them will also affect wine style (see "The Taste of Wine," page 34, and "Pairing Food and Wine," page 38). Such choices are the wine-maker's prerogative—part of a vision or philosophy that is transferred to every bottle.

The Language of Wine

All wines can be described in simple terms according to their style or taste characteristics. Words like *big*, *bold*, *full-bodied*, *rich*, *lush*, and *fruity* will surely give you an idea of what awaits you in your glass. By contrast, words such as *light*, *tart*, *zippy*, *bright*, and *tangy* convey a very different meaning. How wine style affects the way you taste food is discussed further in "The Taste of Wine" (page 34) and in "Pairing Food and Wine" (page 38).

Following are lists of the most common wine varietals that have been recommended for pairings in almost all of the recipes in this book. As noted above, not all wines within a varietal are created equal. But these varietal summaries should help give you a sense of what to expect from a wine before you open it. We also address a few commonly enjoyed wines that defy varietal labeling, such as sparkling, rosé, and dessert wines. But don't look for Concord grapes. They are not members of the grape species commonly associated with fine wine. For more about Concord grapes and their history in Jewish winemaking see "Kosher Wine: The Basics" (page 22).

White Wine Varietals

Chardonnay

The classic Burgundian white wine, Chardonnay, is now grown throughout the world and made in varying styles. Rich, full-bodied Chardonnays are often fermented in, or at least aged in, oak barrels, which can give them a creamy, toasty quality. Unoaked Chardonnays tend to be more austere—leaner on the palate and showing more obvious stone fruit (as in peaches or nectarines) or citrus notes.

Sauvignon Blanc

This varietal is typically made in a style that is higher in acid—and thus brighter or crisper—than Chardonnay. Sauvignon Blanc is known for its refreshing citrus-like flavors. Those wines produced in cooler climates, such as New Zealand, France's Loire Valley, and the coastal regions of California, will often exhibit distinctive gooseberry or grassy notes. Warmer-climate Sauvignon Blanc may be more redolent of sweet pea, fresh figs, and passion fruit.

Riesling

Riesling was once more popular than Chardonnay in America, and it's still the king of white grapes in Germany. It is best known for its spicy, peach-like flavors and bright acidity. The classic German style of Riesling includes some sweetness—used to balance the grape's naturally high acidity. But Riesling can also be made in a dry (not sweet) style or as a supersweet dessert wine (see "Dessert Wines," page 32). How do you know if you are buying a sweet or dry Riesling? If you are buying a German Riesling, you can assume it has some measure of sweetness, unless it has been labeled *trocken*, which means "dry" in German. Domestic Rieslings are sometimes marked "off-dry," which is a code for "somewhat sweet." But more often than not, it's hard to know for certain what—if any—level of sweetness awaits you in a bottle of Riesling.

Gewürztraminer

Like Riesling, Gewürztraminer is a traditional German varietal. It serves up distinctively spicy flavors that are more litchee-like than those of Riesling. Gewürztraminer is also found in both dry and sweet styles. Dry, barrel-fermented Gewürztraminer can be an extraordinarily complex and delicious treat.

Chenin Blanc

Chenin Blanc produces fabulous dessert wines in France's Loire Valley. But in the New World, the varietal is more often produced as a dry table wine. Fresh, clean, and somewhat simple, it typically offers excellent value.

Pinot Gris (Pinot Grigio)

Whether called by its French or Italian moniker, this mild-mannered grape generally produces mild-mannered, simple quaffing wines. But like any varietal, if it's grown and fermented with the right attention, Pinot Gris can produce steely, clean white wines that provide layers of complexity.

Roussane

This is the premiere white grape of France's Rhône Valley. It's often blended with (less interesting) Marsanne. But on its own, Roussane can compete with any great Chardonnay, Sauvignon Blanc, or Riesling in terms of quality. It defies the usual generalizations and, instead, produces distinctive wines that are blessed with a fine integration of flavor and terrific acidity.

Viognier

Viognier is a spicy, fruit-forward varietal with Rhône Valley origins, like Roussane. It has become widely planted in California today and is often made in a rich, lush style.

Moscato (Muscat)

More often made in a sweet style than in a dry style, Moscato is a very fruity varietal with a flavor profile that leans toward apricots and nectarines. (The French call it Muscat.) It is often made in a sparkling style as well (see "Sparkling Wine," page 31). Moscato-based wines make excellent aperitifs. But their heightened fruitiness tends to overwhelm savory dishes (see "Pairing Food and Wine," page 38).

Red Wine Varietals

Cabernet Sauvignon

Cabernet Sauvignon is often called the "king" of red wine varietals in warmer wine-growing regions such as California's Napa Valley or France's Bordeaux. At its best, Cabernet Sauvignon produces full-bodied, complex wines redolent of blackberry and cassis, herbs like thyme and sage, and sometimes chocolate or tobacco. It also comes with robust tannins, which give it structure and a slight astringency. At its worst, Cabernet Sauvignon can be a thin, vegetal, astringent wine that no amount of aging or aeration will improve.

Merlot

Where Cabernet Sauvignon grows, so (typically) does Merlot. Merlot is often described as being softer and fruitier than Cabernet, but this is simply not true. Its texture and fruitiness depend on natural growing conditions and on the skill of both growers and winemakers. One of the most famous wines in the world is made in France with nearly 100 percent Merlot (though the varietal is not listed on the label). To be honest, it's really hard to tell the difference between a well-made Cabernet Sauvignon and a well-made Merlot!

Cabernet Franc

Cabernet Franc is genetically closer to Cabernet Sauvignon than to Merlot, but its taste profile can be quite different. This varietal typically has a more herbaceous quality than Cabernet Sauvignon, although it can also be blessed with ripe black-fruit flavors such as plum, and black cherry, too. It is often blended with Cabernet Sauvignon or Merlot.

Pinot Noir

This is the top red varietal (and grape) of France's Burgundy region, where in good years it produces wines of incredible grace and complexity from the best vineyards. It is generally lighter in style than the Cabernet-related red varietals mentioned above, and it sports higher acidity and softer tannins. Cherry flavors are typically at Pinot Noir's core, and the wine is certainly—from a food pairing perspective—the most versatile of all reds. New World Pinot Noir tends to be more full-bodied and fruity than the French versions.

Syrah

Known for its distinctively "meaty" character, Syrah is the premier grape of France's Rhône Valley, where it produces some of the most famous wines in the world. Syrah is now grown throughout the rest of the world, too. It has adapted well to such New World regions as California and Australia (where it is called Shiraz). In addition to its earthy, meaty notes, Syrah can also be quite fruity, showing robust black cherry and blackberry notes framed in firm, ripe tannins.

Petite Sirah

Created more than a century ago in France as a cross between the Syrah and Peloursin grape varieties, Petite Sirah never really caught on in its country of origin, but it has thrived in Northern California. Its dark-hued color and intensely fruity flavors make it an ideal blending wine. (We use it in a number of our Covenant wines.) Some winemakers make Petite Sirah as a single varietal bottling as well.

Grenache

This is another classic Rhône varietal that is less meaty but more fruity than Syrah. Grenache is often marked by its bright cherry notes and soft tannins. In some ways it can resemble Pinot Noir, although it tends to be more full-bodied and lower in acidity.

Malbec

One of the five classic Bordeaux grapes, it has not traditionally been bottled as a varietal. Today, however, some regions (notably Argentina) are producing a lot of fine wine labeled Malbec. On its own, Malbec often has a fruity, cherry-like quality somewhat reminiscent of that of Pinot Noir. But it has more muscular tannins and usually is made in a more full-bodied style.

Zinfandel

Zinfandel—sometimes called Primitivo—is a grape that came to the United States from Italy and/or Croatia long ago, by way of Long Island, New York, and, later, New England. But it didn't hit its stride until it landed in California, where (along with Grenache) it became a serious "workhorse" grape, producing lots of so-called jug wines. When grown in a more artisanal style with reasonably low yields, Zinfandel can produce lively, spicy, fruit-forward wines redolent of raspberries, bing cherries, and plums. Some winemakers produce Zinfandel in a big, fruity full-bodied style, while others craft more mellow, elegantly structured varietals that are lower in alcohol and more subtle in flavor. (White Zinfandel is a pink wine made with red Zinfandel grapes in an off-dry, or sweet, style. It should not be confused with true, red Zinfandel wine.)

Sparkling Wine

Champagne or Champagne Method

Champagne is the region in France most famous for producing sparkling wine of the same name. European labeling laws prohibit the use of the word *Champagne* for similarly styled wines made outside the region. These labeling laws are generally accepted throughout the world today. The refined Champagne style can, however, be reproduced in other winegrowing regions that label their sparkling wines with different names such as Cava (Spain), Champagne Method, or simply Sparkling Wine. Wines made using the Champagne method undergo a second fermentation in bottles that can give them a complex, toasty (yes, as in "toast" or "dough") quality. Aged Champagne takes on seductively nutty notes while losing some of its effervescence.

Prosecco

This Italian sparkling wine is not usually made using the Champagne method. But it is quite refreshing, if simpler on the palate.

Moscato d'Asti

Looking for a sweet bubbly? That's Moscato d'Asti. It's inexpensive and tasty, if you'd like a glass full of effervescent peach, apricot, and spice flavors. And it's great with dessert, served with fruit, or as an aperitif before dinner.

Dessert Wines

Late Harvest

True dessert wines can be made from any grape that is harvested late in the growing season and has accumulated a lot of sugar. There is too much sugar in a late-harvest grape for yeast to consume completely, and the residual sugar creates a sweet wine. The best dessert wines retain good acidity, which balances the sweetness and keeps the wine from being cloying. Sauternes are perhaps the most famous dessert wines; they are made in France. Other well-known dessert wines are produced in Germany and Canada. The United States also makes some distinctive dessert wines, but they are hardly what we are best known for. Israel now makes them, too.

Port

Port is a different kind of dessert wine, originally developed in Portugal. Instead of waiting to pick the grapes until they have too much sugar to produce a dry wine, Port winemakers stop the fermentation of what could become a dry wine by adding brandy—a distilled spirit. The brandy raises the alcohol to a level that is toxic to yeast. Because the yeast die off, there is no further assimilation of sugar in the wine, which therefore remains sweet, richly textured, and full-bodied. Port typically serves up an array of dark berry flavors, spice, and a hint of chocolate. The wine can age a long time and, yes, Port does pair really well with cigars! Port-styled wine is now made around the world. In California, it is often produced with Zinfandel. But there is not much kosher Port in the marketplace today. Perhaps this will change as demand increases.

Wine, Tradition, and Health

In addition to drinking wine on the Sabbath and on holidays when we make *kiddush*, in our home we also drink wine daily, with our meals—always at dinner and often at lunch, too. It's a custom we adopted during the years we lived in France. (Of course, you don't have to live in a wine region to experience wine-country living at the dining table.) Not only does wine complement the food on our plates, it also slows down our eating, so that as we taste and sip, we savor all the flavors of the meal.

It's no wonder that in many cultures, a toast with wine is accompanied by a phrase that translates to some form of good health. In Hebrew, it's *l'chaim* (to life)! In French, it's *santé* (good health)! Epidemiological studies conducted over the last two decades seem to show a relationship between moderate wine consumption and cardiovascular health. This was most famously featured on a *60 Minutes* program in 1991 that reported on the "French Paradox," which appears to show that people living in France consume higher levels of saturated fat but have lower incidents of coronary disease than people in other European countries and in the United States. This was partially attributed to the French custom of regularly drinking wine with meals. There are substances in wine that raise "good" cholesterol, lower "bad" cholesterol, and protect the linings of the blood vessels in the heart. And the antioxidants in wine might help prevent other diseases as well. Of course, you don't need to be a doctor to know that overindulgence in wine or other alcoholic beverages is bad for you. The key to intelligent wine consumption is moderation.

How much is too much? That depends on the individual. Much has been written on this subject by medical professionals. In our personal experience, if you can feel the effects of the alcohol as you drink, you've probably already drunk too much! And don't forget that wine drunk on an empty stomach will quickly go to your head.

We think that the best way to practice moderation is to make wine a regular part of your dining experience. We rarely drink wine without food; it's a part of our meal—not a preview or postscript. Of course the Sabbath and festivals present special moments to honor our Jewish heritage with wine. But for daily consumption, let a glass of wine add to the joy of a good meal. Every meal is a blessing, particularly when enhanced with wine.

The Taste of Wine

Wine's complex flavors have fascinated people for thousands of years. And while wine can be made from any fruit, history has shown us that grapes provide the most interesting and exciting results. Some wine critics wax poetic and describe wines with terms ranging from rose petals and violets to lemons, limes, cherries, chocolate, and even coffee. A lot of people wonder if this is really possible.

We all have different thresholds of taste perception. Some of us are more sensitive to tart flavors, for example, while others are more appreciative of sweet or fruity sensations. Wines are endowed with aromatic and taste components made up chiefly of chemical compounds known as esters and terpenes, also called essential oils. They are present, in varying degrees, in all members of the flowering plant world and give fruits their defining flavor characteristics.

Wine grapes contain a significant number of these natural flavoring agents, which increase in potency post-fermentation. If you smell cherries and chocolate in your wine,

you're probably not imagining it. You're smelling specific chemical compounds redolent of those fruits. (Yes, chocolate comes from a fruit.)

Some two-hundred-plus aromas and flavors have been identified in wine, but no one should try finding all of them. Still, great wines carry their fair share of flavors. Younger wines are fruitier, and with time these primary flavors change to evoke secondary flavors—such as hazelnut, leather, and tea. Some wines are prized for their aging prowess, while others are best drunk when fresh and young. Personal taste also plays a role here, because not everyone appreciates the same qualities in a wine.

Wine's flavor doesn't come only from grapes. Oak barrels also make a contribution. Barrel staves are toasted over an open flame, and that toasty, smoky quality can be imparted

Assessing Wine Quality:
What Makes a Wine Taste Good?

How do you know whether or not a wine is good? The obvious answer—"if you like it or don't like it"—is not really correct. In the wine country we use the term *cellar blindness* to refer to a winemaker who has become so accustomed to tasting his own flawed wines that he uses them as a reference point for quality. In other words, if you get used to drinking something bad, you can come to believe it's good, or at least "normal."

What is a flawed wine? Typically, this would be a wine with some kind of defect brought about through winemaking errors, poor storage, or some other kind of contamination. Wine flaws are not necessarily dangerous to your health, they just diminish an otherwise acceptable wine. One of the most common flaws is cork taint, which results from a chemical compound found in cork or in other forms of wood. Cork taint can impart cork-like or "wet dog" flavors to a wine. Sometimes the taint is very obvious and sometimes it's not. This flaw is found in a small percentage of wines, despite the efforts of cork producers and winemakers to eliminate it. A tainted wine is referred to as "corked."

Other basic winemaking and storage-related flaws have become increasingly rare. But if a wine tastes a bit like vinegar, it's probably heading that way prematurely. If a red wine evokes the sensation of being in a stable or barnyard, it might contain a common spoilage yeast known as *Brettanomyces*, more often referred to as *Brett*. Small amounts of *Brett* can actually be interesting, but *Brettanomyces* is not really something you want to find in wine meant for aging. It usually gets worse with time.

Finally, some wines are just out of balance. They are too acidic or too tannic (astringent). Or they may be too sweet when they should be dry—or too dry when they should be sweet! This could be a question of context. In other words, what is the wine supposed to taste like given where it is made, and what is the appropriate style? Sometimes, a wine is just not so good—perhaps thin, vapid, devoid of character, or just unpleasant to drink. Depending on who is analyzing the wine, a flaw or defect could be subjective or objective. It makes wine criticism both challenging and fascinating.

Ultimately, it's hard to argue with someone's personal taste. But imagine how children experience food, and then how they taste as adults. In general, kids prefer simple, sweet flavors. Foods too high in acidity or too complex in taste are often unpleasant to them. But as their adult palates become more experienced, they learn to appreciate nuance and complexity, which is exactly what should be expected of a great wine.

A top-quality wine unfolds gracefully on the palate in a way that holds our sensual and intellectual attention. It is to be hoped that a fine wine also reflects the talents of the people who make it—including the grape growers—along with regional, cultural, and historical perspectives. Really good wine should tell a story.

But we are not implying that simple, straightforward (and often inexpensive) wines are bad or flawed. Some can be very good. They just might not have the same intensity of flavor or complex tastes as those found in a better wine. Still, a good, simple wine may be just what we are looking for with lunch or a quick dinner. Sometimes an easy-quaffing wine is really all we desire. And that's okay.

A PLETHORA OF STYLES AND TASTES

Now and then we hear comments such as "I don't like red wine" or "I don't like Chardonnay." In truth, there are so many different styles and flavors found among red wines or even in a single varietal, such as Chardonnay, that it would be absurd to lump all wines of the same color or varietal into one category. For more discussion about this, see "Wine Varietals" (page 25).

What's most important in a well-made wine can be summarized as follows:

Body

All wines have some kind of body, an indication of weight or mouthfeel. Is a wine rich and full in your mouth? Or does it leave an impression of being light and fresh? Full-bodied wines lean toward the former; light-bodied wines tend toward the latter. Body is often a reflection of alcohol—more alcohol means fuller body; less alcohol yields lighter body. Neither is an indicator of good or bad quality but, rather, of style. Ideally, a wine's body should enhance its quality. If your wine tastes too big or heavy, it's probably not a good choice for you at that moment. If it's too lightweight for your palate, the same might apply. For more about wine style, see "Pairing Food and Wine" (page 38).

Acidity

Grapes contain natural acidity, which gives a wine structure or backbone. Without enough acidity, a wine might be considered "flabby" or "shapeless." Just as your backbone holds you up, a wine's acidity holds it together. Red wines are generally lower in acidity than white wines. But what's most important in a well-balanced wine is that its acidity tastes right to you.

Texture

Texture is related to acidity, since acidity can give a textural impression in your mouth. Bright, high acidity can feel tangy or tart. Low acidity might cause a wine to feel smooth and round. In red wines, tannins—naturally occurring compounds found in grape skins—can greatly affect wine texture. (Unlike red wines, white wines are made with little skin contact, so they are low in tannins.) Tannins give a wine astringency and can make your mouth feel dry. But the right kind of tannin gives a wine structure, a kind of framework that supports the flavors. Harsh tannins can obliterate the good qualities in a wine and leave only a drying impression in your mouth. With time, some tannins drop out of solution, leaving a wine softer and more enjoyable to drink. That said, if you need to wait ten years for a wine to "come around," you've probably purchased a wine that was originally flawed by being overly tannic. Sometimes those rough tannins never drop out.

Flavor

Yes, wines do have fruit flavors. They also show herbal and vegetal notes as well. This is because grapes are filled with naturally occurring flavor components known as esters and terpenes, which give fruits and vegetables their distinctive tastes and aromas (see "The Taste of Wine," page 34). After fermentation, wine flavors evolve and are carried along your palate with the help of alcohol—an excellent flavor vector. Other wine flavors may come from oak barrels and acidity, as discussed above. We are not all equally sensitive to these flavors and textures, but most of us can taste something that we like in a good wine. Of course, some wines are more flavorful than others. That's part of what makes wine interesting!

Finish

Does a wine's taste linger on your palate in a good way? If so, this says something positive about the wine's quality. "Finish" simply indicates if the wine has staying power. Great wine should have a great finish.

to barrel-aged wines. In addition, natural oak sugars caramelize during the toasting, serving up a hint of crème brûlée. Ultimately, winemakers use oak the way chefs use salt and pepper for seasoning. Too much oak can be overpowering, but the right amount can provide a nice framework for what is in your glass.

Although some wines are worthy of lengthy discussion and analysis, most are best appreciated for their simple beauty, fresh acidity, and food friendliness. Indeed, wine's greatest contribution to living well may simply be the way it makes eating just a little more special.

Pairing Food and Wine

What wine should you drink with dinner? With just a few guidelines, you will be able to answer this question yourself.

At our home, the main pairing guideline is simple: Lighter foods go with lighter wines; heavier, richer foods pair best with richer, more full-bodied wines.

For example, a meaty beef stew is rich. So is chocolate cake. One may be sweet and the other savory, but they are both rich. A tossed green salad is light textured, and so is lemon meringue pie. The same concept applies to wine: Some are richly textured; some are not. As a rule, red wines tend to be richer or more full-bodied than white wines. White wines—with the exception of dessert wines—are typically lighter bodied. If you can describe what's on your plate as well as what's inside a wine bottle with simple terms like these, you can eliminate the guesswork about matching food and wine.

Pairing similarly styled dishes and wines is known as complementary pairing. A big, rich Cabernet Sauvignon paired with a juicy, robust steak is a complementary pairing. A lighter-styled Chardonnay might work very well with a light salad. But sometimes very different kinds of food and wine do attract. These would be called contrasting pairings. Consider a bright, tangy Sauvignon Blanc enjoyed with salmon with aioli. (Salmon is a rich, oily fish; aioli is a very rich mayonnaise sauce.) The natural acidity of the Sauvignon Blanc balances the richness of the food. In a similar vein, a light-textured, semi-sweet Riesling with good acidity can be a lovely match for rich, fatty, savory duck.

And the "perfect match"? It doesn't exist. Personal wine preferences and distinctions among wine varietals offer multiple taste perspectives. That's why one person may prefer a Pinot Noir—a red wine—with grilled salmon, while another may favor a Chardonnay, which is white, with the same salmon dish. Both wines can be equally enjoyable with that grilled salmon.

Style Versus Color

It's important to note that a wine's style is more important than its color or varietal designation. Just ask yourself, "Is the wine light or heavy? Bright or lush? Full-bodied? Lean and crisp?" These are the terms that define both style and food friendliness.

Typically, white wines have higher natural acidity than red wines. As a result, white wines appear lighter and fresher on the palate. Their higher acidity encourages us to drink them chilled, which mitigates their bright edge.

Red wines tend to be lower in acidity than white wines. They often have a higher alcohol content, too. That makes red wines more full-bodied and rich. They are best when drunk at room temperature (provided the room is not too hot). Dry rosé—or pink wine—is usually made with red grapes but in a style reminiscent of white wine. What renders the wine pink is the relatively short time the fermenting grape juice remains in contact with the red grape skins. Minimal contact prevents the juice from soaking up too much red pigment—which is found in the skins but not the juice. Rosé is drunk a bit like a red wine and also like a white wine. As a result, it pairs well with just about everything from salads and fish to burgers and steaks. Enjoy rosé chilled. It may be the most versatile of all wines.

What if you just don't like white wine as much as red wine? No problem. There is plenty of stylistic variation among red wines. Light-bodied Pinot Noir, for example, is different from full-bodied Cabernet or Zinfandel. And if you prefer whites, the same applies. Barrel-fermented Chardonnay is richer than light-textured, unoaked Sauvignon Blanc. But with so many different wines available today, it would be a shame not to sample wines of all colors.

The next time you open a bottle, ask yourself, "Is this wine rich and lush? Or is it light and fresh?" With a little practice, you'll be tasting wine like a pro!

Sweet Stuff

Sweet foods can make dry wines (i.e., wines that are not sweet) taste bitter. That's why savory dishes that include sweet ingredients such as fruit are challenging for dry wines. Your best pairing bet for sweet-styled dishes is a fruity wine that can stand up to the fruit on your plate. Think Riesling (among whites) and Zinfandel (among reds).

Dessert requires a truly sweet wine for best pairing results. Think vintage Port with cookies or chocolate cake. Lush, elegant dessert wines can also work well alone as a liquid dessert.

Cooking with Wine

We often cook with wine, which has the natural acidity to tenderize meats and brighten a sauce or soup. However, the primary flavors we love in bottled wine are destroyed through cooking. This is why we don't recommend cooking with a great or expensive wine, especially if you need more than a "glug." Remember to cook with dry wine, too. (Sweet wine will sweeten whatever you are cooking.)

When a recipe calls for cooking wine, use a dry (not sweet) inexpensive table wine. It won't hurt the sauce; and it won't hurt your pocketbook. Save the good wine for your glass!

Glassware

Does the shape and size of a wineglass really affect the way your wine will taste? In a word: yes. Much of what we taste is really what we smell. So the way in which a wine's

aromas reach your nose is critical. Essentially, the aromas in wine are volatized, or carried up toward the nose, through the air. A glass with concave edges that curve inward helps harness these aromas and direct them in a more precise manner toward your nostrils.

Swirling wine in the glass prior to smelling and sipping is definitely advisable. This is not some useless, affected custom, but a simple way of aerating the wine, which facilitates the movement of the aromas to your nose. In addition, swirling coats the sides of the glass with wine, thereby increasing the exposed surface area of liquid in close proximity to your olfactory receptor.

But all of this swirling can be a messy affair if your glass contains too much wine. That's why seasoned wine drinkers rarely fill their glasses more than halfway. Adequate headspace in your glass also serves as a kind of storage area for aromas that would otherwise quickly dissipate.

The exception to the rule is the narrow, tall glass—often called a flute—used for sparkling wine. Bubbly is blessed with carbon dioxide, which efficiently carries aromas directly to your nose—no swirling required! The narrow glass provides a direct pathway to the bubbles. So feel free to fill your flute to the top.

How big should a wineglass be? Because a five-ounce pour is commonly enjoyed as a single serving and you don't want to fill your glass more than halfway, ten to twelve ounces is a good all-purpose size. Larger wineglasses, which leave more headspace to collect aromas, may enhance your drinking pleasure, but they are hardly required for enjoying good wine. We like to use larger glasses (fourteen to sixteen ounces) just for fun when drinking special wines paired with a special meal.

What about the many different shapes of wineglasses available today? From a consumer's perspective, too many choices can be overwhelming. The best solution to the question of designer glassware is to find a shape—or several shapes—that appeal to you. Let's keep the simple act of drinking wine as simple as possible!

Cellaring Wine

We are often asked, "When will our wine be ready to drink?" It's a question that is impossible to answer with any authority. Different wines evolve in different ways. And the conditions of storage will also affect the speed at which a wine will age.

The bottom line is this: Wine doesn't need to age to taste good. Most wines are made to be drunk upon release. Some varietals, like Cabernet Sauvignon, may age better than other varietals. But a good Cabernet should taste good in its youth too. In young wines, primary fruit flavors are more apparent. But with age, their flavor profiles change from fruit-driven to something more redolent of earth and leather. In their senescence, they become softer in texture. It's all good. This is what's supposed to happen.

Some people prefer the flavors of aged wines, while others prefer younger wines. We like both.

How to Store Your Wine

Age-worthy wines are fun and filled with surprises. The only way to find out what's inside is to pop the cork (or twist open the screw cap). But if you don't provide your wine with a reasonably good cellar environment, you might discover some unpleasant surprises. Wine is not as fragile as many people think. But if stored consistently at higher temperatures (over 65°F), it will age more quickly than at lower temperatures. If the temperature fluctuates a lot, the cork seal could expand and contract in a way that allows air to enter the bottle. This will oxidize your wine prematurely.

The best environment for wine storage is a dark, cool place, with an air temperature somewhere around 55° to 65°F. A temperature-controlled wine cellar is ideal, but any reasonably cool place—like a basement—will suffice. (If you are storing wine in your basement, don't store the wine near the boiler!) Remember to lay your wine bottles in a horizontal position or securely place them upside down. This will keep the corks moist and prevent them from drying out.

One last piece of advice: If you are planning on aging a wine for an extended period, it's wise to purchase a number of bottles—at least three to six. With only one bottle in stock, you can't possibly gauge how it is going to age. Opening it too soon shouldn't be a problem, but waiting until it's over the hill would be a shame. Alas, a lot of great wine has been aged too long by collectors who discovered that top-flight wine does not continue to improve indefinitely with age. With multiple bottles from the same vintage in your cellar, you can sample a wine from time to time and get a feel for how it is evolving. That's how you gauge aging potential. Ideally, the last bottle will still be full of life when you drink it.

The Price of Wine: What's a Bottle Worth?

In some ways wine is like real estate, where value is often measured by *perception* of quality. For example, two comparable homes may be valued at wildly different prices depending on where they are located. The same thing could apply to two Chardonnays of compa-

Decanting

Transferring a wine from its original bottle to a decanter is hardly a requirement for the enjoyment of fine wine. But it may make a wine taste better for several reasons.

Young wines—particularly red ones—can benefit from aeration. That's what happens when a wine is poured from a wine bottle into a decanter. The contact with air may soften astringent red wine tannins and encourage the wine to "open up," or better reveal its flavors. At our home, we often decant young red wines with this in mind. Today, it's easy to purchase a wine aerator that attaches to a freshly opened bottle. It essentially does the same thing as a decanter, although decanting typically gives wine more time to open up from the air contact. Still, a wine aerator is a good substitute for decanting when the purpose is to soften a wine's texture.

Older wines can also benefit from decanting even though they may already be quite soft and drinkable. The harmless sediment that settles at the bottom of the bottle over the years can be bitter or render a wine cloudy. So it's not a bad idea to decant older wines, too. Slowly pour the wine from the bottle into the decanter, watching for sediment in the shoulder of the bottle as you come to the end of the pour. (That's when you stop pouring!) You may lose an ounce or two, but you'll improve your overall drinking experience.

We can't remember ever decanting a white wine.

Neophytes can rest assured that decanting requires no special training or technique. You don't need a candle or special light to see what you're doing, either. Simply pour the wine from the original bottle into the decanter. End of story. Unlike wineglasses, where shape does make a difference, decanters require no specific shape other than one that pleases you. Any glass bottle—even an old milk bottle—will do the job.

rable quality—one produced with grapes from a renowned vineyard in Burgundy and the other, equally good, with grapes from a less famous site in, say, California's Russian River Valley.

As the saying goes, "Location, location, location!" Wine provenance is a key to its price. Location affects land costs, grape costs, and building and labor costs, which all affect bottle price. Napa Valley grape varieties may be valued at five to ten times the value of the same grape varieties grown in a less prestigious California wine-growing region. The unprocessed juice—not yet wine—for high-end Napa Valley Cabernet can be worth sixty-five dollars per gallon and more. Are Napa grapes really that much better?

Sometimes, perhaps, depending on the variety, the vineyard, and the care that goes into growing the grapes. But sometimes the answer is no. All Napa Valley grapes are not created equal.

Then there is winemaking equipment—barrels, presses, pumps, tanks, etc. Investment in these essential winemaking tools is certainly linked to the cost of wine. A relatively small, new winepress can easily set a winery back seventy-five thousand dollars. Fortunately, a winery doesn't have to buy a new press every year. New French oak barrels come in at about a thousand dollars each—perhaps a little more, depending on the euro. Small wineries purchase ten or twenty every year. Large wineries might purchase hundreds! And if a new winery wants to outfit itself with new tanks, they can run high. Even small stainless steel tanks can cost well over fifteen thousand dollars each. And this is just the proverbial tip of the iceberg.

Mundane supplies such as bottles, corks, labels, and the act of bottling also influence pricing. At Covenant, we've purchased glass bottles that cost as much as two dollars each

(that would be twenty-four dollars per case) and as little as seventy-five cents each (about nine dollars per case). Corks can cost up to almost a dollar per cork, but we try to find high-quality corks for less. Do the math, and you'll find that a wine bottle might cost four to six dollars (or more) before it ever sees any wine!

And let's not forget about the costs of doing business. Winemakers must navigate a complex, national three-tier distribution system that automatically erases half (or more) of a wine's retail value for the producer. Transportation and storage costs are also high. And if there's anything left in the budget, it's a good idea to hire a marketing and sales force—but not, one hopes, at the expense of paying for a good wine production crew in the cellar. There are also permits to be obtained, taxes and insurance to be paid, and a seemingly endless array of related costs. In truth, it never ends.

There is something to be said about economies of scale. A winery producing a lot of wine can afford to make less money on each bottle. Profits accrue from high-volume sales—less profit per bottle, but more money in the grand scheme of things. To stay solvent, small wineries often need to charge more per bottle. Does this mean high-volume wineries make bad wine? Of course not. But the odds are that you'll find more distinctive flavors in what we call "small-lot" production. And you will often have to pay more for it.

Expensive Wine or Cheap Wine: Can We Really Tell the Difference?

Sometimes it's obvious, and sometimes it's not. If you *can* tell the difference, then it's worth paying a premium. If not, buy something inexpensive. And if your budget doesn't necessarily fit your expensive taste, look for good, inexpensive wines for everyday drinking. (They are out there and available.) But for special occasions—like the Sabbath, holidays, or just a great meal with friends—you might want to splurge a bit. In the end, wine is more than just a beverage. Its value is linked to what it means to you.

Appetizers

Whether you serve them as a prelude to a meal or enjoy them as a first course, appetizers, as their name implies, are meant to whet the appetite. They are not meant to be filling. A little goes a long way.

Some evenings, we indulge in a few olives (page 48), some radishes, and perhaps a glass of Sauvignon Blanc for a very simple preprandial interlude. If guests are coming over, we might put more thought into what we serve, focusing on easy-to-share items like hummus (page 51), feta cheese spread (page 57), or our savory onion tart (page 61). This is all finger food that can be enjoyed in your living or dining room.

Some appetizers in this chapter are more easily enjoyed at the dinner table, where a knife and fork come in handy. These include dishes like Fried Green Tomatoes with Saffron Aioli (page 67), Roasted Red Peppers with Olive Oil and Garlic (page 54), and Sautéed Carrots with Cumin Seeds and Fresh Cilantro (page 65). The recipes are mostly inspired by our dining experiences in France and Israel, where appetizers and small plates—or *meze*—are a mainstay of local dining tradition.

We tend to drink white wine at the beginning of a meal, but there's no rule that says you should. Still, these opening dishes are generally light and fresh, like many white wines we enjoy. We'd call this complementary pairing (see "Pairing Food and Wine," page 38).

Olives with Lemon Zest and Thyme

pareve | serves 4

When we first moved to Napa Valley, we discovered two hundred-year-old olive trees planted behind our farmhouse. We planted three more trees, but the olives from the old trees always tasted better than those growing on the younger ones. Inevitably, it was the olives from the old trees we picked for curing, marinating them in salt brine in our cellar for about a year. If you don't have your own home-cured olives, it's easy to buy ready-to-eat olives at the grocery store.

For special occasions, dress your olives with the ingredients below and serve with a glass of any wine you like. We prefer bright, crisp whites, such as sparkling wines, Sauvignon Blanc, or Chardonnay. The lemon zest in the olives and the lemony acidity in many white wines make a perfect match. If you like, you can add a little heat with chipotle pepper flakes, but it's not necessary. Either way, your friends will say they didn't know olives could taste this good!

2 cups cured olives (drained of
    their brine)

2 tablespoons extra virgin olive oil

1 tablespoon minced lemon zest

¼ teaspoon dried thyme or
    rosemary

¼ teaspoon chipotle pepper flakes
    (optional)

In a medium bowl, toss together all the ingredients. Transfer the olives to a smaller serving bowl, with another small bowl for the olive pits on the side.

Sautéed Padrón Peppers

pareve | serves 4

If you have a garden, summer is the best time to grow the tiny, tender, green Spanish peppers known as padróns. We pick them right before dinner, sauté them in olive oil, and serve them to guests as an appetizer before sitting down to eat.

Those of you who don't grow your own padróns can find them in any food store with a good produce section, from late June through August. The little green peppers range in size from 2 to 3 inches in length and have fairly thin skins, which makes them really easy to eat. Just hold them by the stem and munch down to the seeds, which are edible too. As an appetizer, three or four peppers per person is perfect. But it's easy to eat twice that many.

Most of these peppers are sweet, but now and then you'll get a really hot one. It's a little like culinary Russian roulette, but the consequence of getting a hot pepper is a good excuse to sip some cool white wine.

We like to drink Sauvignon Blanc with padróns. The herbaceous, lemony notes in the wine blend beautifully with the salty peppers. Sparkling wine is also a great match.

2 tablespoons extra virgin olive oil

¼ pound padrón peppers (about 16)

Coarse salt

In a large skillet, heat the olive oil over medium-high heat. Add the peppers to the pan and sauté until they are blistered on one side, about 2 minutes. Using tongs or a wooden spoon, flip the peppers and cook until the other side has a similar appearance. (The larger peppers will cook more slowly than the small ones and you might need to roll the peppers around a bit; they are not uniform in shape.) If the oil begins to smoke, reduce the heat to medium.

When the peppers are done, drain them on a plate lined with paper towels. Then transfer to a serving platter and sprinkle with salt to taste. Serve with a small bowl on the side for discarded stems.

Hummus with Toppings and Pita Bread

pareve | makes enough hummus for 3 plates; serves 4 to 6 as an appetizer

In Israel, hummus is ubiquitous. In the States, it has a rapidly growing following. We usually eat it with friends as an appetizer, but you could certainly make a full meal out of it—especially when you serve it with toppings like caramelized onions with mushrooms, or marinated red peppers, or ground lamb—all featured on page 52. (*Note that the recipe will become "meat" if the chopped lamb topping is used.*) For ease in the kitchen, prepare the toppings before you make the hummus; each topping can be enjoyed at room temperature. When you are ready to serve, place a mound of topping in the center of each hummus plate.

Scoop up the hummus with warm pita bread—homemade (page 239) or store-bought. If you are making pita at home, prepare the dough first; then make the hummus; and then bake the bread quickly in a preheated oven. Make sure the oven is hot enough, or the bread will not cook thoroughly.

Today there are many good, store-bought hummus brands in the marketplace. You can buy them and simply dress them up with any or all of the toppings below. But it's really easy to make hummus from scratch. And when it's homemade, it always tastes better.

We also like to garnish hummus with a dollop of spicy harissa, a Middle Eastern condiment available in many fine food shops. If you don't have any harissa, try chipotle pepper flakes.

Hummus lends itself to an accompanying beverage with good acidity, such as sparkling wine, Sauvignon Blanc, dry Chenin Blanc, Roussane, or a crisp, light Chardonnay.

Basic Hummus

1 can (15 ounces) chickpeas, drained, or 2 cups home-cooked (page 242)
½ cup plus 1 to 2 tablespoons extra virgin olive oil
½ cup water
¼ cup tahini (roasted sesame seed paste)
2 tablespoons fresh lemon juice
2 cloves garlic, minced

1 teaspoon salt
½ teaspoon ground cumin
¼ cup small black olives
1 to 2 teaspoons harissa or ½ teaspoon chipotle pepper flakes (optional)
Pita bread, homemade (page 239) or store-bought

In a food processor or blender, combine the chickpeas, ½ cup of the olive oil, the water, tahini, lemon juice, garlic, salt, and cumin. Pulse on low, stopping to stir as needed, until the hummus becomes smooth and thick. Use immediately or cover and refrigerate for up to 3 days.

Spread the hummus in a thin layer on a plate about 9 inches in diameter. Drizzle with 1 to 2 tablespoons olive oil (to taste) and garnish with the olives. If desired, place a dollop of harissa at the center of the plate or sprinkle with the chipotle flakes.

Scoop up with pita bread.

Optional Hummus Toppings

marinated red peppers (pareve)

3 to 4 marinated red peppers, store-bought
   or homemade (page 54),
    coarsely chopped

onions and mushrooms (pareve)

1 tablespoon extra virgin olive oil

½ onion, diced

4 large button mushrooms, sliced or chopped

In a small skillet, heat the olive oil over medium heat. Add the onion and cook until translucent, about 3 minutes. Add the mushrooms and cook until wilted, about 5 minutes.

chopped lamb (meat)

1 tablespoon extra virgin olive oil	½ teaspoon ground cumin
2 green onions, white and green parts, sliced into rounds	½ teaspoon dried rosemary
	¼ pound ground lamb
1 clove garlic, minced	¼ teaspoon salt

In a small skillet, heat the olive oil over medium heat. Add the green onions and garlic and cook until fragrant, about 1 minute. Stir in the cumin and rosemary. Add the lamb and salt. Sauté, stirring occasionally, until the meat is cooked through, about 5 minutes.

Sweet and Spicy Pecans

dairy | makes 2 cups

These spiced nuts are great for nibbling. Enjoy them as a midday snack or prior to a meal, alone or alongside cheeses.

The pecans are terrific when paired with mildly sweet wines such as Moscato or Riesling.

2 tablespoons unsalted butter

2 teaspoons brown sugar

1 tablespoon maple sugar

¼ teaspoon cayenne pepper

½ teaspoon ground cinnamon

Pinch of salt

2 cups pecans

Preheat the oven to 325°F.

In a saucepan, melt the butter over low heat. Stir in the brown sugar, maple sugar, cayenne, cinnamon, and salt. Mix well and stir in the pecans until they are evenly coated with the other ingredients.

Spread the pecans on a baking sheet. Bake for 15 minutes, stirring the pecans every 5 minutes to keep them from sticking or burning. Let cool before eating.

A Note on Salt

Not all salt is equally salty. Sea salt, table salt, and kosher salt all have varying degrees of intensity. But it's not easy to find universal agreement about which is saltiest. Salt's crystal size and origin—from the sea or from the earth—can make a difference. In our kitchen, we generally use sea salt, which is minimally processed. For cooking and general seasoning, we'll use sea salt with fine crystals. But when garnishing a dish, we might use a coarser salt because we like the crunchy texture.

Unless it has been processed with non-kosher additives, all salt is kosher. Those salts marketed as kosher are simply certified to be free of anything not kosher. In addition, kosher salt has a coarseness favored by chefs, who like to really feel that pinch of salt they might add to a dish.

When you add salt to taste, that's exactly what it means. Add a little at a time. It's easy to add more, but you can't remove it.

Roasted Red Peppers with Olive Oil and Garlic

(pareve) | serves 4 to 6

Roasted red peppers are easy to prepare and versatile. We use them as a topping for hummus (page 51), but they can be outstanding on their own as an appetizer drizzled with a little garlic-infused olive oil. It's something you see regularly on dinner tables throughout southern France and Italy, but not as often in the States. We don't know why. Scoop up any remaining olive oil on your plate with a piece of crusty, country bread.

In California, we often serve these fruity peppers with a glass of lush, barrel-fermented Chardonnay or bracing Sauvignon Blanc. Rosé would be a good choice too.

6 red bell peppers
(about 3 pounds)

⅓ cup extra virgin olive oil

2 cloves garlic, minced

Salt and freshly ground pepper

Preheat the oven to 400°F.

Arrange the peppers on a rimmed baking sheet, roasting pan, or baking dish. Roast until the tops of the peppers begin to change color from red to black, 20 to 30 minutes. Remove from the oven and let cool.

While the peppers are cooling, in a medium glass bowl, combine the olive oil and garlic.

Peel off the pepper skins and remove the seeds by partially pulling the peppers apart under cold running water, using your fingers to rub the seeds away. Pull the peppers lengthwise into quarters or halves, discarding the stems, and pat them dry with paper towels.

Add the peeled peppers to the olive oil and mix gently so as not to tear them. Let the peppers marinate at room temperature for about 2 hours prior to serving. (The peppers can also be made in advance. Place the marinating peppers in a covered bowl in the refrigerator for up to 24 hours. Remove them from the refrigerator 30 minutes prior to serving.)

Divide the peppers equally among 4 to 6 salad plates. Drizzle some of the garlic olive oil over the peppers and season with salt and pepper to taste.

Feta Cheese with Lemon, Fresh Rosemary, and Olives

dairy | serves 4 to 6

This exceedingly simple preparation is ideal as an appetizer when friends visit. Bright hues make it quite attractive as well. The briny accents of feta cheese—made from sheep's or goat's milk—work well in tandem with herbs and olives. You can also substitute other fresh, soft goat's- or sheep's-milk cheeses for the feta if you'd prefer.

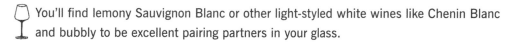 You'll find lemony Sauvignon Blanc or other light-styled white wines like Chenin Blanc and bubbly to be excellent pairing partners in your glass.

3 tablespoons extra virgin olive oil

1 tablespoon fresh lemon juice

½ teaspoon freshly ground pepper

A pinch of coarse salt

½-pound chunk or wedge feta cheese

1 tablespoon fresh rosemary leaves, coarsely chopped

Zest of 1 lemon, chopped fine

⅓ cup pitted olives, such as Niçoise or Kalamata, coarsely chopped

Crackers, toasts, or country bread or baguette slices

In a medium bowl, whisk together the olive oil, lemon juice, pepper, and salt. Place the cheese on a serving plate and pour the oil mixture on top of it. Garnish with the chopped rosemary, lemon zest, and olives. Spread onto crackers, toasts, or crusty bread slices.

Fava Bean Puree with Truffle Oil on Parmesan Crostini

dairy | serves 4 to 6

This pale-green, creamy, smooth spread tastes like our garden in the springtime, when the fava beans reach maturity and produce a prodigious crop of fat, round bean pods on the vine. Soft herbal notes mingle with a hint of earthy truffle oil. The puree is spread on crunchy, tangy Parmesan toasts—perfect finger food. (*To make this dish pareve, prepare the crostini toasts without cheese.*) Truffle oil can be found in most fine supermarkets. Fortunately, it is far less expensive than truffles themselves. And a little goes a long way.

This appetizer is terrific with a glass of crisp Sauvignon Blanc or sparkling wine, though it will pair nicely with just about any other cool, refreshing white wine or dry rosé.

2 pounds fresh fava beans in their pods (about 3 cups shelled)

4 tablespoons extra virgin olive oil, plus more for the bread

2 medium cloves garlic, minced

2 sprigs fresh rosemary (about 4 inches long each)

1 cup water

1 teaspoon truffle oil

2 teaspoons fresh lemon juice

Salt and freshly ground pepper

1 French baguette

½ cup grated Parmesan cheese (optional)

To shell the beans, use the tip of a paring knife to open the pods. (Do not cut into the beans.) Using your fingers, slide the beans into a large bowl.

In a medium pot, bring 3 inches of lightly salted water to a boil over high heat. Add the fava beans and boil until they are bright green but still firm, about 2 minutes. Drain and rinse under cold running water. With your fingers, gently squeeze the outer skin of each bean and pop out the inner bean (discard the skins).

In a large pan, heat 2 tablespoons of the olive oil over medium-high heat until it shimmers. Add the garlic and sauté until fragrant, about 30 seconds. Add the fava beans and stir to coat with oil. Stir in the rosemary. Add ¾ cup of the water and bring to a boil. Reduce the heat to low and simmer for 5 minutes. (If necessary, add more water as needed, one tablespoon at a time, to keep the beans from burning.) Discard the rosemary sprigs.

Add the remaining ¼ cup water to a blender. Add the fava bean mixture and any liquid remaining in the pan as well. Blend at low speed until the beans become fairly smooth. Stir the mixture occasionally if needed (when the blender is off) to facilitate blending. Add the remaining 2 tablespoons olive oil and continue to puree until very smooth. Transfer to a bowl and stir in the truffle oil and lemon juice. Season with salt and pepper to taste.

Preheat the oven to 350°F.

With a sharp bread knife, slice the baguette on an angle into twelve ½-inch-thick slices. Brush one side of each slice with olive oil. Place the slices on a baking sheet and sprinkle the Parmesan evenly over the bread slices. Bake until the crostini turn golden brown, about 20 minutes.

Let the crostini cool until they are easy to handle. Spread a dollop of puree onto each toast, garnish with additional pepper, and serve at room temperature.

Onion Tart

pareve | makes about 36 tartlets or 4 main-course servings

Cut this tart into 2 × 3-inch squares and it becomes a pass-around finger food appetizer. Or slice it into larger portions, like pizza, and serve it alongside a salad for a light meal or first course. In Nice, France, where we used to live, the locals top the tart with anchovies and call it *pissaladière,* but we like it best without the little fish. Note that you can serve this tart hot, warm, or at room temperature, all with excellent results!

For the tart crust, we use a mixture of all-purpose and high-gluten flours. You can also substitute bread flour for both flours (see page 62 for more on flours). The dough will need to rise for a few hours, during which time you can prepare your topping.

When it comes to wine, this onion tart is quite versatile. It pairs equally well with both reds and whites. If you're starting off with the tart as an appetizer, offer your guests a white wine like bubbly or perhaps a glass of crisp Chardonnay. The caramelized onions have a hint of sweetness—great with Riesling or Moscato too.

tart dough

1 envelope (¼ ounce;
    2¼ teaspoons) active dry yeast

1¼ cups warm water

½ cup high-gluten flour

2 cups all-purpose flour, plus more
    for kneading and rolling

½ teaspoon salt

2 tablespoons extra virgin olive oil,
    plus more for the bowl and pans

tart topping

¼ cup extra virgin olive oil

6 cloves garlic, minced

5 teaspoons dried thyme

6 large onions, thinly sliced

1½ teaspoons salt

½ teaspoon freshly ground pepper

30 to 40 pitted Niçoise or
    Kalamata olives

MAKE THE TART DOUGH: In a large bowl, combine the yeast with 1 cup of the warm water. Using a wooden spoon, stir in the high-gluten flour. Add the all-purpose flour, salt, and olive oil. Stir until a sticky dough begins to form on the bottom of the bowl. Add the remaining ¼ cup warm water and, using your hands, shape the dough into a large ball.

When your hands become sticky, dust them with a little all-purpose flour. Knead the dough in the bowl by pushing it down with the heel of your hand and then pulling it together in a mound. Repeat until the dough becomes firm yet elastic, about 5 minutes.

Lightly oil the surface of another large bowl. Place the dough in the bowl, cover the bowl with plastic wrap, and set it aside at room temperature to rise for 2 hours. It should double in size.

While the dough is rising (during the second hour), MAKE THE TART TOPPING: In a large skillet, heat the olive oil over medium heat. Add the garlic and thyme to the oil and cook for 30 seconds. Add the onions, separating the slices with a wooden spoon and stirring to coat them evenly with the oil and thyme. Add the salt and the pepper and stir well. Reduce the heat to low and cook, stirring every 5 minutes, until the onions are soft, about 20 minutes. Set aside.

Get out two nonstick 12- to 14-inch round pans or two nonstick 9 × 13-inch baking sheets or pans. If the pans are not nonstick, oil each with 1 teaspoon olive oil.

When the dough has risen, remove it from the bowl and set it on a floured work surface. Cut it in half and use a rolling pin to roll out two crusts that will fit your pans. Raise the edge of each crust with your thumbs to make a rim.

Preheat the oven to 500°F.

Spread the cooked onions and the olives evenly over each tart crust. Bake until the outer crust is golden brown, 12 to 15 minutes.

Cut into 2 × 3-inch pieces to make appetizer portions (or cut in quarters to serve as a main course).

All-Purpose, High-Gluten, and Whole Wheat Flours

For baking pizza (or onion tart) dough, we often don't use all-purpose flour alone. Instead, we blend it with high-gluten flour (sometimes labeled "gluten flour"). High-gluten flour is milled from hard wheat. It gives bread a slightly chewy texture that is different from the softer crumb of cakes or muffins. In many stores, you can also purchase bread flour, which has a higher gluten content than all-purpose flour. This is what we use to make Challah (page 237).

Using all-purpose flour alone can give your bread or pizza dough the texture of cake. But the right blend of high-gluten flour and all-purpose flour produces an onion tart crust that reminds Jeff of the old-style *pissaladière* he grew up eating in France.

In addition, there is whole wheat flour, which contains nutritious wheat bran and germ. Unfortunately, breads made with 100 percent whole wheat flour don't rise as well as those made with white flour. They can be quite heavy. In a nod to good health, we sometimes bake bread with a blend of white and whole wheat flours.

Lavender Goat Cheese Tart

dairy | serves 6 to 8

This quick-cooking tart serves up a blend of zippy flavors and creamy texture, all enhanced by fragrant lavender. (Look for dried lavender in your supermarket spice rack.) The tart can be enjoyed as an appetizer alone or accompanied by a Green Salad with Mustard Vinaigrette (page 75) for a light lunch.

   While it is possible to make puff pastry from scratch at home, we don't recommend it. Commercial (kosher) dough is readily available and quite good. Also, remember to choose fresh, soft, mild goat cheese for the best results.

Any bright-edged white wine such as bubbly, Sauvignon Blanc, or Chardonnay would make an excellent match.

1 sheet puff pastry (about 10 × 4 inches), thawed to room temperature

1 stick (8 tablespoons) plus 1 tablespoon unsalted butter, at room temperature

8 ounces soft goat cheese

¾ cup whole-milk cottage cheese

3 egg yolks

¼ cup all-purpose flour

½ teaspoon salt

2 tablespoons dried crushed lavender flowers

Preheat the oven to 375°F. Use the end of the stick of butter to lightly butter a 9-inch tart pan with a removable rim. Reserve the rest of the stick.

On a floured surface, gently roll out the puff pastry to stretch and shape it to cover the bottom and sides of the tart pan. Press the dough into the base and sides of the pan and trim excess dough to hang just slightly over the top edge of the pan. This allows for some shrinkage as the dough cooks. Use extra dough to patch up any uncovered spots on the pan.

In a small saucepan, melt 1 tablespoon of the butter over medium-low heat. Using a pastry brush, brush the dough with the melted butter. Place the tart shell in the oven and bake until slightly puffy and light gold in color, 10 to 12 minutes. Remove from the oven but leave the oven on.

While the tart shell is baking, prepare the filling. In a food processor or in a large bowl, with an electric mixer, combine the remaining stick of butter with the goat cheese, cottage cheese, egg yolks, flour, salt, and lavender, blending until the ingredients are creamy smooth.

Scrape the filling into the tart crust, leaving about ¼ inch of space below the top of the crust. The surface of the filling should be smooth.

Return the tart to the oven and bake until the filling appears firm to the touch and the surface is light brown in color, about 20 minutes. Let the tart cool for 15 minutes before removing the sides of the pan. The tart is best when served warm.

Chickpeas with Toasted Cumin Seeds and Fresh Mint

pareve | serves 4 to 6 as an appetizer or side dish

Despite sharing a core ingredient, this dish offers a completely different dining experience from our Chickpea Salad with Red Onion, Red Pepper, and Fresh Cilantro (page 87). Laced with cumin and mint, this appetizer is best served in the company of other simple dishes such as Roasted Red Peppers with Olive Oil and Garlic (page 54) or Olives with Lemon Zest and Thyme (page 48). These chickpeas can also stand in for rice or other side dishes, especially with lighter-styled seafood, such as Grilled Sardines with Marinated Onions, Green Peppers, and Freekeh Salad (page 133) or vegetarian fare.

Light, fresh-tasting white wines such as Sauvignon Blanc, Chardonnay, Viognier, or Roussane are your best bets here. If you prefer a red wine, look for one blessed with good acidity, like Pinot Noir or Sangiovese.

2 carrots, cut into ¼-inch-thick rounds

4 tablespoons extra virgin olive oil

2 cloves garlic, minced

2 cans (15 ounces each) chickpeas, drained, or 3 cups home-cooked (page 242)

1 tablespoon fresh lemon juice

1 tablespoon cumin seeds, toasted (page 243)

3 tablespoons minced fresh mint

Salt and freshly ground pepper

In a small pot, bring 3 inches of water to a boil over high heat. Add the carrots and cook just until tender, about 5 minutes. Drain in a colander and rinse under cold running water to stop the cooking. Transfer to a medium bowl and set aside.

In a medium skillet, heat 2 tablespoons of the olive oil over medium heat. Add the garlic and sauté until fragrant, about 30 seconds. Add the chickpeas and stir to coat evenly with the oil. Sauté until the beans are hot, another 5 minutes, stirring occasionally to prevent burning.

Add the chickpeas to the carrots. Drizzle with the remaining 2 tablespoons olive oil and the lemon juice. Mix thoroughly. Add the cumin seeds and mint and mix again. Adjust the seasoning with salt and pepper to taste. Serve warm or at room temperature.

Sautéed Carrots with Cumin Seeds and Fresh Cilantro

pareve | serves 4

These tender, sweet carrots are brimming with flavors that remind us of both California and Israel. Cumin is found in many Middle Eastern dishes, while fragrant cilantro permeates the kitchens of the West Coast. You can serve these carrots as an appetizer, but they also make a fine side dish.

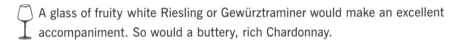 A glass of fruity white Riesling or Gewürztraminer would make an excellent accompaniment. So would a buttery, rich Chardonnay.

1 pound medium carrots, cut into ¼-inch-thick rounds

1½ tablespoons extra virgin olive oil

1 teaspoon cumin seeds

⅛ teaspoon salt

2 tablespoons minced fresh cilantro

Fill a medium pot two-thirds full with lightly salted water and bring to a boil over high heat. Add the carrots and cook until barely tender, about 5 minutes. Drain in a colander and rinse under cold running water to stop the cooking.

In a medium skillet, heat the olive oil over medium heat. Add the cumin seeds and sauté for about 1 minute, or until the seeds are fragrant and turn dark brown. Add the carrots and salt and stir to coat the carrots thoroughly with the cumin seeds. Cover and continue to cook until the carrots can be easily pierced with a fork, 8 to 10 minutes.

Remove the pan from the heat and stir in the cilantro. Transfer the carrots to a serving bowl or platter and serve at once.

Fried Green Tomatoes with Saffron Aioli

dairy | serves 4

In early summer, our tomato plants are heavy with unripe, green fruit. We can never wait for them to turn red, so we pick some early for frying. Cornmeal and grated Parmesan cheese temper their unripe tanginess, as does the rich, golden aioli sauce—its gorgeous color comes from the saffron, and it is so easy to prepare. Make the aioli first and refrigerate until ready to use.

If you don't have a garden, you can buy green tomatoes or Green Zebra tomatoes in many supermarkets, or at farmers' markets in the summer. This recipe can also be made with red tomatoes; just make sure they are not too soft or ripe, or they will fall apart in the pan.

What do we drink with fried tomatoes? Any light-bodied white wine is an excellent choice. We favor crisp Sauvignon Blanc, Chardonnay, or Riesling. Sparkling wine or dry rosé would also make a fine match.

1 cup yellow cornmeal

1 teaspoon salt

⅓ cup grated Parmesan cheese

1 teaspoon dried tarragon

¼ teaspoon cayenne pepper

2 eggs

2 tablespoons milk

1 cup unbleached all-purpose flour

Canola oil, for frying

6 to 8 medium green tomatoes, cut into ¼-inch-thick slices

1 cup Saffron Aioli (page 244)

In a large bowl, combine the cornmeal, salt, Parmesan, tarragon, and cayenne. Stir with a whisk or fork to blend thoroughly. In a second bowl, whisk or beat the eggs and milk together. Place the flour in a third bowl.

In a large skillet, heat 1 inch of canola oil over medium-high heat until it starts to shimmer. If necessary, reduce the heat to medium to prevent smoking.

One at a time, dredge the tomato slices first in the flour, then in the egg, and finally in the cornmeal mix. Dip each one again in the egg and then dredge once more in the cornmeal. Using tongs or a slotted spoon, carefully slip the prepared tomato slices into the hot oil. Work in batches so as not to crowd the pan. Fry the tomatoes, flipping once, until they are golden brown, about 2 minutes per side. Transfer the slices to a platter with paper towels to drain.

Serve hot with the aioli for dipping. Or you can top the tomatoes with a dollop or two of the sauce.

Stuffed Summer Squash Flower Beignets

dairy | serves 4 to 6

In June, the squash in the garden start to flower. It's a sign that summer is coming. These are a special favorite of Jeff's, who first encountered squash flower *beignets* (the French word for "fritters") while living in France as a young musician. His French neighbors cooked up a batch of these large tender flowers and washed them down with the local white wine—a perfect accompaniment!

You can use the flowers of any summer squash, such as zucchini or sunburst. And if you don't grow them yourself, the flowers are often available in supermarkets with good produce departments, or at summertime farmers' markets. You can cook them in canola oil to save money, but pricier olive oil will give you a richer, more layered taste.

This recipe calls for stuffing the flowers with cheese. But if you want to make the dish pareve, it's easy not to use any cheese at all. Just sprinkle some of the mint and lemon zest in each flower. The unstuffed version is lighter but equally satisfying.

In addition to a simple, fresh-tasting white wine such as Sauvignon Blanc, Chenin Blanc, or Roussane, we would recommend a light-textured dry rosé, another classic accompaniment throughout France and now a popular choice in the United States as well.

¾ cup ricotta cheese, at room temperature

¼ cup fresh goat cheese, at room temperature

1 tablespoon minced fresh mint

1 tablespoon minced lemon zest

⅛ plus ½ teaspoon salt

18 to 24 summer squash flowers

Canola oil or extra virgin olive oil, for frying

1 cup all-purpose flour

1 cup water

1 egg

In a medium bowl, combine the ricotta, goat cheese, mint, lemon zest, and ⅛ teaspoon of the salt. Using a wooden spoon or a fork, stir to mix well.

Remove the stamen inside each flower by pinching it off with your fingers. Carefully fill each flower with approximately 1 tablespoon of the cheese filling. (Smaller flowers will require less filling. If you have as many as 24 flowers, make sure they are small ones, or you will run out of cheese.) Gently twist and pinch the tips of the petals to seal the filling inside the flower. Lay the stuffed squash flowers on a large plate and set aside.

In a large skillet, heat 1 inch of oil over high heat until it begins to shimmer.

While the oil is heating, in a large bowl, whisk together the flour and remaining ½ teaspoon salt. Whisk in the water and egg until the batter is smooth and resembles pancake batter.

When the oil is shimmering hot, reduce the heat to medium-high. Working in batches, gently dip the stuffed flowers one at a time into the batter, coating them evenly and allowing excess batter to drip off. Place each battered flower into the hot oil. Cook until the undersides are golden brown, 1 to 2 minutes. Use tongs to gently flip the flowers. Fry for another minute, until they are crisp and golden brown on both sides. Transfer the flowers to a plate covered with paper towels to drain.

Serve hot.

Gravlax

dairy | serves 4 to 6 as a first course, more as a pass-around appetizer

Gravlax, or cured salmon, has been a staple in our house for years. Although it takes a little time (4 days) to cure in your refrigerator, it requires very little prep time in the kitchen. Note that the salmon is not smoked, but rather "slow-cooked" by the salt, sugar, and vodka in which it is wrapped. The result is an elegant, rich-tasting fish that is marked by both savory and sweet notes.

We serve very thinly sliced gravlax on small toasts and topped with a dollop of crème fraîche as an appetizer. Or we lay out larger slices drizzled with lemon juice and garnished with capers as a first course. A little bread and butter on the side adds a nice touch, and you can also enjoy gravlax in a sandwich, surrounded by nothing more than sweet butter or cream cheese on rustic country bread or a bagel. But this is not essential, particularly if you want your gravlax to remain pareve.

The best wines for gravlax would be fresh-tasting bubblies—like Champagne— or steely clean Sauvignon Blanc. Other whites such as Chardonnay, Riesling, and Roussane are excellent options as well.

2 skin-on salmon fillets
   (about 1½ pounds total)

¼ cup sugar

¼ cup salt

1 tablespoon coarsely ground
   pepper

1 cup chopped fresh dill

2 tablespoons vodka

optional garnishes

Crème fraîche (omit if you want
   the recipe to be pareve)

Juice of 2 lemons and capers

Place the fillets, skin-side down, on a large plate. Coat the flesh evenly with the sugar, salt, pepper, and dill. Drizzle both fillets evenly with the vodka. Lay one of the fillets on top of the other, with the flesh sides facing each other and the skin on the outside.

Wrap the sandwiched fillets tightly in plastic wrap and lay them down in a broad, shallow bowl. (Leave the ends of the plastic wrap slightly open to allow liquid to run out.) Set a heavy weight on top of the fish. (We use a 28-ounce can of tomatoes.)

Refrigerate for 4 days. Flip the sandwiched fillets twice a day, once in the morning and once in the evening. Discard any liquid that collects in the bottom of the bowl and replace the weight every time you flip the fillets. After 4 days, unwrap the fish and remove any excess dill that may have clumped up or is thickly covering the fish. Use your hands and/or a paring knife to peel or slice away the skin. (You'll want to get all the tough skin off the fish; it is not good to eat.) Cut the fillets into thin slices and eat plain, or serve as suggested above.

Salads and Soups

The salads in this chapter vary from simple greens to more complex fare such as Frisée Salad with Poached Egg and Beef Fry (page 89). However, some, like Lentil Salad with Cilantro and Spices (page 86), resemble the *meze*-inspired small plates in the appetizers chapter. Truly, many salads and appetizers are interchangeable. And it's not uncommon for us to sit down for dinner with an appetizer followed by a green salad. Or we'll just forget about the salad and have an appetizer.

We also substitute soup for salad. And sometimes we'll eat both, especially during special occasions like Shabbat. But even on a normal weeknight, "soup and salad" can provide a satisfying meal. For example, Endive and Asian Pear Salad with Walnut Vinaigrette (page 80) followed by our rich, heartwarming Salmon Chowder (page 96) should provide plenty of sustenance for even the heartiest appetites.

Salads and soups cry out for a slice of crusty, country bread. If you want to make your own bread at home, try our recipes for Rustic Challah (page 237) or Pita Bread (page 239).

We've heard it said that wine and salad don't mix. But this couldn't be farther from the truth. At issue is the vinegar used in many salad dressings. It can make a rich, red wine taste tart. But if you pair your salad with a white wine or rosé that's blessed with bright acidity, you'll find a pleasing, complementary pairing.

And if you've got only one bottle of red wine at home, so what? You might find you like the red wine with your salad anyway. Food and wine pairing guidelines are not written in stone.

Green Salad with Mustard Vinaigrette

pareve | serves 4

In California, we are blessed with beautiful, fresh salad greens year-round. Typically, we enjoy them as a first course dressed in this simple vinaigrette, which takes about a minute to prepare. After eating this dressing, you will never go back to the sweet, store-bought dressings that you find at grocery stores. We disagree as to whether this salad is better with or without tomatoes. Suffice it to say, you can't go wrong either way, so we'll leave it up to you to decide.

Make sure you use enough mustard (Dijon or similar) in the vinaigrette. It acts as an emulsifier, holding the dressing ingredients together. Dried thyme is also a key element, as it offers a fresh, country taste. Make your dressing whenever it's convenient. Add the greens prior to serving, and toss.

It's important to dry your greens thoroughly after washing them. Residual water on the leaves prevents the dressing from evenly coating the lettuce. To dry lettuce leaves, we use an inexpensive salad spinner that can be purchased in most shops that carry kitchenware.

Any salad made with a vinaigrette will pair best with an equally bright-textured white wine that's higher in acidity, such as sparkling wine, Sauvignon Blanc, Roussane, and Riesling. But most nights at home, we open only one bottle of wine—and that might be a red wine, not a white. So we just don't worry about it and drink a little red wine with our salad. Invariably, it tastes good too!

vinaigrette

3 tablespoons extra virgin olive oil

1 tablespoon balsamic or other white or red wine vinegar

1 teaspoon Dijon mustard

½ teaspoon dried thyme

1 small clove garlic, minced

A pinch of salt (optional)

salad

8 to 10 very thin slices onion (optional)

1 medium head Bibb lettuce or 6 to 8 ounces mixed baby greens, rinsed and dried

1 or 2 tomatoes, quartered (optional)

1 avocado, diced (optional)

MAKE THE VINAIGRETTE: Place all the ingredients in a large salad bowl. Use a wooden spoon to stir and blend evenly.

ASSEMBLE THE SALAD: If using, place the onion in the vinaigrette and stir to coat thoroughly. Add the greens and any of the other optional ingredients. Toss well.

Beet Salad with Arugula, Feta Cheese, and Orange Vinaigrette

dairy | serves 4

This colorful presentation serves up a tantalizing array of flavors. Sweet, earthy red beets lie on a bed of spicy, green arugula. On top of that sits creamy white feta cheese. Coriander and aniseed add a subtle, exotic crunchiness. And the vinaigrette, spiked with fresh orange juice, provides an almost tropical garnish.

Sip a refreshing white wine such as Sauvignon Blanc, Chardonnay, Roussane, or Viognier alongside.

6 small red beets

1 teaspoon coriander seeds

1 teaspoon aniseed

Juice of 1 orange (about ½ cup)

2 tablespoons white wine vinegar

⅓ cup extra virgin olive oil

Coarse salt and freshly ground pepper

4 to 6 ounces arugula

1 cup crumbled feta cheese (about ¼ pound)

Preheat the oven to 400°F.

If the beet greens are attached, remove them, leaving about ½ inch of the stalks. Do not peel the beets. Wrap the beets—2 or 3 together—in foil, leaving the top of the foil open. Roast until they are tender when pierced by a fork, 1 to 1¼ hours. When they are cool enough to handle, peel the skins and trim off the tops. Depending on the size of the beets, cut each into 4 to 8 cube-like pieces.

With a mortar and pestle, or using the side of a wide, flat knife, coarsely crush the coriander seeds and the aniseed. (They should still be crunchy.) Set aside.

In a medium bowl, whisk together the orange juice, vinegar, and olive oil. Season with salt and pepper to taste.

Divide the arugula among 4 salad plates. Place the beets on top of the greens. Sprinkle the feta on top of the beets and sprinkle with the coriander/aniseed mixture. Whisk the vinaigrette one last time to blend, and drizzle 1 to 2 tablespoons over each salad. Season with salt and pepper to taste.

Arugula Salad with Toasted Pine Nuts, Shaved Parmesan, and Lemon Vinaigrette

dairy | serves 4

This simple salad features arugula, one of our favorite greens. With its spicy edge and vaguely licorice-like flavor, arugula requires little more than a light dressing to highlight its unique qualities. A blend of olive oil and walnut oil offers a nutty note, enhanced by toasted pine nuts and their hint of smoky sweetness. (*To make the salad pareve, forgo the cheese. It will still be quite tasty.*)

If you are toasting the pine nuts yourself (see "Toasting Seeds and Nuts," page 243), it takes only a few minutes on the stovetop. Remember to do this first; then set the nuts aside until you've made the dressing.

Lemony vinaigrettes are not particularly wine friendly and can be tricky to pair with wine. Drink a bright-edged bubbly or snappy Sauvignon Blanc—wines with enough acidity to stand up to the vinaigrette—for best results.

1 tablespoon extra virgin olive oil

1 tablespoon roasted walnut oil

2 teaspoons fresh lemon juice

1 teaspoon dried tarragon

¼ teaspoon coarse salt

1 tablespoon minced shallots

2 tablespoons pine nuts, toasted (page 243)

6 ounces arugula

1 ounce Parmesan cheese (optional; omit for pareve)

Salt and freshly ground pepper

In a large salad bowl, use a wooden spoon to stir together the olive oil, walnut oil, lemon juice, tarragon, and salt. Stir in the shallots and then the pine nuts. Add the arugula and toss to coat well. Make sure the pine nuts are evenly distributed throughout.

Using a cheese slicer, a vegetable peeler, or a sharp knife, shave the cheese into paper-thin, 2 × ½-inch shavings. You should have about 20 shavings.

Divide the greens evenly among 4 salad plates. Garnish each serving with the Parmesan shavings and pepper. Individual diners can add salt to taste.

Arugula, Radish, and Avocado Salad

pareve | serves 4

Salad doesn't get much easier than this. The spicy arugula and radish will wake up your palate, but they are mellowed by creamy avocado.

With its own lemony finish, this simple dish has a good dose of acidity and doesn't really need wine. But if you do want a glass of wine to go with your salad, try a crisp Sauvignon Blanc or a sparkling wine.

1 cup firmly packed arugula

1 avocado, cut into ¼-inch-wide slices

4 large radishes, thinly sliced

3 thin slices red onion

½ teaspoon dried tarragon

3 tablespoons extra virgin olive oil

1 tablespoon fresh lemon juice

Salt and freshly ground pepper

Spread the arugula leaves evenly across a large serving platter. Frame the outside edge of the salad with avocado slices and line up the remaining avocado in the center of the arugula. Garnish the avocado with the radishes and red onion. Sprinkle with the tarragon.

Drizzle with the olive oil and lemon juice. Season with salt and pepper to taste.

Endive and Asian Pear Salad with Walnut Vinaigrette

pareve | serves 4

We have enjoyed this wonderfully refreshing salad for many years. Crunchy endive pairs well with the subtle, barely sweet, round Asian pear. (You can substitute Bosc pear if you can't find Asian pear.) It's all dressed in a lovely tarragon vinaigrette that's easy to prepare.

Any crisp, fruity white wine would make a fine match here. Riesling and Gewürztraminer are at the top of our list. Their fruit-driven quality makes them complementary pairings for a dish featuring Asian pears. Bright-edged Sauvignon Blanc would offer a different, but equally interesting, perspective—more contrasting than complementary.

3 tablespoons roasted walnut oil

1 tablespoon extra virgin olive oil

1 tablespoon white wine vinegar

1 teaspoon Dijon mustard

1 small shallot, finely diced

1 clove garlic, minced

½ teaspoon dried tarragon

4 endives (white and/or red), cut into ½-inch-thick rounds

1 head frisée lettuce, coarsely chopped

¼ Asian pear, cut into matchsticks (about ⅓ cup)

Salt and freshly ground pepper

In a large salad bowl, combine the walnut oil, olive oil, vinegar, mustard, shallot, garlic, and tarragon. Whisk until the sauce thickens and all the ingredients are thoroughly blended. Add the endive and frisée and toss to coat evenly. Add the pear and gently toss again.

Divide evenly among 4 salad plates and season with salt and pepper to taste.

Smoked Salmon Caprese with Endive

dairy | serves 4

This is our family's take on the classic Italian salad made with mozzarella cheese, tomato, and fresh basil. It's easy to prepare and lovely to behold. As kids in New York, we grew up with cream cheese and lox, but we never did like cream cheese. Instead, we prefer our lox—or smoked salmon—with mozzarella. The fresher the cheese, the better.

 We often eat this salad as a weekend lunch accompanied by a glass of cool, crisp white wine or rosé.

2 endives, cut into ½-inch-thick rounds

2 tomatoes, cut into ¼-inch-thick slices

8 ounces fresh mozzarella cheese, cut into ¼-inch-thick slices

4 ounces sliced smoked salmon, each slice rolled up

3 tablespoons minced fresh basil

3 tablespoons extra virgin olive oil

1 tablespoon fresh lemon juice

Salt and freshly ground pepper

Evenly spread the endive rounds across the surface of a large serving platter. Place the sliced tomatoes, spaced evenly apart, over the endive. Place a slice of mozzarella on top of each tomato and a rolled salmon slice on top of the mozzarella cheese. Garnish with the basil and drizzle with the olive oil and lemon juice. Season with salt and pepper to taste.

Wilted Spinach Salad with Mushroom Vinaigrette

pareve | serves 4

Salads don't have to be cold or served at room temperature. This one, made with spinach tossed in a fresh mushroom vinaigrette, is warm. Earthy mushrooms and a bright-tasting sauce coat the spinach leaves. The spinach is not really cooked, just wilted from the heat of the sauce in the pan.

Note that the ingredients include Worcestershire sauce, a kosher-certified flavoring that may list fish among its ingredients. As such, Worcestershire sauce would be considered a fish product. According to the laws of *kashrut,* fish products cannot be eaten together with meat, but they can be eaten as a separate course within a meat meal.

This kind of dish pairs beautifully with many different wines—both red and white. Sweet Riesling, zippy Sauvignon Blanc, and creamy-rich Chardonnay will all find complementary qualities in the salad. Meaty mushrooms are also good with most dry red wines. So take your pick!

1 tablespoon plus ¼ cup extra virgin olive oil

½ pound (8 to 10) button mushrooms, sliced

1 clove garlic, minced

1 teaspoon dried thyme

1 tablespoon balsamic vinegar

2 tablespoons Dijon mustard

1 tablespoon Worcestershire sauce

¾ pound spinach

4 thin slices red onion

Salt and freshly ground pepper

In a Dutch oven or deep-sided skillet, heat 1 tablespoon of the olive oil over medium heat. Add the mushrooms, gently stirring to coat well with the oil, and sauté for 5 minutes. (If necessary, add a few tablespoons water to the pan to prevent burning.) Stir in the garlic and thyme. Reduce the heat to low and sauté until the mushrooms are soft, another 3 minutes.

Whisk in the remaining ¼ cup olive oil, the vinegar, mustard, and Worcestershire sauce. Remove the pan from the heat. Add the spinach and toss until all the leaves are evenly coated with dressing. The spinach will wilt in the warm pan.

Add the onion and toss again. Season with salt and pepper to taste and serve warm.

Summertime Tomato Salad with Tahini Dressing

pareve | serves 4

Jeff visited Israel for the first time as a teenager in the summer of 1973. Left to his own devices, he managed to run out of money just outside Bethlehem, where an acquaintance told him about a group of monks who lived up in the hills. They offered room and board to weary (or broke) travelers in exchange for work.

For a hungry teenager, it sounded like a good deal. Jeff located the monastery at the end of a goat trail, and settled into a work routine that began at dawn and ended at noon, when it was too hot to continue laboring outside. Every day, without exception, lunch started with this salad. We've been eating it ever since. It's perfect in summertime, when ripe tomatoes and green peppers weigh heavy on the vines in the garden.

Adding feta cheese would make this a dairy dish. Try it both ways, with and without the cheese, for a slightly different taste.

 A light, fresh-tasting white wine or rosé is the ticket for this salad.

¼ cup extra virgin olive oil

2 tablespoons tahini (roasted sesame seed paste)

1 tablespoon ground cumin

½ medium onion, finely chopped

2 green bell peppers, cut into ¼-inch dice

4 to 5 tomatoes, cut into ¼-inch dice, or 1 pint cherry tomatoes, halved

¼ pound feta cheese, crumbled or diced (optional)

In a large serving bowl, stir together the olive oil, tahini, and cumin. Mix in the onion to coat well with the dressing. Add the green peppers and tomatoes and toss to coat them evenly. If using, add the cheese and toss the vegetable mixture once more before serving.

Lentil Salad with Cilantro and Spices

pareve | serves 4

You can almost taste the sun-drenched Israeli street markets when you take a bite of this lightly spiced lentil salad. Serve it as a first course, garnished with fresh-cut tomato wedges, or enjoy it as a side dish with any number of recipes, including Smoked Salmon Frittata with Gruyère and Fresh Herbs (page 110). Any lentils will do here, but we prefer the small green ones (sometimes called French green lentils) because of their texture. They take a little longer to cook than regular brown lentils but tend to be less starchy.

Rosé would be our first choice of wine to pair with this dish. But any dry wine, white or red, would also taste good.

1 cup dried lentils

3 cups lightly salted water

½ cup diced red bell pepper

½ cup diced carrots

2 tablespoons minced red onion

3 tablespoons finely chopped fresh cilantro

¼ cup extra virgin olive oil

2 tablespoons fresh lemon juice

½ teaspoon ground cumin

½ teaspoon curry powder

¼ teaspoon salt

Fresh tomato wedges, for garnish (optional)

Rinse the lentils and pick through them to remove any pebbles. In a 2- to 3-quart saucepan, bring the salted water to a boil over high heat. Add the lentils, cover, and reduce the heat to low. Cook until the liquid is completely absorbed and the lentils are tender, about 20 minutes. (If the liquid disappears before the lentils are tender, add another ¼ cup water and simmer until it is absorbed.) Remove the pan from the heat and allow the lentils to cool to room temperature. If not using right away, cover and refrigerate for up to 3 days.

In a large bowl, gently mix the lentils, bell pepper, carrots, onion, and cilantro. In a smaller bowl, whisk together the olive oil, lemon juice, cumin, curry powder, and salt. Pour the sauce over the lentils and mix thoroughly. Garnish with tomato if desired.

Chickpea Salad with Red Onion, Red Pepper, and Fresh Cilantro

pareve | serves 4

In Israel, where they make some of the best salads in the world, we've enjoyed dishes similar to this chickpea salad. Not only is it loaded with flavor, it is also easy to prepare, especially if you use canned chickpeas. Purists can cook their own dried chickpeas—also known as garbanzo beans—from scratch, but it's really hard to tell the difference. Serve this small salad on its own, with a variety of small plates, or with a main course such as Baked Stuffed Rainbow Trout (page 139). (Just substitute the chickpeas for the butter beans in the trout recipe.)

Any crisp, fresh white wine would make an excellent accompaniment. Steely Sauvignon Blanc is a favorite in our home. (The term *steely* really means just that: a steely, mineral-like taste that we find very attractive in certain dry white wines. The verdict is still out on exactly where this taste comes from. Some say it comes from the soil, and some might even infer that aging in steel barrels or tanks could be a cause. To be honest, most simple questions in wine have complex answers that defy pat explanations. We don't know exactly why some wines are more steely or mineral-like than others, but most likely, this quality originates in the vineyard. Regardless of why it's there, we love this taste in lighter-styled, bright-edged white wines.)

2 cups home-cooked chickpeas (page 242) or 1 can (15 ounces), drained

½ cup pitted Kalamata or other black olives

⅓ cup finely chopped red onion

½ cup finely chopped red bell pepper

⅓ cup minced fresh cilantro

½ teaspoon salt

1 tablespoon fresh lemon juice

2 tablespoons extra virgin olive oil

Freshly ground pepper

In a large bowl, combine the chickpeas, olives, onion, bell pepper, and cilantro. Sprinkle with the salt and mix well.

In a small bowl, stir the lemon juice and olive oil together. Pour the dressing into the chickpea mixture and toss thoroughly. Season with black pepper to taste.

Frisée Salad with Poached Egg and Beef Fry

meat | serves 4

For best results, use the freshest of eggs in this homage to a renowned, colorful French salad. Note that this isn't breakfast. We eat this salad as a first course prior to lunch or dinner. Walnut oil adds a special dimension as well, and a little truffle salt makes a fine addition—but it's not required. Take care not to overcook your eggs. You want the bright yellow yolk to run across the lettuce and blend with the dressing and smoky beef fry. (*Frisée,* in French, means "curly." The lettuce leaves look like curly green hair.)

Eggs and wine are natural partners. White wines such as Chardonnay, Roussane, Viognier, or Chenin Blanc would make excellent pairings. So would fruity Riesling and Gewürztraminer. Lighter-styled red wines like Pinot Noir or Sangiovese would also complement the flavors on your plate.

2 tablespoons roasted walnut oil

3 tablespoons extra virgin olive oil

2 tablespoons white wine vinegar or apple cider vinegar

1 teaspoon Dijon mustard

1 clove garlic, minced

1 shallot, minced

2 teaspoons dried tarragon

Salt and freshly ground pepper

4 slices beef fry, sliced into thin matchsticks

4 eggs

2 heads frisée lettuce (about ¼ pound each), coarsely chopped

Truffle salt (optional)

In a large salad bowl, combine the walnut oil, 2 tablespoons of the olive oil, 1 tablespoon of the vinegar, the mustard, garlic, shallot, and tarragon. Whisk until the sauce thickens and all the ingredients are thoroughly blended. Season with salt and pepper to taste. Set aside.

In a small skillet, heat the 1 remaining tablespoon olive over high heat. Add the beef fry and cook until crisp and brown, 5 to 7 minutes. Using a slotted spoon, remove the fry from the pan and drain on paper towels. Set aside.

To poach the eggs, fill a large pot with 3 to 4 inches of water. Add the remaining 1 tablespoon vinegar. Bring to a boil over high heat, then reduce the heat to a simmer. Gently crack the eggs into the water. Cook until they begin to firm up and the whites are no longer translucent, about 3 minutes.

While the eggs are poaching, add the frisée to the dressing in the salad bowl and toss. Make sure to coat the leaves evenly. Divide the lettuce among 4 salad plates.

Using a slotted spoon, remove the eggs from the water, draining as much water from the spoon as possible, before gently placing directly on top of the salad. Garnish each serving with beef fry. Season with salt and pepper to taste.

La Soupe au Pistou

dairy | serves 4 to 6

In Nice, France—where we spent years learning how to eat, drink, and cook—the locals are proud of their vegetable soup topped with a spoonful of pistou—or pesto, as the Italians refer to this basil sauce. It adds terrific flavor to the soup, which regularly graces our table in both summer and winter.

The word *pistou* comes from the Niçois word *pista*, which means "to crush," evoking the way the basil leaves were once crushed with a mortar and pestle. You can still make pistou like this, but we now prefer to use a blender. Pistou contains Parmesan cheese, also used separately as a garnish, but if you want to make this soup pareve, you can do so by simply leaving out the cheese. It won't be quite the same, but it will still taste great.

Note that a little prep work will make this simple dish even easier to prepare. It takes only a few minutes to make the pistou (page 246). You can do it while the soup is cooking; or you can make it in advance and refrigerate it for up to 3 days. If you plan to cook your cannellini beans from scratch (page 242), you'll need to plan for that as well. We typically use canned beans. It's so much easier, and no one can tell the difference. You'll also need to cook your elbow pasta separately before adding it to the finished soup. But that's something that can be done in 10 minutes anytime before you are ready to serve your meal.

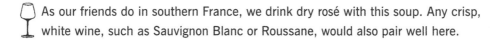 As our friends do in southern France, we drink dry rosé with this soup. Any crisp, white wine, such as Sauvignon Blanc or Roussane, would also pair well here.

3 tablespoons extra virgin olive oil

1 onion, diced

5 cloves garlic, coarsely chopped

2 medium leeks (white parts only), well washed and cut crosswise into ¼-inch-thick rounds

3 plum tomatoes, coarsely chopped

1½ teaspoons salt

2 quarts water

1 medium turnip, diced

2 carrots, cut into ¼-inch-thick rounds

In a large soup pot or Dutch oven, heat the olive oil over medium heat. Add the onion and sauté until it becomes translucent, about 5 minutes. Add the garlic and sauté for another minute. Add the leeks, stir to mix well, and cook for about 3 more minutes. Add the tomatoes and salt and continue to cook, stirring occasionally, until all the ingredients have reduced in volume by one-third, about 15 minutes.

Meanwhile, in a separate pot, bring the water to a boil over high heat.

Add the boiling water to the onion-tomato mixture. Add the turnip, carrots, kale, and sage. Bring to a vigorous boil, then reduce the heat to medium and continue to cook, uncovered, for 30 minutes.

After the ingredients have simmered for 30 minutes, stir in the beans, turn off the heat, and cover to keep warm.

3 cups firmly packed chopped kale
  leaves

3 or 4 fresh sage leaves

2 cups home-cooked cannellini
  beans (page 242) or 1 can
  (15 ounces), drained

8 ounces elbow macaroni, cooked
  (about 2 cups)

Pistou (Pesto) Sauce (page 246)

Grated Parmesan cheese,
  for garnish

When ready to serve, reheat the soup. Place about ⅓ cup cooked pasta in each diner's soup bowl and ladle in the soup. Add a soupspoon of pistou sauce to each bowl and garnish with Parmesan to taste.

Curry Ginger Butternut Squash Soup

pareve | serves 4 to 6

This rustic, fragrant soup is easy to make and has great texture. The squash is only coarsely pureed, leaving tiny chunks that give a full, rich mouthfeel. Curry turns up the heat a bit, but not enough to offend, while grated ginger leaves a zippy, fresh finish.

Full-bodied white wines are recommended for pairing. Fruity Riesling—dry or off-dry—would make an exceptional match. So would lush, barrel-fermented Chardonnay or Viognier.

1 medium-to-large butternut squash (about 3 pounds)

3 cups Vegetable Stock (page 240) or store-bought low-sodium broth

3 tablespoons extra virgin olive oil

1 onion, diced

2 teaspoons grated fresh ginger

1½ teaspoons curry powder

1 teaspoon salt

Freshly ground pepper

Trim the ends off the squash and cut it in half. Remove the seeds with a tablespoon. Using a vegetable peeler, peel the squash and cut the flesh into 2-inch cubes.

In a Dutch oven or large soup pot, bring the vegetable stock to a boil over high heat. Add the squash, reduce the heat to medium, cover, and simmer until the squash is tender, about 20 minutes.

Meanwhile, in a medium skillet, heat the olive oil over medium heat. Add the onion and cook until translucent, about 3 minutes. Add the fresh ginger and cook until fragrant, 30 seconds. Add the curry and mix thoroughly.

Add the sautéed onions and the salt to the squash pot, gently mix, and continue cooking until the squash can be easily pierced with a fork. Strain the liquid through a colander or fine-mesh sieve into another pot. Working in batches if necessary, in a blender or food processor, puree the squash, adding small amounts of the strained broth (¼ cup at a time) as needed to puree. However, do not puree too finely—you want to leave small pieces of solids for the soup.

Return the pureed squash to the soup pot and add the rest of the strained broth, whisking thoroughly to incorporate both. Reheat the soup over medium heat.

Season individual servings with pepper to taste.

Cauliflower Soup with Crispy Garlic and Curry Oil

dairy | serves 6

There's a hint of India in this richly textured soup. It comes from a curry oil you can make in just 2 minutes on your stovetop. Fried garlic croutons—also exceptionally easy to prepare—add a zesty, crunchy dimension that's hard to resist.

This soup calls for a full-bodied white wine, such as barrel-fermented Chardonnay or perhaps a more fruit-driven dry or semi-dry Riesling or Gewürztraminer. You will experience the soup differently depending on what kind of wine you are drinking, because different flavors and textures in a wine will highlight or enhance different qualities in a dish. A rich, toasty (but not-so-fruity) Chardonnay will bring out the curry and garlic notes; but a fruit-forward Riesling will tone down those flavors.

1 tablespoon curry powder

3 tablespoons plus ½ cup canola oil

2 tablespoons unsalted butter

1 onion, diced

12 cloves garlic—2 minced and 10 thickly sliced

1 large cauliflower, cut into large chunks (about 5 cups)

3 cups Vegetable Stock (page 240) or store-bought low-sodium vegetable broth

1 cup heavy cream

¼ teaspoon salt

Freshly ground pepper

In a small saucepan, toast the curry powder over medium heat, shaking the pan frequently to prevent burning, until fragrant, about 1 minute. Add 3 tablespoons of the canola oil, stir to mix thoroughly, and remove the pan from the heat. Set the curry oil aside.

In a large soup pot, melt the butter over medium heat. Add the onion and minced garlic and sauté until the onion is translucent, about 3 minutes. Add the cauliflower, vegetable stock, cream, and salt. Stir thoroughly. Bring the liquid to a boil, then reduce the heat to a gentle simmer. Continue to simmer, uncovered, until the cauliflower is soft, about 20 minutes.

Transfer the soup to a blender or food processor—in batches if necessary—and puree until very smooth. (When pureeing in a blender, cover the top of the blender with a kitchen towel to prevent dangerously hot soup from escaping.) Return the pureed soup to the pot, cover, and set aside.

In a small saucepan, heat the remaining ½ cup oil over medium heat until it starts to shimmer. Add the garlic slices and cook until crisp and golden brown, about 10 minutes. Using a slotted spoon, remove the garlic slices and set them on paper towels to drain excess oil.

Reheat the soup over low heat. Ladle it into bowls, placing 5 or 6 garlic slices on top of the soup at the center of each bowl. Drizzle each serving with ½ teaspoon curry oil and garnish with the pepper. (When serving the curry oil, do not remix the curry powder into the oil. Tilt the pan and spoon off just the oil, leaving the curry powder on the bottom of the pan.)

Salmon Chowder

dairy | serves 6

This creamy chowder has been a favorite at our house for years. It's substantial enough to serve as a main course, too, packed with chunks of salmon and potato. But it's not "fishy." Instead, you'll find this to be a mild-flavored soup that appeals to a broad range of tastes. Tomatoes, corn, leeks, and mushrooms provide additional interest, along with subtle heat from the jalapeño pepper.

We recommend white wine or rosé in your glass. In fact, we really can't think of any white varietal that wouldn't work well here—from Chardonnay to Chenin Blanc and Riesling to Gewürztraminer.

2 tablespoons extra virgin olive oil

1 medium onion, diced

2 cloves garlic, minced

½ jalapeño pepper, seeded and finely chopped

2 medium white potatoes, diced

2 leeks (white part only), well washed and cut into ¼-inch-thick rounds

1 can (28 ounces) whole Italian plum tomatoes, drained and coarsely chopped

4 cups Vegetable Stock (page 240) or store-bought low-sodium vegetable broth

1½ cups dry white wine

2 teaspoons salt, plus more to taste

1 pound fresh salmon fillets or steaks, skinned, bones removed, and cut into 1-inch chunks

1 cup fresh corn kernels (from 2 ears corn)

6 white mushrooms, sliced

1 cup half-and-half

½ cup finely chopped fresh cilantro

Freshly ground pepper

In a Dutch oven or large soup pot, heat the olive oil over medium-high heat. Add the onion, garlic, and jalapeño and sauté until the onion is translucent, about 3 minutes.

Add the potatoes and leeks and continue to sauté until the leeks have wilted, about 5 minutes. Add the tomatoes, vegetable stock, wine, and 2 teaspoons salt. Increase the heat to high and bring to a boil. Reduce the heat to low, cover, and simmer for 10 minutes.

Add the salmon and continue to simmer, covered, for another 10 minutes. Stir in the corn and mushrooms, cover, and simmer for 10 more minutes. Add the half-and-half and cook, uncovered, for 3 minutes.

Stir in the cilantro and adjust the seasoning with salt and pepper to taste.

Fish Soup with Matzo Balls and Aioli

pareve | serves 6 as a first course

We love fish soup. One long-ago Passover, we suddenly wondered, "Why don't we make matzo ball soup with fish stock instead of chicken stock?" This saffron-colored variation on a traditional theme has now become our standard.

You'll probably want to double the ingredients for Passover (and remember to use the Passover recipe for the aioli, with lemon juice instead of mustard), but you don't need to wait for the holiday to enjoy this lovely dish. It's not hard to make and will provide lots of pleasure for you and your dining companions at any time of the year. (You can also enjoy it without the matzo balls.)

The list of ingredients may seem long, but most of them are simply thrown in the pot, boiled, and then strained. You will also need to purchase a 3- to 4-pound ocean fish. (Remember that kosher fish must have fins and scales.) If you are using the fish head, don't bother removing the gills, as some cookbooks traditionally advise. Contrary to popular belief, we haven't found they add any bitterness.

Both the matzo balls and soup are best made a day in advance—or at least the morning before you serve them. First make the matzo balls. They need to be chilled for about 3 hours prior to cooking or the mix will not harden enough to form balls. Make the fish soup when the matzo balls are chilling in the refrigerator. For ease of presentation, we have kept the recipe for the soup and the matzo balls separate.

Aioli, or garlic mayonnaise (page 244), adds richness. It is added to the broth when serving. Diners can just mix it into the liquid themselves. No more than 5 or 10 minutes are required to whip up an aioli from scratch. Make it in advance and refrigerate for up to 3 days.

From a wine-drinking perspective, the French would most likely enjoy this soup with a glass of dry rosé. (We have enjoyed countless fish soups in southern France paired with crisp, chilled local rosés. It's a tradition.) Other fine options would include any racy, dry white wine such as Sauvignon Blanc, Chenin Blanc, or Chardonnay.

soup

2 tablespoons extra virgin olive oil

2 onions, sliced

3 carrots, coarsely chopped

3 celery stalks, coarsely chopped

Make the matzo balls (see recipe on page 100) and refrigerate while you make the soup.

To make the soup, in a large saucepan or a soup pot, heat the olive oil over medium heat. Add the onions, carrots, and celery and sauté until tender, about 5 minutes. Add the fish (cut in pieces, if necessary, to fit into the pot)

One 3- to 4-pound saltwater fish (with or without head), such as cod, flounder, salmon, or halibut, scaled and gutted

½ teaspoon dried thyme

1 bay leaf

2 to 4 sprigs flat-leaf parsley

1 large head garlic, halved

2 tablespoons tomato paste

2½ pounds fresh tomatoes, chopped, or 1 can (28 ounces) whole Italian plum tomatoes, chopped, with juice

1 teaspoon saffron threads

¼ teaspoon cayenne pepper

1 large potato, peeled and coarsely chopped

1 teaspoon sea salt

1½ cups Aioli (page 244), for serving

Freshly ground pepper

and cook, turning frequently, until the flesh begins to fall off the bones, about 10 minutes.

Add the thyme, bay leaf, parsley, garlic, tomato paste, tomatoes, saffron, cayenne, potato, and salt. Add enough water to cover the contents. Bring to a boil, reduce the heat to medium, and simmer, covered, until the potato is tender, about 45 minutes.

Let the soup cool for about 15 minutes. Working in batches if necessary, in a blender or food processor, coarsely pulse the fish soup. Strain the puree through a fine-mesh sieve or colander into a large bowl or pot, forcing the liquid through by pressing on the solids with the back of a large spoon or—even better—the bottom of a (pareve) coffee mug. Discard all the solids. Strain the soup one more time through a fine-mesh sieve into a large pot to remove as many remaining solids as possible.

To serve, add the cooked matzo balls to the soup that is now in a large pot and reheat over medium-high heat. When the soup starts to bubble, reduce the heat to medium, cover, and continue to heat until the matzo balls are hot throughout, about 10 minutes. Ladle the soup with one or two matzo balls per serving into individual soup bowls. You or your dinner guests can add a dollop or two of aioli to the broth in each bowl. Season with pepper to taste.

Matzo Balls | makes 10 to 15 matzo balls

4 eggs

¼ cup extra virgin olive oil

¼ cup water

1 cup matzo meal

2 cloves garlic, minced

2 tablespoons minced fresh cilantro

1 teaspoon salt

Freshly ground pepper

In a large bowl, combine the eggs, olive oil, water, matzo meal, garlic, cilantro, and salt. Add a few grinds of pepper. Using a whisk or wooden spoon, gently mix to incorporate all the ingredients. Cover and refrigerate for at least 3 hours or overnight.

When the matzo mix is firm to the touch, remove it from the refrigerator and shape it into 10 to 15 balls the size of Ping-Pong balls. Rinse your hands with cold water now and then to prevent sticking. Lay the matzo balls out on a flat surface coated with wax paper.

Fill a large skillet halfway with lightly salted water and bring to a boil over high heat. Use a large spoon to gently lay the matzo balls in a single layer into the water. They should not be stacked on top of each other. Cover the pan and reduce the heat to medium-low. Cook until the matzo balls have expanded and are firm to the touch, 45 to 50 minutes. Use immediately or let cool and refrigerate for up to 3 days.

Eggs, Rice, Latkes, and Pasta

Eggs and grains are the building blocks for many recipes you'll find throughout this book. In this chapter, we've included a number of our favorite stand-alone egg, rice, and pasta dishes. Some, like Gnocchi with Sage Butter (page 117) or Fresh Mushroom Risotto (page 113), can also make excellent side dishes, as can potato latkes (page 107), a traditional Chanukah favorite. Each one, however, provides enough substance for a main course.

The chapter starts with Shakshouka (page 105), which in Israel and throughout the Middle East is a wildly popular baked egg and tomato dish. We've adapted it to our California kitchen with the addition of large, flat butter beans, avocado, and feta cheese. Our version is more filling than what we have enjoyed in Israel. We love it equally for lunch or dinner.

We feel the same way about omelets—while many people think of them as breakfast fare, we prefer them for brunch, lunch, or dinner, especially when served with a glass or two of wine.

Two noodle recipes featured here represent different ends of the culinary spectrum. Lemon-Rosemary Pasta (page 121) is distinctly Mediterranean, while Ginger Sesame Noodles (page 124) are inspired by the flavors of Japan. Both require minimum preparation time and deliver maximum pleasure to your palate. Two others—Eggplant, Tomato, and Ricotta Rigatoni (page 119) and Pink Sauce Fettuccine (page 115)—are more in tune with each other, as they are both tomato based. They have long been family favorites.

There's a reason these recipes have become staples at our house—they are satisfying in an elemental way. We hope you like them as much as we do!

Shakshouka

Baked Eggs with Tomato Sauce

dairy | serves 4

We first discovered this colorful, satisfying dish in Israel, where it is made with many variations. All seem to include eggs and some kind of bright, tangy tomato sauce. We've added meaty butter beans, avocado, and feta cheese. (*To make this pareve, leave out the cheese.*) Like so many egg dishes, shakshouka is versatile—perfect for brunch, lunch, or dinner. Enjoy it as a first course, a main course, or even a side dish.

Try not to leave the eggs in the oven too long, though, or you risk overcooking them. For best results, the yolks need to be runny. Butter beans resemble lima beans, but are usually larger. Typically we use canned or jarred beans because they make cooking so much easier, but purists can start with dried beans (page 242). We just don't see much difference. Other firm-textured beans, such as kidney beans or chickpeas, make fine substitutes. If you are using dried beans, remember to cook them well in advance.

These eggs taste best accompanied by a glass of good wine—white, red, or rosé. We recommend higher-acid whites such as Sauvignon Blanc or Chardonnay. Any dry rosé would be fine, too. Brighter-styled red wines like Sangiovese, Pinot Noir, and Zinfandel also make excellent pairings.

3 tablespoons extra virgin olive oil

1 medium onion, diced

3 cloves garlic, minced

1 green bell pepper, diced

1 can (12.5 ounces) butter beans, drained, or 3 cups home-cooked (page 242)

1 teaspoon paprika

1 teaspoon turmeric

1 teaspoon ground cumin

¼ teaspoon cayenne pepper

½ teaspoon salt

8 medium tomatoes, diced (about 4 cups)

½ cup water

8 eggs

In a large, ovenproof skillet, heat the olive oil over medium-high heat. Add the onion and sauté until translucent, 3 to 5 minutes. Add the garlic and stir until fragrant, about 30 seconds. Add the green pepper and sauté until it has softened, about 5 minutes. Add the beans, paprika, turmeric, cumin, cayenne, and salt. Gently mix to coat all the ingredients evenly with the spices. Reduce the heat to medium-low and simmer for 2 more minutes.

Add the tomatoes, any juices that may have accumulated when dicing them, and the water. Increase the heat to high and bring the liquid to a boil. Immediately return the heat to medium-low, cover, and simmer, stirring occasionally, for 10 minutes. Uncover the pan and simmer until the juice has thickened somewhat, another 5 to 10 minutes. It will have turned a darker shade of red.

Preheat the oven to 425°F.

Remove the pan from the heat. Carefully crack the eggs—trying not to break the yolks—one at a time over the beans and sauce, spacing them evenly apart. Transfer the skillet to the oven, uncovered, and bake for 3 min-

1 avocado, diced

1 cup crumbled feta cheese
(optional; omit for pareve)

⅓ cup chopped fresh cilantro

Freshly ground pepper

Crusty country bread, for serving

utes. Rotate the pan (to ensure that the shakshouka cooks evenly) and bake until the egg whites begin to firm up but the yolks are still runny, about 3 more minutes.

Remove the pan from the oven and let sit for 1 minute to settle the eggs. Garnish with the avocado, feta cheese (if using), and cilantro, spreading them evenly across the surface of the shakshouka.

To serve, use a large spoon to scoop out the eggs with the beans, sauce, and garnishes, keeping the eggs on the top, unbroken. Season with pepper and serve with bread for dipping.

Latkes with Sour Cream, Green Onions, and Masago

dairy | makes about 20 latkes (serves 10 as an appetizer, 4 to 6 as a main course)

Everyone loves latkes, the fried potato pancakes traditionally served at Chanukah, but why wait all year? We love latkes so much that we eat them from January through December. In this recipe, we top our latkes with tangy sour cream, green onions, and masago—tiny fish eggs from the capelin fish. You can find the roe in specialty fish markets and food stores. As a substitute, feel free to use salmon roe, which are larger and somewhat saltier. (*To make this pareve, serve it without sour cream.*)

For us, latkes are really all about potatoes and oil. We don't use egg or matzo meal to "bind" the main ingredient, but you will need to use russet (baking) potatoes here. They are high in starch, which serves as a natural binding agent.

The latkes are cooked crisp on the outside and soft inside. We prefer to fry in extra virgin olive oil. It's a little more expensive than other oils, but in our opinion, its fruity flavor is worth it. However, some people find that olive oil smokes faster than other oils, such as canola or vegetable oil. We have not had this experience, but you should feel free to use whatever frying oil you are accustomed to.

Serve latkes as a main course or an appetizer. Or try them (without any garnish at all) as a side dish for our Smoked Salmon Frittata with Gruyère and Fresh Herbs (page 110). Just cut the latke recipe in half to serve 4 since leftovers don't hold up well (after the first day, they lose their perfect crispiness).

Rich white wines, such as barrel-fermented Chardonnay and Viognier, would be our first choice for drinking. Fruity Riesling and Gewürztraminer would pair well too.

5 pounds russet (baking) potatoes (about 8 potatoes), peeled

2 onions, peeled

2 teaspoons salt

Extra virgin olive oil, for frying (2 to 3 cups)

8 ounces sour cream

2 ounces masago or salmon roe

10 green onions (white part only), sliced into very thin rounds

Freshly ground pepper

Preheat the oven to 200°F.

In a food processor fitted with the shredding blade, grate the potatoes. (You can also grate them by hand, but it is very time-consuming.) Transfer the potatoes to a large bowl. Grate the onions and add them to the bowl with the potatoes. Add the salt. Using your hands, thoroughly mix the potatoes, onions, and salt. Set aside.

In a deep-sided skillet, heat ½ inch of olive oil over medium-high heat until the oil begins to shimmer and show small bubbles.

While the oil is heating, form the potato pancakes. Using a ⅓-cup measuring cup, scoop out enough shredded potato mix to fill the cup. Hold the cup over a separate bowl and press as much liquid as possible out of the potatoes. Tap the contents of the cup into the palm of your hand and shape it into a thick pancake, pressing as much additional liquid from the pancake as possible. Set the latke on a large plate. Repeat until you have used up all the potato mix. (You may need 2 large plates to hold all the pancakes. Discard the pressed liquid from the potatoes.)

When the oil is hot enough, cook the latkes in batches. Use a spatula to lift the latkes off the plate and gently set them in the boiling olive oil. (If the oil starts to smoke or splatter, reduce the heat slightly.) Do not crowd the pancakes. Fry until the latkes are crisp on the outside and both sides are dark tan or very golden brown, about 10 minutes per side.

Transfer each batch of cooked latkes to a paper towel–lined baking dish and keep warm in the preheated oven until ready to serve.

To serve, top each latke with a dollop of sour cream. Place a small spoonful of masago on top of the sour cream. Sprinkle with the green onions. Garnish with pepper to taste.

Smoked Salmon Frittata with Gruyère and Fresh Herbs

dairy | serves 4

A frittata is simply an omelet that is finished under the broiler. This method gives the egg a hint of smokiness and a firmer texture without burning or drying out the bottom.

Gruyère cheese is a mild, nutty cow's-milk cheese made in both Switzerland and France. If you can't find one to your liking, feel free to substitute other mild cheeses such as cheddar or Gouda.

Remember that the wider and shallower the pan, the faster the egg will cook. Serve the frittata with buttered toast on the side or—with a little advance preparation—with Lentil Salad with Cilantro and Spices (page 86) or Chickpea Salad with Red Onion, Red Pepper, and Fresh Cilantro (page 87). It would also be terrific served with latkes (page 107) or a simple Green Salad with Mustard Vinaigrette (page 75).

This frittata is especially good for brunch, perhaps with a glass of sparkling wine. But eggs pair very well with both white and red wines. The saltiness of the smoked salmon leads us to a cool, crisp white wine. But on a cold winter day, red wine would be our choice.

---

2 tablespoons extra virgin olive oil

1 cup diced white onion

2 green onions (white and green parts), cut into ¼-inch-thick rounds

8 eggs

¼ pound smoked salmon, sliced into short strips about ¼ inch wide

¼ pound Gruyère cheese, cut into thin, narrow slices

¼ cup coarsely chopped fresh oregano or 1 tablespoon dried

Freshly ground pepper

Preheat the broiler.

In a large, broilerproof skillet, heat the olive oil over medium heat. Add the onion and green onions and sauté until the white onion is translucent, 3 to 4 minutes.

Meanwhile, crack the eggs into a large bowl and whisk to blend thoroughly. Stir in the salmon.

Reduce the heat to medium-low, push the onion to the edge of the skillet, and pour in the egg/salmon mixture, making sure the salmon is evenly distributed throughout the egg. Use a wooden spoon or rubber spatula to spread the onion in the pan throughout the egg. Lay the cheese slices evenly across the top of the egg. Garnish with the oregano. Cook until the bottom of the egg has set, 3 to 5 minutes. The top of the frittata should still be runny.

Transfer the skillet to the top oven rack directly under the broiler. Cook the frittata until the top sizzles and takes on a golden brown hue, 3 to 5 minutes.

Remove the pan from the oven, cut the frittata into quarters, and serve immediately with freshly ground pepper to taste.

Fresh Mushroom Risotto

dairy | serves 6 as a first course, 4 as a main course

Over the years, Jodie has become known as the "risotto queen" of our home. She uses a wide array of ingredients to enhance this Italian staple built on creamy Arborio rice. However, her mushroom risotto is our favorite. Usually we enjoy it as a main dish, although the Italians tend to eat it as a first course.

In winter, wild mushrooms grow in hidden spots throughout Northern California. We make this dish with a variety of whatever the local forests or hillsides are offering—usually a blend of porcinis and chanterelles, but you can use any wild or commercially grown mushrooms that you can find in your grocery store or farmers' market. Even the little button mushrooms and shiitakes commonly found at the supermarket work just fine. Blending two or three types of mushrooms adds flavor and texture, but using a single variety will also yield excellent results.

Another key element here is the vegetable stock. It's easy to make from scratch (page 240), but you'll need to start making it at least an hour before you plan to begin cooking the risotto. Or you can use a low-sodium store-bought vegetable stock. Just be careful not to purchase squash- or tomato-based stocks (or broths), which are too rich. The idea is to use a light, aromatic liquid that enhances—but doesn't overpower—the mushrooms.

You'll also need ½ cup of red wine for the pot, which translates to about one glass of wine. If you're serving a great wine for dinner, we recommend using a different, inexpensive, dry red wine in the risotto. Save the good stuff for your glass! For drinking, we propose just about any top-notch red wine ranging from Pinot Noir to Cabernet Sauvignon. The mushrooms have a wholesome, earthy quality that we find particularly complementary with red wines, which may also have an earthy component. And because the risotto cooks in red wine, the concept of complementary pairing (page 38) is reinforced. Why a top-notch wine? Because any great-tasting dish merits a great-tasting wine!

5 tablespoons extra virgin
   olive oil

1 pound fresh mushrooms, sliced

Salt and freshly ground pepper

1 onion, finely chopped

2 cloves garlic, minced

1 cup Arborio rice

In a Dutch oven or large pot, heat 2 tablespoons of the olive oil over medium-high heat. Add the mushrooms and ¼ teaspoon salt. Stir to partially coat with the oil. Cover the pot and cook, stirring occasionally, until soft, 12 to 15 minutes. Transfer the mushrooms and their juice to a bowl and set aside.

In the same pot used to cook the mushrooms, heat the remaining 3 tablespoons olive oil over medium heat. Add the onion and garlic and sauté until

4 cups Vegetable Stock (page 240) or store-bought low-sodium vegetable broth

½ cup dry red wine

½ cup freshly grated Parmesan cheese

2 tablespoons finely chopped fresh chives

the onion is translucent, 3 to 5 minutes. Stir in the rice and ¼ teaspoon salt and sauté for another 2 minutes. Add 2 cups of the stock or broth, ½ cup at a time. (Allow most of the liquid to be absorbed before adding another ½ cup.) Let the liquid simmer and stir it regularly—about every 3 minutes—until most of the liquid has been absorbed. Then add the wine. When most of the wine is absorbed, add the remaining 2 cups broth, ½ cup at a time, as before, until most of it is absorbed. (The risotto should remain creamy. Do not let it dry out.)

Add the mushrooms and their juices to the rice and gently stir to incorporate. Keep the risotto simmering gently and continue to stir regularly until cooked through. (The rice should be creamy but remain slightly chewy.) This should only take a few more minutes.

Turn off the heat and stir in the Parmesan and then the chives. Serve at once garnished with salt and pepper to taste.

Pink Sauce Fettuccine with Fresh Rosemary

dairy | serves 4

A creamy tomato sauce spiked with fresh rosemary neatly coats these wide pasta noodles. Despite our usual quest for freshness, we don't typically use fresh tomatoes in this recipe. It's one of those year-round dishes we generally whip up at the last minute.

Pinot Noir or Zinfandel would be our initial wine choices here. Sangiovese or Tempranillo—both reds—would also work well.

2 tablespoons extra virgin olive oil

1 onion, diced

3 cloves garlic, minced

¼ teaspoon red pepper flakes

3 tablespoons minced fresh rosemary

½ cup red wine

1 can (15 ounces) tomato puree

1 can (28 ounces) whole tomatoes, drained and coarsely chopped

Salt and freshly ground pepper

1 pound dried fettuccine

¾ cup heavy cream

¾ cup freshly grated Parmesan cheese, plus more for garnish

¾ cup grated Fontina cheese

In a large saucepan or Dutch oven, heat the olive oil over medium heat. Add the onion and sauté until translucent, about 3 minutes. Add the garlic, pepper flakes, and rosemary and sauté until fragrant, about 1 minute. Add the red wine, increase the heat to medium-high, bring to a boil, and cook until the wine reduces by half, 2 to 3 minutes.

Stir in the tomato puree, chopped tomatoes, and ½ teaspoon salt. Reduce the heat to low and simmer, uncovered, for 20 minutes.

Bring a large pot of lightly salted water to a boil. Add the fettuccine and cook until al dente, about 10 minutes. Drain in a colander and shake dry. (Do not rinse the pasta with water.) Set the colander aside.

Meanwhile, in a small saucepan, combine the cream, Parmesan, and Fontina. Simmer over low heat, stirring until the cheese is completely melted. Add the cheese sauce to the tomato sauce and stir gently. The tomato sauce will turn a dark pink. Season with salt and pepper to taste.

Place a small amount of the pink sauce (about ¼ cup) in the bottom of a large serving bowl. Add the cooked pasta to the bowl and then pour the remaining pink sauce over the pasta. Gently toss the fettuccine until it is evenly coated with the sauce.

Garnish with pepper and additional Parmesan, if desired.

Gnocchi with Sage Butter

dairy | serves 6 as an appetizer or first course, 4 as a main course

Gnocchi—the soft dumplings that are synonymous with Italy—are often made with potatoes. This version, made with ricotta cheese and flour, is lighter and fluffier. It's easy to make these gnocchi from scratch. They are quite filling. But they can be served as a first course, as long as you don't eat too many!

We like to melt the sage butter with fresh sage from our garden, but you can also find fresh sage in most supermarket produce sections. It has a kind of earthy, mineral-like quality that we love in food as well as in Fresh Herb Tisane (page 231). What if you can't find fresh sage? Fresh tarragon would make an interesting substitution. Or you can just eliminate the herbs. Simply garnish with a good dose of freshly ground pepper to lighten things up.

Butter-dressed gnocchi pair beautifully with white or red wines—especially ones with bright acidity that can balance the rich sauce. We recommend many different varietals; each will enhance your dining experience in a different way. Try Chardonnay, Gewürztraminer, and Viognier among full-bodied whites; Sauvignon Blanc, Riesling, or Chenin Blanc for white wines that are lighter in style. If you want a red wine, bring up a Pinot Noir or Syrah from the cellar.

1 pound whole-milk ricotta cheese (about 2 cups)

2 eggs, lightly beaten

¼ cup freshly grated Romano cheese

2 cups all-purpose flour, plus more for dusting

Salt and freshly ground pepper

8 tablespoons (1 stick) unsalted butter, cut into 6 large pieces

¼ cup chopped fresh sage leaves

In a large bowl, combine the ricotta, eggs, Romano, 1 cup of the flour, and 1 teaspoon salt. Using a wooden spoon or rubber spatula, stir to blend well. The texture should become light and fluffy. Refrigerate the ricotta mixture for at least 30 minutes or up to 1 hour to allow it to firm up.

Pour the remaining 1 cup flour onto a work surface. Using a large spoon, scoop out 4 equal portions of the ricotta mixture onto the floured surface. Dust your hands with flour and pick up one scoop of the ricotta mixture. Roll it in the flour and very lightly knead it to form a soft dough. Repeat with each of the remaining ricotta scoops.

Using your hands, shape each portion of ricotta dough into a rope or cylinder ½ to ¾ inch in diameter and about 12 inches long. Cut each rope crosswise into 1-inch-long sections and gently roll each section in additional flour to prevent sticking.

Bring a large pot of lightly salted water to a boil. Fill a large bowl with ice and water and set by the stove. Line a baking sheet with parchment paper.

Using a slotted spoon, carefully place 15 to 20 gnocchi into the boiling water. As the gnocchi float to the surface (after 1 to 2 minutes), use the slotted spoon to transfer them to the ice bath. (The cooling firms them up and makes them easier to sauté later.) Once the gnocchi are cool, use a slotted spoon to transfer them from the ice water to the parchment paper.

In a skillet or sauté pan large enough to hold the gnocchi in a single layer, melt the butter over medium-high heat. (If you don't have a large enough pan, divide the gnocchi, butter, and sage between 2 pans.) When the butter has melted, reduce the heat to medium and gently stir in the sage. Add the gnocchi and sauté until each side is slightly browned, 2 to 3 minutes per side. (Use a spatula or slotted spoon to carefully flip the gnocchi.)

Divide among 4 plates and season with salt and pepper to taste.

Eggplant, Tomato, and Ricotta Rigatoni

dairy | serves 4

We make this homey, wholesome dish whenever we discover, last minute, that guests are coming for dinner. It's quick, and we haven't met anyone who doesn't like it! Tube-like rigatoni noodles hold the sauce nicely, but you can really use any kind of pasta you like.

Red wine would be best here. Drink anything that's celebratory but not too complex or expensive. This is simple, country fare. Look for Zinfandel, Malbec, Sangiovese, or varietal table wine blends from producers whose wines you love.

6 to 8 tablespoons extra virgin olive oil

2½ pounds eggplant (unpeeled), cut crosswise into ¼-inch-thick slices

5 cloves garlic, minced

⅛ teaspoon chipotle pepper flakes

½ cup red wine

3 pounds fresh tomatoes, coarsely chopped, or 1 can (28 ounces) whole Italian plum tomatoes, coarsely chopped, with juice

Salt and freshly ground pepper

½ cup chopped fresh basil

1 pound rigatoni pasta

½ cup fresh ricotta cheese

⅓ cup grated Parmesan cheese

In a large skillet, heat 3 tablespoons of the olive oil over medium-high heat until it starts to shimmer. Working in batches, place the eggplant slices in a single layer in the pan and sauté until golden brown on the bottoms, about 3 minutes. Turn them over and sauté until the other side is golden brown, 3 more minutes. If necessary, add more olive oil to the pan, 1 to 2 tablespoons at a time, to prevent burning. Continue until all the eggplant has been cooked. Transfer the eggplant to a platter covered with paper towels to drain excess oil. When the slices are cool enough to touch, cut into 2-inch squares and set aside.

If a lot of oil remains in the pan, use a paper towel to wipe most of it away, leaving only a sheen on the pan surface. Reduce the heat under the pan to medium, add the garlic and chipotle pepper flakes, and sauté until fragrant, about 30 seconds, being careful not to let the garlic burn. Add the red wine and stir and scrape up any browned bits on the bottom of the pan. Stir in the tomatoes and ¼ teaspoon salt. Reduce the heat to medium-low and simmer for 10 minutes. Add the reserved eggplant and mix gently. Continue to cook for 10 more minutes, stirring occasionally. Stir in the basil. Remove the pan from the heat, cover, and set aside until ready to serve. (The sauce can be made in advance and reheated over low heat.)

Bring a large pot of lightly salted water to a boil. Add the rigatoni and cook until al dente, about 12 minutes. Drain the pasta in a colander and shake dry. (Do not rinse the pasta.)

In a large bowl, mix together the eggplant sauce, ricotta, and Parmesan. The sauce will turn light pink. Add the pasta to the sauce and toss to mix thoroughly. Season with salt and pepper to taste.

Lemon-Rosemary Pasta

dairy | serves 4

This is a dish Jeff started to make years ago in France, when he lived in an apartment located directly above a Niçois pasta producer. At lunchtime he'd cook his fresh pasta and toss it with whatever local ingredients happened to be in his kitchen. In southern France, fresh herbs, olive oil, and lemons are ubiquitous.

Today, we enjoy making this simple, delicious dish at home in California. To make the pasta sauce, simply mix the ingredients in a bowl. It requires no cooking. And for those of you without access to a rosemary bush, look for fresh rosemary in your local produce department. Dried rosemary makes a reasonable substitute, but it won't have quite the same vibrant flavor. You can make the sauce in the time it takes to cook the pasta. (Remember that fresh pasta cooks faster than dried pasta.)

The best accompaniment in your glass would be bright, lemony Sauvignon Blanc. Other white wines such as Pinot Grigio, Chenin Blanc, and dry Gewürztraminer would also serve well.

¾ cup extra virgin olive oil

Juice of 2 lemons

¼ cup minced fresh rosemary or 1½ tablespoons dried

1 cup freshly grated Parmesan cheese

1 pound linguine or other dried pasta, or 1½ pounds fresh pasta

Coarse salt and freshly ground pepper

Bring a large pot of lightly salted water to a boil.

Meanwhile, in a large bowl, stir together the olive oil, lemon juice, rosemary, and Parmesan.

Add the pasta to the boiling water and cook until al dente, about 10 minutes for dried pasta, 4 minutes for fresh pasta. Drain the pasta in a colander and shake dry.

Add the pasta to the bowl with the sauce and toss to coat evenly. Season with salt and pepper to taste.

Truffled Macaroni and Cheese

dairy | serves 4 to 6

The pungent truffle oil used here is not nearly as expensive as a real truffle. (However, those with money to burn can purchase a small truffle and shave it into thin slices to garnish for something really delicious.) If you've never used truffle oil, look for it in most well-stocked food shops.

Red wines with an earthy character, such as Syrah or Cabernet Sauvignon, would pair well with this dish. The earthy truffle aroma screams out for something equally pungent or assertive. But lush, full-bodied white wines like barrel-fermented Chardonnay or Viognier would be delicious as well. Instead of earthiness, these wines bring to the table rich, forward flavors that can stand up to intense truffle character.

1 pound elbow macaroni

6 tablespoons unsalted butter, plus more for greasing the baking dish

1 medium white onion, diced

¾ pound button mushrooms, sliced

2½ cups whole milk

3 cups grated cheddar cheese

1¼ cups freshly grated Parmesan cheese

½ cup panko breadcrumbs

4 tablespoons flour

Salt and freshly ground pepper

3 tablespoons truffle oil

Truffle shavings (optional)

Bring a large pot of lightly salted water to a boil. Add the macaroni and cook until al dente, about 5 minutes. (Do not overcook the noodles or they will become soft and lose their shape when baked.) Drain the macaroni in a colander and rinse under cold water. Return the noodles to the pot and set aside.

Position a rack in the center of the oven and preheat to 350°F. Grease a 9-inch square baking dish with ½ tablespoon of butter.

In a large skillet, melt 2 tablespoons of the butter over medium heat. Add the onion and sauté until translucent, about 3 minutes. Add the mushrooms and sauté until wilted, about 5 minutes. If significant liquid from the mushrooms remains in the pan, increase the heat to high and let most of the liquid evaporate, 1 or 2 minutes. Remove the pan from the heat and set aside.

In a medium pot, heat the milk over medium heat until small bubbles begin to form around the sides of the pan; do not let it boil. Reduce the heat to low and keep the milk warm.

In a small bowl, combine the cheddar and ½ cup of the Parmesan. In another small bowl, combine the remaining ¾ cup Parmesan with the panko.

In another medium pot, melt the remaining 4 tablespoons butter over medium heat. Add the flour, whisking frequently to prevent burning. Cook until the butter and flour thicken and turn golden brown, about 2 minutes. Add the warm milk to the butter/flour mix in a slow stream, whisking constantly to prevent the flour from clumping. Once you have added all the milk, remove the pot from the heat and whisk in the cheddar/Parmesan cheese mix until it is melted into the sauce, about 1 minute.

Add the cheese sauce to the macaroni in the pot and mix well to coat all the pasta. Add the mushrooms and ½ teaspoon salt and mix well. Add the truffle oil and mix thoroughly but gently. Season with pepper and additional salt, if desired, to taste.

Pour the macaroni into the greased baking dish. Bake, uncovered, for 15 minutes. Remove from the oven and turn on the broiler, positioning a rack about 4 inches below the broiler. Sprinkle the top of the macaroni with the panko/Parmesan cheese mix. Place the macaroni back in the oven and broil until the top is golden brown and crisp, 3 to 5 minutes.

Serve hot. If desired, garnish with truffle shavings.

Ginger Sesame Noodles

pareve | Serves 4 to 6

In our much younger days, we lived on New York's Lower East Side, where a local caterer made the most delicious sesame noodles. We couldn't get enough of these spicy, crunchy noodles and would regularly ask for the recipe. But we were always refused. Eventually we figured out how to make the noodles ourselves, and we have enjoyed them at home ever since.

Sesame chili oil and toasted sesame oil are generally available among the Asian condiments or vegetable oils at your supermarket. And don't shy away from toasting your own sesame seeds—it's really easy (see page 243). You don't absolutely have to use the seeds, but we think it's a worthwhile addition—they are what give these noodles their delightful crunch. Toast them first, before you begin the rest of the dish.

If you have access to edible flowers, use them to garnish the top of your noodles for a beautiful presentation.

After we moved to California, we discovered that this dish goes especially well with a glass of chilled Sauvignon Blanc or dry rosé.

1 pound dried noodles, such as linguine or fettuccine

3 tablespoons toasted sesame oil

1 tablespoon sesame chili oil

6 tablespoons soy sauce or tamari

1 clove garlic, crushed through a press or minced

½ teaspoon ground ginger

½ teaspoon ground allspice

12 to 14 ounces firm tofu, cut into ½-inch cubes

1 red bell pepper, cut into ¼-inch dice

4 green onions, white and green parts, cut crosswise into ¼-inch rounds

3 tablespoons toasted sesame seeds (optional)

Edible flowers, such as nasturtiums (optional)

Bring a large pot of lightly salted water to a boil. Add the noodles and cook until al dente, about 10 minutes.

Meanwhile, in a large serving bowl, stir together the sesame oil, chili oil, soy sauce, garlic, ginger, and allspice. Add the tofu and toss to coat with the sauce.

When the pasta is done, drain in a colander and rinse under cold running water to bring to room temperature. Shake the noodles dry and add them to the tofu and sesame sauce, tossing until evenly coated.

Add the bell pepper and green onions and toss again. Add the sesame seeds (if using) and toss once more. Serve at room temperature in shallow bowls or on large plates. Garnish with edible flowers, if desired.

Fish

We eat a lot of fish. Not only does it taste good, it's also good for us. Some fish—like salmon and sardines—are loaded with omega-3 fatty acids, which can lower cholesterol and help maintain cardiovascular health. Just about all fish seem to be low in the kind of fats that are bad for us, and as protein, they make a fine foil for many wines, both red and white.

Jeff's mom always told him that she didn't know how to cook fish. But really, it's not hard to do. Even better, fish cooks fast—whether baked, broiled, or grilled. Just be careful not to overcook it. Dried-out fish is never appetizing.

Because fish tends to be more subtly flavored and light-textured than red meat, it often pairs best with lighter-styled white wines (see "Pairing Food and Wine," page 38). But that's not always the case. Rich, oily sardines and salmon can also stand up to big red wines.

Many of you are likely already well versed in the rules regarding kosher seafood. The basic parameters are simple: For a fish to be considered kosher, it must have scales and fins. That knocks shellfish, sharks, skate, and squid, for example, out of the running. Shrimp don't pass muster either.

Unlike meat, fish can be eaten with dairy products in a kosher diet. That means butter- and cream-based sauces can be included in your fish recipe repertoire. In this chapter, you'll find dishes like Pacific Rock Cod Fillets with Beurre Blanc and New Potatoes (page 150) and Sea Bass with Corn Relish and Braised Baby Bok Choy (page 145) that fall into the dairy camp (as does Salmon Chowder, page 96, in the soups and salads chapter). Remember that kosher dietary rules prohibit eating fish together with meat, although fish (without dairy) can be enjoyed as a separate course during a meal that includes meat.

We particularly enjoy eating whole fish. While some home cooks and diners are daunted by filleting a fish, we promise that you'll find Grilled Sardines with Marinated

Onions, Green Peppers, and Freekeh Salad (page 133) and Baked Stuffed Rainbow Trout with Garlic and Tomato Butter Beans (page 139) quite satisfying and easy to prepare. Look for tips on how to debone whole fish on page 135.

If you shop in a non-kosher fish market, you may have concerns about kosher varieties of fish being cleaned on surfaces or with knives that have been in contact with non-kosher seafood. We recommend you ask your rabbi for guidance on this front.

How fresh should your fish be? Today, many fish are frozen at sea where they are caught. As a result, they come in very "fresh." Ironically, locally caught fish can sometimes languish, decomposing, in transit. It's too bad, because, if possible, we prefer to eat fresh-caught seafood that has not been frozen. If you are buying a whole fish, it is important that the eyes still be clear, not cloudy, and the flesh should be firm to the touch, not mushy. The flesh of fish fillets should have a bright, shiny appearance. Dull or dry-looking fillets are best avoided. Obviously, if the fish you are thinking about cooking smells "fishy," don't buy it! A good fish store should smell like the sea, and not much else.

In this chapter, you'll discover an array of great-tasting seafood recipes. Enjoy each one with suggestions for an equally great bottle of wine—white, red, or rosé! The old thought that white wine is always best for fish has pretty much been discounted of late. Wine pairing is really a question of style. Lighter wines—often whites and rosés—will work best with lighter fish dishes. But meaty fish and rich, full-bodied sauces will handle your favorite Cabernet quite well!

Grilled Salmon with Aioli

pareve | serves 4 to 6

In southern France, aioli—or garlic mayonnaise—is eaten with a variety of different fish. You can substitute any meaty fish for the salmon in this recipe, which is quite simple to prepare. It offers a colorful array of healthy ingredients that would be equally perfect for a casual family supper or a weekend dinner party. We've grilled the fish here, but you can also bake it following the method in Baked Salmon Fillets with Gingered Celery Root Puree (page 130).

Make your aioli from scratch. It's easy! Frankly, we don't recommend using store-bought mayonnaise for an aioli. Rarely is mayonnaise made with fine, extra virgin olive oil, and we've never met a store-bought mayonnaise that isn't made with some kind of sweetener.

Most dry white wines and rosés will pair up nicely with this dish. Lighter-styled reds, such as Pinot Noir or Sangiovese, would also be appropriate.

Aioli (page 244)

6 red potatoes (about 3 pounds), quartered

4 medium carrots (about 1½ pounds), cut into 2-inch lengths

1 pound green beans

2 pounds salmon steaks or fillets

Salt and freshly ground pepper

2 teaspoons extra virgin olive oil

Preheat the grill.

Make the aioli. It's best at room temperature, but if you make the aioli well in advance, cover and store it in the refrigerator for up to 2 days.

Fill a large pot two-thirds full of lightly salted water and bring to a boil over high heat. Add the potatoes and carrots. Once the water has returned to a strong boil, reduce the heat to medium-high and cook until the vegetables are tender, about 15 minutes. Drain in a colander and cover to keep warm.

While the potatoes and carrots are cooking, steam the green beans or boil them in water until tender, 6 to 8 minutes. Drain and cover to keep warm.

When the grill is ready, lightly season the salmon with salt and pepper. Using your hands, coat both sides of the fillets with the olive oil. Place the fish on the grill rack and grill, turning once, until almost opaque throughout, 4 to 5 minutes per side. Remove the fish from the grill and cut into serving-size pieces.

To serve, arrange the vegetables, grouped separately, on a large serving platter. Place the salmon on another serving platter and the aioli in a small serving bowl. Let the diners help themselves, family style, to the fish and vegetables. The aioli is a dipping condiment. Diners should place a dollop on their plates and alternately dip their fish and vegetables in it.

Baked Salmon Fillets with Gingered Celery Root Puree

dairy | serves 4

These meaty salmon fillets paired with a creamy-rich puree provide a fine centerpiece for any dinner. Celery root looks nothing like the celery stalks you buy in the produce section. It's a big, round, knobby, yellowish root that is commonly eaten in France. But it's also fairly easy to find in most good produce sections. The puree from celery root is an excellent alternative to mashed potatoes, offering a hint of earthiness to back up the subtle ginger and spice notes.

This is one of those dishes that fairly screams for a wine with good acidity—whether red or white. That could mean bracingly bright Sauvignon Blanc, fruity Riesling or Gewürztraminer, a lush-textured Chardonnay, or a fine-tuned sparkling wine, one that shows excellent balance between acidity and richness. Pinot Noir, perhaps the most versatile of all red wines, would also certainly make the cut. So would a leaner-styled Syrah.

2 celery roots (about 3 pounds total), peeled and cut into 2-inch cubes

2 tablespoons unsalted butter

1 cup heavy cream

1 teaspoon ground ginger

⅛ teaspoon cayenne pepper

Salt and freshly ground pepper

1½ tablespoons extra virgin olive oil

4 salmon fillets (about 6 ounces each)

1 tablespoon dried rosemary

4 lemon wedges

In a medium saucepan, combine the celery root with enough cold water to just cover the celery root. Bring to a boil over high heat. Reduce the heat to medium-high and simmer until the celery root is tender, about 15 minutes. Reserving about 2 cups of the cooking water, drain in a colander. Place the warm, empty saucepan over an unlit burner and put the butter in the pan.

Transfer the warm celery root to a blender or food processor and process to a smooth puree. (If using a blender, you might need to work in batches.) Add some of the reserved cooking water as needed to reach a smooth consistency. Return the puree to the saucepan with the butter. Stir in the cream, ginger, cayenne, and 1 teaspoon salt. Mix well, cover, and set aside until ready to serve.

Preheat the oven to 400°F. Lightly oil a baking pan or dish with ½ tablespoon of the olive oil.

Lightly salt and pepper the fillets on both sides. Drizzle the remaining 1 tablespoon olive oil over the fillets. Sprinkle them, flesh side only, with the rosemary. Place the fillets, skin-side down, in the baking pan and bake until the flesh begins to flake but remains moist, about 15 minutes.

A few minutes before the fish has finished cooking, gently reheat the celery root puree over medium heat, stirring occasionally. When the fish is done, place a generous mound of the celery root puree in the middle of each dinner plate. Using a spatula, remove the fillets from the pan. (Most of the skin, which can be discarded, will remain in the pan.) Lean each fillet at an angle against a mound of puree on each plate.

Garnish each serving of fish with juice from a lemon wedge. Sprinkle both the fish and the puree with pepper to taste.

Grilled Sardines with Marinated Onions, Green Peppers, and Freekeh Salad

pareve | serves 4

Fresh meaty sardines (not those little canned ones) are tasty, rich in nutrients like omega-3 fatty acids, and cheap. They are also easy to prepare. When we lived in France, we ate grilled sardines regularly—it was part of the local culinary custom—but here in California, we don't often see these sleek, silver fish at the market. Whenever we do, though, we purchase them for the grill.

The bones in fresh sardines are generally too big to eat. They won't hurt you, but they might be distracting. If you don't know how to eat a fish that has not been filleted, see "How to Fillet a Cooked Whole Fish" (page 135). Ask your fishmonger to gut the sardines for you before taking them home. There's really not much to clean, but it will save you a few minutes, and a lot of mess, in the kitchen.

Freekeh is a wheat cereal commonly eaten in the Middle East. Because it is roasted, it has an enticing smoky quality. You can substitute bulgur (tabouli) or any other grain here, but you might need to adjust your cooking time accordingly. Look for freekeh in any well-provisioned supermarket. Make the freekeh salad first; then prepare the sardines.

With its lemon-marinated onions, this dish is all about bright acidity. Pour an equally bright-edged wine into your glass. Think Sauvignon Blanc or Pinot Gris, for example—something that's not too rich or oaky.

freekeh salad

4 cups water

1 cup freekeh

¼ cup extra virgin olive oil

2 tablespoons fresh lemon juice

2 cloves garlic, minced

¼ cup diced onion

¼ teaspoon salt

1 cup finely diced cucumber

¼ cup minced fresh flat-leaf parsley

3 tablespoons minced fresh mint

Freshly ground pepper

MAKE THE FREEKEH SALAD: In a medium saucepan, bring the water to a boil over high heat. Stir in the freekeh. Bring the water to a boil again, reduce the heat to low, and cook until all the water has been absorbed, about 25 minutes. Remove from the heat and set aside.

In a small bowl, whisk together the olive oil and lemon juice. Mix in the garlic, onion, and salt. Set the dressing aside.

In a large bowl, combine the cucumber, parsley, and mint. Fluff the freekeh with a fork and add it to the cucumber mix. Pour the olive oil dressing over the freekeh salad and stir gently to incorporate. Season with pepper to taste. Set aside until ready to use. Eat warm or at room temperature.

sardines

1 large yellow onion, sliced into thin rounds

1 cup diced green bell pepper

¼ cup plus 2 tablespoons extra virgin olive oil

Juice of 2 lemons

3 teaspoons dried thyme

1¼ teaspoons coarse sea salt or kosher salt

2 pounds whole fresh sardines (10 to 12 fish)

Freshly ground pepper

MAKE THE SARDINES: Preheat the grill.

In a large bowl, combine the onion, green pepper, ¼ cup of the olive oil, the lemon juice, 1 teaspoon of the thyme, and ¼ teaspoon of the salt. Thoroughly toss all the ingredients and set aside.

Rinse the sardines under cold water to eliminate any excess blood. Rub them with the remaining 2 tablespoons olive oil. Sprinkle them on both sides with the remaining 2 teaspoons thyme, 1 teaspoon salt, and black pepper to taste.

Set the sardines on the grill and cook until the flesh is firm and opaque, about 10 minutes. Use tongs or a spatula to flip them over every 2 minutes. (Regularly turning the fish from side to side will prevent sticking. Be careful not to overcook the fish.)

Before serving, toss the marinated onions and peppers one more time in their bowl. Place a mound of freekeh salad on each dinner plate. Set 2 or 3 sardines alongside the freekeh. Garnish the fish liberally with the onion mixture and pepper. Spoon some of the lemon juice marinade over each serving.

How to Fillet a Cooked Whole Fish

Removing the bones from a cooked whole fish is easy, yet many people are put off by the prospect. Once the fish is cooked, the flesh is soft, and it virtually melts away from the bones.

1. Using your dinner knife, slice down the middle of the side facing up, starting at the gills and moving down to the tail.

2. Use your knife to lift the meat up from the incision and away from the fish onto your plate.

3. Make a small cut with your knife on the underside of the tail and hold the end of the tail between your thumb and forefinger.

4. Slowly pull the tail up from the body. The backbone, ribs, and head will come up with it. (Make sure you have an empty plate or bowl handy for the bones and head.)

Remember to watch for small bones that may still be lodged where the top and bottom fins were once attached.

Gefilte Quenelles with Braised Leeks and Lemon Zest

pareve | serves 6 as a main course, 10 to 12 as a first course

Jeff's grandmother Alice Solomon used to make gefilte fish from the fresh northern pike that Jeff's grandfather Lester would catch in the lake outside their summer cabin in Wisconsin. Alice's gefilte fish bore little resemblance to the store-bought gefilte fish dumplings typically seen at Passover, but they did resemble the light-textured fish quenelles—or fish dumplings—we have often enjoyed in France. Which is how we came up with this recipe!

Don't wait for Passover to enjoy them. They make a wonderful year-round first course or main course. Leftovers are great for lunch too. A hint of ginger, fennel, and coriander adds a subtle, exotic touch. (Horseradish is not recommended.) These quenelles can be served chilled or at room temperature.

For best results, prepare these pink-hued salmon dumplings a day in advance and let them soak, refrigerated, in their broth. They can be plated in minutes

Pair with a refreshing, chilled white wine such as Sauvignon Blanc, Roussane, Chenin Blanc, or Chardonnay. Fruity Riesling or Gewürztraminer would be good too.

2 pounds salmon fillets, skinned, cut into 1- to 2-inch cubes

4 cloves garlic, chopped

2 teaspoons grated fresh ginger

¼ cup chopped onion, plus 1 onion, sliced

2 eggs

2 tablespoons fresh lemon juice

2 teaspoons salt

2 tablespoons extra virgin olive oil

3 carrots, cut into ¼-inch-thick rounds

1 fennel bulb, trimmed and sliced into ¼-inch-thick crescents

1 teaspoon dried thyme

½ teaspoon coriander seeds

1 bottle (750 ml) or 3 cups dry white wine

Place the fish, half the chopped garlic, the ginger, chopped onion, eggs, lemon juice, and 1 teaspoon of the salt in a food processor. In pulse mode, finely chop (but do not puree). Transfer the fish mixture to a large nonreactive bowl. Stir with a wooden spoon or rubber spatula until all the ingredients are well incorporated. Cover and refrigerate for at least 2 hours or overnight. (If the fish is not cold enough, it will not hold its shape when you mold it into balls. You can speed up the cooling process by putting the fish in the freezer. But be careful not to let it freeze.)

While the fish is chilling, in a large pot, heat the olive oil over medium-high heat. Add the sliced onion and remaining chopped garlic and sauté, stirring occasionally, until the onion is translucent, about 3 minutes. Add the carrots and stir to coat with the oil. Add the fennel and stir until it is coated as well. Continue to sauté, stirring occasionally, until the fennel is soft and fragrant, about 10 minutes. Stir in the thyme, coriander, and the remaining 1 teaspoon salt. Add the wine, water, and bay leaf. Bring the liquid to a boil over high heat, reduce the heat to medium, and simmer, uncovered, for 45 minutes.

6 cups water

1 bay leaf

6 to 12 leeks (white part only), well washed (Allow 1 leek per individual portion.)

2 tablespoons finely chopped lemon zest

Freshly ground pepper

Remove the pot from the heat and let the broth cool slightly, about 15 minutes. Strain the broth through a fine-mesh sieve and reserve the vegetables from the broth in a covered container and refrigerate. Divide the strained broth between 2 large pots or deep-sided skillets.

Roll the chilled fish mixture into 10 to 12 balls and arrange them on a flat surface covered with wax paper. (If necessary, wet your hands occasionally with cold water to prevent sticking.) Bring the broth in the pots to a boil over high heat. Use a large spoon to gently lay the quenelles into the broth, dividing them between the 2 pots so that they have room to cook without touching each other. Reduce the heat to medium and if the quenelles are not completely submerged, spoon a little broth over the tops. Cover and braise (which means simply to cook in any liquid—in this case the vegetable broth) for 15 minutes.

Turn off the heat, uncover the pots, and let the quenelles cool slightly in the broth for 10 to 15 minutes. Transfer the fish and the broth together to a large covered container and refrigerate overnight or up to 2 days.

A few hours prior to serving the fish, prepare the leeks. Fill a large deep-sided skillet or pan with about ½ inch water and bring to a boil. Lay the leeks in the pan, cover, and cook until they are tender, about 10 minutes. Remove the leeks from the liquid and let cool for 10 or 15 minutes. Cover and reserve in the refrigerator until ready to use.

To serve, halve each leek lengthwise. On individual plates, lay 2 leek halves in an "A" or "teepee" shape, touching at the top but leaving a wide space at the bottom. Set 1 quenelle in between the leeks for a first course; 2 quenelles for a main course. Place a spoonful or two of the reserved broth vegetables around the sides of the fish. Garnish the quenelles with additional juice from the fish broth, the lemon zest, and pepper to taste.

Baked Stuffed Rainbow Trout with Garlic and Tomato Butter Beans

(pareve) | serves 4

With minimal preparation required, whole fish are a snap to cook. We like to use fresh rainbow trout because they are generally easy to find in stores. But you can use any whole fish of similar size for this recipe. Eating whole fish is almost as easy as cooking it. The bones can be removed with little effort ("How to Fillet a Cooked Whole Fish," page 135). And don't be concerned about buying too much: ½ pound of fish on the bone yields only about ¼ pound of soft, tender, edible flesh. The fish skin will be crisp on top; less so underneath. You can eat it or not, depending on your taste.

Once the fish is plated, diners can pull the kale stuffing out of the fish cavity. It becomes a fragrant green vegetable accompaniment. Also on the side are large, flat white beans known as butter beans. But you can use any white beans, such as navy or cannellini beans. We admit we are lazy and often purchase canned or jarred beans.

Start with the beans on the stovetop. When they begin to simmer with the tomatoes, it's time to prepare the fish. Both the beans and fish will be ready to eat at the same time. (If you need to reheat the beans at the last minute, do so over medium-high heat. Just remember to stir them to prevent burning.)

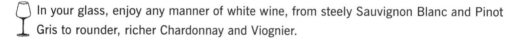 In your glass, enjoy any manner of white wine, from steely Sauvignon Blanc and Pinot Gris to rounder, richer Chardonnay and Viognier.

tomato butter beans

3 tablespoons extra virgin olive oil

6 cloves garlic, minced

¼ teaspoon chipotle pepper or red pepper flakes

4 sprigs fresh rosemary, each about 5 inches long

½ cup dry white wine

2 pounds fresh tomatoes, coarsely chopped, or 1 can (28 ounces) whole Italian plum tomatoes, drained and coarsely chopped

MAKE THE TOMATO BUTTER BEANS: In a large pot or Dutch oven, heat the olive oil over high heat. Add the garlic, pepper flakes, and rosemary and sauté for 1 minute. Reduce the heat to medium, add the wine, and simmer for 3 to 4 minutes. Stir in the tomatoes and simmer for 10 more minutes. Stir in the beans and salt, cover, reduce the heat to low, and simmer for 15 more minutes. Discard the rosemary sprigs. Cover the pot to keep the beans warm and set aside.

MAKE THE STUFFED TROUT: Preheat the oven to 400°F. Drizzle 2 tablespoons of the oil into a medium baking pan that will snugly hold the fish.

In a large skillet, heat 2 tablespoons of the oil over medium-high heat. Add the garlic and sauté until fragrant, about 30 seconds. Add the sun-dried tomatoes and paprika and sauté for 1 minute.

4 cups home-cooked butter
beans (page 242) or 2 cans
(15 ounces each) butter beans,
drained and rinsed

½ teaspoon salt

stuffed trout

5 tablespoons extra virgin olive oil

4 cloves garlic, minced

½ cup chopped marinated sun-
dried tomatoes

2 teaspoons paprika (sweet, not
hot)

4 cups firmly packed chopped kale

3 tablespoons water

⅓ cup chopped, pitted Kalamata
olives

Salt and freshly ground pepper

4 whole rainbow trout, heads
intact (about ½ pound each)

2 teaspoons dried thyme

Add the kale and mix well. Add the water to the pan to prevent burning and mix again. Reduce the heat to medium, cover the pan, and cook the kale until it wilts, about 5 minutes. (If necessary, add more water 1 tablespoon at a time to prevent burning.) Stir in the olives and ½ teaspoon salt. Remove the pan from the heat and set aside.

Drizzle the remaining 1 tablespoon olive oil over the fish and rub the oil on both sides. Salt and pepper the fish and sprinkle with the thyme.

Fill each fish cavity with 2 tablespoons of the kale mixture, firmly tucking the stuffing into the fish. Lay the fish in the oiled baking pan and place the pan in the oven. Bake until the fish is tender to the touch and the flesh is white-opaque, about 20 minutes.

Serve each fish with beans on the side.

Baked Chilean Sea Bass with Tomatoes, Green Peppers, Artichoke Hearts, and Jasmine Rice

pareve | serves 4 to 6

This colorful dish is built around tender Chilean sea bass, bathed in a fragrant sauce served over yellow rice. The recipe is not complicated and cooks quickly, which makes it practical for entertaining at home.

Just for the record, Chilean sea bass is not really bass at all (and it is not an endangered species either). The fish is a large, deep-water, white-fleshed swimmer that lives in the waters near Antarctica. Sold by its original name, *Patagonian toothfish*, Chilean sea bass never got much attention, despite its lush-textured flesh. Even though it is not necessarily caught in Chilean waters, the toothfish's new name has made it a marketing sensation. Note that you can substitute any other meaty, white fish, such as halibut or opah.

Look for cardamom pods in the spice rack of most supermarkets. These small pods are opened easily; inside you'll find the little black seeds that define the distinctive, yet subtle, aromas in this dish.

Two cups of white wine are required for the sauce. We recommend using any inexpensive dry white wine for cooking (see "Cooking with Wine," page 40). Reserve a better wine for your glass. Try pairing with Chardonnay, Sauvignon Blanc, Riesling, Gewürztraminer, or Chenin Blanc, for example. Each varietal will provide you with a different kind of dining experience.

20 cardamom pods

3 to 4 tablespoons extra virgin olive oil

2 large white onions, cut into quarters

4 cloves garlic, minced

1 tablespoon grated fresh ginger

4 pinches of saffron threads

1 teaspoon aniseed

½ teaspoon Spanish hot paprika (pimentón picante)

4 medium plum tomatoes, quartered lengthwise

Using a paring knife, remove the cardamom seeds from their pods. Crush them using a mortar and pestle or the flat side of a large knife. Set them aside. You should have about 1 teaspoon of crushed seeds in total.

Preheat the oven to 400°F.

In a large, deep-sided, ovenproof skillet or Dutch oven, heat 3 tablespoons olive oil over medium-high heat. Add the onion wedges and cook until they start to brown on the edges and become translucent, about 10 minutes. Push the onions to the side of the pan, reduce the heat to medium, and add the garlic and ginger. (If there is no oil left in the bottom of the pan and the garlic begins to stick, add another tablespoon of olive oil.) Sauté until the garlic is fragrant, about 30 seconds, then mix with the onions.

2 large green bell peppers,
　　cut into long strips

1 can or jar (12 to 15 ounces)
　　water-packed whole artichoke
　　hearts, drained

Salt and freshly ground pepper

2 cups dry white wine

1 can (12 to 15 ounces) chickpeas
　　or 2 cups home-cooked
　　(page 242)

1½ pounds Chilean sea bass
　　fillets, cut into 2- to 3-inch
　　chunks

4 cups water

2 cups white jasmine rice

½ teaspoon turmeric

Stir the crushed cardamom, saffron, aniseed, and paprika into the onions. Add the tomatoes and sauté until they begin to soften, about 2 minutes. Add the green peppers, artichokes, and ½ teaspoon salt. Gently stir to mix all the ingredients. Sauté until the peppers begin to soften, about 5 minutes, stirring occasionally. Add the wine and bring to a boil over high heat. Stir in the chickpeas, reduce the heat to medium, and simmer for 5 minutes.

While the vegetables are simmering, lightly salt and pepper the fish. Turn off the heat and gently tuck the fish chunks into the vegetable mixture, submerging the fish as deeply as you can into the liquid. (It's OK if the tops of the fish are not covered by the sauce.)

Cover the skillet and transfer to the oven. Bake until the fish is tender, about 20 minutes.

While the fish is baking, make the rice. In a medium pot, lightly salt the water and bring to a boil over high heat. Add the rice and stir gently. Stir in the turmeric and mix well. Reduce the heat to low, cover, and cook until all the water is absorbed, 12 to15 minutes. Prior to serving, use a fork to scrape the top of the rice and fluff it.

Place a mound of jasmine rice in the middle of each dinner plate. Spoon the fish, vegetables, and sauce over the rice.

Sea Bass with Corn Relish and Braised Baby Bok Choy

dairy | serves 4

Sea bass has virtually become a generic term for a variety of meaty, mild-flavored, white-fleshed fish. (This does not include Chilean sea bass, page 141, which could nonetheless be used for this recipe.) Whichever kind of fresh sea bass you find at your fishmonger will work just fine here.

It's the creamy, sweet corn relish that really makes this dish distinctive. A touch of cayenne gives it a pleasing hint of heat. Look for leafy, green bok choy in most supermarkets. The "baby" version used here is the smallest and most tender kind.

Before you start cooking, separate your ingredients as they are listed below. This is the preparation order; following it will make your work in the kitchen much easier. The relish and bok choy do not need to be served piping hot. They will still be warm when the fish is ready to eat. (But you can quickly reheat them on the stovetop if you desire.)

A rich, barrel-fermented Chardonnay would be our first choice as a wine companion. But many other kinds of white wines would pair nicely as well. Try an off-dry Riesling or Gewürztraminer, for example, or a dry Roussane or Chenin Blanc.

corn relish

2 tablespoons unsalted butter

½ cup diced onion

3 cups white corn kernels, fresh (4 or 5 ears) or frozen

1 red bell pepper, diced

⅛ teaspoon cayenne pepper

2 plum tomatoes, coarsely chopped

¼ teaspoon salt

Freshly ground pepper

½ cup heavy cream

braised baby bok choy

1 tablespoon unsalted butter

1 tablespoon extra virgin olive oil

3 cloves garlic, minced

MAKE THE CORN RELISH: In a large skillet, melt the butter over medium heat. Add the onion and cook until translucent, about 3 minutes. Add the corn, bell pepper, and cayenne. Stir to mix well. Simmer, stirring occasionally, until the kernels are soft, about 10 minutes. Add the tomatoes and salt. Sprinkle in black pepper to taste. Reduce the heat to medium-low and simmer for 10 more minutes, stirring occasionally to prevent burning. Stir in the cream and simmer for 2 more minutes. Remove the pan from the heat, cover, and set aside.

MAKE THE BOK CHOY: In a large skillet, melt the butter with the olive oil over medium-high heat. Add the garlic and sauté until fragrant, about 30 seconds. Add the bok choy, cover, reduce the heat to medium-low, and cook until the greens are wilted and the fleshy parts are tender, about 5 minutes. Uncover, increase the heat to high, and cook until the liquid evaporates, about 2 minutes. Remove the pan from the heat and adjust the seasoning with salt to taste. Cover and set aside.

MAKE THE FISH: Preheat the oven to 425°F.

1½ pounds baby bok choy
  (about 4 bunches),
  ends trimmed and heads
  halved lengthwise

Salt

fish

4 sea bass fillets (6 to 8 ounces
  each), with or without skin

Salt and freshly ground pepper

2 tablespoons extra virgin olive oil

2 tablespoons unsalted butter

1 tablespoon minced lemon zest

Season the fillets on both sides with salt and pepper. In a large, ovenproof skillet, heat the olive oil over high heat. When the oil begins to shimmer, place the fillets in the pan skinned-side down (or skin-side down if the fillets have skins), reduce the heat to medium, and cook until golden on the bottoms (or until the skin is crisp), about 3 minutes. Using a spatula, gently turn the fillets, taking care not to let them fall apart. Transfer the pan to the oven and bake until the flesh is opaque throughout, about 3 minutes. Remove the pan from the oven and add the butter to the pan alongside the fillets. When it melts, baste the tops of the fillets with the butter. Garnish the fillets with the lemon zest.

To serve, divide the corn relish among 4 plates. Arrange each fillet to rest slightly on the relish. Place the bok choy to the side of the corn and fish. Season with pepper to taste.

Baked Opah with Smoked Paprika, Tomatoes, Green Olives, and Brown Rice

pareve | serves 4

When visiting Israel, we like to shop at the outdoor market by the port in Jaffa. There's a great fish shop at the water's edge where local fishermen haul in their daily catch. It usually includes palamida, a small member of the tuna family also referred to as bonito. The silvery Israeli palamida are about 2½ feet long, and one fish can easily feed eight people. To our taste, these meaty fish resemble mackerel more than tuna.

We can't easily find palamida in California so we've substituted opah, another meaty fish—but one that hails from Hawaii. In fact, you can use any large, firm-textured fish such as tuna, salmon, or halibut here as well. Just make sure the fish is cut into thick steaks (with or without the bone)—one per person. For ease in the kitchen, make the fish while the rice is cooking.

Smoked paprika gives the sauce a sweet, smoky edge and a red tint. Look for it on most supermarket spice racks. But don't confuse smoked paprika with *hot* paprika, or you will have a very different dining experience!

Conveniently, there's a nice wine shop at the Jaffa port, where we stock up on Israeli wines. Many pair well with this dish. The key is selecting a wine with good acidity. Think about whites such as Chardonnay, Sauvignon Blanc, Chenin Blanc, Viognier, or Roussane. Reds like Syrah, Pinot Noir, and Merlot would also be excellent matches. Cabernet Franc would work well too. And don't forget about cool, refreshing rosé—especially on a hot summer evening.

rice

1 tablespoon extra virgin olive oil

½ medium onion, finely diced

1 cup brown rice

¼ teaspoon turmeric

¼ teaspoon ground coriander

⅛ teaspoon salt

2 cups water

fish

2 tablespoons extra virgin olive oil

MAKE THE RICE: In a medium pot, heat the olive oil over medium heat. Add the onion and cook until translucent, about 3 minutes. Add the rice, stir to coat well with the oil, and cook for about 30 seconds. Stir in the turmeric, coriander, and salt. Mix well.

Add the water and bring to a boil over high heat. Reduce the heat to low, cover, and cook until all the water is absorbed and the rice is tender, about 40 minutes. Remove from the heat, keep covered, and set aside until ready to use.

MAKE THE FISH: Preheat the oven to 400°F.

In a Dutch oven or large ovenproof pot, heat the olive oil over medium heat. Add the onions and garlic and cook, stirring occasionally to prevent burning, until the onions are translucent, about 7 minutes. Stir in the oregano.

3 medium onions, sliced into thin rounds

4 cloves garlic, minced

1 teaspoon dried oregano

8 plum tomatoes (about 2 pounds), coarsely chopped

2 teaspoons smoked paprika

1 cup pitted green olives, coarsely chopped

4 opah steaks, 1 inch thick (about ½ pound each)

Salt and freshly ground pepper

Zest of 1 lemon, chopped fine

Add the tomatoes, increase the heat to high, and sauté, stirring occasionally, until the tomatoes begin to soften, about 3 minutes. Add the paprika and mix well. Add the olives and let simmer for about 3 more minutes, stirring occasionally.

Remove the pot from the heat. Season the fish with salt and pepper. Push the onion/tomato mix to the sides of the pot and lay the steaks in a single layer on the bottom of the pot. Cover the fish with the onions and tomatoes.

Cover the pot, transfer to the oven and bake until the fish steaks are white/opaque throughout and firm but still moist, 15 to 20 minutes.

To serve, place a mound of rice on each dinner plate. Carefully remove the fish steaks from the pot and lay one over the rice on each plate. Spoon the onion, tomato, and olive sauce over the fish to taste. Garnish with the lemon zest.

Pacific Rock Cod Fillets with Beurre Blanc and New Potatoes

dairy | serves 4

Light, flaky Pacific rock cod fillets are similar to red snapper. If you can't find rock cod or red snapper, any white or light-colored fish fillets no more than ½ inch thick will do. This dish is inspired by the many panfried fish dishes we have enjoyed over the years in France, where fish fillets are often bathed in a white wine and butter sauce called beurre blanc. Capers add extra zing! Both the fish and the sauce are quickly prepared. It's one of those simple recipes perfect for a weeknight when you're too tired to make something complicated but still want something elegant.

Wine, of course, transforms even the simplest of meals into something special. Dry, moderate- or light-bodied white wines are the best choice of beverage here. Chardonnay, Sauvignon Blanc, Viognier, Chenin Blanc, Gewürztraminer, or Riesling (on the dry side) would all be excellent. But don't use your fine drinking wine for the sauce. That would be a waste. (See "Cooking with Wine," page 40.)

1½ pounds new potatoes or other thin-skinned potatoes such as Yukon Gold

1 egg

½ cup all-purpose flour

Salt and freshly ground pepper

4 rock cod fillets (about 6 ounces each)

3 tablespoons extra virgin olive oil

½ teaspoon Spanish paprika

2 cups white wine

3 tablespoons butter

2 tablespoons capers

¼ cup finely chopped fresh parsley

1 lemon, cut into quarters

Scrub the potatoes but do not peel. Cut them into quarters or eighths, depending on their size. In a large pot of boiling water or in a steamer, boil or steam the potatoes until tender when poked with a fork, about 20 minutes.

While the potatoes are cooking, prepare the fish. In a medium bowl, whisk the egg. Pour the flour into another medium bowl. Salt and pepper the fillets. Dip each fillet in the flour, then in the egg, and then in the flour again until both sides are well coated. Set the fillets aside on a plate.

In a large skillet, heat the olive oil over medium-high heat. When it starts to shimmer, lay the fillets in the pan. (They can touch, but should not overlap.) Sprinkle half the paprika over the fillets and cook until the underside of each fillet is golden brown, 3 to 4 minutes. Using a spatula, carefully flip the fillets and sprinkle them with the remaining paprika and cook until the underside is golden brown, about 3 more minutes. Remove the fillets from the pan, set them on a plate, and tent with foil to keep warm. Reduce the heat to low under the skillet to keep it hot but not burning.

By this time, your potatoes should be done, or almost done. If you are steaming the potatoes, simply turn off the heat when they are tender. Keep the pot covered only halfway or the potatoes will continue to cook. (You just want them to stay warm.) If you have boiled the potatoes, drain them in a colander and return them to the pot. Keep the pot half covered, so the potatoes will stay warm.

Increase the heat under the skillet to high, add the wine, and stir with a wooden spoon to scrape up any browned bits stuck to the bottom of the pan. Cook to reduce the wine by half. Reduce the heat to medium and add the butter and capers. Stir occasionally as the butter melts. When the butter has completely melted, transfer the sauce to a gravy bowl. Divide the potatoes among 4 plates and set a fillet next to each portion. Liberally drizzle both the fish and potatoes with the sauce. Garnish with parsley and freshly squeezed lemon. Season with salt and pepper to taste.

Halibut Pockets with Spiced Olive Tapenade and Kasha

pareve | serves 4

Halibut is a light-fleshed fish well suited to being dressed in this fragrant olive tapenade—a variation on traditional Mediterranean olive spreads. This exquisitely simple preparation uses parchment paper, shaped into a "pocket" for cooking the fish with minimal loss of moisture. (If you don't have parchment paper, you can use foil.)

You'll notice that the cumin and coriander seeds are lightly crushed. Start with whole seeds and use a mortar and pestle to crush them. If you don't have a mortar and pestle, set the seeds on a cutting board and use the flat side of a large knife to gently, but firmly, press down on them.

Kasha, or roasted buckwheat groats, has a lovely nutty quality that frames the halibut well, but rice or another grain can be substituted.

In your wineglass, enjoy any refreshing, light-textured wine. Among whites, Sauvignon Blanc, Viognier, Roussane, Riesling, and Chenin Blanc come to mind. Reds tend to be too rich, but a light-bodied Pinot Noir would make a fine choice. So would a dry rosé—technically a red wine that drinks more like a white.

Salt and freshly ground pepper

2 cups water

1 cup kasha

7 tablespoons extra virgin olive oil

1 cup green olives, pitted and diced

2 cloves garlic, sliced into thin rounds

2 teaspoons cumin seeds, lightly crushed

2 teaspoons coriander seeds, lightly crushed

4 halibut steaks (about 6 ounces each)

4 thin, round slices of lemon

¼ cup coarsely chopped fresh cilantro

Preheat the oven to 400°F.

In a medium saucepan, salt the water and bring to a boil. Add the kasha, cover, reduce the heat to low, and simmer until the water has been absorbed, about 10 minutes. Remove from the heat, keep covered, and set aside. Just prior to serving, add 3 tablespoons of the olive oil and gently fluff the kasha with a fork to mix well.

While the buckwheat is cooking, make the olive tapenade: In a medium bowl, use a wooden spoon to thoroughly mix the olives, garlic, cumin, and coriander seeds.

Cut off 4 sheets of parchment paper (or foil) 12 × 12 inches. Place a halibut steak in the center of each sheet. Crimp the edges of the paper to prevent any liquid from seeping out as you prepare the fish. Lightly season both sides of the fish with salt and pepper. Drizzle each steak with 1 tablespoon olive oil. Dividing evenly, coat the top of each steak with the olive tapenade. Place a slice of lemon on top of the tapenade. Pull the sides of each parchment sheet together over the fish steaks to cover them. Pinch or fold the sheets firmly together at the top to create a closed pocket.

Place the packets on a baking sheet and bake for about 15 minutes. When done, the fish should be completely white and firm to the touch.

Set a mound of buckwheat on each plate. Unwrap the fish pockets and gently remove the contents, leaning each steak up against the buckwheat. Drizzle both the fish and the grain with juices remaining in the pockets. Garnish with cilantro and additional salt and pepper to taste.

Tuna Steaks with Shiitake Mushroom Fried Rice

pareve | serves 4

These tender tuna steaks have a meaty quality that makes them very red wine–friendly. Use any high-quality tuna, such as ahi, for best results in the pan. Shiitake mushrooms also have a meaty character. But if you can't find them in the produce section, substitute common button mushrooms. Note that we use brown rice instead of white rice here and in most recipes. In general, we prefer its taste; plus, its higher fiber content makes it healthier.

We'd recommend fruity reds such as Pinot Noir or Zinfandel to accompany this dish. Rich, full-bodied white wines like Chardonnay or Viognier would also make a fine match.

Salt

4 cups water

2 cups short-grain brown rice

¼ cup plus 2 tablespoons soy sauce or tamari

2 tablespoons toasted sesame oil

1 teaspoon ground ginger

¼ teaspoon cayenne pepper

4 tuna steaks (about 6 ounces each)

¼ cup plus 1 tablespoon canola oil

4 green onions, chopped

2 cloves garlic, minced

4 ounces shiitake mushrooms, stems discarded, caps thinly sliced

½ red bell pepper, diced

2 eggs, lightly beaten

In a medium pot, lightly salt the water and bring to a boil over high heat. Add the rice, reduce the heat to a simmer, cover, and cook until all the water is absorbed, about 40 minutes. Remove the pot from the heat and set aside.

Meanwhile, in a bowl or pan large enough to hold the tuna steaks, stir together ¼ cup of the soy sauce, the sesame oil, ginger, and cayenne. Place the steaks in the marinade and let sit at room temperature for 15 to 30 minutes, turning them now and then to make sure both sides are sufficiently moistened.

In a large skillet, heat ¼ cup of the canola oil over medium-high heat. Add the green onions and garlic and sauté until the onions have softened, about 1 minute. Add the mushrooms and bell pepper and cook, stirring occasionally to prevent burning, until the mushrooms have wilted, about 3 minutes. Push the vegetables to the side of the pan and add the cooked rice to the empty portion of the pan. Stir the remaining 2 tablespoons soy sauce into the rice and continue to cook, stirring occasionally, until the rice is slightly crunchy, 3 to 4 minutes. Mix the rice and vegetables in the pan together and push the mixture to the side of the pan, leaving a portion of the pan surface empty.

Pour the eggs onto the hot pan surface and use a wooden spoon to lightly scramble them. Once the eggs are reasonably cooked (they can still be slightly runny), mix them into the rice. Remove from the heat, cover, and set aside.

In another large skillet, heat the remaining 1 tablespoon canola oil over high heat. When the oil starts to shimmer, place the tuna steaks in the pan. Sear for 1 to 2 minutes per side for rare to medium-rare, 3 minutes per side for medium. (If cooking for more than 2 minutes per side, reduce the heat to medium to prevent burning.) Place a mound of rice on each plate and lean a tuna steak up against it.

Braised Tuna with Lemon Zest and Ratatouille

pareve | serves 4

Ratatouille, the famous French eggplant and tomato dish, can be made in many ways. Our version is influenced by Middle Eastern spices rather than the herbes de Provence that go into the traditional one. We've topped the ratatouille with tender chunks of lemony fresh tuna. Chickpeas provide added interest. And we use Spanish hot paprika (or pimentón picante), which packs a little heat. (But regular, sweet paprika will work just fine too.)

This makes a wonderful meal in summertime, when vine-ripened tomatoes are fresh and juicy. You'll notice that 2 cups of white wine are used to braise the fish. Any dry, inexpensive wine will do the trick. Save the good wine for your glass! (See "Cooking with Wine," page 40.)

Both white and red wines are suitable for pairing. We recommend wines with more pronounced acidity to stand up to the citrus and spice flavors. Try Sauvignon Blanc, dry Riesling, Gewürztraminer, or Chardonnay. Red wines such as Pinot Noir, Cabernet Franc, Sangiovese, or Tempranillo would work well too.

ratatouille

½ cup extra virgin olive oil

1 large onion, diced

4 large cloves garlic, minced

1 large eggplant (unpeeled), cut into 1-inch cubes

3 medium tomatoes, diced

1 teaspoon ground cumin

1 teaspoon turmeric

½ teaspoon Spanish hot paprika (pimentón picante)

½ teaspoon ground cinnamon

⅛ teaspoon cayenne pepper

½ teaspoon salt

1 cup home-cooked chickpeas (page 242) or 1 can (15 ounces), drained and rinsed

¼ cup cold water

MAKE THE RATATOUILLE: In a large skillet, heat the olive oil over medium-high heat. When it starts to shimmer, add the onion and sauté until translucent, about 5 minutes, stirring often to prevent burning. Add the garlic and cook until fragrant, about 30 seconds. Add the eggplant and sauté until it is soft, about 10 minutes, stirring often.

Add the tomatoes, cumin, turmeric, paprika, cinnamon, cayenne, and salt, and gently stir to mix thoroughly. Reduce the heat to low, cover the pan, and simmer for 30 minutes, stirring frequently to prevent sticking or burning.

Stir in the chickpeas and water, cover the pan, and simmer over low heat.

PREPARE THE TUNA: Salt and pepper the tuna chunks and set them aside. In a medium skillet, heat the olive oil over medium heat. Add the garlic and cook until fragrant, about 10 seconds. (Be careful not to let the garlic burn.) Add the wine and stir to scrape up any bits of garlic that may have stuck to the pan surface. Add the thyme, 1 teaspoon of the lemon zest, and the bay leaves. Bring the wine to a gentle boil. Add the tuna chunks. When the liquid begins to bubble slightly again, reduce the heat to medium-low and cover. Cook until the tuna chunks are slightly pink in the center, about 3 minutes.

tuna

Salt and freshly ground pepper

1½ pounds tuna, preferably albacore or yellowfin, cut into 1½-inch cubes

2 tablespoons extra virgin olive oil

2 large cloves garlic, minced

2 cups dry white wine

1 teaspoon dried thyme

2 teaspoons minced lemon zest

2 bay leaves

With tongs or a slotted spoon, transfer the tuna chunks to a large bowl. Add the remaining 1 teaspoon lemon zest and salt and pepper to taste and gently toss.

Divide the ratatouille among 4 plates. Top it with the tuna chunks and season with additional salt and pepper if desired.

Meat and Poultry

The Talmud states that "there is no happiness without meat and wine." We don't take this literally, but we do love meat and, without question, a glass of wine makes any good meal even better.

As most people know, red wine generally pairs better with red meat than white wine (see "Pairing Food and Wine," page 38). But exceptions abound. Full-bodied white wines can also hold their own with meat dishes, such as bell peppers stuffed with lamb and veal (page 175).

Poultry is a more wine-versatile companion than red meat. We enjoy poultry regularly with both whites and reds (rosés too). You'll find that our wine selections for such dishes as Spiced Chicken Burgers with Kasha and Sautéed Kale (page 160) and Apple-Stuffed Rosemary Roast Chicken (page 165) reflect an equal-opportunity approach to drinking.

Whatever your wine preferences, in this chapter you will find a multitude of opportunities to enhance your meals. Every dish is a star in its own right, but in our opinion each one shines brightest paired with a glass of fine wine!

Spiced Chicken Burgers with Kasha and Sautéed Kale

(meat) | serves 4

These chicken patties are fragrant with curry and cumin. And just because we call them "burgers" doesn't mean we eat them on a bun with ketchup. The spiced meat holds its own without any condiments at all. You can also substitute ground turkey breast for the chicken. Either way, it's a tasty low-fat burger! And with kasha (roasted buckwheat) and garlic-scented kale on the side, your main course will be as good for your health as it is good to eat. (Note that you can also make the kasha while the chicken patties are refrigerating. However, we typically make the kasha first as in the method below.)

What wines go with curried foods? Typically, fresh, fruity whites such as Riesling, Chenin Blanc, and Sauvignon Blanc. Fuller-bodied white wines like Viognier and Chardonnay can also pair nicely. If you insist on drinking red wine with this dish, try a soft, fruity one like Pinot Noir or Zinfandel.

Salt and freshly ground pepper

2¼ cups water

1 cup kasha

3 tablespoons canola oil

½ onion, chopped

4 cloves garlic, minced

1 egg

6 tablespoons panko breadcrumbs

1½ teaspoons curry powder

½ teaspoon ground cumin

¼ teaspoon cayenne pepper

1 pound ground chicken (or turkey) breast

2 tablespoons flour

3 tablespoons extra virgin olive oil, plus more for drizzling

1 pound kale leaves, coarsely chopped

In a medium saucepan, lightly salt 2 cups of the water and bring to a boil. Add the kasha, cover, reduce the heat to low, and simmer until the water has been absorbed, about 10 minutes. Remove from the heat, keep covered, and set aside.

In a large skillet, heat 1 tablespoon of the canola oil over medium heat. Add the onion and 1 minced clove of garlic and sauté until the onion is translucent, about 3 minutes. Transfer to a large bowl. Reserve the skillet for cooking the burgers.

Add the egg, panko, curry, cumin, cayenne, and ½ teaspoon salt to the onion and garlic mixture. Use a fork to thoroughly blend all the ingredients. Add the ground chicken and mix well. Divide the chicken mixture evenly into 4 balls and flatten into patties about ½ inch thick.

Place the flour on a plate and gently dip each burger in the flour on both sides. Pat the patties with both hands to evenly distribute the flour. Place them on a plate, cover with plastic wrap, and refrigerate for at least 30 minutes or up to 4 hours.

When you are ready to cook the burgers, in the reserved skillet, heat the remaining 2 tablespoons canola oil over medium-high heat. Cook the patties on one side for 5 minutes. Then reduce the heat to medium, flip them, and cook for 5 more minutes. To finish the burgers, cook each side for 1 more minute until they are golden brown on the outside and white/opaque on the inside.

While the burgers are cooking, prepare the kale. In a large skillet, heat the 3 tablespoons olive oil over medium-high heat. Add the remaining 3 cloves minced garlic and stir until fragrant and evenly coated with oil, about 30 seconds. Add the kale and toss to cover the leaves with oil. Add the remaining ¼ cup water, stir, and cover. Cook until the leaves are tender, about 5 minutes. Season with salt and pepper to taste.

If desired, briefly reheat the kasha over medium-high heat, stirring to prevent burning. Place a mound of kasha flanked by a serving of kale on each dinner plate. Drizzle a little olive oil over the kasha and lightly season with salt and pepper. Add a burger to the plate, adjacent to the kasha, and you are ready to sit down to your meal.

Kosher Meat and Salt

According to the laws of *kashrut*, eating the blood of an animal is prohibited (see "Shechita," page 16). That's why kosher poultry and meats are typically salted long before they arrive in your kitchen. The salt draws out the blood. How much salt is used can vary depending on who does the *kashering*. We've tasted kosher meats that display no overt saltiness and others that are obviously heavily salted.

It is impossible for us to gauge just how salty your kosher meats might be, as this varies from butcher to butcher. As a result, we have decided to treat all meat and poultry in this book as if they did not taste salty. The modest quantities of salt used in the recipes in this chapter are appropriate for raw meats of this genre. But it is not uncommon for cooks to prepare kosher meats without any additional salt seasoning. Remember that you can always add salt later, to taste.

Chicken Stew with Leeks, Zucchini, Root Vegetables, and Wehani Rice

meat | serves 4 to 6

This is our go-to dish for cold winter nights. It's both hearty and elegant, and quite simple to prepare. The only prep required is chopping vegetables. (If you buy a whole chicken, which we prefer, ask your butcher to cut up the chicken and remove the skin. If that option is not available to you, buy an assortment of precut, skinless chicken breasts, drumsticks, and thighs.)

The rich broth is balanced by good acidity, which comes from the wine. As we have noted elsewhere, choose an inexpensive dry wine for cooking. Don't waste the good stuff in the pot! (See "Cooking with Wine," page 40.)

We add the vegetables in stages to prevent some of them from becoming soggy. You can be creative, too, and substitute or add other vegetables as desired; it's a great way to clean out your vegetable drawer and use what you have. What we love most about this dish is that it is extremely satisfying—a bit like our grandmother's chicken soup, but more substantial!

Wehani rice is a reddish-brown rice with a nutty aroma and chewy consistency. It will add color and texture to your dining experience. Look for Wehani rice in most specialty food stores, but feel free to substitute any brown or other whole-grain rice if you prefer.

As a wine pairing, drink any white wine that you like—from Chardonnay to Riesling to Champagne! Rosé would be nice too. But most red wines would be too heavy.

---

2 tablespoons extra virgin olive oil

3 cloves garlic, minced

1 medium onion, diced

Salt and freshly ground pepper

1 whole chicken (3 to 4 pounds), skinned and cut into 8 pieces (drumsticks, thighs, wings, and breasts)

1 tablespoon dried rosemary

1 tablespoon dried thyme

4 cups dry white wine or 1 bottle (750ml) plus 1 cup water (most wine bottles contain only 3 cups of wine, so feel free to add water to get the right quantity of liquid)

In a Dutch oven or large, heavy pot, heat the olive oil over medium heat. Add the garlic and onion and sauté until the onion is translucent, about 3 minutes. Lightly salt and pepper the chicken pieces and place them in the pot. Brown them lightly on all sides, 3 to 5 minutes. Stir in the rosemary and thyme. Add the 4 cups wine (or wine plus water) and bring the liquid to a boil over high heat. Reduce the heat to medium-low. Stir in 1 teaspoon salt, add the bay leaf, cover, and simmer for 40 minutes, stirring occasionally.

While the stew is simmering, make the rice: In a medium pot, lightly salt the water and bring to a boil over high heat. Add the rice, reduce the heat to low, cover, and cook until all the water is absorbed, about 40 minutes. Keep covered and set aside.

After the stew has cooked for 40 minutes, add the carrots, potatoes, turnip, leek, and fennel. Cover and cook for 20 more minutes. Add the zucchini,

1 bay leaf

4 cups water

2 cups Wehani rice

2 carrots, cut into 1-inch lengths

3 small red or white potatoes, cut into 1-inch cubes

1 turnip, cut into 1-inch cubes

1 large leek, well washed and cut into ½-inch rounds

1 bulb fennel, trimmed and cut crosswise into ¼-inch-thick, round slices

3 small zucchini, cut into ½-inch-thick rounds

¼ cup chopped fresh dill

then cover and cook for 10 more minutes. Season with additional salt and pepper to taste.

To serve, set a mound of rice in a shallow, wide bowl for each diner. Use a ladle to spoon the stew over each portion of rice. Garnish with the dill.

Apple-Stuffed Rosemary Roast Chicken with New Potatoes

meat | serves 4

This is surely one of the easiest recipes to prepare among the main courses in the book. But that doesn't mean it holds back on flavor. The apple that bakes inside the chicken gives the bird a slightly fruity quality. (Don't forget to eat the baked apple with the chicken.) And the heady scent of roasting rosemary, garlic, and olive oil is an aromatic treat that permeates the kitchen.

Sometimes we like to make a wine gravy to go with the baked chicken. It requires little more than 2 cups of wine (see "Cooking with Wine," page 40) and an additional 5 minutes of stove time. At other times, however, we simply spoon drippings from the roasting pan over the carved meat. Either way, this simple, soulful dish is always a hit in our home.

From a wine perspective, chicken is perhaps the most versatile of meats. It tastes great with red, white, or pink wines. Among reds, robust Cabernet or Syrah would make a marvelous match here. But so would lighter-styled Pinot Noir or spicy Zinfandel. If you prefer white wine, try a fruity white Riesling or Gewürztraminer. A rich, barrel-fermented Chardonnay would be nice too.

1 whole chicken (4 to 5 pounds)

Salt and freshly ground pepper

3 tablespoons extra virgin olive oil

3 tablespoons dried rosemary

1 medium apple

6 to 8 new potatoes (about 2 pounds), cut into quarters

1 sweet potato, cut into 2-inch cubes

8 cloves garlic (unpeeled)

2 cups red or white wine (optional)

Preheat the oven to 425°F.

Sprinkle the chicken, inside and out, with salt and pepper to taste. Using your hands, rub the skin with 1 tablespoon of the olive oil. Then gently rub with 2 tablespoons of the rosemary until the skin is evenly covered. Stuff the cavity with the apple. Set the chicken on a roasting rack in a baking pan, but do not place it in the oven yet.

In a large bowl, toss the potatoes, sweet potato, and garlic with the remaining 2 tablespoons olive oil and 1 tablespoon rosemary. (Use your hands for easiest mixing.) Season with additional salt and pepper and toss again.

Place the potatoes in the baking pan around the roasting rack and under the chicken. Place the garlic cloves on top of the potatoes (or they will burn and stick to the pan). Roast the chicken for 15 minutes, then reduce the oven temperature to 400°F. Continue to roast until the chicken skin is crisp, and the juices run clear when the thigh is pierced, about 1 hour 45 minutes. (The potatoes should be firm but tender. The garlic should be soft, although some cloves may be a little crunchy.)

Transfer the chicken to a carving board and let it rest for 10 minutes before carving. Remove the apple from the bird and carve it into wedges or slices. Transfer the potatoes and garlic cloves to a large bowl and set aside.

If you are making a wine gravy, remove the roasting rack from the pan and pour out half the fatty drippings that have collected in the pan. Set the pan over high heat and add the wine. Use a wooden spoon to scrape up any browned bits that may be sticking to the pan. Let the wine reduce by half and pour it into a gravy bowl.

Serve the chicken with the potatoes and garlic on the side and a slice or two of apple. Drizzle with wine gravy or pan drippings.

Curried Chicken with Baby Spinach and Jasmine Rice

meat | serves 4 to 6

This creamy, curried chicken is filled with fragrant spices. Jasmine rice is a subtly scented, medium-grain white rice that serves as an excellent foundation, but feel free to substitute any other white rice. If you prefer brown rice, remember that brown rice takes twice as long to cook as white. Once the rice starts cooking, prepare the rest of the recipe.

With spicy curry, chilled, fruity white wine is the ticket. One of the best choices for this dish would be an off-dry (or semisweet) Riesling. Other fruit-driven white wines, such as Chardonnay, Chenin Blanc, Gewürztraminer, and Moscato, would also do nicely, depending on their level of sweetness. (A little sweetness is good; but too much sugar in a wine will challenge the food.) Sparkling wine would also make a fine selection.

4 cups water

2 cups jasmine rice

3 tablespoons canola oil

1 large onion, diced

4 cloves garlic, minced

2½ teaspoons curry powder

2½ teaspoons ground coriander

1½ teaspoons ground cumin

1 teaspoon turmeric

⅛ teaspoon cayenne pepper

4 boneless, skinless chicken breasts (about 3 pounds total), each cut into 4 pieces

1 can (14 ounces) unsweetened coconut milk

1 teaspoon salt

1½ pounds baby spinach

¾ cup chopped fresh cilantro

In a medium saucepan, bring the water to a boil over high heat. Add the rice and stir briefly. Reduce the heat to medium-low, cover, and cook until the rice is tender and all of the water is absorbed, 15 to 20 minutes. Remove from the heat, keep covered, and set aside.

Meanwhile, in a large skillet, heat the canola oil over high heat. Add the onion and garlic and sauté for 2 minutes. Add the curry powder, coriander, cumin, turmeric, and cayenne and stir well. Add the chicken and sear each side for 3 to 4 minutes. Add the coconut milk and salt. Stir well, cover, and reduce the heat to low. After 10 minutes, flip the chicken pieces and cover again. Cook until the chicken is opaque, about 10 more minutes.

Stir in the spinach, cover, and cook until wilted, about 5 minutes. Then stir in the cilantro, cover, and cook for 2 more minutes.

Set a mound of rice in the middle of each dinner plate and serve the curried chicken over the rice.

Couscous with Chicken and Lamb Sausage

meat | serves 6

Although it looks like a small grain, couscous is actually a grain-like semolina wheat that serves as a foundation for the riotously rich, spiced stew that sits atop it. It is an excellent complement to both meat and poultry, and works well with both at the same time. This version features chicken with lamb sausage. If you can find them, you might enjoy using the North African spiced lamb sausages called merguez, but any lamb sausage will add an earthy richness to the dish; or you can make it with chicken alone, for a cleaner, simpler flavor. Spicy harissa chili paste gives the sauce a special kick. It can be found in many supermarkets and certainly any food shop that specializes in Middle Eastern ingredients. Use harissa sparingly. It is really hot.

Try not to be intimidated by the long list of ingredients. You just throw them all in the pot at various times and wait until everything cooks. If you really want to cook your chickpeas from scratch, feel free to do so (you'll need to soak them overnight; see page 242), but we rarely do this ourselves.

A cool, refreshing quaff is what you want with spicy food. And without question, the best wine pairing for couscous is dry rosé. It's got some of the red fruit notes found in red wine, but it's drunk chilled. You could also enjoy opulent white wines such as Chardonnay or Viognier. But if you'll settle for nothing other than red wine, select a fruity one like Pinot Noir or Zinfandel, slightly chilled in the refrigerator for 10 to 15 minutes.

1 tablespoon cumin seeds

1 tablespoon coriander seeds

2 pinches of saffron threads

2 cinnamon sticks

4 lamb sausages (about 1 pound total)

¼ cup plus 1½ teaspoons extra virgin olive oil

2 large onions, coarsely chopped

5 cloves garlic, minced

1 tablespoon grated fresh ginger

4 plum tomatoes, quartered

2 cups coarsely chopped fresh cilantro

In a small pan, toast the cumin and coriander seeds over medium heat until fragrant, about 2 minutes. Shake the pan or stir the seeds frequently to prevent burning. Remove the seeds from the pan and crush them using a mortar and pestle or the back edge of a wide knife. Place the crushed seeds in a medium bowl and add the saffron and cinnamon sticks. Set aside.

Fill a medium skillet with 1 inch of water and bring to a boil over high heat. Using a fork, prick 3 holes on the top and 3 holes on the bottom of the sausages and place them in the boiling water for 2 minutes. Turn them over and cook for another 2 minutes. Transfer the sausages to a plate and set aside. Discard the water. Once the sausages have cooled, cut them into 3-inch lengths and set aside.

In a Dutch oven or large soup pot, heat ¼ cup of the olive oil over medium-high heat. Add the onions and sauté until softened, about 3 min-

3 chicken thighs, skinned

2 chicken breasts, skinned, cut in half

2 teaspoons salt

5½ cups Chicken Stock (page 241) or store-bought low-sodium chicken broth

4 large carrots, cut into 1-inch lengths

1 large fennel bulb, trimmed and cut into eighths

3 small zucchini, cut into 1-inch lengths

1 can (15 ounces) chickpeas, drained and rinsed, or 2 cups home-cooked (page 242)

2½ cups water

1½ cups couscous

1 tablespoon harissa

utes, stirring occasionally to prevent burning. Add the garlic and ginger and sauté for 1 minute, stirring frequently. Add the cumin/coriander/saffron/cinnamon from the bowl and stir to mix thoroughly. Stir in the tomatoes and simmer until they have softened, about 3 minutes. Stir in the cilantro. Add the chicken and 1½ teaspoons of the salt and stir well. Add the chicken stock, increase the heat to high, and bring to a boil. Reduce the heat to low, cover, and simmer for 30 minutes.

Add the lamb sausages, carrots, and fennel. Cover and simmer for 20 more minutes. Add the zucchini and chickpeas and simmer for 10 more minutes.

While the ingredients are simmering, prepare the couscous. In a medium pot, bring the water to a boil over high heat. Add the remaining ½ teaspoon salt and 1½ teaspoons olive oil to the water. Place the couscous in a glass or metal baking dish. Pour the boiled water over the couscous, mixing with a fork to moisten all the grains. Cover the baking dish with plastic wrap and set aside for 10 minutes. Prior to serving, rake a fork across the couscous to fluff it up.

Remove ½ cup broth from the pot and place it in a small serving bowl. Add the harissa and use a fork to stir it into the broth until completely dissolved. (If you want a bit more heat, use more harissa.)

Place a generous portion of couscous in the middle of each diner's plate. Top the couscous with chicken, sausage, vegetables, and broth. Garnish with the harissa sauce to taste.

Duck Breasts with Red Wine Gravy, Wild Rice, Mushrooms, and Toasted Pine Nuts

meat | serves 4

With their rich, red meat, duck breasts are more like steak than like chicken. Easy to cook, here they are graced with a golden crisp topping that tastes as good as it looks. The red wine gravy is prepared simply. In addition to the mushrooms, we've spiked the wild rice with toasted pine nuts, which give it a slightly sweet and smoky quality. Pine nuts are commonly used throughout the Mediterranean. And they are also found throughout Asia. You'll find them in most supermarkets with a good selection of nuts.

Any full-bodied red wine, such as Cabernet Sauvignon, Merlot, Zinfandel, or Syrah, would be an excellent choice at the dinner table. But remember to save the good wine for your glass! Use inexpensive wine for the sauce.

4 cups water

Salt and freshly ground pepper

1 cup wild rice

2 tablespoons extra virgin olive oil

⅓ cup diced onion (about ½ onion)

5 medium button mushrooms, finely chopped

½ cup pine nuts, toasted (page 243)

2 boneless, skin-on duck breasts (about 1 pound each)

2 cups red wine

In a medium pot, combine the water and ½ teaspoon salt and bring to a boil over high heat. Add the wild rice, return to a boil, and reduce the heat to simmer. Cover and cook until the water is absorbed, about 1 hour. (If there is still water in the pot after 1 hour, drain the rice in a colander.) Cover and set aside.

In a large skillet, heat the olive oil over medium heat. Add the onion and sauté until translucent, about 3 minutes. Add the mushrooms and gently stir to coat with the oil. Reduce the heat to medium-low, cover, and cook until the mushrooms are soft and have released their liquid, about 10 minutes. Add the wild rice, pine nuts, and salt and pepper to taste. Stir to blend well, cover, and set aside. (The rice can be served warm or reheated on the stovetop prior to serving.)

Cut each duck breast in half and trim away excess fat from around the edges of the skin. But *do not remove* the skin on top of each breast. Using a fork, poke the skin of each half breast about 5 times to make holes that will allow the fat to drain. Season the breasts on both sides with salt and pepper.

Heat a large skillet over high heat. After a few minutes, once the skillet is very hot, add the duck breasts, skin-side down. Cook until the skin is crisp and golden brown, about 8 minutes. Reduce the heat to medium and turn the breasts over. Cook until medium-rare, 4 to 5 more minutes. Remove the breasts from the pan, set them on a platter, and tent with foil. Let them rest for about 10 minutes.

While the breasts are resting, make the red wine gravy. Carefully pour the fat that has collected in the skillet into a medium bowl and set aside. Return the skillet to the stovetop over high heat. Add the wine to the pan and stir with a wooden spoon to scrape up any browned bits that may be sticking to the surface. Let the wine reduce by about two-thirds until it is dark and viscous, 5 to 10 minutes. Just before the gravy is ready, add 2 tablespoons of the melted duck fat from the bowl to the pan and stir to incorporate into the gravy. Turn off the heat.

Carve the duck breasts into ¼- to ½-inch-thick slices. Place a mound of wild rice on each dinner plate. Divide the duck slices into 4 portions and set them on or against the rice. Pour any juices that collected when carving the breasts back into the gravy and stir to blend. Spoon the gravy over the duck.

Stuffed Bell Peppers with Sautéed Baby Spinach and Garlic

meat | serves 4 to 6

Bell peppers are made to be stuffed. Any color will do, but we like to use a mix of red, yellow, and green. Not only do they make a pretty picture together on the plate, but the varied tastes of the different colored peppers add a subtle nuance. All the peppers have a fruity quality, and they are stuffed with an array of ingredients that include earthy lamb, sweet pine nuts, and smoky paprika. Sautéed spinach adds a simple, refreshing counterpoint.

You can stuff these peppers with any kind of ground meat, but we particularly like the blend of lamb and veal called for here.

Wine options are legion. Fruity reds such as Zinfandel and Pinot Noir would work well. So would meaty Syrah. Or try a rich white wine, such as barrel-fermented Chardonnay, Viognier, or Roussane.

stuffed peppers

2 cups water

1 cup brown rice

2 tablespoons extra virgin olive oil

½ onion, diced

4 cloves garlic, minced

½ pound button mushrooms, chopped

1 cup diced fennel

4 plum tomatoes, diced

1 tablespoon ground coriander

2 teaspoons smoked paprika

Salt and freshly ground pepper

½ pound ground lamb

½ pound ground veal

½ cup pine nuts, toasted (page 243)

6 large bell peppers (red, yellow, and/or green)

MAKE THE STUFFED PEPPERS: In a medium pot or saucepan, bring the water to a boil over high heat. Stir in the rice, return to a boil, cover, reduce the heat to low, and cook until all the water has been absorbed, 30 to 40 minutes.

Meanwhile, in a large skillet, heat the olive oil over medium heat. Add the onion and garlic and sauté until the onion is translucent, 3 to 5 minutes. Add the mushrooms and sauté, stirring occasionally, until they begin to soften and wilt, about 5 minutes. Add the fennel and cook until it softens, about 5 minutes. Add the tomatoes and cook until they begin to release some of their juices, about 3 minutes. Stir in the coriander, smoked paprika, and ½ teaspoon salt, to create a sauce that will be fairly thick.

Increase the heat to medium-high and stir in the lamb and the veal. Sauté, breaking the meat into small bits as needed and stirring occasionally until it is cooked through, about 10 minutes. (Stir regularly to prevent the meat from sticking to the bottom of the pan.)

Reduce the heat to medium, stir 1½ cups of the cooked rice into the meat, and mix well. (Refrigerate any remaining rice for a leftovers snack.) Stir in the pine nuts and mix well. Remove the pan from the heat.

Preheat the oven to 400°F.

spinach and garlic

2 tablespoons extra virgin olive oil

3 cloves garlic, minced

1 pound baby spinach leaves

Cut off a ¼-inch-thick slice from the stem end of each bell pepper. Discard the ends and remove the seeds. Carefully fill each pepper with the meat and rice mixture, dividing it evenly. Place the stuffed peppers in a baking pan, standing them upright. Pour water to a depth of ¼ inch in the bottom of the pan.

Cover the pan (and the peppers) with foil and bake until tender, 30 to 40 minutes. Remove them from the oven and set aside.

MAKE THE SPINACH AND GARLIC: In a large skillet, heat the olive oil over medium-high heat. Add the garlic and sauté until it starts to sizzle, about 30 seconds. (Don't let the garlic brown or it will start to burn.) Add the spinach (depending on the size of your skillet, you may have to start with half the spinach and add the rest as the first batch reduces) and sauté, stirring constantly with a wooden spoon to prevent burning. Scrape any bits of garlic off the bottom of the pan as well, or it could burn. If this begins to occur, add a tablespoon or two of water to the pan. When all the spinach has wilted, after a minute or two, remove the pan from the heat.

Set a mound of spinach on each dinner plate. Garnish with a pinch of salt and freshly ground pepper. Carefully lean a stuffed pepper against the spinach, making sure it doesn't fall over and spill the stuffing.

Korean-Style Flanken with Asian Slaw and Red Potato Salad

meat | serves 6

Flanken are strips of beef cut lengthwise across the short rib bones. Korean-style flanken is sliced thinner than the Jewish version (page 181), then marinated and grilled. The Korean cut can be found in most supermarkets, but you may have to look for Korean-style "short ribs," not flanken. Or, just ask your kosher butcher to slice his flanken into ¼- to ½-inch-thick slices.

Because it is sliced so thin, Korean-style flanken is very tender and cooks quickly. These juicy ribs have a nutty, smoky edge and an almost fruity quality that teams up well with the tangy Asian slaw and spiced potato salad—perfect for summertime dining outdoors. This dish is also ideal for parties, because you can prepare everything well in advance and then be free to socialize with guests. The grilling takes literally only minutes, but you'll need to prepare the meat in the morning or early afternoon to let it marinate.

In your glass, pour any fruity red wine such as Zinfandel, Syrah, Grenache, or Pinot Noir. Chilled rosé would also make an excellent accompaniment.

flanken

2 tablespoons brown sugar

12 Korean-style beef ribs
   (about 2½ pounds)

¼ cup soy sauce or tamari

¼ cup rice vinegar

¼ cup toasted sesame oil

3 tablespoons sesame chili oil

3 cloves garlic, minced

1 tablespoon grated fresh ginger

4 green onions (white parts only),
   cut into ¼-inch-thick rounds

asian coleslaw

2 tablespoons soy sauce or tamari

2 tablespoons rice vinegar

¼ cup toasted sesame oil

1 tablespoon sesame chili oil

PREPARE THE FLANKEN: Sprinkle the brown sugar on both sides of the beef strips and set aside. In a glass or nonreactive bowl, whisk together the soy sauce, vinegar, both sesame oils, garlic, ginger, and green onions. Place the meat in a large zip-seal plastic bag. Pour the marinade over the meat and gently squeeze the bag to expel any excess air. Seal the bag and turn it over several times to cover all the meat with the marinade. Place the bag on a plate (in case it leaks) and refrigerate for 6 to 8 hours, flipping the bag every 2 hours or so.

While the meat is still marinating, MAKE THE COLESLAW: In small glass bowl, whisk together the soy sauce, vinegar, both sesame oils, lime juice, garlic, and ginger. Place the sliced cabbage, carrots, and green onions in a large bowl. Pour the dressing over the cabbage mixture and toss gently. Add the cilantro and toss again. (The slaw can be made in advance and stored in the refrigerator for several hours. For best results, remove it from the fridge 1 hour prior to eating and allow it to return to room temperature.)

MAKE THE POTATO SALAD: In a large pot, bring 3 to 4 inches of water to a boil over high heat. Add the potatoes, reduce the heat to a gentle boil, and simmer until the potatoes are tender enough to be poked easily with a fork,

Flanken Pot au Feu

meat | serves 6

In Eastern Europe, the short-cut short ribs known as flanken were traditionally boiled and served with horseradish. However, we don't boil flanken. Instead, we slowly braise it like a French pot-au-feu until the meat is so tender it literally falls off the bone. The bones give the broth extra flavor, and on a cold winter night, this dish will warm the heart. But forget the horseradish. Its spicy sharpness will ruin your wine!

Lush, full-bodied red wines are exactly what this dish calls for. So take your pick: Cabernet, Merlot, Pinot Noir, or Syrah, for example. All would pair nicely.

4 pounds flanken

1 bay leaf

1 teaspoon dried thyme

1 teaspoon dried rosemary

8 whole cloves

½ teaspoon black peppercorns

8 cups water

2 teaspoons salt

Freshly ground pepper

1 onion, cut into eighths

4 large red potatoes, quartered

4 large carrots, cut into 1-inch lengths

2 leeks (white parts only), well washed and cut into ¼-inch rounds

2 turnips, peeled and cut into eighths

¼ cup minced fresh parsley

Rinse and pat the flanken dry. Set aside.

Make a bouquet garni by combining the bay leaf, thyme, rosemary, cloves, and peppercorns in a 4-inch square of cheesecloth. Tie it closed with a piece of kitchen twine. Trim the ends of the string and any excess cheesecloth. Set aside.

Place the flanken in a Dutch oven or other large ovenproof pot. Add the water and the bouquet garni. Bring the water to a boil over high heat, cover, reduce the heat to medium-low, and bring to a simmer. Wait a few minutes, and then using a large spoon, skim the surface of the water to remove any foam that may develop. (You may need to do this a few times.) Cover and let simmer for 3 hours.

Remove the pot from the heat and discard the bouquet garni. Use a ladle to scoop up enough broth to fill a fat separator. Then remove and discard the fat from the broth. (If you don't have one of these simple, handy devices, use a spoon or meat baster to skim whatever fat you can off the top of the broth.) The meat should be very tender, and it may have broken into large pieces. This is OK.

Return the pot to the stove over high heat and add the salt and pepper to taste. Add the onion, potatoes, carrots, leeks, and turnips. Bring to a boil and reduce the heat to medium. Cover and cook for 1 hour.

To serve, place a piece of the flanken and a portion of the vegetables in a wide shallow bowl for each diner. Ladle a generous serving of broth over the meat. Garnish with the parsley and additional pepper to taste.

Cowboy Cholent

meat | serves 6 to 8

We rarely see our friend Judge Scott Snowden without his trademark boots and cowboy hat. (The judge, when not practicing law, also owns a beautiful hillside vineyard in Napa Valley.) His claim to fame—locally, that is—may be a homemade specialty he prepares for his friends. He calls it "Outlaw Chili."

Judge Snowden's aromatic chili reminds us of traditional cholent—the slow-cooked, meat-filled casserole typically enjoyed by Jews on the Sabbath. With Outlaw Chili as inspiration, we created our own cholent. How could we call it anything but Cowboy Cholent?

Because certain forms of cooking on the Sabbath are prohibited, we start cooking our cholent on Friday afternoon. It is kept warm overnight and eaten for lunch on Shabbat afternoon. There are quite a few rules and regulations on the proper way to prepare cholent—whether it's in a pot inside an oven, or in a pot on a stovetop—so that prohibited forms of cooking do not occur on Shabbat, and the OU has given us the step-by-step instructions (see "How to Prepare Cholent for Eating on Shabbat," page 185). If you want to make your cholent in a slow cooker, consult a rabbinic authority for instructions on how to do this for Shabbat. It's a bit more complicated.

We think this rich, hearty dish tastes great anytime, especially on a cold winter night. We offer two cooking methods here: one overnight and one shorter method that takes about 4 hours. Readers should note that both methods require soaking the dried beans. Which method is best? In our opinion, both are equally delicious; you should use the method that best suits your time and the occasion.

For variety, we use a blend of lamb sausage, beef, and veal shank. The tender veal has a nice, marrow-filled bone for added richness. But you can use any meat you want. If you substitute other meats, or simply use one or two cuts, remember you'll need 4 to 5 pounds total.

What wines go best with cholent? Big, rich red ones! Serve Cabernet Sauvignon, Zinfandel, or Syrah, for example. Cabernet Franc or Petite Sirah would also make excellent selections. Pinot Noir lovers will be happy to hear that this versatile varietal—which goes with just about anything—won't let you down with cholent either.

---

1 cup dried white beans (such as navy)

3 tablespoons extra virgin olive oil

Rinse and pick over the beans to remove any pebbles or misshapen beans. Place the beans in a large bowl and cover with water by 2 inches. Let soak for 6 to 8 hours or overnight. Drain when ready to use.

2½ pounds beef brisket,
excess fat trimmed,
cut into 2-inch cubes

1½ pounds lamb sausages, halved

1 piece of veal shank
(about 1 pound)

2 onions, coarsely chopped

5 cloves garlic, minced

4 cups Chicken Stock (page 241)
or store-bought low-sodium
chicken broth

3 cups dry red wine

2 tablespoons ground cumin

1 tablespoon chili powder

1 tablespoon dried oregano

1 teaspoon salt

3 carrots, cut into 1-inch lengths

½ cup pearl barley

In a 6-quart Dutch oven or heavy ovenproof pot, heat 2 tablespoons of the olive oil over high heat. Add the beef and sear until it is browned on all sides, 5 to 7 minutes. Using a slotted spoon, remove the meat from the pot and set aside in a large bowl. Add the sausages to the pot and sear on two sides until the skin begins to blister, 3 to 4 minutes. Remove from the pot and set aside with the brisket. (Be careful not to let the pan burn while searing the meat. If you start to see smoke or burning, reduce the heat a little.) Add the veal shank to the pot and brown on both of the cut sides, about 2 minutes per side. Remove it from the pot and set aside in the bowl with the other meats.

Reduce the heat to medium and add the remaining 1 tablespoon olive oil. Add the onions and garlic and cook, stirring occasionally, until the onions are translucent, 6 or 7 minutes.

Return all the meat to the pot. Add the chicken stock, wine, cumin, chili powder, oregano, and salt. Gently stir to mix without spilling any liquid. Increase the heat to high and bring to a boil. Skim off any foam that collects on top. Add the carrots, drained beans, and barley, gently stirring to distribute evenly. (The liquid will be close to the top of the pot at this point. Just stir slowly and you won't spill.) Reduce the heat to medium, cover, and cook for 30 minutes.

If you are preparing your cholent for eating on Shabbat, see opposite.

FOR THE OVERNIGHT COOK: While the cholent is simmering on the stovetop, preheat the oven to 200°F or as low as it will go. After the cholent has simmered for 30 minutes, place the pot, covered, in the oven and let cook overnight until ready to serve for lunch. You will lose a certain amount of liquid during the long, slow cook. If possible, check on the pot prior to leaving it in the oven unattended overnight. Add a little water, stock, or wine to bring the liquid level back up near the top edge of the pot.

FOR THE QUICKER METHOD: While the cholent is simmering on the stovetop, preheat the oven to 350°F. After the cholent has simmered for 30 minutes, place the pot, covered, in the oven and let cook until the meat and beans are tender, about 3 hours.

Serve each portion with a mix of the meats, as well as a robust selection of the beans, barley, and vegetables.

How to Prepare Cholent for Eating on Shabbat
(as Explained by Our Friends at the OU)

If the cholent is cooked on a gas or electric stovetop and will not yet be edible when Shabbat begins, the burner must be covered before Shabbat with a *blech,* a large square sheet of aluminum or steel that can be purchased in hardware stores or grocery stores in Jewish neighborhoods, or on some Judaica websites. If the cholent *will be* edible by sunset, a *blech* is not an absolute requirement, but using one is preferable for various reasons. If you start cooking the cholent on a stovetop and then move it into the oven before Shabbat, the cholent *should be* edible when Shabbat begins, because setting up a *blech* inside an oven is not something that can easily be done.

According to many rabbinic opinions, it is best to open the oven door on Shabbat only when your oven is in the "on" cycle. Once you have removed the cholent from the oven or the stovetop and have served it on Shabbat afternoon, it can't be returned to the oven or the stovetop if there is any cholent left over.

You may add water to a cholent on Shabbat, provided the following criteria are met:

1. The cholent is fully cooked.

2. The water added to the cholent is hot.

3. The cholent pot is lifted off the *blech* before the water is added. And either:

   a. one person holds the pot as another person adds the water, or

   b. when you set the pot down on your countertop, you continue to hold the pot with one hand (with a pot holder, of course) while adding the hot water with the other hand, or you have someone else add the water while you are holding on to the pot.

4. The cover is put back on the pot before putting the pot back onto the *blech.*

You may return the cholent pot only to an area covered by a *blech*. Because an oven does not lend itself to a *blech,* a cholent pot cannot be returned to an oven.

Chili-Rubbed Rib-Eye Steak with Sautéed Onions and Rosemary Potatoes

(meat) | serves 4

Rib-eye steaks are among the most tender cuts of kosher meat. They are also very large, and can weigh up to a pound. To keep them tender, don't overcook them. (We like them medium-rare.) This chili rub is inspired by the Mexican cooking enjoyed by so many of us in California. It gives the meat a tangy kick, but is not excessively hot. Sweet onions temper the heat. There's a reason "meat and potatoes" is a household phrase. We really haven't discovered a better food match!

On the wine front, big, rich, fruity reds are recommended. We suggest Zinfandel. But Syrah, Grenache, and fruit-driven California Pinot Noir would also work well.

chili rub

2 tablespoons chili powder

1 tablespoon light brown sugar

½ teaspoon salt

½ teaspoon ground cumin

½ teaspoon garlic powder

½ teaspoon ground coriander

½ teaspoon oregano

¼ teaspoon cayenne pepper

meat and potatoes

3 pounds small white potatoes, halved or quartered

2 rib-eye steaks, 1½ to 2 inches thick (about 1 pound each)

6 tablespoons extra virgin olive oil

5 large onions, thinly sliced

2 teaspoons salt

¼ cup fresh rosemary leaves, finely chopped

2 tablespoons canola oil

MAKE THE CHILI RUB: In a medium bowl, combine all the rub ingredients and use a spoon or fork to mix thoroughly. Set aside.

PREPARE THE MEAT AND POTATOES: In a steamer or pot of boiling water, steam or boil the potatoes until they are tender, about 20 minutes. Drain the potatoes in a colander if boiling them, or remove them from the steamer and empty the water from the steamer pot. Return the potatoes to the pot and set aside uncovered. When the potatoes are cool enough to handle, cut them into ½- to ¼-inch cubes and set aside.

Meanwhile, set the steaks on a large cutting board and trim off any excess fat. Spoon 2 teaspoons of the rub onto each steak. Using your hands, gently massage the rub into the surface of the meat. Turn the steaks over and do the same thing to the other sides. Coat the edges of each steak with the rub as well. Set the meat aside for 30 minutes.

In a large skillet, heat 3 tablespoons of the olive oil over medium-high heat. Add the onions and stir them to separate the slices and coat them with the oil. Reduce the heat to medium, add 1 teaspoon of the salt, and continue to cook—stirring occasionally—until the onions are tender, about 25 minutes. Remove the pan from the heat, cover, and set aside. Shortly before serving, reheat the onions over medium-low heat.

Meanwhile, in another large skillet, heat the remaining 3 tablespoons olive oil over medium-high heat. When the oil starts to shimmer, add the potatoes, the remaining 1 teaspoon salt, and the rosemary. Cook, stirring occasionally to mix the ingredients and prevent burning, until the potatoes have a slightly golden hue, 10 to 15 minutes. Remove the pan from the heat, cover, and set aside.

Preheat the oven to 475°F.

In a large ovenproof skillet, heat the canola oil over high heat. When the oil begins to shimmer, place the steaks in the pan and sear them for 2 minutes on each side, turning them with tongs or a large fork. Transfer the steaks to the oven and roast until the internal temperature of the thickest part of the steak registers 140°F for medium-rare, about 8 minutes.

Remove the steaks from the oven and let them sit for 3 to 5 minutes. (This is a good time to reheat the potatoes and onions.) Cut each steak in half and divide the meat among 4 plates. Set a mound of potatoes and onions alongside each steak.

Brisket with Juniper Berries, Bay Leaves, Red Wine Gravy, and Mashed Potatoes

meat | serves 4 to 6

This is comfort food at its finest. Long, slow braising (about 3 hours) in the oven makes brisket—typically an inexpensive, tough cut of meat—tender and quite flavorful. The juniper berries and bay leaves cook with the brisket to give it a wonderfully earthy, minty quality. Mashed potatoes soak up the rich gravy created from the meat's natural juices and a little wine.

Many traditional brisket recipes use sugar, which can make dry wines taste bitter. That's why we don't use any sugar in this dish. We think brisket is best served with fruity (but dry) red wines like Zinfandel or Pinot Noir. More robust Cabernet Sauvignon and Syrah will also make excellent pairings.

3 pounds brisket

Salt and freshly ground pepper

3 tablespoons plus 1 cup extra virgin olive oil

5 medium onions, sliced into thin rounds

5 cloves garlic, minced

15 juniper berries

2 bay leaves

1½ tablespoons tomato paste

1½ cups dry red wine

2 cups Chicken Stock (page 241) or store-bought low-sodium chicken broth

3 pounds small, think-skinned potatoes, such as Yukon Gold

Preheat the oven to 325°F.

Season both sides of the brisket with salt and pepper. In a Dutch oven or large ovenproof pot, heat 2 tablespoons of the olive oil over high heat. Add the brisket and sear on both sides until browned, about 3 minutes per side. Transfer the meat to a platter and set aside.

Reduce the heat to medium and add 1 tablespoon of the olive oil to the pan. Add the onions, garlic, ½ teaspoon salt, and pepper to taste and stir well. Sauté until the onions have wilted, 5 to 7 minutes, stirring regularly to prevent burning.

Add the juniper berries and bay leaves and mix well. Add the tomato paste and mix well. Add the wine and chicken stock, increase the heat to high, and bring to a boil. Return the brisket to the pot. Cover and bake for 1½ hours. Flip the meat over, cover, and bake until the meat is very tender, another 1½ hours.

Thirty minutes before the meat has finished cooking, prepare the potatoes. Wash but do not peel them, then cut them into quarters or eighths. Steam or cook in lightly salted boiling water until they are tender, about 20 minutes. Drain the potatoes in a colander if boiling them, or remove them from the steamer and empty the water from the steamer pot. Return the potatoes to the pot.

Using a potato masher, mash the potatoes while adding the remaining 1 cup olive oil, ¼ to ½ cup at a time. Continue mashing until the potatoes are fairly smooth. (It's OK if some lumps remain.) Using a wooden spoon, stir in 1 teaspoon salt. The potatoes will become smoother but remain dense, not runny. Season with additional salt to taste. Cover and set aside. The potatoes should remain hot enough to serve with the meat. But if not, reheat them over medium-high heat before serving, stirring to prevent burning.

Take the meat out of the oven and transfer it to a large serving platter. Tent with foil until ready to slice. While the meat is resting, fish out the juniper berries and bay leaves and discard. Season the gravy and the onions in the pot with salt and pepper to taste.

Slice the meat against the grain on the platter and top with the onions and gravy. Serve the meat and potatoes family style. Extra gravy from the pot can be served in a gravy boat on the side.

Braised Beef Short Ribs with Root Vegetables and Garlic Confit Mashed Potatoes

meat | serves 4 to 6

Braising in wine may be the simplest and most effective way to cook meats. Wine's natural acidity and the moist heat it creates in the oven make the meat on these ribs practically melt in your mouth. Pan juices and cooking wine create a lush gravy for both the meat and garlic-infused potatoes. (Garlic confit is not hard to make: It's just garlic cloves slow-cooked in olive oil.) For easier preparation, we don't peel our potatoes, which gives a slightly more rustic quality to the dish. But you can peel yours if you really want to.

A big, meaty dish like this cries out for a full-bodied red wine like Cabernet Sauvignon, Merlot, or Syrah.

Salt and freshly ground pepper

10 beef short ribs
  (about 4 pounds)

1 onion, coarsely chopped

3 carrots, cut into 2-inch lengths

2 leeks (white parts only), well
  washed and cut into ½-inch-
  thick rounds

2 parsnips, peeled and cut into
  2-inch lengths

21 cloves garlic—6 peeled and
  halved, 15 peeled and whole

1 bay leaf

6 to 8 sprigs fresh thyme or
  2 teaspoons dried thyme

1 bottle (750 ml) dry red wine
  (about 3½ cups)

3 tablespoons plus 1 cup extra
  virgin olive oil

3 pounds medium thin-skinned
  white potatoes, quartered

Lightly salt and pepper both sides of the short ribs.

In a large zip-seal plastic bag, combine the short ribs with the onion, carrots, leeks, parsnips, 6 halved garlic cloves, bay leaf, thyme, and wine. (If you need 2 bags, divide the ingredients evenly between them.) Gently massage the ingredients for a minute and refrigerate for a minimum of 6 hours or up to 24 hours. Turn the bag(s) over two or three times during marination.

Preheat the oven to 350°F.

Reserving the marinade and the vegetables in the bag(s), remove the meat from the marinade.

In a Dutch oven or large ovenproof pot, heat 3 tablespoons of the olive oil over medium-high heat. Working in batches if necessary, add the meat to the pan and sear on each side until browned, about 3 minutes per side. Remove the ribs from the pot and set them aside.

Reduce the heat to medium and add the vegetables from the marinade. Sauté until the vegetables soften, about 10 minutes, stirring regularly to prevent burning. Add the marinade to the pot, increase the heat to high, and bring to a boil. Remove from the heat.

Return the short ribs to the pot, tucking them into the marinade. Cover and bake, turning the ribs over in the pot every 45 minutes, until the meat is tender and easily separates from the bone, 2 to 2½ hours. If the liquid in the pan runs low, add an additional cup of wine or water and mix thoroughly.

While the meat is cooking, prepare the garlic confit and potatoes. Place the remaining 15 whole garlic cloves in a small saucepan and cover them with the 1 cup olive oil. (Add a little extra olive oil, if necessary, to fully submerge the cloves in the oil.) Heat the oil over medium heat until it starts to bubble. Reduce the heat to low and simmer until the garlic is golden in color and soft textured, about 30 minutes. Remove the pan from the heat and set aside.

Fill a large pot one-third with cold water and add the potatoes. Bring the water to a boil over high heat. Reduce the heat to medium and cook the potatoes until they can be easily pierced with a fork, about 20 minutes. Drain the potatoes in a colander and return them to the pot. Add the garlic cloves, the olive oil they cooked in, and ¾ teaspoon salt. Using a potato masher, mash the potatoes until they are fairly smooth. (We like a few lumps, but mash for longer if you prefer.) Cover the pot and set aside. (The potatoes can be reheated for 5 minutes over low heat, stirring occasionally, prior to serving.)

When the meat is ready, discard the bay leaf and any visible thyme stems. Divide the potatoes among individual plates and place one or two short ribs angled up against the potatoes. Garnish with the vegetables and gravy from the pot.

Spiced Lamb Meatballs with Tomato Sauce and Freekeh

meat | makes about 16 meatballs (serves 4)

Filled with the flavors of the Middle Eastern *shouk*, or marketplace, these fragrant meatballs have just a hint of heat. They are bathed in a bright tomato sauce and served over smoky freekeh, a wonderful wheat cereal found all over Israel and now becoming popular in the United States. You can substitute brown rice for freekeh, if you can't find it. Remember, though, that freekeh takes a little longer to cook than rice and requires more water. Whether you use freekeh or rice, start by cooking it first. When it's done, just keep it warm and covered, until you are ready to serve.

Don't be afraid of the long list of ingredients. Most are simply spices. And the tomato sauce is a snap to prepare. (We don't recommend seeding or peeling the tomatoes. It's not worth the effort.) However, because there are three steps here, the best way to keep it simple is to lay out the ingredients for all steps prior to cooking. You'll breeze through the rest!

And from your wine cellar, look for a rich, spicy California Zinfandel or an earthy Syrah.

freekeh

4 cups water

½ teaspoon salt

1 teaspoon extra virgin olive oil

1½ cups freekeh

meatballs

1 pound ground lamb

½ onion, finely chopped

3 cloves garlic, minced

½ teaspoon salt

⅓ cup panko or other breadcrumbs

1 egg

1 tablespoon ground cumin

1 tablespoon ground coriander

1 teaspoon Spanish hot paprika
   (pimentón picante)

MAKE THE FREEKEH: In a medium saucepan, combine the water, salt, and olive oil. Cover and bring to a boil over high heat. Add the freekeh and let the water come to a boil again. Reduce the heat to medium, cover, and let simmer until all the water has been absorbed, about 45 minutes. Set the pot aside, covered, until ready to use. Prior to serving, fluff the freekeh with a fork.

MAKE THE MEATBALLS: In a large bowl, use your hands to thoroughly blend the lamb, onion, garlic, salt, panko, egg, cumin, coriander, paprika, cardamom, cilantro, and 2 tablespoons of the olive oil. Shape the mixture into balls the size of golf balls and set aside on a platter.

In a large, heavy-duty skillet, heat the remaining 1 tablespoon olive oil over medium-high heat until it starts to shimmer. Gently set the meatballs in the pan and brown them on all sides, turning them now and then to brown them evenly and keep them from sticking to the pan, about 5 minutes. Transfer the meatballs to on a platter. Leave the oil and any bits of meat remaining in the pan (you will be cooking the tomato sauce in this pan).

1 teaspoon ground cardamom

3 tablespoons chopped fresh
   cilantro

3 tablespoons extra virgin olive oil

tomato sauce

1 medium onion, diced

4 cloves garlic, minced

1 cup red wine

2 pounds fresh tomatoes,
   chopped, or 1 can (28 ounces)
   whole Italian plum tomatoes,
   chopped

2 tablespoons dried oregano

1 teaspoon ground cumin

½ teaspoon salt

¼ teaspoon cayenne pepper

1 bay leaf

1 cinnamon stick

¼ cup chopped fresh cilantro,
   for garnish

Freshly ground pepper, for garnish

MAKE THE TOMATO SAUCE: Reduce the heat under the pan to medium. Add the onion and garlic and sauté until the onion is translucent, about 3 minutes. Add the wine, increase the heat to high, and use a wooden spoon to scrape up any bits of meat or other solids sticking to the pan. Let the wine reduce by half, about 3 minutes.

Add the tomatoes, oregano, cumin, salt, cayenne, bay leaf, and cinnamon. Reduce the heat to medium, cover, and simmer, stirring occasionally, until the tomatoes are soft and the sauce has thickened, about 20 minutes. Remove and discard the cinnamon stick.

Add the meatballs to the sauce, cover the pan, and let simmer until the meatballs are cooked through, another 20 minutes.

To serve, place a mound of freekeh in the middle of each dinner plate. Then top the freekeh with 3 or 4 meatballs and the sauce. Garnish with the cilantro and pepper to taste.

Lamb Shepherd's Pie

meat | serves 4 to 6

Many years ago, Jeff spent several summers working as a shepherd in the Swiss Alps. He was charged with herding cattle and goats—but not sheep. Maybe that's why he doesn't remember eating anything that resembles this dish—commonly referred to as shepherd's pie. It's not really a pie at all, and it's typically made with lamb topped with a potato crust.

Meaty red wines like Syrah are particularly good with lamb. So are Cabernet Sauvignon, Zinfandel, and Pinot Noir. And if you've got an aged red wine in the cellar, use it to brighten up the evening. Simple dishes such as this one can really make a complex, classy wine shine.

3 pounds small thin-skinned potatoes (red or white)

8 tablespoons extra virgin olive oil

1 onion, diced

2 cloves garlic, minced

8 large button mushrooms, coarsely chopped

2 pounds ground lamb

2 teaspoons dried rosemary

1 teaspoon dried thyme

2 teaspoons salt

2 pounds fresh tomatoes, unpeeled and coarsely chopped, or 1 can (28 ounces) whole Italian plum tomatoes, drained and coarsely chopped

1½ cups shelled fresh or frozen peas

½ cup red wine

Wash the potatoes but do not peel. Halve or quarter the potatoes, depending on their size. Fill a large pot about two-thirds with water. Add the potatoes and bring to a boil over high heat. Reduce the heat to medium and cook until easily pierced with a fork, about 20 minutes.

Preheat the oven to 300°F.

In a Dutch oven or large ovenproof pot, heat 3 tablespoons of the olive oil over medium-high heat. Add the onion and garlic and sauté until the onion is translucent, about 3 minutes. Add the mushrooms, stir, cover, and cook until tender, about 3 more minutes.

Increase the heat to high and add the lamb, rosemary, thyme, and 1 teaspoon of the salt. Sauté, stirring occasionally, until the meat has browned, about 5 minutes. Reduce the heat to medium and add the tomatoes, peas, and wine. Stir to blend all the ingredients, cover, and simmer for 10 minutes.

When the potatoes have cooked, drain them in a colander and return them to the pot. Add the remaining 5 tablespoons olive oil and 1 teaspoon salt, and mash them with a potato masher. (We like hand-mashing. Lumpy potatoes have character!)

Spread the mashed potatoes over the meat and vegetables in the Dutch oven or pot. Cover and bake in the oven for 20 minutes.

Spiced Lamb Tagine with Currants and Israeli Couscous

meat | serves 4 to 6

A North African tagine typically features slow-cooked meat, braised until it is tender. This richly textured stew is brimming with exotic spices, a touch of heat, and a hint of sweetness. The heady aromas that arise from the pot remind us of the *shouk*—or marketplace—in Jerusalem, where spice merchants line the ancient corridors of commerce. You can easily find all the spices in this recipe on the spice rack at your local supermarket too. Israeli couscous is a large-grain, round-shaped pasta widely enjoyed in Israel. It has a growing following in the United States as well.

In your glass, a fruity red wine will provide a complementary pairing to the currants (see "Pairing Food and Wine," page 38). Pinot Noir and Zinfandel might be your best bets. Syrah could work well too. But don't rule out more herbaceous varietals like Cabernet Sauvignon, Merlot, or Malbec. They will also have their charm.

1 teaspoon ground cardamom

1 teaspoon ground cinnamon

1 teaspoon ground coriander

1 teaspoon ground cumin

¼ teaspoon cayenne pepper

⅛ teaspoon saffron threads

Salt and freshly ground pepper

2 pounds lamb shoulder, cut into 1½-inch cubes

½ cup dried currants

¼ cup extra virgin olive oil

2 tablespoons plus 2½ cups water

2 medium onions, coarsely chopped

3 cloves garlic, minced

1 tablespoon grated fresh ginger

5 medium carrots, cut into 1-inch lengths

2 tablespoons tomato paste

In a small bowl, combine the cardamom, cinnamon, coriander, cumin, cayenne, saffron, and ½ teaspoon salt. Mix thoroughly. Place the lamb on a large plate and sprinkle the spice mixture over it. Place the seasoned lamb in a zip-seal plastic bag, close the bag, and massage the lamb to evenly to coat the meat with the spices. Refrigerate for 4 to 6 hours. Remove the lamb from the refrigerator 15 minutes prior to cooking.

Place the currants in a small bowl and cover with warm water. Set aside.

In a Dutch oven or heavy-duty pot, heat the olive oil over medium-high heat. Working in batches if necessary, sear the lamb on all sides, about 2 minutes per side. Remove the seared meat from the pot and set aside on a plate.

Add 2 tablespoons water to the pot and use a wooden spoon to scrape up any browned bits that have formed or might be sticking on the surface.

Add the onions and sauté until translucent, about 5 minutes. Add the garlic and ginger and sauté until fragrant, about 1 minute. Add the carrots, stir to coat with the onion mixture, and cook for 2 minutes. Drain the water from the currants and add them to the pot. Stir in the tomato paste. Add the chicken broth and stir to mix well. Return the lamb to the pot, add 1 teaspoon salt, and mix well. Increase the heat to high, bring the liquid to a boil, then

4 cups Chicken Stock (page 241)
    or store-bought low-sodium
    chicken broth

2 cups Israeli couscous

½ cup minced fresh cilantro

reduce the heat to low and partially cover the pot, leaving a small sliver of space open at the top. Simmer for 2 hours, stirring occasionally.

Uncover and simmer for another 30 minutes to thicken the sauce.

In a medium pot, lightly salt 2½ cups water and bring to a boil over high heat. Add the Israeli couscous, stir, and reduce the heat to medium-low. Cover and cook until all the water is absorbed, about 8 minutes.

To serve, place ½ cup couscous in a wide, shallow soup bowl. Top with the lamb, the carrots, and a generous portion of sauce from the pot. Garnish with cilantro and pepper.

Lamb Chops with Cilantro Chimichurri Sauce and Warm Quinoa Salad

meat | serves 4

We love lamb, and we love the ease with which this dish is made. It offers a welcome variation on the classic theme of meat and potatoes.

Both quinoa and chimichurri have South American roots. Quinoa are small, grain-like seeds that have become popular today not only for their slightly crunchy texture, but also for their high nutritional value. You can find quinoa in most well-stocked supermarkets, but rice can also be substituted. Green chimichurri sauce is said to have originated in Argentina. It adds a wonderfully fresh-tasting edge to the lamb.

This is a recipe that calls for red wine in your glass, unless perhaps you'd like a chilled, dry rosé on a warm summer evening. Rosé and lamb make a marvelous match; just ask anyone who's lived in southern France. Among red wines, we can't think of a well-made varietal that wouldn't do well here. But truth be told, when it comes to lamb chops, we are partial to earthy Syrah or densely structured Cabernet Sauvignon.

chimichurri sauce

2 cups firmly packed coarsely chopped fresh cilantro

¾ cup extra virgin olive oil

2 tablespoons fresh lime juice

1 clove garlic, minced

1 teaspoon ground cumin

⅛ teaspoon cayenne or chili powder

¼ teaspoon salt

quinoa salad

2 cups Chicken Stock (page 241) or store-bought low-sodium chicken broth

1 cup quinoa (white, red, or multi-colored)

2 tablespoons plus ¼ cup extra virgin olive oil

MAKE THE CHIMICHURRI SAUCE: In a blender, combine the cilantro and olive oil and puree to a smooth sauce. Add the lime juice, garlic, cumin, cayenne, and salt. Pulse to incorporate thoroughly. Transfer the sauce to a small serving bowl, cover, and set aside. (Refrigerate for up to 2 days if you plan to store the sauce for more than a few hours before using.)

MAKE THE QUINOA SALAD: In a medium pot, bring the chicken stock to a boil over high heat and stir in the quinoa. Cover, reduce the heat to low, and simmer until all the stock is absorbed, about 15 minutes. Remove the pot from the heat.

While the quinoa is cooking, in a medium skillet, heat 2 tablespoons of the olive oil over medium-high heat. Add the leek and carrot and sauté until tender, 10 to 12 minutes.

In a large bowl, gently mix the quinoa with the leek and carrot. Add the tarragon and chives and mix well. Drizzle with the remaining ¼ cup olive oil and add the lemon juice. Stir gently to mix thoroughly. Adjust the seasoning with salt and pepper to taste. Serve warm or at room temperature.

PREPARE THE LAMB CHOPS: Preheat the grill or the broiler.

1 medium leek, well washed and diced

1 large carrot, diced

2 tablespoons minced fresh tarragon

3 tablespoons minced fresh chives

2 tablespoons fresh lemon juice

Salt and freshly ground pepper

lamb chops

8 lamb chops (about 2½ pounds), trimmed of excess fat

1 clove garlic, peeled and halved

Salt and freshly ground pepper

1 tablespoon extra virgin olive oil

1 tablespoon dried rosemary

Rub the meat with the cut sides of the garlic. Lightly salt and pepper the chops, then rub them with the olive oil. Coat the chops with the rosemary.

Grill or broil the chops for about 7 minutes per side for medium-rare. Let the meat sit for 5 to 10 minutes prior to serving.

To serve, place a mound of quinoa salad on each plate. Lean 2 chops at an angle against the quinoa. Drizzle the chimichurri sauce onto the chops to taste.

Veal Osso Buco with Butter Beans and Gremolata

meat | serves 4

Osso buco is a classic Italian dish that will please anyone who loves tender yet richly textured meat. (Ask your butcher to tie the veal shanks so they won't fall off the bone while cooking.)

In this recipe, the veal is topped with a gremolata, a simple garnish made with parsley, lemon zest, and garlic to balance the richness. The dish is served on a colorful backdrop of golden butter beans, tomatoes, and carrots—all dressed in a luscious white wine sauce.

If you can't find large, flat butter beans, use any white beans, such as cannellini. And if you're starting with dried beans, you will need to cook them in advance (see page 242). We find the canned version to be fairly indistinguishable from the dried beans.

You can also make this dish with lamb shanks. But veal is so exceptional, it's worth the additional cost.

In your glass, any rich, full-bodied wine—red or white—will complement pale-hued veal. Try Cabernet Sauvignon, Merlot, Syrah, or Sangiovese, for example, among reds. Pinot Noir would also make an excellent red wine match, even though it's lighter in style than those previously mentioned. Barrel-fermented Chardonnay or Viognier would do well among white wines.

veal shanks

4 pieces of veal shank, cut for osso buco, ⅔ to 1 pound each

Salt and freshly ground pepper

1 cup all-purpose flour

¼ cup extra virgin olive oil

1 medium onion, diced

1 carrot, diced

2 celery stalks, diced

½ teaspoon dried rosemary

½ teaspoon dried thyme

1 bay leaf

1 cup dry white wine

2 cups Chicken Stock (page 241) or store-bought low-sodium chicken broth

---

Preheat the oven to 350°F.

PREPARE THE VEAL SHANKS: Pat the veal shanks dry with paper towels to remove any excess moisture. If your butcher has not already done it, secure the meat to the bone by tying a piece of kitchen twine around each shank's perimeter. Season the meat with salt and pepper. Dredge the shanks in the flour, shaking off any excess clumps.

In a Dutch oven or large ovenproof pot, heat the olive oil over medium-high heat. When it shimmers, add the veal shanks and brown on both cut sides, about 3 minutes per side. Transfer the shanks to a large plate and set aside.

To the same pot, add the onion, carrot, and celery. Sauté over medium heat until the vegetables are soft, about 10 minutes. Add the rosemary, thyme, bay leaf, and ½ teaspoon salt. Stir to mix well and cook for 30 seconds. Add the wine and chicken stock, increase the heat to high, and bring to a boil. Return the shanks to the pot, spoon a bit of the wine sauce over the shanks,

gremolata and beans

⅓ cup chopped flat-leaf parsley

1 tablespoon chopped lemon zest

3 cloves garlic, minced

1 tablespoon extra virgin olive oil

15 cherry tomatoes, halved

2 cans butter beans (15 ounces each), drained and rinsed, or 4 cups home-cooked (page 242)

½ teaspoon dried rosemary

¼ teaspoon salt

Freshly ground pepper

cover, and transfer to the oven. Bake until tender, about 2 hours, turning the shanks over every 45 minutes.

While the meat is cooking, MAKE THE GREMOLATA: In a blender or food processor, combine the parsley, lemon zest, and 1 minced garlic clove. Do not puree. Instead pulse 3 to 4 times to retain a coarse texture. Set aside.

PREPARE THE BEANS: In a large pan, heat the olive oil over medium heat. Add the 2 remaining minced garlic cloves and sauté until fragrant, about 30 seconds. Add the cherry tomatoes and mix well. Sauté until the tomatoes have softened, 2 to 3 minutes. Stir in the beans, rosemary, salt, and pepper to taste. Reduce the heat to medium-low and cook until the beans are hot and the flavors are integrated, about 5 minutes. If necessary, add 2 to 3 tablespoons of water to prevent the beans from burning. (If the beans are ready to eat long before the meat, cover the pan, remove from the heat, and set aside. Reheat over medium heat for a few minutes prior to serving.)

To serve, divide the beans evenly in a wide circle on each plate. Carefully remove the cooked veal shanks from the pot and place one on top of the beans on each plate. Cut the kitchen twine from each shank. Spoon 3 to 4 tablespoons of the vegetables and sauce from the pot over the meat and beans. Garnish each veal shank with the gremolata.

Veal Rib Roast with Wild Mushrooms, Black Rice, and Red Wine Sauce

meat | serves 4

There is a reason veal costs a lot. It is simply one of the best meats you can buy. You may not make this recipe every week, but it is certainly worth splurging on for a special occasion. Wild mushrooms add intriguing earthiness. If you can't find them, commercially grown button mushrooms will suffice.

Black rice (sometimes called Forbidden Rice) is a flavor-packed, chewy dark rice once reserved for the emperor of China in ancient times and forbidden to everyone else. Fortunately, times have changed. Not only do we love its taste, but the rice's black hue creates a lovely contrast with the white veal. However, any whole-grain rice can be substituted.

Enjoy this robust dish with an equally robust red wine such as Cabernet Sauvignon, Cabernet Franc, Merlot, or Syrah.

1 veal rib roast with 4 chops
(about 3½ pounds),
fat trimmed off

Salt and freshly ground pepper

5 tablespoons extra virgin olive oil

1¾ cups water

1 cup black rice

1 leek (white part only), well
washed and cut into thin rounds

2 teaspoons minced fresh thyme
or ½ teaspoon dried

1 pound mixed wild mushrooms,
such as porcini, shiitake,
or chanterelles, thinly sliced

2 cups red wine

2 teaspoons flour

Preheat the oven to 375°F.

Season the roast with salt and pepper on both sides. In a large ovenproof skillet, heat 1 tablespoon of the olive oil over high heat. Place the roast in the pan, meat-side down, and sear for about 5 minutes until it is browned and crisp on the bottom. Remove the pan from the heat and turn the veal roast over with the bone side facing down. Set the pan in the oven and roast until the meat's internal temperature registers 145°F, about 1 hour.

While the meat is roasting, prepare the rice and the mushrooms. In a medium pot, combine the water, the rice, and a pinch of salt. Cover and bring to a boil over high heat. Reduce the heat to medium-low and cook, covered, until all the water is absorbed, about 30 minutes. Remove the pot from the heat and set aside. Keep covered.

In a medium skillet, heat 2 tablespoons of the olive oil over medium heat. Add the leek and sauté until it is wilted, about 3 minutes. Add the thyme and mushrooms, mix well, and sauté until the mushrooms have wilted, about 10 minutes. Remember to shake the pan or stir the mushrooms occasionally to prevent burning. Remove the pan from the heat and set aside.

When the veal is done, place the roast on a cutting board and tent it with foil.

Pour out and discard any fat or oil in the pan. Return the pan to the stovetop over medium-high heat. Add the red wine to the pan and stir thoroughly to scrape up any bits of browned meat or fat stuck to the surface. When the wine begins to bubble, reduce the heat to low and simmer, stirring occasionally, until the wine reduces by half, about 5 minutes.

Several minutes before the wine has finished reducing, in a small saucepan, heat the remaining 2 tablespoons olive oil over medium heat for 1 minute. Remove the pan from the heat and use a whisk to smoothly blend the flour into the oil. Add the olive oil/flour mixture to the red wine reduction and use the whisk to thoroughly blend it into the wine. Continue to simmer for a few more minutes until the reduction becomes a thick, dark sauce.

As the sauce finishes reducing, reheat the mushrooms on the stovetop over medium heat.

Slice the veal roast into 4 chops, starting at the meaty end and cutting alongside the bone. Place a generous portion of rice on each individual plate. Lay a veal chop at an angle over the rice with the mushrooms bordering the rice as well. Pour the wine sauce on and around each veal chop.

Desserts

Sweets, like wine, make a meal complete. They can transform a daily dinner into an exceptional one. And as anyone who has enjoyed cookies and tea in the afternoon knows, sweets can also enhance any ordinary moment. Perhaps most important, dessert makes the moment worth savoring.

Baked goods and many desserts are made with dairy products like butter and cream. However, for kosher meals, dairy-based desserts are not appropriate when meat has been served. For us, that's easy. We just serve a dessert designed without dairy. But many people prefer to substitute nondairy ingredients like margarine for butter in order to enjoy a dairy-style dessert and still keep kosher. In the following recipes, substituting margarine for butter is an option. Look for non-salty brands made without trans fats (see "A Word About Margarine," page 13). Alas, we haven't found anything we can recommend as a reliable, tasty stand-in for cream or milk.

Pairing wines with desserts can be tricky. Sweet things make dry wines taste bitter or tart. So you won't typically see dry wine pairings accompanying our dessert recipes. (Pistachio Cardamom Butter Cookies, page 212, are the exception. At the end of a meal, we like nothing better than to dip them into the last drops of whatever wine remains in our glass.)

Sweet wines are different. These late-harvested whites and reds can pair wonderfully with all kinds of desserts. (But forget about Cabernet Sauvignon and chocolate. It's a bad idea; the chocolate might taste great, but the dry wine will be severely diminished.)

Sometimes, dessert wine *is* the dessert in our home. A great bottle of French Sauternes, for example, needs no accompaniment.

Finally, after all the wine has been drunk, we might enjoy a refreshing Fresh Herb Tisane (page 231), an herbal tea made with fresh herbs from the garden. It's a custom adopted from our days in southern France, where thyme, rosemary, and sage grow in profusion.

We have enjoyed the desserts in this chapter with family and friends for many years. We hope some of them will become part of your ongoing mealtime repertoire as well.

Pistachio Cardamom Butter Cookies

dairy | makes about 25 cookies

These cookies are almost as easy to make as they are to eat! They are light-textured and slightly crunchy; not too sweet with just a subtle hint of cardamom.

Great for snacks or after a meal with a cup of Fresh Herb Tisane (page 231). You can also dip them into whatever wine might be left in your glass. From our perspective, cookies and wine is certainly an improvement upon cookies and milk!

½ cup unsalted pistachio nuts, plus 25 for garnish

2 cups unbleached all-purpose flour

2 teaspoons ground cardamom

2 sticks (8 ounces) unsalted butter, at room temperature

½ cup powdered sugar

1 teaspoon vanilla extract

Using a blender or small food processor, grind the ½ cup pistachios into coarse bits the size of rice grains. Set aside.

In a medium bowl, combine the flour and cardamom. Set aside.

In a large bowl, with an electric mixer, cream together the butter and powdered sugar until fluffy, about 2 minutes. Add the vanilla and continue to beat for another 30 seconds. Add the flour/cardamom mixture and continue to mix for another minute. The dough will become coarse grained and resemble little pebbles. Add the ground pistachios and mix well for another 30 seconds.

Cover the bowl with plastic wrap and refrigerate for 30 minutes.

Position a rack in the center of the oven and preheat to 350°F. Lightly grease a baking sheet (or use a nonstick sheet).

Using your palms, roll 2 tablespoons chilled dough into a small ball. Repeat with the rest of the dough and place the dough balls on the baking sheet.

With the heel of your palm, gently press on each dough ball to flatten to a thickness of about ½ inch and a diameter of about 1½ inches. Gently press a pistachio into the top of each cookie, being careful not to crack the cookies.

Bake until the cookies turn golden brown, 15 to 20 minutes.

Set the cookies on a wire rack to cool to room temperature.

Toasted Coconut Macaroons with Chocolate Drizzle

pareve | makes about 18 cookies

These light-textured cookies are not too sweet—but sweet enough to mark the end of any great meal, like a Passover Seder, for instance. The coconut is the star flavor here, with chocolate serving as a garnish and pleasing visual element. Make sure you use unsweetened shredded coconut for best results.

With their sweetness and hint of chocolate, these macaroons would marry well with a red dessert wine such as Port. They are also quite satisfying when enjoyed with our Fresh Herb Tisane (page 231).

3 cups unsweetened shredded
   coconut

4 egg whites

½ cup sugar

¼ teaspoon salt

1 teaspoon vanilla extract

3 ounces semisweet chocolate,
   chopped

Position a rack in the center of the oven and preheat to 350°F.

On a baking sheet, evenly spread the coconut and bake until it begins to turn golden brown, about 10 minutes. (Occasionally, use a wooden spoon to stir the coconut. This will prevent burning along the edges.) Remove from the oven and let cool, but leave the oven on. Slide the toasted coconut off the sheet into a bowl and set aside. (You can reuse the baking sheet for the next step.)

Line 2 baking sheets with parchment paper.

In a large bowl, with an electric mixer, beat the egg whites until they are frothy. Add the sugar and continue to beat for about 1 minute. Add the salt and vanilla and beat for another minute. Use a rubber spatula to mix the coconut into the batter. Stir until just blended, but do not overmix. Let the batter sit for about 1 minute to firm up.

Slightly moisten your hands with water to prevent sticking. Then, using your hands, shape cookie balls the size of Ping-Pong balls from the batter. Place the cookies about 2 inches apart on the baking sheets with parchment paper. (They will spread as they bake.)

To bake evenly, bake one sheet at a time until the cookies are golden, 15 to 20 minutes.

Remove the baking sheets from the oven and gently slide the parchment paper with the cookies off the pan onto a flat surface. Let the cookies cool to room temperature on the parchment paper.

Melt the chocolate in a double boiler or in a small pot over low heat, stirring occasionally with a rubber spatula, until smooth. Remove from the heat and whisk 3 to 4 tablespoons warm water into the chocolate until it can be easily poured in a thin stream. Using a teaspoon, slowly drizzle a small stream of the chocolate in a circular pattern over each cookie.

Eat the cookies the same day or store, refrigerated, in an airtight container for up to 1 week.

Cherry Coconut Rice Pudding

pareve | serves 4

This simple dessert blends a taste of Italy with that of the Caribbean. Dried cherries add color along with a delightful fruitiness, but if you can't find dried cherries, substitute raisins or dried currants. Arborio rice is a short-grained Italian rice that has a high starch content and a creamy, chewy texture. It is used to make classic Italian risotto but is also ideal for making this delicate, mildly sweet rice pudding. Look for Arborio rice in most supermarkets. In addition, the coconut milk adds a dairy-like richness but still keeps the dish pareve.

If you'd like a glass of wine with this dessert, try something honeyed, like a late-harvest Sauvignon Blanc made in the style of French Sauternes. Sweet Riesling or Gewürztraminer would make excellent choices as well.

1 can (14 ounces) unsweetened coconut milk

1 cup water

¼ cup sugar

⅓ cup unsweetened shredded coconut

⅓ cup Arborio rice

⅛ teaspoon salt

¼ cup coarsely chopped dried cherries

¼ teaspoon vanilla extract

In a medium saucepan, combine the coconut milk, water, sugar, shredded coconut, rice, and salt and bring to a gentle boil over medium-high heat, stirring frequently. Reduce the heat to low, cover partially, and simmer for 15 minutes. (Stir and scrape the bottom and sides of the pan occasionally with a rubber spatula to prevent burning.)

Add the dried cherries to the pudding and mix thoroughly. Continue to cook until most of the liquid is absorbed and the pudding has the consistency of soft oatmeal, about 15 more minutes. Remove from the heat and stir in the vanilla.

Evenly divide the pudding among 4 dessert bowls. It can be served hot or at room temperature. You can also refrigerate and serve cold.

Lavender Panna Cotta

dairy | serves 6

This creamy, light pudding ends with a lemony-fresh finish. A sprinkling of lavender on the top reminds us of our herb garden. Because it's not too sweet, panna cotta leaves you refreshed even after a big meal. The recipe calls for a vanilla bean, which is easy to locate in the spice rack of most supermarkets. Bean pods have more flavor than the internal seeds, which you'll discard.

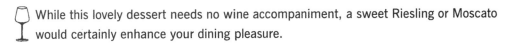 While this lovely dessert needs no wine accompaniment, a sweet Riesling or Moscato would certainly enhance your dining pleasure.

½ vanilla bean, about 3 inches long

¼ cup cold water

2 teaspoons kosher gelatin

1½ cups heavy cream

⅓ cup sugar

1 tablespoon lavender buds, plus more for garnish

1½ cups buttermilk

Lay the vanilla bean flat on a cutting surface. Using a sharp paring knife, slice the bean open lengthwise. Scrape out the pasty seeds from the interior and discard them. Set the bean pod aside.

Pour the cold water into a small bowl and sprinkle the gelatin on top. The gelatin will absorb all the water in about 2 minutes.

In a medium saucepan, combine the cream, sugar, 1 tablespoon of lavender, and the vanilla bean. Heat until almost boiling over medium heat, stirring frequently until the sugar is dissolved. Remove the pan from the heat just before the cream mixture boils. (You'll see it start to bubble around the edges of the saucepan.)

Use a rubber spatula to slide the gelatin out of the bowl and into the hot cream. Use a whisk to mix the gelatin into the liquid. Add the buttermilk in a slow stream and whisk the cream mixture for about 1 minute until it has cooled a bit, and all the ingredients are thoroughly blended.

Strain the cream mixture through a fine-mesh sieve into a medium pitcher. Divide the strained cream evenly among six 4-inch-wide (4-ounce) rame-kins and chill until set, about 4 hours. Once the panna cotta is firm, garnish each ramekin with a few lavender buds, cover with plastic wrap, and refrig-erate until ready to serve or for up to 3 days.

Orange Chiffon Cake

pareve | serves 10 to 12

Chiffon cake is known for its lightness, making it an excellent choice to follow an otherwise filling meal. Orange zest and orange juice give this elegant cake a particularly refreshing quality. Sometimes we serve it with homemade Whipped Cream (page 247). This would, of course, transform the cake into a dairy dessert.

🍷 Because it's not too sweet or too heavy, chiffon cake pairs very well with most white dessert wines, should you have any on hand. An herbal tea, such as Fresh Herb Tisane (page 231), would also make a fine accompaniment.

Cooking spray, such as grapeseed spray oil

2½ cups cake flour

1½ cups superfine sugar

1 tablespoon baking powder

1 teaspoon salt

5 egg yolks

½ cup canola oil

⅓ cup coarsely grated orange zest (from 2 to 3 medium oranges)

¾ cup fresh orange juice

8 egg whites

½ teaspoon cream of tartar

3 tablespoons powdered sugar

Preheat the oven to 325°F. Lightly coat a 10-inch tube pan with a removable center with cooking spray.

In a large bowl, sift (or stir) the flour, superfine sugar, baking powder, and salt to blend thoroughly. Set aside.

In a medium bowl, with an electric mixer, beat the egg yolks, canola oil, orange zest, and orange juice until frothy and pale orange in color, about 1 minute. In a larger bowl, with an electric mixer, beat the egg whites and cream of tartar until soft peaks form, about 1 minute.

Pour the egg yolk mixture into the flour mixture and beat until the ingredients are thoroughly incorporated, about 2 minutes. Scrape the sides of the bowl as needed. Using a rubber spatula, gently fold the egg whites into the batter, being careful not to deflate it.

Pour the batter into the tube pan and bake until the cake is golden brown and the center is firm yet spongy, about 1 hour.

Remove the cake from the oven and immediately turn the pan upside down onto an oiled wire rack until it cools, about 30 minutes. If the cake does not drop out of the pan by itself, run a sharp long knife along the sides of the pan to loosen it. Then invert the pan onto the wire rack to remove the cake. Run the knife under the base of the cake to remove the pan base.

When the cake has completely cooled, dust it with the powdered sugar.

Frangipane Tart with Poached Pears

dairy | serves 8 to 10

This is a wonderful crowd-pleaser, since it's sweet enough for sugar lovers, but not too sweet.

Almonds and pears work together beautifully here. The almond flavor comes from the almond paste, also known as frangipane. You can find it in the baking section of any grocery store. Prepare the crust first; you'll need to let it sit in the refrigerator for at least 2 hours before making the rest of the tart.

🍷 This is the kind of light-styled dessert that works with many sweet wines, from late-harvest whites to bold, rich Port or Madeira.

crust

1 stick (4 ounces) plus
   1 tablespoon unsalted butter,
   at room temperature

⅓ cup sugar

1 egg

1 cup all-purpose flour,
   plus more for kneading

½ teaspoon salt

filling

1 cup water

1¼ cups sugar

1 Bosc pear, cut into 8 slices

⅓ cup almond paste
   (about 3 ounces)

3 eggs

4 tablespoons unsalted butter,
   at room temperature

⅓ cup all-purpose flour

MAKE THE CRUST: In a large bowl, with an electric mixer, cream the 1 stick of butter with the sugar until they turn pale yellow. Add the egg and beat until the mixture is fluffy and light. (Use a rubber spatula to scrape down the sides of the bowl, if necessary.) Add the flour and salt. Mix until all the ingredients are incorporated into a soft dough.

Remove the dough from the bowl and place on a lightly floured surface. Using the heel of one hand, push the dough forward. Then use both hands to fold it back onto itself. Repeat five or six times until the dough has a smooth, firm texture. Roll the dough into a ball and very slightly flatten it with the palm of your hand. Wrap with plastic wrap and refrigerate for at least 2 hours or up to 2 days.

Preheat the oven to 350°F. Grease the bottom and sides of a 10-inch tart pan with a removable bottom with the remaining 1 tablespoon butter.

On a lightly floured surface, use a rolling pin to roll out the tart dough into a round about 12 inches in diameter. Carefully place the dough inside the tart pan and pinch off the top edge so that it does not hang over the sides of the pan.

MAKE THE FILLING: In a small pot, combine the water and 1 cup of the sugar. Bring to a boil over high heat. Reduce the heat to medium-high, stirring occasionally, until the sugar has dissolved, about 1 minute. Add the pear slices to the syrup and simmer until they are firm-tender, 3 to 4 minutes. Transfer the pear slices from the syrup to a plate and set aside. (Discard the syrup.)

In a food processor, combine the almond paste and the remaining ¼ cup sugar and process until the mixture has a grainy consistency. Add the eggs, one at a time, and continue to mix until smooth, about 1 minute. Add 2 tablespoons butter and mix for 30 seconds. Repeat with the remaining 2 tablespoons butter. Use a rubber spatula to transfer the almond/butter mix from the food processor to a large bowl. Sift (or slowly pour) the flour into the almond mix, using the rubber spatula to thoroughly blend the ingredients.

Fill the tart crust with the almond paste mix. Arrange the pears in a fan-like or circular pattern across the top of the tart.

Bake until the top is firm and golden brown, about 30 minutes.

Pear Tart

dairy | makes one 12-inch tart (serves 6 to 8)

We've been making tarts like this one for years, much to the delight of our daughters, who—now grown up—continue to request them when they come home to visit. A tart, unlike a pie, has no top crust. Jeff first encountered this kind of tart when he lived in southern France as a young music student. He found that French tarts were not as sweet as American pies and could double for breakfast as well as dessert!

 And yes, enjoy with any white dessert wine or (for breakfast) your cappuccino!

1 stick (4 ounces) plus
   3 tablespoons unsalted butter,
   at room temperature

⅓ cup plus 1 tablespoon sugar

1 egg

1 cup all-purpose flour,
   plus more for dusting

½ teaspoon salt

3 Bosc pears (unpeeled),
   halved and cut lengthwise
   into ¼-inch-thick slices

In a large bowl, use a wooden spoon to beat together the 1 stick butter and the ⅓ cup sugar until they are fluffy. Beat in the egg. Add the flour and salt and mix thoroughly until a dough forms. Transfer the dough to a floured work surface and collect it into a rounded mound. Push down on the dough with the heel of your hand and spread it forward over the floured surface. Fold it back onto itself and repeat these movements several times to knead the dough until it is smooth and elastic. (Lightly flour your hands or the flat surface occasionally to prevent the dough from sticking.)

Shape the dough into a ball and wrap it with plastic wrap or place it in a zip-seal plastic bag. Refrigerate for at least 1 hour or up to 2 days.

Remove the dough from the refrigerator and let stand at room temperature for 20 to 30 minutes. On a floured work surface, roll out the dough into a thin round, about 14 inches in diameter. Using 1 tablespoon of the butter, grease the bottom of a 12-inch tart pan with a removable bottom. Gently transfer the dough to the pan and fit it into the bottom and sides. Roll the rolling pin over the top edge to cut away excess dough. (Don't discard these scraps right away. You may need them to patch thin spots in the crust or sides.)

Preheat the oven to 350°F.

Starting at the outer edge of the crust, arrange the pear slices in concentric circles or in a spiral so that they cover the crust completely. Cut the 2 remaining tablespoons butter into small pieces and dot the top of the pears with the butter. Sprinkle the top of the tart with the remaining 1 tablespoon sugar.

Place the tart in the oven and bake until the edges are golden brown, about 45 minutes. Let cool completely on a rack, then remove the pan sides and transfer to a serving platter.

Mocha Cheesecake

dairy | serves 8

This dessert conjures up memories of youthful decadence growing up in New York, where cheesecake continues to be (in our opinion) the king of desserts. As kids, we couldn't get enough, and the taste has stayed with us.

Mocha flavoring is an added treat for anyone who loves not only cheesecake, but also chocolate and coffee. Although many desserts can handle wine, this dessert—with its creamy chocolate and coffee flavors—would in fact make a really bad pairing. Why distract yourself from serious cheesecake with wine? But an espresso afterward would be a fine idea!

15 graham crackers, broken into squares

¼ cup granulated sugar

1 stick (4 ounces) unsalted butter, melted

6 ounces semisweet chocolate, cut into 1-inch squares, plus more for garnish

1 teaspoon vanilla extract

1 tablespoon instant espresso powder

1 pound cream cheese, at room temperature

¾ cup powdered sugar

3 eggs

¼ cup sour cream

⅓ cup mascarpone cheese

¼ cup heavy cream

Preheat the oven to 325°F.

In a blender or food processor, grind the graham crackers into coarse crumbs. In a large bowl, use a wooden spoon to thoroughly mix the graham cracker crumbs with the granulated sugar. Pour in the melted butter and mix well.

Pour the graham cracker mix into a 9-inch springform pan, distributing it evenly. Pat and press the crumb mixture firmly across the pan bottom and 1 inch up the sides. Set the crust in the oven and bake until golden brown, 8 to 10 minutes. Remove the pan from the oven but leave the oven on and reduce the temperature to 300°F.

Let the crust cool on a wire rack. When cool enough to handle, wrap the bottom and sides of the pan with a double layer of foil, crimping the sides to fit snugly around the pan.

Meanwhile, melt the 6 ounces of chocolate in a double boiler. (If you don't have a double boiler, fill a medium saucepan with 2 inches of water and bring to a boil. Reduce the heat to low and keep the water at a low simmer. Place the chocolate in a medium heatproof bowl—slightly larger at its top than the width of the saucepan; too large in diameter to descend into the water. Set the bowl with the chocolate inside the saucepan suspended over the hot water, but do not let the water touch the bowl. Stir to melt.) Add the vanilla and espresso powder to the melted chocolate and stir to fully incorporate. Keep the chocolate soft over very low heat.

In a large bowl, with an electric mixer, beat together the cream cheese and powdered sugar until a thick, creamy texture forms, about 1 minute. Scrape the sides of the bowl with a rubber spatula as needed. Add the eggs one at a time, beating until the cream cheese mixture is pale yellow in color, about 2 minutes.

Add the sour cream and mascarpone and beat for another minute. Add the heavy cream and beat for 1 minute, scraping the sides of the bowl with a rubber spatula as needed. Add the melted chocolate and beat to mix well for another minute or two.

Place the foil-wrapped springform in a roasting pan. Fill the roasting pan with warm water to come halfway up the sides of the springform (but not above the foil).

Pour the batter into the springform and bake until the center is fairly firm but still springy, about 1 hour.

Remove both pans from the oven. Take the springform out of the water bath and place it on top of a kitchen towel. Remove the foil from around the pan, being careful to watch for water that may have become trapped in the foil. Let the cake cool to room temperature, about 15 minutes. Refrigerate the cake (in its pan) for at least 6 hours or overnight.

To serve, remove the cake from the refrigerator. Carefully run the edge of a long knife warmed in hot water between the cake and the side of the pan. Unclip and remove the pan side. Using a vegetable peeler, scrape short, thin slivers of semisweet chocolate for garnish and sprinkle them over the top of the cake. Serve immediately, sliced into wedges. Uneaten cake should remain refrigerated.

Orange Olive Oil Cake

pareve | serves 8

This fruity cake serves up a lovely blend of sweet and tart flavors. If you are wondering about using olive oil in a dessert, just remember that both butter and olive oil are fats. The olive oil works marvelously well here.

This cake is not too sweet to enjoy with a dessert wine like Moscato or other late-harvest varietals such as Semillon or Sauvignon Blanc. A sweet Riesling or Gewürztraminer would also lend itself nicely.

⅓ cup extra virgin olive oil,
   plus more for the pans

1 cup all-purpose flour,
   plus more for the pans

1 orange

1 lemon

¼ teaspoon salt

1½ teaspoons baking powder

2 eggs

¾ cup sugar

½ cup almonds, toasted
   (page 243) and finely chopped

Preheat the oven to 350°F. Coat the bottom and sides of a 9-inch springform cake pan with olive oil. Line the bottom of the pan with a round piece of parchment paper. Evenly spread about 2 tablespoons of flour on the base and sides of the pans. Turn the pan over and tap to remove excess flour.

Using a vegetable peeler, peel the orange and the lemon. Reserve both the rinds and the peeled fruit. In a small saucepan, blanch the rinds in boiling water for 30 seconds. Strain the blanched rinds, rinse with cold water, and let drain. Finely chop the rinds and set aside.

Cut the peeled orange and lemon in half and squeeze the juice from both fruits into a small bowl. (Using a hand juicer is the most efficient way to do this.) Set aside.

In a medium bowl, combine the 1 cup flour, salt, and baking powder and set aside. In a large bowl, with an electric mixer, beat the eggs and sugar until the eggs are pale in color, about 2 minutes. Mix in the almonds. Carefully beat the flour mixture into the egg batter and blend thoroughly, scraping the sides as needed. Add the chopped citrus rinds and the orange/lemon juice and continue to mix. Add the ⅓ cup olive oil and mix until it is evenly blended throughout.

Pour the cake batter into the prepared pan and bake until the cake is firm and golden and a toothpick inserted in the center comes out dry, about 30 minutes. Unclip and lift away the pan sides and gently turn the cake upside down onto a platter. Remove the bottom of the pan and peel off the parchment paper. Place another platter on top of the cake and flip the cake to serve right side up.

Chile Chocolate Soufflé

dairy | serves 6

This bittersweet chocolate dessert may come at the end of a meal, but it steals the show. The chocolate is dark and rich, but the texture is light. Inside, a soft, hot, lava-like core can be found. You'll love the surprise finish—a subtle kick from the cayenne pepper.

If you want to serve these soufflés fresh out of the oven to dinner guests, make the batter in advance. Fill the ramekins, cover with plastic wrap, and store in the refrigerator until ready to use or for up to 4 hours. Remove the ramekins from the refrigerator 5 minutes prior to baking.

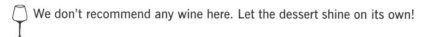 We don't recommend any wine here. Let the dessert shine on its own!

9 ounces bittersweet chocolate, coarsely chopped

1¼ teaspoons ground cinnamon

¼ teaspoon cayenne pepper

¾ teaspoon vanilla extract

¼ cup all-purpose flour, plus more for the ramekins

1½ teaspoons baking powder

2 sticks (8 ounces) unsalted butter, at room temperature, plus 2 tablespoons for the ramekins

⅓ cup granulated sugar

5 eggs

Powdered sugar, for dusting

Preheat the oven to 400°F.

Melt the chocolate in a double boiler, stirring until smooth. (If you don't have a double boiler, fill a medium saucepan with 2 inches of water and bring to a boil. Reduce the heat to low and keep the water at a low simmer. Place the chocolate in a medium heatproof bowl—slightly larger at its top than the width of the saucepan; too large in diameter to descend into the water. Set the bowl with the chocolate inside the saucepan suspended over the hot water, but do not let the water touch the bowl. Stir to melt.) Stir in the cinnamon, cayenne, and vanilla until thoroughly blended. Remove the pot from the stove, but keep over the hot water so the chocolate stays soft.

Meanwhile, in a small bowl, whisk together the ¼ cup flour and baking powder. In a large bowl, with an electric mixer, cream together the 2 sticks butter and the granulated sugar until the mixture is pale yellow, about 1 minute. Add the eggs one at a time and continue to mix until all the ingredients are blended, about 1 minute. Add the flour/baking powder mixture to the egg mixture and blend thoroughly. (The batter will be a little lumpy, but it will smooth out when the chocolate is added.)

Whisk the melted chocolate into the batter until smooth, about 30 seconds.

Lightly coat the insides of six 4-inch-wide (4-ounce) ramekins with the 2 tablespoons of butter. Dust the surface of each ramekin with 1 teaspoon of flour. Turn each ramekin upside down and gently tap to remove excess flour. Set aside.

Using a large spoon or a measuring cup, fill each ramekin three-fourths full. Smooth the top of each soufflé with a rubber spatula. Gently tap the bottom of each filled ramekin to help settle the batter.

Place the ramekins on a baking sheet and bake until the soufflés have risen about ½ inch above the edge of each dish, about 15 minutes. The top of each soufflé will have split open and will be crunchy.

Remove the ramekins from the oven and let cool for 5 minutes. Dust the top of each soufflé with powdered sugar and serve immediately.

Fresh Herb Tisane

pareve | serves 4

After lunch we drink espresso. But after dinner, espresso is not the best way to ensure a good night's sleep. So we've borrowed a custom from our French friends with this fresh herb tisane, a caffeine-free tea that we make from the fresh herbs growing in the garden— sage, lemon verbena, and rosemary. (Sage, by the way, is said to have a particularly calming influence.) You can also use any one of these herbs alone instead of the blend listed below. The exact blend is not critical. Just keep the total amount to 4 tablespoons. Eventually you won't even measure. Israelis enjoy a similar tea made with fresh mint leaves. We like this too.

If you don't have garden herbs at the ready outside your kitchen door, just pick some up at any supermarket with a decent fresh produce department, or at your local farmers' market. A touch of honey rounds off the tisane and will leave you and your guests with a subtle, fresh sweetness in your mouths. It's a great way to end the evening.

2 tablespoons coarsely chopped fresh sage

1 tablespoon coarsely chopped lemon verbena

1 tablespoon coarsely chopped fresh rosemary

4 cups boiling water

Honey

Place the herbs in a teapot or saucepan and pour the water over them. Let steep for 5 minutes. Strain the hot liquid into teacups. Sweeten each cup with ½ to 1 teaspoon honey (to taste).

Flourless Toasted Hazelnut Chocolate Torte

dairy | serves 8

This family favorite will make anyone who loves chocolate very happy. The torte—a word that implies flourless cake—has a rich, chocolaty core highlighted by fresh cream and strawberries. What could be better? Remember to toast the hazelnuts first.

If you've still got the urge for a sweet libation after dessert, pour yourself a glass of Port.

1 stick (4 ounces) unsalted butter, plus 1 tablespoon for the pan

1 cup hazelnuts, toasted (page 243)

8 ounces semisweet chocolate, coarsely chopped

½ teaspoon vanilla extract

5 eggs, separated

1 cup granulated sugar

1 tablespoon powdered sugar

Whipped Cream (page 247)

1 cup sliced strawberries

Preheat the oven to 350°F. Use 1 tablespoon butter to grease the bottom and sides of a 9-inch springform pan. Line the bottom with parchment paper.

In a food processor or blender, pulse the hazelnuts until they are coarsely ground. They should still have some crunch and not be as finely ground as flour. Set aside.

In a small saucepan, combine the chocolate and 1 stick butter and heat over low heat, stirring frequently until they have melted. Gently stir in the vanilla. Keep the mixture warm over very low heat until ready to use.

In a medium bowl, with an electric mixer, beat the egg yolks. Slowly add ½ cup of the granulated sugar in a steady stream. Continue to mix until the sugar is incorporated and the mixture is thick and pale yellow, about 1 minute. Set aside.

In a large bowl, with the electric mixer, beat the egg whites until foamy. Slowly add the remaining ½ cup granulated sugar, continuing to beat until slightly stiff peaks form, about 1 minute. Using a rubber spatula, gently mix the egg yolk mixture into the egg whites. Add the ground hazelnuts and mix well. Pour in the melted chocolate and mix until the color is uniform.

Pour the batter into the springform pan and bake until a toothpick inserted in the center comes out dry, about 30 minutes. Remove the cake from the oven, place the pan on a wire rack, and let it cool to room temperature.

Unclip the springform pan and remove the sides. Gently turn the cake upside down onto a platter and carefully remove the bottom of the pan and the parchment paper. When the cake has cooled to room temperature, use a fine-mesh sieve to evenly dust the top of the cake with the powdered sugar.

Garnish each serving slice with a dollop of whipped cream and sliced strawberries.

Basics

At our house, a number of simple recipes are used as the base for many of our meals. Some, like Vegetable Stock (page 240) or Chicken Stock (page 241), are essential components in soups, sauces, and even grain dishes. Techniques such as toasting seeds (page 243) or cooking dried beans (page 242) are also commonly used and really simple. We've included them here as well.

Bread—very much a basic part of our daily dining regime—is too hard to make at home every day. But homemade Rustic Challah (page 237), traditionally baked for the Sabbath, regularly finds its way to our table. So does Pita Bread (page 239).

Additionally, you'll find other staples from our diet like fresh Mayonnaise and Aioli (page 244), Pistou/Pesto (page 246), and Whipped Cream (page 247). Once you get used to the homemade versions, it's hard to go back to what you get in stores.

Each recipe that follows is easy to make and versatile. That's why we count them among our basic culinary building blocks in the kitchen.

Rustic Challah

pareve | makes 2 loaves

Challah, the braided bread traditionally enjoyed by Jews on the Sabbath and other holy days, has been a part of Jewish life for thousands of years. Most certainly, a book could be written just about challah and its symbolic significance.

But our own perspective on challah is parochial. We are simply concerned with what it tastes like. Jeff likes water challah, a style that is not typically sweet and uses no egg wash. Egg challah—the most commonly made challah in the United States—is too soft and sweet for Jeff, who insists it tastes more like cake than bread!

But even the water challahs we have purchased tend to be too sweet for Jeff's taste. So one day he decided to make his own. The following recipe produces traditionally shaped challah, but one that tastes more like a crusty French country bread or Italian ciabatta.

Note that we use bread flour, a high-gluten, high-protein flour widely available in supermarkets. This is not the same as all-purpose flour. (See "All-Purpose, High-Gluten, and Whole Wheat Flours," page 62.) Use any active dry yeast. We prefer "rapid-rise" yeast, which produces a lighter crumb with more air pockets than traditional active dry yeast. But either yeast will work well. Another factor that affects texture is temperature. Prior to baking, bread that rises in a cool room (say, at 68°F) will be denser than one that rises with an ambient temperature above 70°F.

1 envelope (¼ ounce;
 2¼ teaspoons) active dry yeast

2 to 2½ cups warm water

1 teaspoon sugar

4½ cups unbleached bread flour,
 plus more for the work surface

2½ teaspoons sea salt

1 tablespoon extra virgin olive oil

In a large bowl, add the yeast to 2 cups of the warm water and mix with your fingertips. Add the sugar and mix, using your fingers as well. Set aside until the liquid begins to foam, about 15 minutes.

While the yeast is hydrating, in another large bowl, use a fork or whisk to mix the flour and the salt. Add ½ cup of the flour/salt mixture at a time to the yeasted water and stir, using a wooden spoon. When the flour becomes too thick to stir, massage the dough with your hands to consolidate. However, if the dough becomes too solid or elastic, add another ½ cup of warm water and work it in with your hands. The dough needs to be moist and malleable at this point.

Turn the dough out onto a floured work surface. (It should still be moist, so use extra flour to keep it from sticking to the work surface or your hands.) To knead the dough, use the heel of one hand to push it forward. Then use both hands to fold it back onto itself. Knead until the dough firms up but is still elastic, 5 to 7 minutes. (Continue to use additional flour to prevent sticking.)

Lightly coat the bowl that the ingredients were originally mixed in with the olive oil. Place the dough in the bowl and turn it gently to coat the exterior with oil. Cover the bowl with plastic wrap or a damp kitchen towel. Let the dough rise until it has doubled in size, about 1½ hours.

Without taking the dough out of the bowl, pull one side of the dough up and fold it over the rest of the dough. Repeat 2 or 3 times. Cover with the towel or plastic wrap and let the dough rise until it has doubled again, about 45 minutes.

Turn the dough out onto a floured work surface. (Do not punch the dough down. You want it to retain as many air pockets as possible.) Dust the dough and/or work surface liberally with flour to keep your hands from sticking. Cut the dough in half and then cut each half into 3 equal pieces. Use your hands to roll each into a 12- to 15-inch rope. Try to keep all 6 ropes approximately the same length. You'll be using 3 ropes for each loaf.

Pinch 3 ropes together at one end and tuck the end under. Braid the bread as you would 3 locks of hair: Fold one rope over the middle strand, then fold the remaining outside rope over what has become the middle rope, alternating ropes until you reach the end. Repeat for the second loaf. Let the challah loaves rise at room temperature for another 20 to 30 minutes.

Meanwhile, position a rack in the center of the oven and preheat to 500°F. (If using a baking stone, set the baking stone on the rack to preheat.)

If you've got a hot baking stone in the oven, pull the stone out of the oven and set it on the stovetop. Place the two loaves on the stone or—if you don't have a stone—on a nonstick baking sheet. Bake for 20 minutes. Reduce the oven temperature to 400°F and bake until the loaves are golden brown, 10 to 15 more minutes. Each loaf should sound hollow when tapped on the bottom.

Let cool on a wire rack or wooden cutting board.

Pita Bread

pareve | makes 12 pita breads

It's easy to find good store-bought pita breads in many supermarkets today. But fresh, warm pita from the oven is truly a special treat. The classic pairing for these easy-to-make small round breads would be Hummus (page 51). Pita also stands in easily for any fresh bread, anytime. If you have a pizza/baking stone, use it, although any flat baking sheet will suffice. We like to blend whole wheat and white flours for a more substantial crumb. The bread remains light textured, nonetheless.

1½ cups whole wheat flour

1½ cups all-purpose flour, plus more for kneading and rolling

1 envelope (¼ ounce; 2¼ teaspoons) active dry yeast

1 tablespoon sugar

1½ teaspoons salt

2 tablespoons extra virgin olive oil, plus 1 teaspoon for the bowl

1¼ to 1½ cups warm water

In a large bowl, combine the two flours and the yeast. Mix with a wooden spoon. Add the sugar and salt and mix well. Add the 2 tablespoons olive oil and 1¼ cups water. Mix thoroughly. A ball should form, but if some of the flour is not incorporated, add another ¼ cup lukewarm water.

Transfer the dough to a lightly floured work surface. Using the heel of one hand, push the dough forward. Then use both hands to fold it back onto itself. Knead the dough for 10 minutes until it is smooth and somewhat sticky. (Use additional flour to prevent your hands from sticking.)

Lightly coat the bowl that the ingredients were mixed in with the remaining 1 teaspoon olive oil. Place the dough in the bowl. Cover the bowl with plastic wrap or a damp kitchen towel and set aside. Let the dough rise until it has doubled in size, about 1½ hours.

When the dough has risen, punch it down gently and divide it into 12 pieces. Roll each piece into a ball, place the dough balls on a lightly floured surface, cover with a damp kitchen towel, and let relax for 20 minutes.

Position a rack in the center of the oven and preheat to 500°F. If you have a baking stone, set it in the oven to preheat. If you do not have a baking stone, set a baking sheet in the oven to preheat.

After the dough has relaxed for 20 minutes, dust a work surface lightly with flour. Place 1 dough ball on the surface, sprinkle a little flour on top of the dough, and use a rolling pin or your hands to stretch and flatten the dough into a round about 6 inches in diameter and ⅛ to ¼ inch thick.

Place as many breads as you can fit onto the hot baking surface without overlapping. Bake until they have risen to produce a natural "pita pocket" at the center, about 3 minutes. Repeat with the remaining dough.

Vegetable Stock

pareve | makes about 2 quarts

This easy-to-make stock will come in handy for a number of recipes in this book, including Fresh Mushroom Risotto (page 113) and Salmon Chowder (page 96). Use it as a base for just about any soup or grain to add more flavor than plain water would. And because it is pareve, vegetable stock is more versatile for kosher cooking than chicken stock.

3 quarts water

2 teaspoons salt

1 large onion (unpeeled), quartered

2 celery stalks, tops removed, halved crosswise

4 carrots, quartered

3 cloves garlic, unpeeled

20 to 25 sprigs fresh flat-leaf parsley

1 tablespoon apple cider vinegar or any white vinegar

10 black peppercorns

1 bay leaf

In a large pot (at least 6 quarts), bring the water and salt to a boil over high heat. Add all the other ingredients. Bring the contents to a boil and reduce the heat to medium. Partially cover the pot and cook until the vegetables are soft, about 30 minutes.

Remove the pot from the heat, uncover, and let the liquid cool for about 30 minutes. Strain through a colander. Using a large spoon or potato masher, press on the vegetables in the colander to extract more flavorful liquid. Then use a fine-mesh sieve to strain the liquid one more time to remove solids. Cover and store in the refrigerator for up to 3 days or freeze for up to 3 months.

Chicken Stock

meat | makes about 2 quarts

Unlike chicken soup, chicken stock (or broth) has no solids. (Stock is generally not as rich as a broth, but we use the terms interchangeably.) Chicken stock can enhance all kinds of foods that might otherwise be made with water such as rice, quinoa, or lentils. Of course, using chicken stock will render whatever you are cooking "meat," as opposed to "pareve." Use chicken stock as a base for various soups, sauces, and dishes like Couscous with Chicken and Lamb Sausage (page 169) and Cowboy Cholent (page 183).

To make a stock, use leftover chicken and chicken bones from a roast chicken or raw chicken parts. Fresh chicken may give you a bit more flavor, but leftovers are more practical and economical. Make a little stock each time you roast a chicken. You can then freeze it for future use.

3 quarts water

2 to 3 pounds cooked chicken carcass or raw chicken parts, such as backs, wings, and necks

1 onion, coarsely chopped

1 large carrot, coarsely chopped

4 whole cloves garlic, peeled

½ teaspoon dried thyme

1 bay leaf

1 teaspoon salt

In a large pot (at least 6 quarts), combine all the ingredients and bring to a boil. Reduce the heat to low and simmer, uncovered, for 1½ hours, skimming off any foam that may collect on the surface. Remove the pot from the heat and strain the liquid through a fine-mesh sieve into a clean container. Discard the solids and let the stock cool to room temperature.

Cover and refrigerate until a layer of fat congeals on the surface. With a spoon or spatula, remove and discard the fat. Use the stock immediately or refrigerate for up to 3 days or freeze for up to 3 months.

Dried Beans

pareve | makes about 6 cups

Dried beans are easy to cook, but they require a little foresight. More often than not, we substitute canned beans for the dried version. We can't really tell the difference.

However, dried beans have a tremendous shelf life, which has some advantage. They're also much cheaper than the canned version. And cooking them from scratch allows you to regulate salt content or add ingredients like the onions and bay leaf below.

It's best to soak the beans overnight before cooking. But if you forget, you can still cook them in relatively short order (see Shortcut Method, below). Most presoaked beans will cook in 45 minutes to 1 hour. Chickpeas take more time—nearly 3 hours. (That's why we almost always buy them canned!) Remember that 2 cups of dried beans makes about 6 cups cooked. That's a lot of beans. For smaller groups, cut the quantities below in half.

2 cups dried beans, rinsed

1 bay leaf (optional)

1 onion, quartered (optional)

2 teaspoons salt

OVERNIGHT SOAK METHOD: Rinse and pick over the beans to remove any pebbles. In a large bowl, cover them with water by 2 inches and let soak for about 8 hours or overnight. Drain off and discard any remaining water. Transfer the beans to a large pot. If desired, add the bay leaf and onion. Add fresh cold water to cover by 1 to 2 inches and bring to a boil. Add the salt, reduce the heat to low, and cook, uncovered, until tender, 45 minutes to 1 hour. Drain in a colander. Discard the bay leaf and onion.

SHORTCUT METHOD: Rinse and pick over the beans to remove any pebbles. In a large pot, combine 8 cups water and the salt. If desired, add the bay leaf and onion. Bring to a boil over high heat. Add the beans, cover, and cook for 10 minutes. (If the water starts to boil over, reduce the heat to medium-high.) Turn off the heat, cover, and let the beans soak for 1½ hours. Drain the beans in a colander. Discard the bay leaf and onion. Return the beans to the pot and cover with fresh water by 1 to 2 inches. Bring the water to a boil, reduce the heat to low, and cook, uncovered, until the beans are tender, about 45 minutes. Drain in a colander.

Toasting Seeds and Nuts

pareve

Toasting seeds and nuts is one of the easiest kitchen techniques. The only kitchenware required is a skillet. Toasting intensifies aromas and provides extra crunchiness that we find very attractive. We toast seeds and nuts for such recipes as Ginger Sesame Noodles (page 124), Couscous with Chicken and Lamb Sausage (page 169), and Flourless Toasted Hazelnut Chocolate Torte (page 232). Remember to carefully watch over your toasting: It's a quick process, and perfectly toasted nuts can easily become burned ones if you neglect to remove them quickly from the heat.

Hazelnuts, with their papery outer skin, require a little extra attention after toasting. If you have purchased hazelnuts with the skin still on, place them between two pieces of paper towel and use your hands to gently rub the nuts back and forth to remove the skin.

3 to 4 tablespoons seeds or nuts

TO TOAST SEEDS OR NUTS: Place them in a dry skillet over medium heat. Stir fairly constantly until fragrant, 3 to 4 minutes. Larger nuts, such as hazelnuts or almonds, may require additional time, 8 to 10 minutes. If the seeds or nuts begin to smoke, remove them from the heat. Transfer immediately to a plate to cool.

Mayonnaise, Aioli, and Saffron Aioli

pareve

Our homemade mayonnaise tastes nothing like store-bought mayonnaise. One reason is that we use extra virgin olive oil, which is rarely used by large manufacturers. We also can't figure out why store-bought mayonnaise is sweetened. The sweetness overwhelms whatever is savory on your plate (or in your sandwich).

It takes only about 5 minutes to make mayonnaise. At our house, it's used more often as a dipping sauce than as a sandwich spread.

Unlike store-bought mayonnaise, our homemade version is made with raw eggs. That means salmonella poisoning is a real (if unlikely) threat, particularly for small children, older individuals, or anyone with a compromised immune system. For the record, we have always enjoyed homemade mayonnaise without incident. But if you have health concerns, buy store-bought mayonnaise that relies less on sugar and more on fine ingredients for flavor.

Aioli is a garlic mayonnaise commonly enjoyed in Mediterranean cuisines. It's made the same way as mayonnaise, just with garlic added.

You'll note that we make aioli (and mayonnaise) with mustard, which is made from mustard seeds. Because mustard seeds cannot be used on Passover by Ashkenazic Jews (they fall under the same *kitniot* category as, among other foods, rice, corn, lentils, beans, sesame seeds, and peas: grains and legumes that can be made into food that can resemble *chametz* products), we are also providing a second, Passover-appropriate aioli recipe—one that substitutes lemon juice for mustard. The lemon juice gives the mayonnaise a brightness similar to what comes from the vinegar in mustard.

The best mayonnaise comes from the freshest eggs. But you don't need to raise your own chickens. If possible, purchase eggs from reputable farmers who raise free-range birds. Note that cold eggs don't emulsify easily. So remember to bring your egg to room temperature before whisking.

Regular Recipe (with mustard) | makes about 1½ cups

1 egg yolk, at room temperature

2 teaspoons Dijon mustard

Pinch of salt

1 clove garlic, minced or crushed in
   a garlic press (for aioli)

Pinch of saffron threads
   (for saffron aioli)

1 cup extra virgin olive oil

HAND METHOD: In a medium bowl, whisk together the yolk, mustard, salt, garlic (if making aioli), and saffron (if making saffron aioli). Whisk in a little bit of olive oil until the mayonnaise begins to thicken. Continue adding the oil, a small amount at a time, taking care not to let the mayonnaise liquefy.

PROCESSOR METHOD: In a food processor, pulse the yolk, mustard, salt, garlic (if making aioli), and saffron (if making saffron aioli). With the machine running, add the oil in a fine stream.

Use immediately, or cover and refrigerate for up to 3 days.

Passover Recipe (without mustard) | makes about 1½ cups

1 egg yolk, at room temperature

Pinch of salt, plus salt to taste

1 clove garlic, minced or crushed in a
   garlic press (for aioli)

Pinch of saffron threads
   (for saffron aioli)

1 cup extra virgin olive oil

1 teaspoon lemon juice

HAND METHOD: In a medium bowl, whisk together the yolk, salt, garlic (if making aioli), and saffron (if making saffron aioli). Whisk in a little bit of olive oil until the mayonnaise begins to thicken. Continue adding the oil, a small amount at a time, taking care not to let the mayonnaise liquefy. When you have finished adding the oil, whisk in the lemon juice. Add additional salt to taste.

PROCESSOR METHOD: In a food processor, pulse the yolk, salt, garlic (if making aioli), and saffron (if making saffron aioli). With the machine running, add the oil in a fine stream. Transfer to a medium bowl and whisk in the lemon juice. Add additional salt to taste.

Use immediately, or cover and refrigerate for up to 3 days.

Pistou/Pesto Sauce

dairy | makes about 1½ cups

Pistou is the southern French term for pesto. For a quick and easy dinner, toss pasta with a spoonful or two of this fresh-tasting basil sauce, then garnish with a little fresh pepper and grated Parmesan. We also use this sauce in a traditional soup from southern France called La Soupe au Pistou (page 91). Sure, you can buy reasonably good pesto sauce in many food shops, but there's nothing like making your own with fresh, aromatic basil for added flavor. Even better, kitchen prep doesn't get much easier than this.

¾ cup extra virgin olive oil

1 cup firmly packed fresh basil leaves

2 cloves garlic, peeled

½ cup grated Parmesan cheese

3 tablespoons pine nuts (optional)

Salt and freshly ground pepper (optional)

In a blender, combine all the ingredients except the salt and pepper. Puree until thick and smooth. Season with salt and pepper to taste. Use at once or refrigerate for up to 3 days.

Whipped Cream

dairy | makes enough to garnish 8 to 10 dessert portions

Real, fresh whipped cream (as opposed to what you buy in an aerosol can) is so simple to make, we wonder why anyone buys it premade. The real stuff is rich yet refreshing—the perfect foil for all sorts of desserts from light-textured Orange Chiffon Cake (page 219) to dense Flourless Toasted Hazelnut Chocolate Torte (page 232). With a little practice, you can make whipped cream in less than 5 minutes. We like to use powdered sugar to add subtle sweetness, but granulated sugar will work too.

1 cup heavy cream

2 teaspoons powdered sugar

Place the cream and sugar in a deep-sided bowl. Beat with a handheld whisk or an electric mixer until the cream becomes stiff and peaks form.

Holiday Menus

Jewish tradition provides a richly textured culinary canvas for celebration. Our home holiday traditions transcend geography, because we have been influenced by both Sephardic and Ashkenazic customs. We generally eat in courses, which gives us more time to savor every dish, as well as the company of our friends and family. Nonetheless, some dishes might easily be enjoyed together, such as the break-fast salads and appetizers suggested for Yom Kippur.

Each menu that follows is composed of recipes from this book. And each recipe includes suggested wine pairings. However, we recognize that choosing a separate wine for each course might be a bit overwhelming. Selecting a single "all-purpose" wine—something that goes with every course—is a perfectly fine alternative. We have noted in "Pairing Food and Wine" (page 38) that some red and white wines are more versatile than others, and we encourage you to revisit this section for a wine-pairing refresher. Truth be told, we often start off a holiday meal with some kind of white wine. Later, especially if meat is served, we'll move on to a red. Really big meals at our home, like the Passover Seder meal, feature many different wines—both red and white. Ultimately, what's most important is that you find your own comfort zone. There is no right or wrong choice.

Chag same'ach!

ROSH HASHANAH

The olives are just an excuse for an accompanying glass of chilled sparkling wine—a New Year's tradition for us. We keep drinking bubbly with our first two courses. (Or we might switch to a white wine without bubbles.) But the brisket requires a full-bodied red wine.

Olives with Lemon Zest and Thyme (pareve) (page 48)

Roasted Red Peppers with Olive Oil and Garlic (pareve) (page 54)

Endive and Asian Pear Salad with Walnut Vinaigrette (pareve) (page 80)

Brisket with Juniper Berries, Bay Leaves, Red Wine Gravy, and Mashed Potatoes (meat) (page 189)

Orange Olive Oil Cake (pareve) (page 226)

YOM KIPPUR BREAK-FAST

We are not particularly good fasters, and we tend to be tired, cranky, and really hungry after Yom Kippur. For the break-fast we serve dishes that can be prepared and refrigerated before the fast begins and then served cold or at room temperature when the fast is over. This includes an initial selection of four appetizers/salads for immediate nibbling. The salmon with aioli makes a great follow-up, but instead of grilling the salmon, keep things simple by baking it in advance—an alternative indicated in the recipe—and reheat it if desired.

Herbal tea after dinner has a mellowing influence should any crankiness remain! The tea goes great with the cookies. And which wine? After twenty-five hours of no eating or drinking, we are happy to drink just about anything!

Gravlax (dairy) (page 71)

Hummus with (or without) **Toppings and Pita Bread** (pareve) (page 51)

Sautéed Carrots with Cumin Seeds and Fresh Cilantro (pareve) (page 65)

Lentil Salad with Cilantro and Spices (pareve) (page 86)

Grilled Salmon with Aioli (pareve) (page 129)

Pistachio Cardamom Butter Cookies (dairy) (page 212)

Fresh Herb Tisane (pareve) (page 231)

SUKKOT

We are generally in the midst of our grape harvest during Sukkot. There's a chill in the air, and in the sukkah, too. The idea here is to make sure we eat warm, filling things! Our tangy, bright squash soup is a heartwarming starter that also evokes autumn.

Big, rich wines are best here—both whites and reds. The soup and salad call out for a fruity Riesling or a bold, barrel-fermented Chardonnay. The tagine would pair best with an earthy Syrah or a fruit-driven Zinfandel.

Curry Ginger Butternut Squash Soup (pareve) (page 93)

Wilted Spinach Salad with Mushroom Vinaigrette (pareve) (page 84)

Spiced Lamb Tagine with Currants and Israeli Couscous (meat) (page 199)

Cherry Coconut Rice Pudding (pareve) (page 217)

CHANUKAH

We normally start our meals with lighter dishes, such as salads. But on Chanukah, everyone wants latkes! So why wait? We use the salad as a second-course palate cleanser before tucking into meaty tuna steaks. Dairy is the flavor du jour, not only because it's traditional but also because Jeff insists on eating latkes with sour cream. Drink white wine with your latkes and salad; red wine with the tuna!

Latkes with Sour Cream, Green Onions, and Masago (dairy) (page 107)

Arugula Salad with Toasted Pine Nuts, Shaved Parmesan,
and Lemon Vinaigrette (dairy) (page 78)

Braised Tuna with Lemon Zest and Ratatouille (pareve) (page 156)

Frangipane Tart with Poached Pears (dairy) (page 220)

PURIM

You don't have to be a kid to love Purim! We dress up in funny costumes and are particularly careful to observe the mandate to drink until we can't tell good-guy Mordechai from bad-guy Haman. (Designated drivers take note!)

Because we spend the late morning and early afternoon delivering *mishlo'ach manot* packages to our neighbors, we need a menu for our Purim *se'udah* that consists of dishes that can be made in advance or prepared quickly. Our onion tart and the lamb meatballs can be made well in advance. The tart is delicious at room temperature, and the meatballs are easily heated while the first two courses are being enjoyed. Green salad takes only minutes to prepare.

Red wines are probably your best all-purpose choice with this menu. But the onion tart and salad would pair well with many different white wines too. And seeing as how it's a *mitzvah* to drink, make sure you've got a nice, sweet dessert wine—like Moscato, Riesling, or Gewürztraminer—ready for sipping with the cake.

Onion Tart (pareve) (page 61)

Green Salad with Mustard Vinaigrette (pareve) (page 75)

Spiced Lamb Meatballs with Tomato Sauce and Freekeh (meat) (page 193)

Orange Chiffon Cake (pareve) (page 219)

PASSOVER

With four cups of wine that celebrate the four elements of the liberation from slavery and establishment of the Jewish nation, the Passover Seder is one of the most extraordinary meals of the year. For the Seder meal, macaroons may strike a sentimental chord with many of you, but we know our gefilte quenelles and fish soup with matzo balls will raise a few eyebrows. We like to push the envelope.

Don't even think about red wine with your quenelles (oy!), and stay with white wine through the soup as well. (Rosé is an excellent alternative to white wine, however.) Bring out the big red—such as Syrah or Cabernet—for the short ribs. We love to drink Port with our macaroons.

(And don't forget to check that products you buy for Passover carry the additional Kosher for Passover certification.)

Gefilte Quenelles with Braised Leeks and Lemon Zest (pareve) (page 137)

Fish Soup with Matzo Balls and Aioli (Passover recipe) (pareve) (page 99)

Arugula, Radish, and Avocado Salad (pareve) (page 79)

Braised Beef Short Ribs with Root Vegetables
and Garlic Confit Mashed Potatoes (meat) (page 191)

Toasted Coconut Macaroons with Chocolate Drizzle (pareve) (page 214)

SHAVUOT

Dairy dishes are traditionally enjoyed during this holiday, which celebrates the giving of the Torah to the Jews at Mount Sinai. We like to start our holiday meal with a somewhat traditional Italian caprese salad enhanced with smoked salmon. We also love goat cheese and fragrant lavender (which remind us of the hills of Provence). Together they make a perfect tart. For dessert, the mocha cheesecake will not disappoint. But as a main course, we take a break from dairy and enjoy meaty opah fish steaks in a recipe inspired by our many visits to Israel.

For us, this is a meal made for white wine or rosé. If you prefer reds, look for light-bodied wines with good acidity, such as Pinot Noir or Grenache.

Smoked Salmon Caprese with Endive (dairy) (page 83)

Lavender Goat Cheese Tart (dairy) (page 63)

**Baked Opah with Smoked Paprika, Tomatoes, Green Olives,
and Brown Rice** (pareve) (page 147)

Mocha Cheesecake (dairy) (page 224)

Acknowledgments

One day several years ago Jodie said blithely, "Let's write a Covenant cookbook." We had been writing cookbooks for more than a decade—mostly for other people—and it was time to write one about our own life in the wine country. We are grateful to many colleagues, friends, and family members for their assistance.

Our business partner and close friend, Leslie Rudd, has nurtured and encouraged us for the last fifteen years. Along the way, he has been a source of personal, professional, and spiritual inspiration, helping to transform Covenant from a dream to reality.

America's premier kosher wine family has also been with us from the beginning. Nathan Herzog supported our vision early on, and he convinced family members David, Mordy, and (later) Joseph to help us grow. Back then, we also benefitted from the good graces and knowledge of Herzog winemakers Peter Stern and Joe Hurliman, along with their outstanding cellar crew—including Josh Goodman.

Covenant Associate Winemaker Jonathan Hajdu has been equally indispensable, and he has worked with us on every vintage of Covenant. Jonathan's "can-do" attitude and his understanding of *kashrut* have been as important to us over the years as his considerable cellar skills and our deep friendship. Recently, Covenant cellarmaster Eli Silins has come on board. His attention to detail has freed us to be more creative in the kitchen.

In 1988, Long Island winemaker Larry Perrine ignored his better judgment and hired Jeff—then a New York saxophonist—to work at his North Fork vineyard. Larry gave Jeff the foundation that led Jeff to a wine-writing career. He remains a close friend and mentor today. Some fifteen years later, California winemaker David Ramey showed Jeff how to make Cabernet Sauvignon—Napa Valley style. David has always been there for us, generously sharing his expertise and giving guidance. If there is a Covenant style today, it is thanks to David.

Initially, an OU Press partnership seemed to us like wishful thinking. Rabbi Cary Friedman first saw the potential, and we are forever grateful to Rabbi Menachem Genack and to Simon Posner for considering us worthy. Kudos also go to our troubleshooting OU Press editor, Rabbi Dovid Bashevkin, for keeping a keen eye on our prose, and to Rivki Rosenblatt for her helpful comments on the manuscript. Appreciation also goes to Phyllis Koegel of the OU, who helped get the ball rolling, and to Joelle Delbourgo of Delbourgo Associates for her assistance in keeping the project on track.

Some people don't fit neatly into any category. One such individual is Steve Goldfinger, whose quick wit and Jewish roots inspired the name Covenant. He also contributed the lovely photograph of Leslie Rudd's estate vineyard Cabernet (destined for Covenant Solomon) on page 7. Our multifaceted friend Joel Fleishman is another. Joel has opened many doors for us over the years—including the ones that led to both the OU Press and Schocken.

This brings us to our fabulous editors at Schocken, Altie Karper and Lexy Bloom. Their early enthusiasm and clear vision were critical. Altie's encyclopedic knowledge of *Yiddishkeit* has proved to be a most welcome blessing. And Lexy brought her considerable culinary sensibilities to play, tightening up the copy, the message, and the look of the book. We also thank her second set of eyes—assistant editor Thomas Pold—for his attention to detail. Thanks also go to Rabbi Gary Ambrose, for his helpful comments on the text. In addition, we are grateful to copy editor Kate Slate, who—just when we smugly thought we had taken care of every detail—showed us the error(s) of our ways, and to production editor Rita Madrigal, who cheerfully and patiently turned our scribbled corrections into the seamless text you have just read.

From a visual perspective, we are so fortunate to have Ed Anderson's photography illustrating these pages. Assisting Ed with panache were food stylist Lillian Kang and prop stylist Ethel Brennan. The Covenant logo featured on the cover was designed by Napa Valley artists and sisters Susann and Joann Ortega, who also created our original wine label. Thanks also go to text designer Cassandra Pappas, for the marvelous look of every word, and every photograph, on each page, and to cover designer Janet Hansen for making the book look good enough to eat! And our thanks to production manager Lisa Montebello, who worked with the book's printer to achieve the truly wonderful reproduction quality of all the photographs.

A number of recipes in the book were conceived in Israel, where we have found much culinary inspiration. Special thanks go to our Israeli cousins, Amy and Barak Dukas, as well as their children, Yotam, Itai, and Ma'ayan. We have shared many meals, recipes, and joyful moments eating together.

Without the patience and rock-solid confidence of our literary agent, Carole Bidnick, it is highly unlikely this book would ever have been written. Our appreciation also extends to Carole's colleague Paula Breen, for her deft contract negotiation skills.

Finally, we must pay tribute to our daughters, Skye and Zoë, who have spent a lifetime sampling and critiquing our cooking. *The Covenant Kitchen* is as much a reflection of their taste as it is of ours.

Index

Page references in *italics* refer to illustrations.

RUMBLE, YOUNG MAN, RUMBLE

RUMBLE, YOUNG MAN, RUMBLE

BENJAMIN CAVELL

F
CAVE

ALFRED A. KNOPF ☞ NEW YORK 2003

Published in the United States by Alfred A. Knopf, a
division of Random House, Inc., New York, and simultaneously in Canada
by Random House of Canada Limited, Toronto. Distributed by
Random House, Inc., New York.
www.aaknopf.com

5/03   B+T $22.00

Library of Congress Cataloging-in-Publication Data
Cavell, Benjamin.
Rumble, young man, rumble / Benjamin Cavell. — 1st ed.
p.   cm.
ISBN 0-375-41464-9 (alk. paper)
1. Young men—Fiction.   I. Title.

PS3603.A9 R8 2003
813'.6—dc21   2002027525

Manufactured in the United States of America
First Edition

TO MY MOTHER AND FATHER

THE HANDS CAN'T HIT WHAT THE EYES CAN'T SEE.
FLOAT LIKE A BUTTERFLY, STING LIKE A BEE.
RUMBLE, YOUNG MAN, RUMBLE.

—Bundini

CONTENTS

RUMBLE, YOUNG MAN, RUMBLE

BALLS,
BALLS,
BALLS

On Thursday, a man comes into the store and asks me how to kill his wife. I know, because it's my business to know, that what he really wants to ask is how to kill his wife and not get caught.

The man wears a short-sleeved button-down shirt and dark blue Dockers. His face is cratered with acne scars. It looks like the surface of the moon. I know without being told that this man works at one of the tech firms that have sprung up in the last year or so all along the road from Albany. He has never lifted a weight in his life. He has probably never been in a fight. He has never even been paintballing. But for some reason I feel sorry for this poor, bony fool and so I ask him whether he has a gas furnace.

I explain how to drill a hole in the main line that will allow a tiny stream of gas to trickle into his basement. The emission is so gradual that his wife is unlikely to notice. This is less detectable than disabling the pilot light on a gas stove. Also, it's more controllable than blocking the return-air vents and filling the house with carbon monoxide. Then I tell him that he'll need a spark.

The spark can come from anything. The static electricity

of shoes scuffing a rug, the momentary discharge from the flipping of a light switch, the red power light on a clock radio that usually clicks on when the alarm sounds, a lightbulb that has been filled with gasoline and then screwed back into the socket—each can become a trigger that will *turn out all the lights,* if he knows what I mean. He does. He buys the Taskmaster Tool Kit (Deluxe Set), $179.99 on sale.

In the afternoon, I tell a nineteen-year-old in a fatigue jacket how to make napalm from gasoline and frozen orange juice concentrate (just mix equal parts—diet cola and gasoline works also) and then he buys a superthin Maxi-Grip C-series folding knife ($124.99)—which can be concealed in a boot or even inside a shirt collar for easy access—and a telescoping graphite police baton ($64.95). I tell him two stories about my time in the SEALs and show him my tattoo of Freddie the Frogman and then sell him *The Mercenary's Guide to Urban Survival* ($19.99, paperback), and he leaves smiling and even salutes me, almost dropping his new baton.

The tattoo is temporary (I got a whole box of them two years ago at a novelty shop in Jersey City) and I've never been in the Navy. I've never even been farther than Philadelphia. And I can't swim.

My name is Logan Bryant. I sell sporting goods.

A ctually, I sell sporting goods, hardware, athletic equipment, patio furniture, barbecue grills and hobby literature.

But don't get me wrong: I'm not just some wanna-be. Truth is, I *could* have been a SEAL if I'd ever bothered to learn to swim. I hold at least a green belt in several fighting disciplines and am nearly a black belt in Thai kickboxing (I just haven't had time to take the test). I am the uncontested star of what is generally acknowledged to be the fourth-best paintball team in the tristate area. (We were scheduled to compete for the national title on ESPN2 but were scratched

at the last second. Politics.) I have a full collection of green
and brown face paint in various shades. I was All-Conference
at middle linebacker my junior year of high school and would
have been All-State or maybe even Honorable Mention All-
America the next year if I hadn't quit. I used to have sub-
scriptions to *Soldier of Fortune* and *Guns and Ammo* until
Barry told me that no one reads those anymore. Also, I am
confident in my willingness to take the life of another
human being.

And I can almost bench-press three eighty-five.

Barry arrives as Lou and I are totaling Thursday's
receipts. Lou nods to him and Barry swaggers
around a standing rack of catcher's mitts and ducks under
the counter. Barry is wearing a lime-green New York Jets
warm-up jacket.

"The average American," I am telling Lou, "has an IQ
around seventy-three. At that level of intellect, even basic
functioning requires considerable effort. Decisions that you
or I would consider simple border on impossible for Joe
Citizen. That's why people are so easily swayed by celebrity
pitchmen and Oprah Winfrey and demonstrations of the
new-and-improved Spic and Span. That's why a presidential
candidate can give the same speech over and over—they're
all talking to five-year-olds. People are just like children."

"But all people *were* children at one point," Lou says.

"So?"

"So, if they're children now, what were they then?"

I sigh. "I'm trying to illustrate a point."

"And what is that?"

"What is what?"

"The *point*, guy, the *point*."

"My point is that people, for the most part, have no understanding of the realities of the world. That's why it's so easy
for guys like you and me to get ahead."

Lou finishes with his receipts and lays them down on the counter in a neat stack. "Isn't that the same point you made on Monday?"

"No," I say, exasperated. "My point on Monday was that college degrees are meaningless and that the only useful intelligence is street smarts. And that guys like you and me should really be running this country—and *would* be if we had little pieces of paper that said we'd gone to Princeton. Also, my point on Monday was based on the figure they released over the weekend, which put the average national IQ around seventy-six. In light of the most recent data, the conclusions must be even more extreme."

"And who," Lou says, "is compiling this data?"

I stare at him. "What do you mean? It's a study."

"By who?" He smiles. "Who's 'they'?"

Before I can answer, Barry says, "Do you doubt what he's saying, Louie?"

Lou shrugs. "I just don't know if people are so dumb."

"Don't *know*," Barry says. "Look around you, man. We have the corrupt, liberal media. We have unchecked and unquestioned federal power. We have suppression of the First *and* Second Amendments, babies being murdered, kids' shows that promote homosexuality, twenty-four-hour music videos, political correctness, celebrity magazines that promote homosexuality, celebrity talk shows, school shootings, celebrity profiles, celebrity political campaigns, celebrity fund-raisers for homosexual causes. This country is in the midst of a moral, racial, political, economic, social, sexual, military, environmental, educational, moral, fiscal, ethical, moral, class-based, moral crisis. We have forgotten our morality. We need a leader with *character*, who can provide moral stewardship and protect our kids from nudity and foul language and violence in the media and from entertainment with a homosexual agenda and who will institute a foreign policy to keep the ragheads in check *and* who has the compassion necessary to phase out the welfare system that lets *fifty million* unwed, teenage black mothers live lazily in the veritable lap of luxury by sucking on the overtaxed teat of real, hardworking Americans. Instead, we get these goddamn midwestern smooth talkers, chosen—by *fifty-three percent* of voters according to the most recent statistics— on the basis of *height*, for Chrissake. And you don't know if people are dumb?"

I watch Lou triumphantly.

"That's quite a speech," he says.

"Damn right," Barry says. "I always have one ready for you goddamn bleeding hearts."

Lou frowns. "Are you sure there are fifty million black girls on welfare?"

"Sure I'm sure," Barry tells him.

I'm tired of losing," Barry says.

"At paintball?" I say.

"That's right."

"We don't lose too often."

"Often enough."

We're at our gym, which is called Size, and Barry and I are taking turns on the leg press. He is wearing a tan leather weight belt to support his lower back. I pull the pin out of the weight stack—it was at two hundred, the weight Barry uses—and slide it into the hole marked four twenty-five.

There are only a few sluts in the weight room, stretching on the mats in the corner or else working on the lat pull-down, all of them dressed in spandex and string-strapped tank tops. I wait until a few of them are done with their various sets and then I lie back on the red-padded machine and set my feet shoulder width on the dimpled metal plate and push hard against it. The rack I am on slides away from the unmoving metal plate, and next to me four hundred twenty-five pounds of Bodysmith Nautilus weights creak upward in a quivering pile.

I can't see anything but the white plaster of the ceiling, but I know the sluts must be looking. Even if they hadn't already noticed me, the sound would have gotten their attention.

The ideal weight-lifting sound is never very loud. If you scream, you look like you're trying too hard. The sound should combine the moan of sex with a muted angry roar. It should grow louder with each repetition, ending at about the same volume as a normal speaking voice.

When I am finished with the set, I sit up with my legs hanging off the edge of the machine and blot my face with a towel, looking out the side of my eye at one of the wall-size mirrors, inspecting the veins on my arms and the bulges of my chest and shoulders under the T-shirt.

I stand and Barry lies down for his next set.

"I've decided to bring in an expert," he says.

"What kind of expert?"

"You know—an operator, a specialist, a mechanic."

"Like a mercenary?"

He glances around us to see if anyone heard and motions for me to lean toward him, and when I do, says, "Like a mercenary."

I keep my breathing normal. "Where's he from?"

Barry smiles, our faces still close together, and says, "Israel, I think."

"Why Israel?"

"Because they're experienced."

I groan. "But they don't even *lift*. He probably has skinny little arms."

Barry stares at me.

"Also," I say, "what does some *yid* have to teach me about being hard?"

"He might know more about it than you think. And don't say 'yid.' "

"Sorry, but this all comes as quite a shock."

"He'll be here for our morning session on Saturday."
He waves for me to move away from him and starts his
set.

In the locker room, after we shower, Barry and I examine each other's bodies and give constructive
criticism. I know this sounds bad, but I just want to assure
everyone that I'm not a fag. In fact, I would hate fags except
that I read somewhere that hating fags meant you were a fag
yourself. So I don't hate them. I'm just not one. Really.

My apartment looks onto a grassless soccer field
and the abandoned hulk of a paper mill and then
onto the bright gray surface of Route 90, stretched out between banks of rust-colored trees, separated from the soccer
field by a chain-link fence.

I turn on the television and slouch, sore-limbed, on the
sofa. I drink a ready-mixed vanilla Met-Rx. The light from
the television flickers across my face as I prepare the hypo-
dermic and line up the bottles of pills—Dianabol, Nolvadex,
Maxibolin, creatine phosphate. After I swallow the pills, I
give myself the injection of B-12 and, so that doesn't keep me
up all night, follow it with two Seconal capsules the color of
velvet-red cherries. I take four chalk-white zinc pills to keep
the steroids from putting zits on my back and then I lie back
and watch the bright gray screen.

The champion has teased hair and a sequined dress. She
sings "I'm Still Here." She is seven years old. She would like
to thank God and her parents. She smiles all the time. The
judges give her three and a half stars.

The challenger is an eleven-year-old boy with blond hair
that flops over the sides of his head. He smiles wider than
the girl. He sings "Yankee Doodle Dandy," marching ener-

getically in place. Suddenly, I have a vision of this boy in fifteen years, bruised, crying, track marks all along his arms.
He is curled in a ball on the floor grabbing at the ankles of
a V-bodied stud in leather pants. The big stud is saying, "It's
over, Julian. It's . . . over."

The judges give the challenger two and three-quarters
stars.

The Seconals take hold and I am drifting and my chin sags
to touch my chest. My eyelids droop closed and then pop
open and droop closed again and do this over and over until
finally they do not open anymore and I am asleep and the
television is saying, "Kill, kill, kill."

O n Friday morning a blond slut in a purple tank top
comes into the store and asks me about recumbent stationary bicycles. I am wearing a dark blue T-shirt
with the Navy SEAL crest over the heart and UNITED
STATES NAVY SEAL TEAMS across the back in white. The
sleeves hug my biceps. My jeans are dark and boot-cut (I
never wear a taper). My boots are tan Timberlands ($59.99
with the staff discount).

The slut stares at me hungrily. I lift up my T-shirt, using
the bottom to wipe some imaginary grime from underneath
my eye, showing her the cobblestone abs and the striations of
the obliques.

"Are you an athlete?" she asks.

"I'm captain of the store paintball team."

"Are you any good?"

"Bill Cookston said I was almost the best he ever saw. He
said I could make any team I wanted, including Shockwave."

"What's that?"

"You've never heard of Shockwave? They're only the win-
ningest team in the *history* of the World Cup of paintball."

"So, were you guys ever in that tournament on ESPN?"
she says.

I snort. "ESPN."

"I thought those guys were the best."

"That's what a lot of people think," I say. "But for the serious MilSim competitor, that stuff is a sellout. It dilutes the purity of the sport."

"What's MilSim?"

I look at her for a few seconds and then say, "Military Simulation. What do you think we're talking about?"

"I thought it was called war games."

I can feel the muscles tighten in my shoulders. "It's not a game."

"Sorry."

"Don't worry about it," I say, teeth clenched.

To calm myself, I put my hand on the seat of the Ergometer 9000 with optional heart-rate monitor and reading rack ($1,499.95).

"The recumbent feature," I say carefully, "is particularly important if there will be any men riding the unit. Studies have shown that the upright models tend to promote impotence."

"How do they do that?"

"Excuse me?"

"Promote impotence. The upright bicycles. How do they do it?"

"Well . . . I believe it has something to do with"—I look around for Lou, but I don't see him anywhere—"with the ah . . . the heat of the testicle walls."

Stevie is the only other salesman on the floor. He is showing a Merry Men compound bow ($334.99) to a fat-body in jungle camouflage complete with bush hat. I catch Stevie's eye and he says something to the fat-body and walks toward me. The fat-body lays down the bow and begins fingering various arrowheads and stroking his thick mustache.

"Hello," Stevie says when he reaches us.

"Hello," the slut says. She is looking at Stevie with the same expression she had when I showed her my stomach.

Stevie is taller than I am, but thin, and I wonder whether I am misreading her reaction.

"I was just explaining how upright bicycles cause impotence by overheating the testicle walls," I say.

"Well," Stevie says, smiling at me, "of course, that's part of it. Also, the pressure restricts blood flow and damages the soft tissue."

He walks the slut toward the displays of upright bicycles.

When erect, my cock is nine and a half inches long and as thick as some men's wrists. A year ago, Stevie started working at the store and I heard from some slut we both know that he was packing almost eleven. Since then I have been seriously considering the experimental penile-enlargement surgery, which has been performed (I understand) with great success by two doctors in Sweden.

On the way into Champagne Dreams, the bar we go to on Friday nights, Barry points out two men in suits standing on the corner and tells me that they could be from the secret police.

I say, "This country doesn't have any secret police." I frown. "At least, I've never heard of any."

Barry shakes his head. "Why do you think they call them *secret*?"

Inside, the place glows blue and orange from neon signs that hang outside the windows. The room is full of sluts dressed to show their belly buttons and the narrow strip of skin between their inflated breasts.

"I could never fuck a girl with a tit job," Lou says.

"I don't care if she's had a tit job," I say, "as long as she *looks* like she's had one. And not one of these cut-rate three-grand hack jobs where you can still see the scar. I'm talking about seven thousand *per*."

Ken, who is the fifth member of our paintball team and the only one who doesn't work at the store, is sitting in a horseshoe-shaped corner booth with two brunette sluts. We all slide into the booth, the sluts crowding closer to Ken to make room.

The slut sitting next to Barry looks at the gold that glitters on each of his fingers (including the thumb) and at his platinum necklace, which she probably thinks is silver, and asks him what he does for a living.

"I own a store called Balls, Balls, Balls," Barry says.

"On the highway? 'Everything for the New American Sportsman,' or something like that?"

"That's the one."

"And what about the rest of you?" the other slut says.

"They work for me," Barry says. "Except for Ken. But he used to."

"So you're the boss," she says.

Later, Barry and I will take turns fucking these sluts. We'll tie them up. We'll beat them with phone cords and Spiritbreaker riding crops (two for $79.50). But now I just smile at them and then I go to the bar.

Waiting for the drinks, I talk to Samson Taylor, who is the largest man I know. He is slumped, sullen, close to the surface of the bar. In the dimness the features of his face are nearly indistinguishable. He is a gray-haired, mahogany mountain.

"How many years you play, again?" I ask him.

"Five," he says, his eyes closed.

"All in Minnesota?"

"Yeah."

"So, why'd you stop so early?"

He sighs. "Can we not talk about this right now?"

"Sure, sure. Whatever you want. I heard it was drugs."

"You shouldn't believe everything you hear."

"What do you mean?"

He shrugs.

"Barry's bringing in a professional," I say, "to help with our training. He gets here in the morning. I'm worried that Jew fuck is trying to phase me out of the team. I practically *built* that team for him. You think they'd be fourth-best without me? The fuck they would. None of those bitches has my skills."

He puts one of his enormous hands on my forearm and I almost jerk away. I stare at the hand, imagining that I can smell the blackness rising from it.

"You're my friend, right?" he asks.

"Of course."

"Then leave me alone a while."

"Okay. Leave you alone. No problem. Done and *done*."

He removes his hand from my arm and I take a deep breath.

"I knew you'd understand," he says. "You're the only one who understands."

The bartender brings my drinks and pours two more shots for Samson, who does not open his eyes but smiles slightly when he hears the shots set down in front of him. A tear dribbles down his cheek.

I walk back to the booth, thinking that Samson Taylor is not as tough as I thought.

I am nervous that my cock shrinks too much when it's limp. I read once that black guys don't actually have larger dicks, it's just that they grow less, so they walk around bigger.

Sometimes I even wonder whether I am really as good as I think, whether all the sluts who have screamed my name and begged for more, more, more weren't in it for the sex but were trying to attach themselves to my rising star. I have heard that, sooner or later, all great men have that worry.

One slut I used to know—I think her name was Laura— told me when I broke up with her that I was selfish in bed.

I said, "I tried to give you everything I have. You're just not deep enough."

I drive Ken and Stevie to practice on Saturday morning in my black Pathfinder, which I got for *well* under the list price from some Panamanians Barry knows. I have the tuner set to National Public Radio. The host of the show says, "We're talking America's foreign policy woes. Do you have the solution? Our lines are open."

Sitting in the passenger seat, Ken says, "How can you take this crap?"

I say, "I need to have the information."

"This isn't information, it's opinion."

I wave him off. "It's not my fault if you don't care about being educated."

"But they're all so self-satisfied."

"It's a small price to pay."

He shakes his head. "Carl Kassel can kiss Ken's crevice."

" 'Crack,' " Stevie says from the backseat.

"What?"

"Use 'crack.' It's funnier."

"There's nothing funny about using crack."

"I mean instead of 'crevice.' "

Ken turns around in his seat to look at him. "Just say no, guy."

The practice site is a replica of a few blocks from Beirut circa 1985, contained inside an immense warehouse that is owned by a paintball-organizing company called Marked for Dead. When we arrive, all of us dressed in gray-and-white urban-camouflage jumpsuits, Barry is there already, standing next to a full-scale model of a bombed schoolhouse. He is with Lou and a man I don't recognize. My heart is thumping fast. My face has begun to sweat.

When we reach them, Barry introduces us to the new man, whose name is Jack.

"Jack what?" Ken says.

"Just Jack," Barry tells him.

"Like Madonna," Stevie says.

Jack smiles. "That's right."

He is my height and twenty pounds lighter, which is considerably larger than I imagined. Even so, I doubt he can bench-press three-fifteen. But he *is* thick through the shoulders and awfully cut, the veins in his arms raised like seams. I get a view of him in profile and, I have to admit, he doesn't look too kikey. His nose is short and broad. His head is shaved almost to the scalp. His skin is as dark as mine. I wonder where he does his tanning.

He is wearing a light blue short-sleeved flannel shirt and beige pants, which are made from a horrible, coarse-looking material but which, as far as I can see, do not taper. His shoes are low-top boots that are probably not *half* as expensive as my Timberlands (if I had paid full price), although they might be more durable.

"How old are you?" I ask him.

"Thirty."

"Mmm," I say, "I would have guessed older. But still, thirty might be a little old for this business. Killing, as I'm sure you know, is young men's work."

"I'll be all right."

"Your English is pretty good."

He looks at me for a moment. "I'm from Pittsburgh."

"Barry said you were from Israel."

He shrugs. "I worked there for a while."

"What did you do before that?"

"I was in the Navy."

"Doing what?" Stevie asks.

Jack shrugs again. "Let's just say I wasn't a sailor."

My face is suddenly hot. I sit down on the charred remains of a swing set and lean my head down, pretending to retie my boots, hoping that no one will notice.

Jack makes us run laps around the inside of the warehouse to warm up. He keeps us running for forty minutes. When we stop, I open my duffel bag. Sweat stings my eyes. I take out my goggles, which are made by V-Shock. I put on the goggles and then take out the face mask (also by V-Shock). Jack looks at the mask.

"What are you putting on a mask for?" he says. "This is paint*ball*, not paint*pussy*. Not paint*ovary*. I see why you guys never win."

I open my mouth, but I can't make a sound, so I begin setting up my weapon, which is a Hicap 180-round front-loader with Trimount sight rail and TF90 reflex sight, all from Gods of War. I walk to the high-pressure air pump behind the jagged ruins of a small apartment building and fill the gun's tank (I *never* use carbon dioxide for propulsion).

When I come back, Jack is checking the sight of a pistol that looks like a Beretta automatic.

"Who makes that?" I say. "Spyder? Hardboilers? Gods of War? Bloodsports?"

"No," he says.

"Who then? It looks so real."

He glances up at me. "It *is* real."

Somebody once told me that the average man experiences his greatest rate of hair loss at age twenty-three, so for the last five years (since my twenty-first birthday) I have been using Rogaine (Maximum Strength formula) twice a day, every day. I haven't detected any sign of fallout.

• • •

Sitting on the sofa Saturday night after practice, too tired to move, waiting for the Seconals to kick in, I hear one of the square-jawed network anchormen say that the average American now has an IQ of seventy-one. He starts a story about the stock market and then interrupts himself for breaking news: the national IQ has dropped below sixty. This has resulted in record sell-offs. While he is telling me this, the IQ drops to fifty-three, then to forty-seven. As I succumb to the Seconals, the number continues to plummet. By the time I am completely surrounded by blackness, it is approaching twenty.

For Sunday's practice, we are simulating night fighting. All the windows are covered with blackout blankets. The ceiling of the warehouse is a glowing map of stars with a perfectly rounded moon in the center. The bomb-cratered buildings of our Beirut are lit dimly with recessed floor lights and dull floodlights that line the edges of the course. We sit on broken seesaws in the playground beside the schoolhouse, waiting for our eyes to adjust to the gloom.

"He's not such hot shit," I am whispering to Lou. "It's not like he was in Vietnam or anything. All he's done is ran a lot and swam a lot, and jumped out of some planes. Big deal. I've sky-dived; you've sky-dived."

"I don't know," Lou says. "He seems to know what he's doing."

"He *can't* be better than I am."

We practice house-to-house assaults. Door kicking, Jack calls it. Cardboard silhouettes pop up to confront us as we enter some of the ruined houses and we pepper the targets with small yellow blotches. Occasionally we shoot each other.

We break after finishing each block. During the second-to-last break, all of us lying on the floor of a gutted, roofless mosque, Jack sits next to me and looks at the false sky.

"You have anything you want to say to me, Logan?"

I feel the muscles behind my testicles contract, but I keep my voice as normal as I can and say, "I've been wondering how much combat experience you've had."

"Ah," he says.

"Because I personally don't like someone passing themselves off as some kind of expert when they don't have the *credentials*. Playing soldier in California doesn't do much for me. I mean, being able to swim don't make you a dolphin."

"Mmm," Jack says, nodding. He reaches into the front pocket of his tan windbreaker and comes out with a crumpled pack of Pall Mall unfiltereds.

I smile at him, little chills of relief running along my spine. "You know, everything I've read says that commandos shouldn't smoke. Especially in the dark. Ruins the night vision."

He ignores me, lighting one of the cigarettes and sucking on it until the tip glows orange.

"Don't feel bad that you didn't know," I say, dizzy from the chills. "You've probably never been on long patrol."

He takes the cigarette out of his mouth and looks at me and then presses the burning end to the back of his hand and holds it there as we listen to the quiet sizzling. His expression does not change.

"Jesus Christ," Stevie says.

I feel the circular exterior wall of the mosque begin spinning around us. The stars twinkle like strobe lights. Gray smoke floats from under the edges of the cigarette. Ken and Barry have their hands held against their eyes.

Jack stares at me all the time, not blinking, grinding the flaming tip into his hand. My chills have disappeared. My mouth is hanging open. And then I feel nothing. I cannot move. All I can do is watch the gleaming coal of the cigarette reflected in Jack's eyes.

• • •

can't remember anything else until we are sitting in our booth at Champagne Dreams. Jack is there, laughing with Lou and Stevie. They are talking about Bosnia. I lean my mouth close to Ken's ear. "*Lots* of guys can put cigarettes out on their hands," I whisper.

"Not lots," Ken whispers back.

"I must've seen it in a hundred movies."

"That's *movies*, guy. Can *you* do it?"

"I think so," I say.

Ken shakes his head and turns away from me. I walk to the bar, dazed.

Samson Taylor is in his usual seat, a line of empty shot glasses in front of him. I sit down next to him.

"I thought about what you said," he tells me.

"Yes," I say.

"About the expert. I don't think it's a real challenge to you. I mean, you know Sugar Ray Robinson was a better fighter than the guys who trained him."

"What are you talking about?"

"Sometimes the guy with the knowledge isn't the guy with the skills."

I look at the sluts around the room and wonder how many people know what happened with the cigarette.

"You know," I say to Samson Taylor, "you really are a silly nigger."

"What?" He is blinking, trying to focus his eyes.

"You," I say. "Are. A. Silly. Nigger."

"I don't understand."

"What's to understand?"

"You're my friend."

"Bullshit. I'm not friends with silly-nigger winos. No wonder your kids won't see you. I wouldn't either."

There are tears running down his cheeks. "No," he says. "No, no, no, no."

"What do you mean, no?"

"You're my friend. My friend."

"Wrong, nigger. I'm better than you." I look around the bar. "I'm better than all these stinking people. I'm the kind of man who knows how to get ahead. You're nobody. That's why somebody else gets to fuck your wife every night."

He groans.

"Do you wonder about it?" I say. "You must. You must wonder if she likes it, if she makes different noises with him than she did with you. Maybe that's why she left—you couldn't make her scream."

His groan turns into a growl and then into a roar, and his tree-trunk arm comes around, much faster than I was expecting, and knocks me off the stool and onto the floor. He stands over me, his bulk blocking out everything else. He picks up the stool to smash on my head and I brace for it and then there is someone on his back, who I think might be Stevie, and there is someone else hanging from one of his arms. Then there is confusion and bodies flying through the air above my head and then there is a moment of calm and I see that Samson has thrown off everybody and lifted the stool again and I can only see one other person, who is standing behind Samson and to the side and has one arm extended with a handgun on the end of it. The gun is pointed at Samson's temple, but he does not notice. We are frozen like that.

Then Samson screams again and hurls the stool against a wall and runs out of the bar. I can hear him roaring in the street. I sit up.

Jack is standing above me, his arm still extended, the pistol held steadily in his hand, sighting down the barrel just like the textbooks teach.

"He could have killed me," I say.

He nods.

"Why didn't you put him down?" I say.

"I don't know."

"Well, I guess you *better* fucking know. This is my *life*."

He lowers his arm and shakes his head. "I *wanted* to fire," he says. "I was all ready." He shakes his head again. "Hunting scuds, we always tried to avoid everybody. Never had to shoot. Not in Somalia, either."

I hear sirens in the distance.

Jack kneels beside me. His mouth is inches from my face. "I never killed anybody," he whispers. "But I *could*. I'm sure I could."

ALL THE NIGHTS
OF THE WORLD

In the car, snowflakes floating against the windshield and then melting in the defrost and streaking the glass like tears, Chris tells me how nervous she is. I make the turn. My hands are cold against the steering wheel. "Why should you be nervous?" I say.

"This is *my* audition," she says.

I glance over. She is huddled inside her coat. She has my jacket wrapped around her legs and her hat pulled down low over her ears. The only part of her I see is her nose, peeking from under the mass of clothing, windburn red and tiny and perfect. She is sitting on her hands.

"Is that what you think?" I say. I turn back to the road.

We drive in silence for a while.

Chris says, "Is he going to like me?"

"I told you before," I say.

"Tell me again," she says and I do.

As I am making the turn onto the street that runs in front of the restaurant, Chris says, "Am I going to like him?"

I laugh. "Everybody likes him," I say. "He's a star."

We pull into the parking lot. I ease into a space near the

entrance. I turn off the engine. Then we sit, not moving, the car clicking, and before we open the doors I tell Chris how much I love her and she nuzzles my shoulder.

My father is never late.

He is already at the table when we enter the room. Several of the waiters have recognized him. They are gathered around him excitedly. He is telling a joke. When my father finishes the joke, the waiters laugh too loudly. He half-smiles and picks up his glass of water and drains it. The glass disappears in his fist.

The room is red-carpeted and dark-walled and is filled with men who have never torn off another man's ear. The men are soft and pink-faced. They sit separated from their dates by cream-colored tablecloths. The dates are young models with skeletal fingers and long legs or middle-aged wives with faces like marble floors.

The maître d' leads us to the table. When he sees us, my father stands and steps past the group of waiters. He throws his arms around me and claps me on the back. I am drowning in Old Spice and the familiar smell from his shirt. I am shocked, as I always am, by the size of him. He steps away from me and looks at Chris.

"You must be Christina," he says. He leans down very far to kiss her delicately on the cheek.

The waiters are nervous with my father standing. They disperse quickly.

Without all the coats wrapped around her, Chris seems very small. The men in the room notice her, as they always do. I watch my father notice them noticing.

I pull out Chris's chair for her and we sit.

The menus are leather-bound. They do not list prices.

"What *is* this place?" I say.

"First class," my father says. "It's first class."

Chris reaches into her purse and brings out a black jewelry box. She hands it to my father. "Happy birthday," she says.

He opens the box and peers inside.

"It's a tie clasp," I say.

He begins to nod and then catches himself. He picks up the tie clasp. In his hand it looks like a toothpick.

"Chris made it," I say.

He smiles at her. "It's wonderful," he says.

Chris smiles back at him.

A waiter slides in to take our drink orders. When he's gone, I say, "How was the flight?"

My father shrugs. "Made it in before the storm."

"I suppose we should have come down," I say.

"Please," he says. "I had to fly so much when I was playing, I could practically *pilot* one of those things."

The waiter returns with the drinks.

"Should we order?" I say.

"We're waiting for Don," my father tells me.

"Will you tell one of your stories?" Chris asks him.

"What do you want to hear?"

"I'm not sure. I don't know much about sports."

"Me neither," he says and they laugh. He begins to tell her about Bobby Layne jumping into the pool at the Hyatt in Philadelphia from his window on the third floor, but he stops and looks at the front of the room. When I look, Don Erskine is standing beside the maître d'.

The maître d' walks toward the table. Don Erskine lumbers after him. He is almost as tall as my father and not quite as thick through the shoulders. In front of him he carries a hard-fat gut like a swollen hot-water bottle.

We introduce Don to Chris. He shakes her hand and glances at me. He sits across from me and says, "I hate the winters in this city."

"Move," my father says.

"Play nice. It's your birthday."

The waiter comes back with a gray-haired man in a white dinner jacket. This is the owner. I know it before he tells us. The collar of his shirt is open. The skin of his chest is the same unnatural tan color as his face.

The owner puts his hand on my father's shoulder and says, "I just want you all to know what an honor it is to have you dining with us this evening."

"Glad to be here," my father tells him.

"Does anyone need recommendations? We have some five-pound lobsters. Just got them this morning. Watched them get unloaded myself. Also, I hope you will do me the courtesy of being my guests."

"That would be fine," my father says. "Thank you."

"After your meal, perhaps we could take a picture together for the wall."

"Why not?"

"I'd like to bring my son over to meet you. If he's going to run this place, he's got to learn how to treat our special guests."

"We'll help you break him in."

We order the food. The waiter and the owner disappear.

Chris says, "You never finished your story."

Don Erskine says, "What story?"

"Bobby Layne at the Hyatt," my father tells him.

"That's a good one."

"I'm always telling stories," my father says. "I want somebody to tell me a story for a change. I want Chris to tell me the story of her life."

"That's not so easy," she says.

"It's easier than you think. There are only tiny parts of it that anyone wants to hear."

"Where should I begin?"

"Tell what you do for a living."

"He hasn't told you?"

"He doesn't tell me much."

"I'm a dancer."

"Ballet?"

"I'm with a jazz company."

"I don't know anything about jazz dancing," my father says.

The waiter brings the salads.

When Chris is in the ladies' room, Don Erskine says, "A shiksa?"

"I'm not exactly Jackie Mason," I tell him.

He nods. "But you're not Pat Boone, either."

"He never liked the Catholic girls," my father says.

"Jesus Christ, Pop," I say, "you haven't been inside a church in twenty years."

"First of all, you're too young to remember what I did twenty years ago. Second, not going to church doesn't make me not a Catholic. Sure as hell doesn't make me a *WASP*."

He eats a bite of his steak.

"You going to marry this girl?" Don Erskine says.

"It's a little early for that. She only just met the old man."

"So what?"

"So he'll charm her for me. Then I won't have to marry her."

"Careful. Your old man might not be as glamorous as you think." Don smiles. "Anyway, answer me seriously."

"Seriously, I don't know."

"What's to know?"

"What if I don't love her?"

"Don't marry her."

"I mean, what if it turns out I don't?"

"It never *turns out*. Either you do or you don't. When you're under the covers in the dark, either you're the only two people on earth or you aren't."

"That's not much."

"That's all there is."

"That's all you need," my father says. His face is a picture of solemnity.

We look at him for a moment. Then I say, "How lyrical of you."

He can't hold it. His lips force their way up at the sides and he smiles and then he laughs with his head thrown back.

"Jesus," Don Erskine says. "I'm just trying to give your son a little fatherly advice."

My father's eyes are shining. He says, "If the earth moves then she's the one? That's not advice, that's pillow talk. The only romantic advice you need is give her an enema before you fuck her in the ass. That and abs. Girls like abs. Don't let yourself go the way Don has."

"Fuck you, you prick. It's part of the aging process."

"I weigh thirty pounds less today than I did the day I quit playing."

"Different metabolisms," Don mutters.

My father pours himself more wine. He looks at me. "I assume you inherited your father's cock. That'll keep a woman better than any ring."

"Comes a time when a woman needs you to settle down," Don says.

"If you're poking her in the kidneys every night, she'll deal with the uncertainties."

"So why'd you get married?"

My father looks at him. "I don't have bastard kids."

Don shakes his head. "Never take romantic counsel from a man who can't invite his ex-wife to his fiftieth birthday."

When the owner brings his son over, my father tells them about the night he broke Mike Webster's nose. The owner's son is tall, nearly my height. The top of his head would be even with my father's chin. He has blow-dried hair and caps on his teeth. He smiles as often as possible.

My father tells about reaching under Webster's face mask and grabbing and tearing and how he felt the bone give and how the blood poured as though someone had turned on a faucet. He tells about the sound that Webster made and how he clawed at my father's hand and pulled the index finger out of its socket and bent it back so far that it touched the back of the hand. My father shows them the crooked finger.

The owner and his son are very happy. My father tells them about thumbing Gene Upshaw in the Adam's apple and how Upshaw went down on his hands and knees and vomited. The other men from the Raiders' line were insane with rage. They tried to get even on every play. Finally Art Shell stomped my father in the groin near the end of the third quarter and he pissed blood for a week.

I examine Chris's face while my father speaks. I expect her to be excited or disgusted. She only looks sad.

"You know," the owner says, "my son was a halfback in college."

"Mine, too," my father says.

"Where?" the son asks and I tell him.

My father says, "Nobody your age knows how to play ball."

"There are a few," Don Erskine says.

"Maybe," my father allows. "Who's that boy they have now—the one with hands the size of pie plates?"

"I don't think you can say 'boy,' " I tell him.

"You can't say anything these days."

The waiter brings coffee and the dessert cart. After he leaves, my father says, "I'm twenty-five years old in every story I tell."

"We're famous for playing a little boys' game," Don tells him.

"You're not really *famous*."

Don smiles. "No, I suppose not."

"I'm not complaining, you understand. It keeps me fed. They put my name on the letterhead and give me an office and a partner's salary, and all I have to do is sit around and tell war stories. I haven't really worked in fifteen years."

"Wonderful," Chris says.

I clear my throat. "We need to think about going. It's only supposed to get worse out there."

"All right," my father says. "I still have to give the jock sniffer his picture. Don'll drive me to the hotel."

We stand. Chris kisses my father and Don Erskine.

In the coatroom, I say, "Every time I see the way he affects people, I feel like I'm going to be a failure."

Chris turns around and looks at me. "That's the dumbest thing you've ever said."

Before I can ask what she means, the girl is back with our coats and then my father has come up behind us and put an arm around each of us and is walking us to the parking lot. I decide to ask her on the way home, but by the time we are in the car I have forgotten what it is I was going to ask.

C hris is so cold when we get back to my apartment that she is unable to speak. Her teeth chatter wildly. She strips off her clothes and throws herself onto my bed. She wraps the blankets close around her.

I undress more slowly and fold my clothes and then fold hers and lay them all at the foot of the bed. I turn on the stereo with the volume low. I light an orange candle that smells like ginger tea.

Chris is still shivering when I climb in next to her. She has bedclothes clutched against her chin. I slide down under the covers and blow warm breath on her body. I take each of her feet between my hands and rub it hard until the sole loses its iciness. Then Chris turns on her side and I emerge from under the bedding, dripping sweat. I wrap myself around her and breathe hot against the back of her neck.

She stops shaking. Her breathing slows. I go back under the sheets and kiss my way down her back. She squirms slightly each time I press my lips against her. When I reach her underwear, I kiss along the waistband and then gently turn her over onto her back. I kiss the front of her panties and the soft outlines of what is underneath. She moans.

When I come up again, we are both breathing deeply. She pushes her mouth against mine very hard.

"I think you impressed my father," I say in a voice I don't recognize.

"It wasn't him I was trying to impress."

We push our mouths together again and then we lie together. Light from the candle flickers over us. Snow falls past my window in bloated flakes. Below, the street bustles silently.

We lie like that a long time.

KILLING TIME

Ray sits with his eyes half closed and does not look at the girls. The girls look the way they always look. They sit across the room all in a row on the banquette, whispering to each other, giggling, staring at our table. We order a second round and Milt Bailey says, "Maybe I should go show those three a little piece of Philadelphia."

Davey Manzelli says, "A very little piece," and we laugh. Dave's face looks like a boiled dinner.

"Fuck you, Garlic," Milt Bailey says.

"Up your ass, you jungle-bunny fairy."

Frank Patterson, the bodyguard, sits beside Ray and does not watch the girls, either. He is wearing a white suit. He leans far back in his chair. The only parts of him that move are his eyes.

"What time is it?" Davey asks.

"Eleven-thirty," Milt tells him.

"You sparring in the morning, Ray-Ray?"

Ray shrugs without looking up. "Ask Sunshine."

"Well?" Davey says.

"Well, what?" I say.

"Are you sparring in the morning or not?"

"Fuck should I know? It's up to Doc. I'm not the trainer."

"Well, Doc ain't here. I think maybe we ought to call it a night."

"Hey, Dave," I say, "I already have a mother. And a wife."

"Hey, fuck you, Mike. I'm just trying to be the voice of reason. These niggers would stay out all fucking night. Can't even hardly tell time."

"Why are you in such a rush?" I ask him. "The new *Playgirl* just come out?"

Ray smiles for the first time. "Hey, Dave," he says, "did you suck cock before Dannemora or did the spade sodomites make you into a bitch and one day you discovered you liked it?"

Dave smiles slightly. "It was Folsom, and who you calling a spade?"

Ray brightens further. "You mean the pot and the kettle? Well, get one thing straight: I ain't no spade, Daddy. I'm a high-yellow, gold-colored African prince with a cock that hangs to my knees."

Dave says, "Doesn't it get in the way when you *drop* to your knees?" and we laugh and Ray reaches across the table and musses Dave's hair and Dave slaps his hand away.

"You're Ray Martin," the girl says.

"That's right," he tells her.

"We think you're the sexiest. Except for Oscar De La Hoya."

Ray nods. "Fuck Oscar De La Hoya."

The girl smiles nervously.

"Who's your friend?" one of the other girls says.

"That's Mike Larkin."

"Are you a fighter too?" she asks.

"Not anymore," I tell her.

The third girl is brunette and prettier than the others. She wears a black wrap skirt that clings to her hips. She smells like a peach. "Don't you worry about your face?" she says.

Ray laughs. "It's not much to begin with."

"Doesn't it hurt when you get hit?" one of the others asks. "Whenever I hit my head—getting out of a car, or whatever—I always want to cry."

"Not Ray," I tell her. "Ray didn't even cry when the doctor slapped him on the ass. They thought he was stillborn."

Ray's smile fades, but does not disappear. He says, "Mike is so tough he doesn't even have to throw punches. He just *scares* them to death."

"Would it hurt if I hit you?" asks one of the girls who is not the pretty girl.

"Depends," Ray says. He looks only at the pretty one.

She smiles. "On what?"

"On what you hit me with."

"What about with my fist?"

"Try it on Mike first."

Her eyes are wide. "Can I?"

"He doesn't mind."

When Ray takes the two girls into the men's room with him, I am alone with the pretty one and I ask her why she didn't go.

"I'm no groupie," she says.

"Of course not."

"What's that for?"

"Sorry. Sometimes this gets me down."

"This happens often?"

"Fight week is nasty," I tell her.

"So why are you here?"

"Because I'm his friend."

We are silent for a while. I sip my drink.

She says, "Have you known him a long time?"

"Ten years."

"How did you meet?"

"We used to fight sometimes in the amateurs."

"Who won?"

"We split pretty even."

"What about now?"

"What do you mean?"

"Could you beat him now?"

Across the room, Ray has reappeared, smiling hard, one of the girls on each arm. When she sees them, the pretty girl shakes her head.

"I'm glad you didn't go with them," I tell her.

On the street, mist makes the lights stretch out long. Frank Patterson sits beside me while I drive. The Navigator rides high in front like a motorboat.

"You guys won't say anything to Doc?" Ray says.

We are silent.

"Come on," he says. "The whole worry is the legs, right? Well, I was sitting the whole time. I made them do all the work. All I had to do was stay hard. I didn't even move the hips."

I listen to the breathing sound our tires make against the wet pavement.

"Fuck this," Ray says. "Who's the fucking champ here, anyway?"

"You are," Davey says.

"So I must be doing something right. If clean living won titles, Mike would be champ. Hey, Frank, you're on my side, aren't you?"

Frank shifts in his seat.

"Well, then fuck you too," Ray screams. "You want to shut me up, you big fuck? I don't care that you're Man-Mountain Dean. You think you can whup me?"

"No, Ray," Frank mumbles.

"What's that?"

"No," he says. "I can't."

. . .

We lie in the twin beds with the lights out, staring at the ceiling, unable to sleep. We listen to the cars passing and to the sounds from the sidewalk outside the casino. Ray says, "These beds make me feel like we're at camp."

"You never went to camp," I say. "Besides, they don't sleep two to a room there. They sleep in cabins with lines of beds. Like a barracks."

"All right. College, then."

"You never went to college, either."

"Fuck you, man."

After a while I say, "You want to play cards?"

"I don't have the energy. I wish we could just sleep."

"I miss my wife," I say.

"Mikey," he says some time later.

"Yeah."

"I don't know if I can take it."

"Just two more days," I tell him.

Ray walks into the gym from the lobby wearing track pants and a white T-shirt with a gold lion's head in the center. He sits on a folding chair at the gray plastic table next to the ring and Davey comes over and sits across from him. They do not speak. Ray puts his right hand on the table, palm down, and Davey lifts it gently and begins wrapping it in a light-brown cloth bandage.

"We on colored-people time this morning?" Doc says from across the room.

Ray shakes his head. "Too early for bullshit, Doc."

"Sorry. I thought we were training for a fight."

"Nobody else has to spar the day before."

"What if, for a little while, I was the trainer and you were the fighter?"

Ray shrugs.

When Ray is finished having his hands wrapped, I put in

my mouthpiece and strap on the headgear and check my cup.
I slide on the pillowy sparring gloves and mount the portable
metal steps and duck through the ropes and into the ring.
The chinstrap from the headgear is chafing and I try to adjust
it by rubbing it with my shoulder. Davey helps Ray into his
gloves and then Ray climbs into the ring and stands in front
of me.

"Light," Doc tells us. "Light."

"Careful of the face," Ray says through his mouthpiece.
"Press conference tonight."

We circle. Ray hops easily from foot to foot. I stalk,
crouched low, forcing him into the corner, narrowing his
angles of escape, cutting off the ring. I throw a short combination to his body, pulling the punches so that they thud
harmlessly against his belly and his pulled-in forearms.
He counters by hammering a left hook behind my ear. He
bobs once and then throws an uppercut into my ribs. He slips
my next few punches. He works his way out of the corner
with jab-jab-hook. I hook him as he weaves past me and
he counters with a right hand over the top that lands on
the bridge of my nose and makes white flashbulbs explode
in my head. I shake the haze away and I can see again and
now the flashbulbs are like furry white bees that dart around
the edges of my vision. I bully Ray into a corner again and
he brings his right leg even with his left and squares his
shoulders and pounds uppercuts just above my belt. I pound
him back. I lean my head against his shoulder and weave
with him. I watch the muscles in his chest to know when
he's punching. He works his way out this time with a seven-
punch combination to my head. The punches are so fast that
the sound of them runs together. As he dances away, I throw
a big, looping hook at him that misses terribly. He winks
at me.

Doc lets us go for fifteen minutes before he rings the bell.

. . .

The first two Mexicans come in and stand by the entrance, working hard to look tough. After a few seconds, Bennie Suarez sweeps in behind them. And then comes Pachanga, flanked by one of his brothers and a kid with a mean-looking puckered pink scar running along his jaw. Pachanga is wide-shouldered and shorter than Bennie Suarez. Bennie is thin and careful in his movements. He spots us and oozes toward the table. Pachanga follows. The four Mexicans move with Pachanga.

"Good evening, Raymond," Bennie says.

Pachanga looks only at Ray. Pachanga's brother and the first two Mexicans glower at each of us in turn. Davey glowers back. The kid with the scar looks only at Frank Patterson. Frank seems about to fall asleep.

"You been working on your accent there, *vato*?" Ray says to Bennie Suarez.

"I am making an effort at assimilation," he says.

Ray snorts. "Wearing a mink shirt?"

Bennie shrugs. "I forgive myself a few little eccentricities."

"You just buy one of those word-a-day calendars?" I say.

"There's nothing wrong with sounding educated."

"Maybe you ought to teach your boy a little something," I say. "How long's he been here and he still can't speak the language? People are starting to think he's retarded."

Bennie half-smiles. "He knows what he needs to know."

"Doesn't take too much education for 'No mas,'" Ray says.

There is grumbling from the Mexicans. Pachanga raises his hand.

"I haven't quit yet," he says quietly.

"He hasn't *queeeet*," Davey says.

Pachanga does not look at him.

"Maybe," Ray says. "But you're at middleweight now, *cabrón*. I ain't no hundred-thirty-five-pound spic."

"You going to say that to the cameras?" Bennie asks.

Ray smiles. "You using an interpreter?"

"Of course."

"Too bad. Throws off my timing."

"All apologies."

A blue-jacketed hotel security guard comes through the double doors and says, "Five minutes."

Bennie says, "Time to get mean."

Ray says, "You tell your boy, he pulls any shit today and I'll ruin him for you."

The Mexicans head for the exit from which they will enter when the reporters are seated. When they are almost to the side door, Pachanga stops and turns around. "You piss blood tomorrow, *mayate*," he says.

Ray blows him a kiss.

"He *peeees* blood," I say.

We are already on the stage when the reporters are let in. Milt Bailey and Bennie Suarez are standing behind us with the promoters and the head of the commission, in front of the white sheet dotted with Budweiser crests that hangs at the back of the platform. When the reporters are seated, Pachanga enters behind Cleveland Henderson, his trainer. They are followed closely by Pachanga's brother and the kid with the scar. Cleveland Henderson sits next to Doc at the center of the table. Pachanga flops into the chair beside him, calm and brown and tough. Ray leans forward and grins at Pachanga. Pachanga pretends not to notice. He keeps staring straight ahead.

The reporters begin asking questions.

"How do you feel?" they say.

Pachanga mumbles into the microphone. The interpreter says, "I am an Aztec warrior. I have heart. I fight no matter how I feel."

"How's the eye?" they say.

"I am an Aztec warrior. I feel no pain."

"The bell hasn't rung yet," Ray says and everyone laughs.

"How long will the fight go?" they ask Pachanga.

"If he faces me like a man and does not run, the fight will be very short. If he runs like a rabbit, we will be there longer."

"I have no question that I will win," the interpreter says. "I am an Aztec warrior."

When it's Ray's turn, he says, "I've been in with Hopkins. I've been in with Jones. Who's *he* been in with?"

Ray says, "I'm not an idiot. I'm not going to bang with him. But I'm not planning on doing much running. He's used to guys standing in front of him. I don't do that. I can't see him being able to find me."

Ray says, "As far as that rabbit business, ask him about it after the sixth when he can't breathe and I'm still bouncing. I don't like watching these clumsy guys fight. It's not artistic. Makes me feel like a thug."

Ray says, "Sure, he has a chance—there's always a *chance*. But if you're asking me where to put your money, I'd have to think that's easy." He smiles. "When you're at a bullfight, you don't bet on the bull."

They are weighed on a black balance scale. The head of the commission slides the weights along the beam and calls out the numbers. The cameras chatter and flash. Pachanga wears sunglasses. Ray smiles and flexes his biceps.

Afterward, they pose together for the photographers. They face each other, hands up, trying to look bored.

The morning of the fight, we eat pancakes and eggs in our suite. We watch television. We do not answer the phone. Ray drinks as much water as he can handle. We play rummy and don't keep score.

At noon Ray eats two bananas and two hard-boiled eggs.

When he's finished with the second egg, he says, "You pissed at me?"

"Don't break your concentration," I say.

"You want me to apologize 'cause I'm better than you?"

I am silent.

"You don't have nothing you want to say?" he says. "I can look in your eyes and see what you're thinking. Why don't you grow some balls and tell me?"

"Careful, Ray."

"Careful of what? If you was my friend you'd tell me what you thought. But you get *paid* to be my friend, so you have to shut up and take what I give you. I throw my punch a little faster than you throw yours and it lands a little harder and that means you spend your life with your tongue in my ass. What do you think of that?"

"I think fight week is a tough week."

"Yeah, it's *my* tough week."

"Fine," I say.

It is hot in the locker room under the arena. Ray dances between us over the cement floor and throws combinations in the air. Sweat pours off him. He is dressed in gray sweatpants and his ring shoes. The noise of the crowd breaks in above our heads. The walls shake with the force.

When Ray stops shadowboxing, he stands shuffling his feet, unable to keep still. Davey sits on a high stool in front of him and massages the sweat into his chest and shoulders.

"I'm ready," Ray says.

"Goddamn right," Milt Bailey tells him.

"Bring that motherfucker," Ray says, his voice rising.

"He don't even belong in the same ring with you. He's never been in with anybody serious."

"He hits like a bitch."

"He can't break popcorn."

"I'm gonna take that motherfucker *out.*"

"It's your ring, baby. It's *your* ring."

Milt is almost screaming now. Ray, his eyes wild from the tension, pulls himself away from Davey and begins flying around the room again and throwing bombs with both hands. Milt screams at him as he throws. "There ain't nobody else, baby. They can't *see* you. He'll be lucky to make it through the first."

One of the security guards appears in the doorway. Thunder from the crowd pours in behind him. He shouts over the roar, "You boys ready to exchange trainers? They want to wrap Pachanga."

Doc is sitting on one of the benches in front of the banks of lockers. He glances up and nods.

"I'll go," I tell him.

He nods again.

The security guard motions into the hallway. Cleveland Henderson glides past him. Cleveland Henderson is small and caramel-colored. His fists are the size of grapefruits.

"Doc," he says. "Ray."

"Cleve," Doc says.

Ray sits on the high stool in front of Dave Manzelli. I walk toward the door.

"Your boy looks a little edgy," Cleveland Henderson tells me as I pass him.

"You know how he gets," I say.

The security guard leads me down the hallway. We pass lines of event staff and cameramen with laminated cards hanging from chains around their necks. We pass ring-card girls in sequined bikinis craning their necks for a glimpse of the crowd.

The Mexicans are gathered outside the dressing room, near the entrance to the tunnel. The kid with the scar slouches elaborately against one of the walls and looks fierce.

Inside the room, Pachanga sits on a padded table, staring at the floor. His brother sits next to him on a wooden chair. The inspector from the commission is the only other person in the room. In the corner, an immense radio blasts Tito Puente. Pachanga's brother nods at me and does not speak. He begins wrapping Pachanga's hands with white gauze. Pachanga does not move. When the hands are wrapped, I inspect them. I check the knuckles for lumps. The inspector takes the gloves out of his bag and sets them on the table. The brother puts the gloves on Pachanga and laces them and covers the laces with tape. I examine the gloves and the covered laces. I pull a fat marker from my pocket and write "M. Larkin" over the tape on each wrist.

As I leave, the brother nods again and still does not speak. Pachanga is still staring at the floor.

Ray is standing in the center of the room when I get back. He is stripped down to his shorts. The sweat on his body gleams. Davey is on his knees in front of him, retying the laces of the ring shoes.

"How'd he look?" Ray asks me.

"Scared," I tell him. He nods.

Cleveland Henderson chuckles.

Ray jerks his head at me. I cross the room and lean in close to him.

"Thanks, Mikey," he says.

I look at him.

He lays a gloved hand on my shoulder.

Dave finishes with the shoes. Ray takes his hand from my shoulder and then he is weaving again. He uses the back of his forearm to wipe the sweat from his eyes.

"How we gonna do it?" he shouts at Milt Bailey.

"Limb from limb!" Milt Bailey shouts back.

"All night long!" Milt Bailey shouts.

Cleveland Henderson watches them peacefully, half-smiling. The rest of us stand back and let Ray get himself ready.

EVOLUTION

PART ONE: SEX

On our first date, Heather Gordon orders the Maryland crab cakes with red-pepper polenta and when I walk her home she asks me to take her to bed. On our second date, she has portabello and endive salad followed by veal tenderloin with poblano chiles and we make love on the swing set of an empty playground. On our third date, she tells me she is going to marry me.

For our one-month anniversary, Heather lights candles all around my bedroom and strips me naked and walks me to the bathtub, which is filled with warm water and rose petals. After three months, she takes me to Paris for the weekend. When we have been dating for six months, she asks me to kill her father.

• • •

"The first thing we have to do," Kelly says when I tell him, "is cross over."

"Cross over," I say.

"Cross over the line between the good people and the bad people."

"There's a line?"

"Sure," he says. "Actually, there are several. We'll cross them in stages. We'll work slowly. We'll keep upping the ante."

"Did you get this from a book?"

He shakes his head. "No books. This is about personal experience. We must walk the path."

"The path."

"The path to emotional detachment."

"Are you making this up?"

He shakes his head again. "It's in all the latest literature."

I stare at him. "I thought you said no books."

He frowns. "From now *on*," he says.

We are sitting on the sofa in our apartment watching Kelly's high-definition television, which is shaped like a fish tank. The picture is so sharp that it reveals the individual pores in human faces.

Kelly says, "Everything's going cerebral these days. If we want to resist that trend, we have to master the physical world. If we want to be masters of the physical world, we have to know about life and death."

"Kel," I say, "are you sure you want to do this?"

He looks at me in silence for a while. Then he says, "This is what we've been waiting for."

The room is cavernous and blue-carpeted and honey-combed with tiny cubicles. The analysts sit in the cubicles between eighty and a hundred hours each week. The traders come in at eight-thirty and leave at five.

A green digital stock ticker rushes along the edges of the ceiling.

Kelly and I are sitting in brown leather armchairs outside a glass-walled conference room. Inside the conference room is a long cherry table with a podium at one end.

A kid about our age wearing Ferragamo lace-ups strolls past the analysts and pours himself a cup of coffee from the cart next to us.

Kelly says, "You have to come all the way over here every time you want coffee?"

The kid shrugs. "Can't put it on the trading floor. Someone would crash into it."

"You a trader?" Kelly says.

"Apprentice. You the boys from Merrill?"

Kelly shakes his head.

"We work for a start-up," I say.

The kid frowns. "But you're wearing suits."

"We're in new investment."

"You're here to pitch us?"

"Something like that," Kelly says.

The kid nods. "You guys have one of those cute tech names where you change the first couple letters of an existing word? Like Verizon. Or Cinergy."

"We're called eVolution," I tell him.

"Small ee, big vee?"

"That's right."

He smiles. "So what does it do?"

"The small ee, big vee?"

"The *company*."

I look around the room at analysts hunched over keyboards and at traders in shirtsleeves shouting into telephones. "I really don't know," I tell him.

• • •

You can open a car door without a slimjim by bending a hanger into a squared hook and inserting it between the window and the weather stripping and using it to catch the lock rod. Sometimes you can open the door by using a key from the same manufacturer.

It is possible to hot-wire the car from the inside, but to do this you need to remove the ignition mechanism and complete the circuit manually. This risks severe electric shock. It also damages the car.

It is better to pop the hood and run a wire from the positive side of the battery to the positive side of the coil wire. The coil wire is red. Use a pair of pliers to hold the starter solenoid to the positive battery cable. This fires the engine. To unlock the wheel, insert a screwdriver into the steering column and use it to push the locking pin away from the wheel.

Kelly says, before you can kill you have to know what it is like to die.

Before you can know what it is like to die, he says, you have to know what it is to live.

"Do you know the life span of the common housefly?" he asks me.

"One day."

"One day," he says. "Twenty-four hours in which to pack all his loving and hating and living and dying."

I say, "I don't think a housefly does much loving and hating."

I change the channel on the high-definition television. The news is running a feature on school shootings.

Kelly sighs. "You're missing the point."

I shrug. "His life isn't short if he doesn't know it's short."

Kelly frowns and wrinkles his forehead and then says, "He only gets one sunrise and one sunset."

"And you only get a few thousand."

"Hopefully more than a *few*."

"Even so," I say.

Kelly nods. "Even so."

We are in a taxi. The driver wears a green knit hat and loafers with no socks. He has a stick of incense burning on the dashboard, which makes the air smell and taste like hot soap. I am sitting in the middle, between Kelly and my boss. My boss wears a linen suit. His tan is perfectly even.

Looking out the window at skyscrapers like enormous gray wafers, I say, "I don't understand my job."

My boss says, "What's to understand?"

"Shouldn't we bring a programmer with us?"

"Didn't I explain this to you last week?"

My scalp itches. I say, "It's just that I've been thinking some more about it and I figure it couldn't hurt to have an expert along."

My boss sighs. I look at Kelly. He is shaking his head. My boss says, "Our investors didn't grow up covered with zits."

"Excuse me?" I say.

"These people made their money the old-fashioned way— they inherited it. And they'll *never* give it away to some fruitcake in clear-framed glasses who wears his jeans two sizes too small. The key is charm, not knowledge. You were born for this."

Kelly is smiling at me. I ignore him. "But what if they ask me"—I lean close to my boss and whisper—"*technical* questions?"

"Do they ever?"

"They *could*."

He rolls his eyes. "Make something *up*. We're *salesmen*, for Chrissake."

"What are we selling? We don't make anything."

He looks at me. "We make *money*, kid. I sell experience. Kelly sells cool. You sell cheekbones and green eyes and leading-rusher-in-Ivy-League-history."

"Second-leading."

"My mistake," he says.

"It's just," I say, "that I don't know anything about computers."

He shakes his head. "This isn't about *computers*. Do you think Rockefeller knew anything about oil? Do you think Carnegie knew anything about steel? All you have to know is what people want and how to tell them they want it from you."

"But what if you don't know what people want?"

He shrugs. "Then you have to know how to tell them what they want."

W hen you die violently, your bowels let go. It's called involuntary-sphincter-release response and it means that you spew all the foul waste from inside you, more than you ever imagined possible.

Kelly says the next step after crossing over is the planning phase.

Really, he says, the two steps are simultaneous.

I am sitting in our living room, listening to the steam heat, and Kelly is telling me that evolution means the extinction of the weak.

"Every human and animal characteristic is the result of random genetic mutation."

"Yes," I say.

"Think of the creatures who lived before certain features developed. Think of the ones whose mutations failed to increase their fitness."

I close my eyes and picture ancient sea creatures with

squat bodies and tails like embryonic alligators', bobbing on the tide, near powerless with their shrunken fins, watching one of their fellows crawl out of the surf and onto the beach. He will go on to populate the world. The rest will be prey for prehistoric sharks or else will have descendants who will be less and less suited to the sea and will eventually drown as infants or occasionally flop their way onto the sand. I wonder whether these creatures know that they are the footnotes of history while their friend on the beach is the ancestor of an entire planet. I think of all the animals not selected for a place on the ark. I think of the thieves crucified next to Jesus.

"Eyelids," Kelly says.

I open my eyes. "What?"

"Eyelids are the result of random genetic mutation."

"Yes," I say.

"You have to be able to imagine how it felt before eyelids. If you looked at the sky during the day, your retinas would burn. You'd have to walk with your face pressed into the ground, dirt in your mouth all the time. You'd have to sleep with your eyes open."

"Yes," I say.

Kelly nods. "You need to be able to imagine the time before tear ducts."

Heather's father leaves his office between six-eighteen and six-fifty-one, Monday through Friday. On Saturday and Sunday he works noon to five. It takes him between four and seven minutes to make his way down to the garage, depending on the elevators. He drives a black Lexus sedan.

There ought to be two men in bland suits who drive Heather's father to and from work and sit all day behind Plexiglas in the hallway outside his office and shadow him wherever he goes.

This would make for more of an operation.

In that case, we might use a pipe bomb. We might use an incendiary device underneath the backseat. We might use a sniper. If the bodyguards blocked sight lines to the subject whenever they were out in the open (as they should), we might use the sniper to take out the bodyguards and use a chase man to go after the subject if he broke and ran. Of course, it is better to snipe in two-man teams. And neither of us knows how to use a rifle.

I am pressing my face into Heather's neck and smelling her perfume and her shampoo and the soap she uses, which is goat's milk and honey and costs twenty dollars a bar. Even through all of that, I can still catch the scent of her skin.

Heather is wearing a pair of my boxer shorts and a T-shirt from the gym I go to, which is called Advance.

We are watching *2001* on my DVD player.

I stop nuzzling Heather's neck and sit back into the sofa with my legs extended in front of me. Heather rests her head on my chest. The light from the television twinkles all around us.

"It's less than two thousand years since the fall of the Roman Empire."

"Is that right?" Heather says.

"That's right," I say. "Less than two thousand years after chariot races, we have airplanes and space shuttles and movie-theater popcorn."

"Amazing."

She shifts the position of her body and nestles into my chest.

I say, "We weren't even the same *species* until about twenty thousand years ago. Before that we were Cro-Magnons."

"Fascinating," Heather murmurs. Her breathing is becoming deep and slow.

"Until recently, we were carrying clubs and living in caves."

She is silent.

I watch the television. Keir Dullea has just shut down the supercomputer. This is immediately before the part I don't understand, in which he imagines himself sitting in a room that looks like the smoking room from the world's fanciest mental hospital and then sees himself as an old man and a fetus.

I say, "Kelly and I are making preparations."

Heather stirs for a moment and then relaxes back onto me. "Mmm," she says sleepily. "Preparations for what?"

"Never mind," I say. "It's all right if you don't want to talk about it."

Kelly says, "You're the bastard who gave measles to the Yanomami." He is talking to the waiter, whom he has just accused of sneezing over his Parmesan-and-onion tartlet. "These people lived in isolation for hundreds of years and then you goddamn sociobiologists and you save-the-rain-forest fairies came in and gave them a measles vaccine, except that there *were* no measles in the rain forest until you brought them. And when the vaccine made some of the people sick, you refused them treatment on the grounds that you wanted to study a society completely free from outside influence."

The waiter is trying to figure out whether Kelly is making fun of him. The men sitting next to Kelly are laughing. One of them says, "This guy is a card. A goddamn *card.*"

The other one nods and says, "The genuine article."

Kelly says, "Do you have any *idea* how many germs live in the mucus inside your nose?"

We are in a restaurant called Neoterra in which each of the tables has a different shape than the others and none of them is round. Our table is shaped like a lima bean or like a slug writhing to death under a blanket of salt.

The men we are eating with all wear suspenders and Kenneth Cole glasses and have their sideburns trimmed every other day. There are five of these men. They are venture capitalists. I cannot remember any of their names, so I have assigned names to them at random. When I cannot remember the name that I have assigned, I say the first name I can think of. They do not seem to notice.

One of the men next to Kelly is saying, "The plain ones are always the most suggestible. The pretty ones tend to be too uppity and the ugly ones are too wary. The plain ones are up for what*ever*."

Kelly says, "How do you know who's pretty and who's ugly?"

The man says, "You *look*."

"But how do you assign categories? Certain features make you feel physical attraction, but these features are different from culture to culture and even, sometimes, from person to person. It is a selection-based instinct to want to combine your genes with the genes of someone physically attractive, in order that you will have attractive offspring whose appearance will make them more likely to have reproductive success. Of course, you have a chicken-and-egg problem there. Also, that does not account for differences of opinion."

The man stares at him.

Kelly says, "Do you ever try to imagine the time before dilating pupils?"

When I open my eyes, the man to my right is speaking earnestly to my boss. He is asking to see the business plan.

My boss shifts in his chair.

"You do *have* a business plan," the man says.

My boss clears his throat. "Of course we have a plan," he says. "But we're not planning to be captains of industry. This isn't industry. We're not planning to be the world's leading distributor of butt plugs. We're sure as *hell* not planning to build the world's best shuffleboard Web site so that some Daddy Warbucks can stroll up and pat us on the head and pay us twenty-five million to split twenty-four ways, so we can buy a town house and a Benz and some pussy and live goddamn upper-middle-class. Upper-middle-class means *dick*. Fuck the suburbs. Fuck commuting. Fuck neighbors. Our plan here is to be rich enough not to *have* neighbors. To be able to stand in front of your house and turn around in a circle and own everything you see. Not season tickets, not even courtside. I'm talking about owning your own team. No Internet millionaires here. Fuck that, too. I'm talking about Internet *billionaires*. What we're offering you is the opportunity to be part of that."

The man to my left, whom I have decided (I think) to refer to as Gill, looks at me and says, "So, you played halfback at Princeton?"

"Not Princeton," I tell him.

"Of course not," he says. "How tall are you? Six feet?"

"Why not?"

"You weigh around two hundred?"

"One-ninety."

He smiles. "What's your forty time?"

"My forty time."

He nods.

"I don't know these days."

He frowns.

"I'm not really an athlete anymore," I explain.

"Hmm," Gill says.

We drink in silence for a while. Suddenly Gill looks at me. I lean back toward him.

Gill says, "What's your body-fat percentage?"

· · ·

We are standing at the urinals in the bathroom at Neoterra and Kelly is saying, "The difference between assault and aggravated assault is mostly about the severity of the injuries."

I say, "How bad does it have to be to be aggravated?"

"It's subjective."

We zip up. The urinals flush automatically when we walk away.

We hold our hands under the faucets, waiting for the sink to recognize that we are not just dust particles blowing in front of the electric eye.

Kelly says, "Last night I was reading about the human botfly."

"I thought you said no books."

He nods. "I think we're going to have to forget that rule."

"I already did," I tell him.

The water begins to spray from our faucets.

He glances at me. "When?"

"From the beginning."

"Why didn't you tell me?"

I shrug. "I don't care much about it. As long as we don't say no movies."

"Of course not," he says. "That would ruin everything."

"The human botfly," I remind him.

"Right, right. Anyway, when it bites you, it raises a bump like a mosquito bite. Except that the fly has burrowed its way into your arm and the bump is covering it. It incubates for a while until it gets hungry and then it begins to consume you. You can feel it eating its way up your arm."

We take our hands from under the faucet and the water stops. We stand with our hands under the nozzles of the hand dryers.

Kelly says, "There are tiny parasitic worms that can live

in drinking water. Once they're inside you, they gather in sores on your legs. The only way to get rid of them is to immerse them in water and allow them to flow out of the hole they'll open in your skin."

They are laughing when they leave the club and weaving as they walk. Both of them wear white baseball caps emblazoned with the letters of their fraternity.

Kelly says, "Are you ready for this?"

I nod.

"Deep breaths," he says. "Try to swallow."

I nod again.

The frat boys do not notice us until they are only a few feet away. Then they stop.

Kelly is wearing a long black overcoat and leather gloves with lead studs sewn into the knuckles on the inside. He says, "You boys sure you're all right to drive? You look a little under the weather."

The frat boys are silent.

Kelly says, "Is this your car?"

"Yeah," one of them says.

"This a Corvette?"

The frat boy snorts. "Try Lamborghini."

"Ah."

He narrows his eyes. "You fuck with the alarm or something?"

Kelly smiles. "Now why would you think that?"

"Should be going off with you sitting on the hood."

"Well," Kelly says, "we're not as heavy as we look. The camera adds ten pounds." He laughs.

The frat boy says, "If you get off the car by yourselves, we'll give you a running start." He spreads his hands, palms up. He is thick through the chest and shoulders. His friend is taller than he is and wide.

Kelly slides off the car onto his feet. The frat boy smiles and turns his head to glance at his friend and when he turns back Kelly throws a straight right hand into the middle of his face. The gloved fist makes a dull-hollow slapping sound when it lands, followed immediately by the crunch of the nose breaking, and the frat boy's head disappears in red mist and then he has fallen to his knees. His friend is staring, openmouthed, and does not notice me standing up off the hood. He is reaching for Kelly when I kick him in the groin as hard as I can. He crumples next to the other one. And then we are on top of them.

I take the big one, who is curled into a ball with his hands cupped between his legs. He is dry-heaving. White lines of saliva hang from his chin. I kick him a few times in his kidneys and he rolls onto his back and I stomp his forearm with the heel of my boot and I am pretty sure I feel bones breaking. He screams. I kick him in the stomach and listen to him gasp as the air rushes out of him. Now he has no breath to scream and he is gagging. I drop onto his chest and, as I do this, I bring my elbow straight down into his mouth and feel the teeth give. He brings his arms up to cover his face and I punch the broken forearm. He screams again. When he moves the forearm, I drive my fists into him over and over. The skin splits along his eyebrows and forehead and cheekbones and blood seeps through the cracks like lava. Sweat is rolling down my face, plastering my hair to my forehead. I feel like crying.

Kelly says, "Enough."

I stand up and look at the big frat boy at my feet. His wrist is bent at a terrible angle. His mouth looks like a tomato with ripped skin. There are teeth sticking through his upper lip.

I look at Kelly, who is also standing. "Wallets?" I say, my chest heaving.

Kelly shakes his head. "This is assault, not robbery."

"Two birds, one stone?"

He chews his bottom lip and considers this. "Fuck it," he says. He reaches inside his frat boy's jacket and pulls out his wallet. The frat boy groans. Kelly kicks him in the ribs.

"We taking the car?" I say.

"No," Kelly says. He looks at the frat boy below him. "Don't take it too hard, fellas," he says. "We've just grown past you. You're the giraffes whose necks never stretched." He pulls off his gloves. "You're the elephants with short noses."

"**I** think we're ready for the next level," Kelly says.

I glance at him. The streetlights we pass turn his face ghostly white and run the shadow of the windshield wipers along his profile. I massage the fingers of my left hand against the knuckles of my right, which are scraped bloody and have already begun to swell.

"What's the next level?" I say.

Kelly turns his head slightly so that the wiper shadow now flows over his face asymmetrically, making a jagged line on his nose. He is smiling enough for me to see the tips of his teeth.

"It's time to shoot somebody," he says.

Heather is wearing a red dress with no back. The dress is longer on one side than the other. On the short side, it rises almost above her hip.

The skin on Heather's thighs is the color of butterscotch.

We are standing under an enormous crystal chandelier that hangs over a crimson staircase. Everywhere I look, there are men in tuxedoes. Heather has the fingers of her left hand laced through the fingers of my right.

The poster next to the theater door shows two immense eyes and, above that, the word "Gatsby" in white letters.

Heather is talking to Cynthia Lowell-Wellington and

Vanessa Mather Coppedge Bryson, who are jammed up against us by the crush of people. Cynthia's boyfriend, who is taller than I am and has a dimpled chin, looms on my left, just behind Cynthia. I am fairly certain that he was on the crew team at Brown, but it is possible that he was on the lacrosse team at Penn. He shakes my hand at every opportunity.

For dinner, Heather had the New Orleans–style catfish with chipotle dipping sauce.

She is saying, "If you're going to use a bronzing agent of *any* kind, you *have* to couple it with a good moisturizer."

Cynthia says, "Should I be looking for one with sunblock in it?"

"I suppose it couldn't hurt. But really, you should be keeping yourself out of the sun completely. That's what the bronzer is for."

Vanessa leans toward Heather and says, "So, do you put it *every*where?"

Heather nods. "No white should show."

I say, "Can you picture the time before melanin?"

Heather raises herself on the balls of her feet and kisses the side of my mouth.

The mob surges all around us, moving with tiny shuffling steps.

We are sitting in a private box on the left side above the orchestra. The house lights are down and the women onstage are singing to each other and staring into the audience. According to the program, they are singing in English, but it is impossible to understand them and my attention is focused on the seat backs of the row in front of us where a thin digital screen shows a scrolling transcription of the lyrics.

Heather is sucking my thumb.

Next to me, Cynthia's boyfriend, Clay Harrison Adams, whispers, "When's your IPO?"

I say, "We're not trying to be the world's leading distributor of butt plugs."

He says, "Oh."

The stage is darker now and the women are gone. They have been replaced by a dancing mob and bright-colored balloons. In the background a tiny green light is flashing.

Suddenly I have the urge to climb on top of my seat and throw my head back and scream. I have this urge every time I go to the theater. I believe it is a similar instinct to the one I have to turn on the engine of my car when the mechanic has his hand inside it. Or the impulse I feel on subway platforms to push the man next to me in front of the oncoming train. Or when I imagine swerving my car into a group of pedestrians and feeling the dull cracks of their heads against my windshield and gazing at the wet smears of their blood. Or when I think of diving through the plate glass of the Rainbow Room at Rockefeller Center and plunging, back arched, head up, gleaming shards of glass falling all around me, into the middle of the herd of ice-skaters circling sixty-seven stories below.

Clay says, "Johnson and Johnson?"

"What?" I say, turning to him.

"The butt plugs. Leading distributor."

I sigh. "I don't *know*, guy."

"Oh," he says.

I think about throwing him over our balcony and watching him drop, arms and legs windmilling, into the front row.

With all these impulses, there is the idea stage, then the imagination stage, then the spine-tingle, adrenaline-shot, testicle-clench moment when you *know* that you are actually going to do whatever it is.

But you never do.

• • •

During intermission Heather and I get on one of the mirror-walled elevators and ride it until we are alone. She pushes the Run-Stop button. A voice comes over the intercom asking if everything is all right. Heather begins unbuttoning my shirt. The voice from the intercom says that if the elevator does not begin moving in the next five minutes it will call the fire department. Heather licks my chest. I put my arms around her. The voice tells us not to panic.

Heather pulls away from me and takes two steps backward, smiling slightly, and presses herself against the brass handrail. As she leans onto the handrail, her dress drifts up and I can see the thin black string of her panties. I move close to her and she kisses me hard and runs her hand along the back of my neck and along my shoulder and down my arm and then she takes my hand and puts it gently between her legs. Her underwear is already moist. I grab hold of it and pull so that the narrow strip rubs against her. She gasps. I slide my hand under the wet fabric and touch the soft, slick skin and then I ease my middle finger inside her. She tips her head back and moans. I suck on the skin of her neck. Her perfume has a bitter taste.

She says, "Oh my God."

I kneel down in front of her and grip the backs of her thighs and pull her close to me, resting my head just below her ribs.

She strokes my hair. "How much do you want me?" she whispers.

I groan against her stomach.

Back in my seat, I can smell Heather on my fingers and I can taste her when I lick my lips.

In front of us, dozens of miniature chandeliers hang on long cords from the ceiling. In the hallways behind us, the lights flash off and on and an usher closes the door to our box. The cords begin to retract and the chandeliers float toward the high ceiling.

Heather whispers, "What's wrong with you lately?"

"What do you mean?"

"You've been even more distant than usual."

I say, "I've been walking the path to emotional detachment."

She frowns. "This is Kelly's idea?"

I nod. "We're working in stages."

She opens her mouth to say something else, but the two women are singing again. They are slumped in lawn chairs. They wear straw hats and white dresses. They draw out a single note so long that I have to take a deep breath in sympathy. The urge to scream washes over me again.

The words click by in white block letters on the digital screen in front of me. IT'S HOT, says the screen. IT'S HOT.

PART TWO: VIOLENCE

The man by the door is wearing a beige turtleneck and a leather jacket. He leans us against the wall and frisks us quickly.

Kelly says, "Won't you at least buy me dinner first?"

The man sighs. "Haven't heard that one yet this week."

Dexter is sitting in the far corner on a hydraulic chair that looks like a life raft. The man cutting his hair wears a long white shirt that says MECCA across the chest. The room smells of cocoa butter. The floor is covered with hair.

The man beside Dexter is almost as thick as he is and has

a big jagged scar along his jaw. He wears a cream-colored suit and a silk shirt.

The only other man in the barbershop lounges on a leather sofa in the corner opposite Dexter. His entire body seems frozen, including his eyes, which are locked on mine.

Dexter raises his head and looks at me in the mirror. "Looking good, baby," he says.

I smile. "You remember Kelly?"

He shrugs. "Why not?"

"Good to see you again," Kelly says.

Dexter grunts. He jerks his head toward the window. "That your new whip?"

"Yeah."

"Whip?" Kelly whispers.

"Car," I tell him.

Dexter whistles. "Fuckin' ay. You niggers must be *flush.*"

"We can't complain," I say.

"I thought you were supposed to call me before you went public."

"We will."

He frowns. "So how come you niggers are rolling Bill Gates–style all of a sudden?"

I look around at the bodyguards. "You think you have enough security?"

"Can't be too careful."

"I don't remember anyone ever taking a shot at Butkus."

Dexter grins. "He wasn't a Nubian king."

"All right, I don't remember anyone taking a shot at Willie Lanier."

"That was a different era. It's all haters out there these days. Can't stand to see a brother living the dream."

"Is *that* what you're doing?"

Dexter's barber opens a drawer in the counter in front of him and changes the guard on his clippers.

Dexter says, "You watch me in the Pro Bowl?"

I nod.

He says, "They've never seen anything like me."

The barber removes the guard from his clippers and carefully shapes Dexter's sideburns. He unsnaps Dexter's maroon smock and passes the razor over the back of his neck. He pours alcohol onto a cotton ball and runs it around Dexter's hairline. He douses him with talcum powder.

Dexter says, "That's enough. Don't give me any of that Afro-Sheen shit."

The barber nods.

Dexter shrugs out of his smock and stands. He is an inch or two taller than I am. He is wearing a white knit tank top. His body is like a clenched fist.

"Shame the way you're letting yourself go," I say.

Dexter snorts. He takes a fat wad of bills from his pocket, peels one off the top, and hands it to the barber.

The man in the corner is moving now. He is on his feet and coming toward us. I can't remember seeing him stand up.

Dexter says, "This is Wilton."

"Wilton?" I say.

Dexter smiles. "Him a yardie, y'know."

"What?" Kelly says.

"He's Jamaican," I say.

Wilton looks at Dexter. "That accent's a little Harry Belafonte."

Dexter says, "So are you."

Wilton is wearing gray wool slacks and a black ribbed turtleneck sweater.

Dexter says, "These are the boys I told you about."

Wilton nods. He does not move to shake our hands.

I say, "Dexter tells me you used to work for Mike Tyson."

He shrugs.

"You know what we're working on?"

He shrugs again.

"We're trying to reach the next stage in our development."

Wilton stares at me.

Kelly says, "For most mammals, grooming is a sign of affection. That's why I cut my own hair."

Wilton is saying, "You'd be amazed how long it takes some guys to die."

I say, "Doesn't it depend on where they get hit?"

"Not always."

We are at an outdoor shooting range, lying on our stomachs beside green T-shaped shooting benches, facing white-and-black silhouette targets set up in front of a stone wall. I am leaning on my elbows on the concrete apron, sighting down the barrel of a rifle that looks like it is made out of Legos.

I say, "I wish these things still looked like they used to."

"Why?"

"It would make me feel more real."

Wilton says, "Draw down center body mass on everybody. No head shots."

"What about bulletproof vests?"

"That's just movie shit."

"*Some*one must wear them."

"Sure. But they'll still be incapacitated if they take one in the chest, provided you have enough stopping power. Even with body armor, a heavy load can break ribs and collapse lungs."

I squint through the aperture and place my crosshairs on the center of the target.

"Raise your aim four inches at two hundred yards, ten inches at three hundred."

"Why?" I turn my head to look at him.

"Gravity," he says.

"What do I do past three hundred?"

"You miss."

I nod.

Wilton says, "How you know Dexter?"

"We went to high school together."

"You play ball with him?"

"Sure."

He frowns. "I thought he was from Cleveland."

"So?"

"So, you don't look too Cleveland to me."

I shrug, gently so as not to lose my target picture. "Near Cleveland."

"Shaker Heights?"

"Something like that."

He smiles. "Always knew that motherfucker was wanna-be hard."

"Don't need to be from the ghetto to be hard."

"It helps." He looks at Kelly, who is on his stomach fifty feet to my right, sighting down the barrel of his Lego rifle. "What about the ofay?"

"Why is he an ofay and I'm not?"

He shrugs. "Ain't just about skin color."

"Mmm," I say. "We lived together in college."

Wilton nods. "He's a fuckin' fruit loop."

Sometimes, particularly when you can anticipate the precise location of your target, it is preferable to snipe at a near-flat trajectory. For countersniping, because you cannot predict your target's whereabouts and because the target will likely be concealing himself from anyone on the ground, it is vital to occupy the highest position possible.

In close quarters, the pistol is ideal because of its conceal-ability and ease of use. However, its effectiveness drops sharply as range increases. It is very difficult to be accurate with a pistol at distances greater than fifty feet. Past a hundred, it is almost impossible.

• • •

My boss is riding in the cart in front of us with a man from Goldman who has skin like tapioca. We all wear green sweaters and brown-and-white spikes.

Kelly is driving our cart, bouncing over ruts in the dirt path. The air tastes like the dirt thrown up by the other cart. Kelly is saying, "Why doesn't he have an accent?"

"He told me he lost it."

"He talks like a goddamn Yalie."

"He's self-educated."

Kelly snorts. "You *must* know what that means."

"What?"

"Anytime a Nubian says he's self-educated, ten to one he was reading with his ass to the wall."

"Prison?"

He nods. "Probably has one of those correspondence diplomas."

"That's not fair."

He glances at me. "You two have been getting awful close lately."

"He's been *teaching* me."

"I hope you're not losing perspective."

"Perspective on what?" I say.

"Just make sure you keep in mind what it is we're doing."

The cart in front of us stops dustily. Kelly pulls in behind it. We sit off to the side on a wooden bench while the man from Goldman sets himself over the tee.

Kelly says, "In gorilla societies, each adult male has his own position in the hierarchy. You don't look directly at anyone higher than you. Eye contact indicates provocation for all primates. No one looks at the alpha male, unless they are ready to challenge for his position. If you look him in the eye before you're ready for him, he will tear your limbs off."

· · ·

I am sitting in the backseat, between Heather and her father. We are on the way to the opening of an art gallery called Cave Paintings. Heather is gazing out the window.

Her father is my size with big hands. He has a thin white scar under his right eye. I am trying not to look at him.

He is saying, "Sometimes we would wait all night and not see anyone. Some nights we would all see movement on the road and we would blow the claymores and launch flares and pour fire into the tree line and when we walked down, we wouldn't find anything except the craters we'd made."

I say, "How'd they get away?"

"Who?"

"Whoever was on the road."

He looks at me. "There *wasn't* anybody on the road. We imagined it."

"You all imagined the same thing?"

"The visions are contagious. One guy points at what he sees and you make yourself see it, too."

"So, after a while, why didn't you stop believing something was there?"

"Because sometimes something *was* there."

"What were those nights like?"

He shakes his head. "You don't want to hear about *those* nights."

"Sure I do."

He says, "Later on, I was with Recon and we did less search-and-destroy, but we still had visions."

"Does it give you nightmares?"

"Nightmares?"

"Because you hated it so much."

He frowns. "Did I say that?"

"I just assumed. I thought everybody hated it."

He says, "It was the happiest time of my life."

• • •

We are sitting in a rented van at the curb across the street from Heather's father's office building and Kelly says, "What about knives?"

Wilton looks at him. "This ain't *West Side Story.*"

"It's just that I thought we were supposed to learn these things in stages."

"You niggers want to learn knives, you can do it on your own time."

Wilton is shielding his eyes from the sun and staring up at the building, which looks like a giant milk carton. He says, "Next time we're doing reconnaissance, you ought to bring a jacket."

Kelly says, "Why not just keep the heat on?"

Wilton says, "Three guys sitting by the curb all day in a car with the motor running might as well hang out a sign that says STAKEOUT."

"Why are we here at all? We already know his schedule."

"*You* already know it. I want to see it for myself."

"You don't trust us?"

Wilton shakes his head. "You can't learn this stuff from books."

"And you've learned it through experience."

"That's right."

"So when we have the experience we'll be as good as you."

Wilton shifts his eyes to look at Kelly. He says, "You can't have a late start."

Armor-piercing or KTW rounds can puncture steel doors and pass through bulletproof vests. Their drawback is that they make neat, surgical wounds.

Full-metal-jacketed rounds also have a better penetration value than standard loads, but they are less streamlined than the armor piercers and cause more tissue damage.

Hollowpoints carry low penetration values but expand on impact. This is also true for dum-dums.

You can create a hollowpoint effect by cutting cross-shaped grooves into the tips of your cartridges. On impact, the round will flatten out along the grooves, disintegrating muscle and bone. (Note: Handmade loads may tend to jam an automatic.)

I am kneeling by an open window on the ninth floor of the Ritz, looking past the Public Garden at Beacon Street, and Wilton says, "Blue suit with the grocery bag."

"Got it," says Kelly.

"Why him?" I say.

"I don't know," Wilton says. "Easily identifiable."

Kelly says, "It doesn't pay to stand out."

They are on their feet next to me, binoculars held to their faces. I open and close my hands against the rifle and blink my eyes and watch through the scope as the man scratches his neck, magnified ten times.

"I don't know if I can," I say.

Wilton sighs. "This is what you said you wanted."

"I know. I just wasn't expecting him to be so *alive.*"

Kelly says, "I'll do it."

"Wait your turn," Wilton says.

The man stops walking and checks his watch.

I say, "Won't they be able to tell where the shots came from?"

"Who's 'they'?"

"I don't know. Somebody."

"Unlikely. The flash isn't too apparent in daylight."

"What about the sound?"

"It'll echo off the buildings. It'll seem to come from everywhere."

"What if somebody sees us?"

"The chances of that increase with every second you don't take the shot."

The man is whistling now. I steady the crosshairs on the top button of his suit jacket. I close my eyes and imagine the way his face will look when the bullet hits him and the noises he'll make and the way his body will come apart. I wonder whether he will drop the groceries. I open my eyes.

Wilton says, "Deep breaths. Squeeze, don't pull."

The man smiles suddenly and switches his grocery bag to the other arm. A young girl with blond hair runs into the sight picture. The man bends down and scoops her up with his free hand and spins her around in a circle. She kisses him on the cheek.

I draw back from the scope and lay the rifle on the windowsill and stand up. I shake my head. "Not in front of his daughter."

Kelly looks at me. "The fuck you care?"

"She'll never recover."

"Nobody recovers from anything. Your experiences shape who you are. You have a chance to be the defining influence in this girl's life."

I don't say anything.

"If you're so worried about it," he says, "maybe we should do her too."

"No," I say. "I won't do that."

He groans. "Have Wilton do it."

"The girl can't die."

"She can and she will. The only question is when."

"Not today."

"What difference does it make? Today, tomorrow, eighty years from now. She won't be in a position to care."

"But in eighty years, when she feels it coming, she'll be able to look at all the things she did. Now she could only think of what she didn't do."

"So what if this girl has an unpleasant last few minutes in which she imagines the life she didn't live? It'll probably be better when she imagines it than it would have been to live it. It'll be better than remembering all the things she could never quite do. Besides, it's only a few minutes at the end. And if you hit her right, she won't even have that. Like flipping off a light switch."

Wilton turns to look at him. "I don't wash anybody for free."

"We'll pay you," Kelly says.

On the street below us, the man has put the girl down and is holding her hand. Holding the girl's other hand is a pretty blond woman in a blue cardigan.

Wilton turns back to the window. The family is moving away from us. They round the corner onto Charles Street.

I say, "They'll go home tonight like they do every night and they'll never know that they just lived through the most important moments of their lives. They don't even know we exist."

Kelly says, "Goldfish have thirty-second memories. Everything that happened more than thirty seconds ago is erased to make room for the new things. That means that at the very end, when they look back, they've been dying their whole lives."

Wilton grunts. When Kelly shoots him, his body clenches and he half turns from the waist, head rigid, pupils crammed to the sides of his eyes, trying to look at Kelly behind him. Then he sags against the glass, blood spraying from the big exit wound in his chest. The sound of the handgun is much softer than I am expecting. It is the dry crack of a twig snapping over and over.

"Sorry about that," Kelly tells me.

"You're crazy," I say quietly.

He smiles. "I doubt it. It's just that I've developed a more complete understanding of our situation."

"Do you understand that Dexter's other boys will be looking for us now? Along with God-knows-who-else."

He shrugs. "I hope you see why it was necessary."

I stare at him.

He stands very close to Wilton, who is gurgling. "It's

all perfectly natural. Today we're selecting for people who draw their guns on time." He smiles. "We're selecting against surly tarbabies who don't know how to watch their mouths."

We are sitting on long sofas in the dark-maple locker room at the Harvard Club and my boss is saying, "If poor people were as smart as rich people, they'd be rich by now."

The man next to him is soft everywhere and colors his hair red-brown. He netted eleven million dollars last year. He chuckles.

My boss says, "Every generation of a family has a chance to hit it big. If they keep missing, after a while you have to assume that something's wrong with the genes."

The carpet is blood-colored. The walls of the locker room are covered with lacquered plaques that show vertical columns of men's names. Kelly and I have our legs stuck out in front of us and crossed at the ankles. We are wearing white Izod shirts and gray shorts. We have long-handled rackets laid across our laps.

The television that hangs from the ceiling of the locker room shows a pretty blond woman with straight teeth and a gray-haired man, also with straight teeth, sitting at a curved desk in front of Corinthian columns and windows that show false sky. At the bottom of the screen, stock prices churn by in a blue strip.

Kelly whispers, "Ancient chieftains developed efficient methods of agriculture so that they could throw banquets to show their power."

"What?" I say.

"It wasn't to better provide for their people. For that, the old methods were sufficient."

I stare at him.

"Technology develops not to advance the species but to consolidate the power of individuals."

"Listen," I say, "I don't have any idea what you're talking about."

"I'm talking about the death of emotion and the sublimation of desire."

"I thought the death of emotion was what we wanted. I thought you said we were walking the path to emotional detachment."

He nods. "Yes. I've come to reexamine our position. At the beginning I thought we were working to evolve into things capable of murder. I thought we were trying to divorce mind from body. I thought we were trying to resist going cerebral." He sighs. "I realized recently that our problem is that we had already *gone* cerebral. We had already separated mind and body. We've been denying our instincts. For human beings to be able to kill, they don't need to evolve, they need to regress. All these computer-geek faggots live in the world of the cerebral and they've probably never been in a fight. They can't fight, they can't fuck, they have no physical *presence*. You and I have been trying to regain our instinctive behaviors. We're trying to get back to basics."

"But my instinct was to feel sorry for those frat boys and for the guy I was supposed to shoot."

"You're making the mistake of classifying compassion as a human emotion. Really, your natural instincts are to do what's best for yourself and to eliminate anything that challenges your success. You do for you, I do for me, everyone does for themselves, shake it all up and the cream rises to the top. It's mathematics."

"How can you tell me what my instincts are?"

"Because human behavior has been completely dissected. The genome is mapped. There are no more secrets."

My boss is smoothing a terry-cloth headband over his hairline. He looks at the man next to him, who is still chuckling. My boss says, "Take the Gettys, for example."

The pretty blond anchorwoman looks into the camera and

says something, but I can't hear it because the sound on the television has been muted. Her words appear in a black closed-caption box below her. The black box says, "Now, the day's headlines."

I ignore the first two stories, both of which include videotape of rolling tanks. When the third story begins, a graphic appears over the anchorwoman's shoulder featuring a painting of the Ritz-Carlton Hotel splattered with enormous puddles of blood. Written over this painting in white block letters are the words "Ritz Murder."

Kelly says, "Normally they don't make so much fuss over a shine killing."

My boss says, "Location, location, location."

The man sitting with him says, "Such a waste."

Kelly says, "We don't know if it's a waste. It's not like this was some kid on the honor roll. Maybe this was just a big, mean dog who ran into a bigger, meaner dog. These things happen."

The man turns to look at him.

"Do you know any of the men on the walls?" I say quickly.

"Sure," he says. "Most of them."

"That must be hard."

He turns away from Kelly to look at me. "What must be hard?"

"To lose so many friends."

"Lose?"

"In the war."

He shakes his head. "The war dead are in the lobby, kid. These are the trustees."

"Oh," I say.

Kelly leans close to me and whispers, "Human beings have come to treat death differently than other animals do. When lions get too old, they lose their place in the pride and are forced to wander, scavenging for food, unable to hunt, until eventually they die of starvation or disease or they become immobilized by starvation or disease and are then eaten alive by hyenas. When sharks are injured, other sharks come from miles around and tear them to pieces. Human beings are the only species that tries to prolong life artificially after the subject has outlived his usefulness. We are the only creatures that mourn our dead."

"Elephants," I say.

"Elephants?"

"Elephants mourn their dead."

"That's impossible," he tells me.

We are standing in Dexter's living room, surrounded by Persian rugs and sliding glass doors and a glass-topped coffee table dusted with cocaine residue. The residue is smeared into white streaks. On the floor beside the table are three long-stemmed champagne glasses and a metal ice bucket.

On the other side of the glass doors are the floodlit patio and the swimming pool and the hot tub, both of which have underwater lights, and past all that are evergreen-covered hills that loom black in the darkness.

Dexter is in the hot tub with one of the girls. The other girl, naked and brown and smooth and gleaming, is standing on the edge of the pool and swaying in time to faint music. They are all laughing. I can't tell where the music is coming from.

Kelly motions toward the glass doors. He is dressed entirely in black. His face is covered in greasepaint.

"What if they hear?" I whisper.

"They won't," he whispers back. "And, even so, if they look back at the house they'll be looking from the light into the dark."

"It's not really *dark* in here."

"Dark enough."

I slide one of the doors open. It hisses on its runner. I freeze. Dexter and the girls keep laughing. I slip through the opening and onto the slate of the patio. Kelly follows me. We move slowly, crouched low, careful to keep our footfalls silent.

The dancing girl sees us first. She stops swaying and opens her mouth. Kelly shows her his gun. She does not speak.

I kneel down behind Dexter and press the barrel of my automatic into the back of his neck. His body shudders and tenses. The girl next to him gasps. She has long hair and skin the color of coffee ice cream.

I say, "Where are the roughnecks?"

"We're the only ones here," Dexter says. His voice is very steady.

"Bullshit," Kelly says.

"I swear to God."

Kelly says, "If you're lying, I'm going to slice your eyeballs open with a razor."

"I'm not lying."

"After that, I'm going to pour gasoline into your eye sockets and pull off your fingernails one by one. Then I'm going to tie your hand to the side of this pool and mash it with a cinder block. Then I'm going to take a pair of garden shears and cut your tongue in half while it's still in your mouth."

The girl in the hot tub starts to cry.

Kelly turns to her. "Is he lying?"

She shakes her head.

Kelly says, "If he is, I'm going to do the same thing to you."

She sobs more loudly. She keeps shaking her head.

Kelly looks at me. "I believe it."

I stand and walk around in front of Dexter. "It's me," I say.

He squints at my face. "Jesus Christ," he says. "You almost made me piss myself."

Kelly says, "Don't think I didn't mean what I said."

Dexter says, "What do you want?"

"We need to talk," I tell him.

Dexter is sitting on the black leather sofa in his living room and wearing a white robe that pulls very tight across his shoulders. I am seated facing him on a ceramic barstool that I dragged in from the kitchen. Kelly is on the other side of the room, leaning on a mantelpiece. The girls are upstairs in the windowless walk-in closet in Dexter's bedroom. We slid a heavy bureau in front of the closet door. We balanced a mirror between the bureau and the door. Kelly told the girls that if we heard the mirror break he was going to come upstairs and pull out their teeth with pliers and shove straightened coat hangers into their ear canals to rupture the drums.

"Where'd the hitters go?" I ask Dexter.

He says, "Wilton's disappeared. They're trying to find him."

"They have any ideas?"

He shrugs. "Not that I know of."

I glance at Kelly. He shakes his head.

"I don't believe you," I say to Dexter.

"I can't help that."

Kelly says, "The next time you lie, I'm going to shoot you in the hip. Won't be too many more Pro Bowls after that."

"Tell us," I say.

Dexter says, "They think maybe you two clipped him."

"You try to talk them out of that?"

"I tried. They weren't sure anyway."

"They have a theory?"

"They think Wilton's that thing at the Ritz."

"I thought that guy couldn't be identified."

He looks at me carefully. "Yeah, somebody put some caps

in his face. Blew out his teeth and everything. Also, they took his wallet and cut off the tips of his fingers."

"So what makes them think it's Wilton?"

"It's just a guess right now. That's why you're still walking."

"How long before it's not just a guess?"

"Who knows? Depends what they find."

"Any chance you can get them off of us?"

He shakes his head. "They're looking for payback. I can't call them off."

"What are they doing now?"

"They're checking you out."

"Any prediction about what their conclusion will be?"

"Again," he says, "it depends."

"On what?"

He stares at me. "On what you've done."

"What's your instinct?"

"These guys are pros. They'll put this together in their sleep. They'll take just enough time to be certain." He takes a breath. "Then, Kelly goes for sure. I tried to tell them that *you* couldn't have been involved. They'll spend a little while thinking about that."

"And then?"

"And then I figure you go too."

"Unless?"

He shrugs. "Unless you're gone to somewhere they can't find you."

"Or they aren't good enough," Kelly says.

"They're good enough," Dexter tells him.

"Wilton wasn't."

We are silent for a while.

Dexter says, "I'll try to warn you."

"Why would you do that?" Kelly says.

Dexter jerks his head at me. "He's my friend. It isn't fair for him to get burned just because of the company he keeps."

"You're so sure it was me?"

"Sure enough."

Kelly smiles. "Then how do you know I won't do you too?"

"Because I'm your early-warning system."

"How can you warn us when you don't know where they are?"

"They still check in." He frowns. "That reminds me—how'd you get past the alarm?"

Kelly's smile widens. "I think you may need a new one," he says.

Heather comes out of the dressing room wearing blue jeans made from some kind of stretch material. She lifts the bottom of her sweater, showing a narrow strip of belly. The jeans ride low on her hips.

"What do you think?" she says.

"Great," I say.

"That's what you always say."

"I always mean it."

She examines herself in a long mirror on the wall.

"I like them," she says. "You can wear them with a blouse. You can wear them with a halter."

"You're sexy," I tell her.

She turns her head toward me and smiles. "You're sweet."

The walls of the store are lined with light brown shelves. Most of the shelves hold scented candles and kitchenware and lamps with rice-paper shades. The shelves in back hold thirty-dollar T-shirts.

Heather walks to the narrow doorframe of the dressing room and leans her head inside. She pulls her head out and says, "Still empty."

She takes my hand and leads me into a pine-smelling corridor lined with stalls. The door of one of the stalls is hanging open and Heather pulls me inside. She closes the door behind us and throws the bolt. Her jacket is lying on the gray bench in the corner. Her shoes are on the floor under the bench. Each wall, including the back of the door, is completely covered by a mirror. The mirrors reflect each other's reflections. We are surrounded by infinite versions of ourselves that extend as far as we can see in every direction. We can see ourselves from every angle.

Heather runs her tongue along the edge of my ear. She puts her palm between my legs. I feel myself stirring against the zipper of my pants. I grip her shoulders and gently push her away. She frowns at me.

I say, "I'm sorry if my behavior has been strange lately."

"I hadn't noticed."

"I've been under a lot of pressure."

"Work?"

"Not really. I've been dealing with some personal issues."

She presses me down onto the gray bench and sits across my knees with her arms around my neck. "Like what?" she says.

"Oh, I don't know. I've been working on my development."

"As a person?"

"Sort of."

She strokes my hair. "I want to get married."

"I know. You told me after our third date."

"I mean I want to get married soon. I want to take care of you. I want you to take care of me."

"I don't have *anything*," I tell her. "At least let's wait and see what happens with the company."

"I don't like waiting. Besides, my father is practically *made* of money."

"I don't want your father to take care of us."

"No," she says, "neither do I."

• • •

Kelly's sketch has wide eyes and too much nose. Mine is a cross between Errol Flynn without the mustache and Paul Bunyan without the beard. The sketches are superimposed side by side on the blue-sky background behind the pretty blond anchorwoman with the stock ticker flowing beneath her.

We are sitting on the sofa in our living room.

Kelly says, "I don't like her as much on the HDTV. She wears too much makeup."

"Everyone wears makeup on television."

"She has bumps on her face. She looks like a pickle."

The anchor is talking to a brunette with thin lips who is standing in front of the Ritz in the rain, looking concerned. The anchor also looks concerned.

I say, "Aren't you a little bit worried?"

"About the sketches? You can't tell it's us unless you know what you're looking for. Even then, they're kind of a stretch. They made me look like Groucho, for Chrissake."

"Maybe we ought to lay low. Get out of the apartment. *Something.*"

"Forget it. Those pictures could be almost anybody. The cops aren't gonna find us with these descriptions unless they're already onto us."

"And what about Dexter's boys?"

"The Jamaicans?"

"How do you know they're Jamaicans?"

He shrugs. "Wilton was."

"Fine, then," I say. "What about the Jamaicans?"

He sighs. "The important thing is for us to stay on-mission."

"On-mission?"

"Heather's old man."

"Are you serious?"

"We have to finish what we started."

The back of my neck is hot. "I'm not sure about that."

"You don't have to be sure. I'm telling you it's going to be done."

"I think I may have made some kind of mistake."

"Trust me," Kelly says. "This is best for everybody. This is what you said you wanted."

"I think I've changed my mind."

Kelly nods.

The sketches are gone. The anchorwoman is smiling now.

Kelly stands up from the couch and walks to the door.

"Where are you going?" I say.

He opens the door and walks into the hallway. I listen to the door click shut behind him. I turn back to the television.

When the phone rings an hour later, I pick it up immediately. "Kel?" I say.

There is no answer.

"Where are you?" I say.

I hear the ticking of the open line.

I say, "Just come back and we can talk about it."

I hold the receiver against my ear and listen to buzzing static and then Dexter's voice says, "They're coming."

PART THREE: CLIMAX

"**Y**ou don't look good," my boss says.

"I had to get a hotel room last night."

He half-smiles. "You have a fight with your boyfriend?"

"We're having some work done," I say.

We are looking out the big window of the Credit Suisse

luxury box at the Fleet Center, squinting at tiny players on a tiny floor hundreds of feet below us. It is almost impossible to tell what they are doing. When we want to see the game, we watch wide-screen televisions in the corners of the room.

My boss says, "I was trying to reach you. I called the cell phone."

"It didn't get reception in the hotel."

"You need to be available to me twenty-four hours. Where's Princess Grace?"

"He's not here?"

My boss shakes his head. "If you two want a job where you don't have to come in on Sundays, go work at the post office."

"I *am* in," I say.

A young trader is screaming at one of the televisions. His friends sit in front of the television in leather armchairs, Frisbeeing paper plates at the screen.

My boss says, "Any of these guys would kill for your job."

The skin on my face feels very tight. "So would I."

I imagine throwing my boss through the tinted window and watching him plummet into the middle of the court. I can see the stain of him spreading on the bleached wood.

My boss says, "Let's see some of that."

I pull my gun from inside my coat and touch the barrel to his eyebrow. "Open your mouth," I say.

"What?"

I hit him in the forehead with the side of the gun. He steps back. Blood trickles down his face.

"Get on your knees," I say.

He does.

"Open your mouth."

The traders have stopped making noise. I know that people around the room are looking at us. No one moves. My boss opens his mouth.

"Wider," I say.

I shove my gun deep into his mouth. It clatters against his teeth.

I say, "You're going to have to learn how to treat people."

He nods. He is shivering.

I say loudly, "You're a ridiculous man. You don't even understand your job. I don't know who put you in charge. I'm younger than you, I'm better than you. I don't even need this gun. I could kill you with my *hands.*"

A dark patch has appeared on my boss's light gray trousers. There are tears running down his face.

I say, "You don't have the balls for this kind of work."

I take my gun out of his mouth.

Everyone stares at me uncertainly. A few of the traders applaud.

"Thank you," I say.

My boss is slumped on the floor, moaning. I smile at the room. I put my gun away and give one last wave and then walk quickly to the door.

I say, "If I see this door open while I'm still in the hallway, I'm going to come back and choose two of you at random and shoot you in the balls."

When the elevator opens, it is full of security guards. They have their guns drawn.

I say, "There's some maniac in there with a gun. He has baggies of nitroglycerin taped all over his body. He said he would detonate if he heard anyone trying to come in. If you shoot him, the whole place might go up. Can you imagine what that would be like? You'd spend days sifting through body parts. You'd have to make piles of limbs. Can you imagine an enormous pile of severed arms?"

One of the security guards says, "Get behind us."

They push past me and fan out around the entrance to the luxury box. One of them puts a finger to his lips and leans his ear against the door.

I step inside their elevator and press Lobby.

Standing on the sidewalk next to the Fleet Center, listening to the sirens approaching, I take out my cell phone and call Heather.

I say, "How soon can you be at South Station?"

"Is this a joke?" she says.

"It's not a joke. I'm leaving. Will you go with me?"

"Yes."

I cross Causeway Street. "How soon?"

"Do I have time to pack?"

"No."

"Half hour," she says.

I push the End button and put the phone back in my pocket and look over my shoulder at the Fleet Center and at the squad cars pulling up in front and that is when I see the Jamaicans.

They are on the other side of the street, half a block behind me, watching the cops pile out of their cars. One of the Jamaicans is tall and wide. The other is the one who frisked us at the barbershop. They are moving at the same speed I am. They turn away from the cops and toward me and I snap my head back around, but I am almost certain they saw me see them. I keep walking, sweat dripping down my back, feeling them behind me.

I cross Merrimac Street.

I glance over my shoulder. The Jamaicans are still matching their speed to mine. They are maintaining the same distance.

At Cambridge Street, I reach the corner just as the DON'T WALK sign stops blinking and I slow down and almost stop and then suddenly I dash into the street and hear squealing brakes and slide over the hood of a moving taxi and hear horns screaming behind me and then I am on the other side, running.

Heather's father stands up to meet me. His office is lined with black shelves that hold crystal eggs and lacquered cigar boxes.

"How did you know I'd be here?" he says.

"What do you mean?"

"It's Sunday."

"Oh." I run my tongue along the backs of my teeth. "Heather must have told me."

He looks at me. "Must have," he says.

I take a deep breath. "I need your help." I glance out the window. "By the flower cart."

Heather's father walks to the window and gazes down at the street. "Who are they?" he says.

"I don't know exactly."

"They're pros."

"Yes."

"How'd you make them?"

"I don't know. They just sort of appeared across the street from me."

"I mean, how'd they let you see them?"

"I was looking for them. I knew they were coming."

He shakes his head. "Shouldn't matter."

"But why would they want me to spot them?"

He shrugs. "Maybe they wanted to see whether you'd run. Maybe they figure only a guilty man runs."

We are silent for a while.

Seven stories below us, the big Jamaican crosses the street and walks along the sidewalk and around the far side of the building.

"Why don't they follow me in?" I say.

"They don't know which floor you're on. Also, they'd be worried about the building's security force. And they don't want to trap themselves in case things go south. If they take you in the open, they have escape routes and it's easier for them to avoid the cops. They'll cover the exits and wait to reacquire."

"You learned all this in Vietnam?"

"It's textbook," he says. He lifts his telephone receiver.

"What are you doing?"

"Cops."

I shake my head.

He puts down the receiver. "Sounds like you have something to tell me."

I don't say anything.

He steps away from the window and takes his key ring from his pants pocket and unlocks the top drawer of his desk. He brings out a heavy automatic. He pulls back on the slide and checks the cylinder.

"You keep it *loaded*?" I say.

"Doesn't do much good when it's not." He puts the gun in the waistband of his pants. "You carrying?"

I show him the pistol inside my jacket.

"You any good with that?"

I shrug.

"Who put these guys on you?"

I shrug again.

"This have anything to do with that fairy you hang around with?"

"You mean Kelly?"

"How many fairies you know?"

"But Kelly's just cool."

He snorts. "For a catamite."

"No," I say. "It's his *job*. Kelly sells cool. I sell cheekbones."

He looks at me. "I don't know what the fuck you're talking about. I don't much care. All I want to know is why there are two hard guys waiting for you outside my building."

"It's kind of a long story."

"Give me the broad strokes."

"They think Kelly took out a friend of theirs."

"Did he?"

I stare at him.

Heather's father nods. "I guess that's not too surprising."

"Will you help me?"

He frowns. "You ever do any wet work?"

I take a breath. "Not really."

"Stay close to me. When it happens, hold low and put your man down. Nothing fancy. Keep shooting until he drops."

I am having trouble breathing. "Are we going now?"

He shakes his head. "We'll wait until the game breaks. The more confusion, the better."

When it's time, Heather's father says, "Get yourself frosty. They won't go easy."

"You can tell that by watching them stand on a street corner?"

"That's right," he says. He taps his middle finger against the handle of the gun in his waistband. "Let's go have a little roughhouse."

In the lobby we fall in step with a group of gray-suited corporate lawyers and pass with them through the enormous revolving door. Outside, the street is seething. The sidewalk in front of us is a sea of bobbing heads. We move with the crowd.

I am peering over the people around me, watching the Jamaican leaning against his flower cart on the opposite sidewalk. He is staring into the crowd, trying to keep sight of the door. Heather's father is directly in front of me, crouched slightly, also watching the Jamaican.

Heather's father glances at me over his shoulder. He says, "Cross at the corner. We'll take him as soon as we hit the other side."

I nod. Everything seems far away. I no longer feel shoulders jostling against mine. I no longer feel feet scraping the backs of my heels.

I imagine what would happen if a V-shaped flight of F-4s passed over us and dropped flaming orange sheets of napalm. I see the commuters around me turn black in the heat. I see their melting faces. I imagine an earthquake in which the skyscrapers above us disintegrate into a concrete avalanche. I imagine a world without skyscrapers where we would huddle close together and wait for lions or saber-toothed cats to charge us from the underbrush. We would scatter, lungs burning, tingling-hot all over from the adrenaline burst, and the lions would go after the youngest or the sickest or the weakest and they would bring him down with airborne strikes that break his legs and they would rip him apart.

I imagine meteor showers.

We are almost to the corner when I see Kelly. He is in a second-story window across the street. I do not see his rifle. He nods to me.

I lean toward Heather's father. "We may have a problem," I say.

"You mean your boy in the window?" he says. He does not turn around.

"You saw him."

"When we got out here."

"Why didn't you say anything?"

"I didn't know it was an issue."

"He may not be a friendly," I say.

"Is he a hostile?"

"Possibly."

He turns his head now. "Is there something you're not telling me?"

We have reached the corner.

I say, "I believe there's been a series of misunderstandings and misinterpretations."

"Leading to what?"

"Kelly is probably going to try to kill you."

He stares at me. "Why would he do that?"

I don't say anything.

Heather's father says, "Because you told him to?"

The light changes and we begin moving across the street.

"I've recently come to reexamine some things," I say.

When Kelly appears next to me, Heather's father is still on his knees. The smaller Jamaican is lying next to the flower cart. There is a hole in the center of his face. His cheeks are caved in toward it. The big Jamaican is on the ground next to us. On the ground next to him are the white and gray and blue-veined coils of his guts. He has been cut nearly in half by the exit wound from Kelly's hollowpoint. His face is smooth and unmarked. His eyes are wide open.

Kelly says, "Let's get what we came for."

"I don't think this is what Heather wants."

"Sure it is. You said so."

"I know that. I think I made it up."

"That's crazy."

"Yes," I say.

He shrugs. "I suppose it doesn't much matter. It was never really about her."

"What was it about?"

"Getting back to nature."

Heather's father says, "You don't have to do this."

Kelly draws his pistol. "Don't flatter yourself. It was never really about you either."

I say, "You've already made your progress. You don't need this."

"We need to finish what we started."

I shake my head. "You're being too literal."

"It's what separates us from the animals."

"I thought what separated us from the animals was that we know we're going to die."

"What separates us from the animals," he says, "is our ability to ask what separates us from the animals." He aims his pistol. Heather's father closes his eyes. "The danger," Kelly says, "is to become all talk and no action."

I close my eyes before I fire—holding low, squeezing-not-pulling—so I do not see Kelly's face when the bullet hits him. I imagine him looking at me with enormous, shocked eyes and reaching out his hand and taking a shaky step toward me and I fire again and again with my eyes closed until I hear his body fall.

He is still alive. He sounds like he is trying to clear his

throat. I imagine the way he looks on the ground, flopping like a landed fish, drowning in the air.

I turn away before I open my eyes.

Heather's father is leaning against me. We are shuffling along Purchase Street, trying to seem casual. I have draped my jacket over him to hide his shoulder. Taking the jacket off revealed my gun harness, so I unstrapped it and threw it in a garbage can on Federal Street. I have the pistol in my pants pocket.

There are sirens everywhere now. The cruisers are stuck in the traffic from the Central Artery construction site. The sidewalk is full of people who do not know what has happened. We are lost in the crowd again.

Heather's father drags himself along, stepping as lightly as he can so as not to jostle his shoulder. We do not speak.

Heather is sitting in her Mercedes with the line of taxis in front of South Station.

She says, "Get in."

I open the back door and help her father inside and slide in next to him. Heather pulls away from the curb.

Her father says, "Where are we going?"

"What is he doing here?" Heather says. "What's wrong with him?"

"It's sort of a long story," I tell her. "We can't go home."

"No," her father agrees.

"We need to get out of the city for a while."

"What if they shut it down?"

"The whole city?"

"They could."

"But they don't even know what to look for. They don't know what we're driving."

"Chancy," he says.

. . .

Heather's father closes his eyes and leans against the back of the seat. We creep onto the bridge beside the Children's Museum and sit in the steaming line of stopped cars.

Heather's father is taking deep breaths.

Heather turns her head toward me. "Do it," she says.

"Do what?" I say.

"Kill him."

I feel the inside of the car begin to spin. I open my mouth but no sound comes out.

"What's wrong?" Heather says.

"I thought I imagined it."

"Imagined what?"

"That you asked for this."

"Why would you think that? This is what you wanted."

"*Me?*"

"You said you wanted to take care of me."

"I do."

"Then he's served his purpose."

"So he has to die?"

"You want me, you want money. He has both. I want a man who doesn't *ask* for everything. I want a man who *takes.*"

"Are you sure you want this?"

"Really, I want it for you. I want you to feel like you can be the man in my life."

I rub my neck.

"I'm establishing my independence," she says.

Heather's father says, "You must know she's crazy." His eyes are still closed.

"Shut up," Heather says. She turns back to me. "Kill him."

"I don't know," I say.

Heather's father says, "This can't be the first time you've seen it. She used to sprinkle detergent in the birdfeeder."

"Do it," Heather tells me, "so we can start our new life."

Her father says, "She was thirteen the first time she tried to kill me."

"Why don't you stake out some territory for yourself?" Heather asks me. "Be a man. Get in the *game*, for Chrissake. You can't let people walk all over you. Let's break free. Let's set out on our own."

"Let's," I say.

"Do it, then."

"Why can't we just leave?"

She says, "We have to cut all our ties."

Her father says, "In an hour she'll love me again. She'll blame you for killing me. Every day you'll be wondering who she's going to ask to do *you*. Indecision, kid. It's what separates man from the animals."

"Regret," I say.

"That too."

I take a deep breath and unlock my door.

"Where will you go?" Heather says. "I thought you were on the run."

"I'll have to think of something."

"You're nothing," she sneers. "You always need someone else to do your work. Maybe I'll get Kelly to do it. I'm sure *he* has the balls. Maybe I'll even throw a little pussy his way."

"Good luck with that," I say. "Today we've been selecting against silk-suit thrill killers."

As I am opening the door, I hear Heather say, "I don't need you anymore."

"I love you," her father says. "I want to help you." His voice cracks.

I close the door and leave them there.

Walking back along the bridge, I imagine the beginning of the universe.

THE ART
OF THE
POSSIBLE

You date pretty, brown-haired, apple-cheeked girls who will seem like virgins even after they have children. You stay away from drugs. You drink just enough not to stand out. You use football to get yourself to school, but not to pay for it (your school doesn't give athletic scholarships)—for that you take out loans and get work-study jobs hauling trash and sweeping floors. Your hair is cut short, but not *too* short. You work for various campus political organizations—all of which are liberal, but not *too* liberal.

You are handsome, but not *too* handsome. You are tall, but not *too* tall.

After college, from which you graduate one year early, you go straight to law school and then to the state attorney's office and you establish residency in a district with a congressman who you have heard is about to make a run for the Senate and when he does you run for his seat. And you win it. Election day is two weeks after your twenty-eighth birthday.

You're going to make a name for yourself championing the common man. You're going to get on the Judiciary Committee during your second term. You are not going to cave to big business. You are going to be a senator. You will keep all of your promises; you will never sacrifice your ideals for political gain. You will be president by the time you're forty.

You are going to do some good.

You are pretty sure it's Wednesday, but it might be Monday, and you're dressed in a navy overcoat and black oxfords and you are striding, strong-jawed, projecting quiet confidence, along the edge of a vacant lot in the center of your district where a construction crew is breaking ground for a low-rise affordable-housing complex. You are walking with the contractor, both of you wearing bright orange hard hats, leading a phalanx of reporters. Really, the phalanx is one longhaired photographer and a beat reporter from the city paper with coffee stains on his shirt.

You are wondering when your father will call.

Later, you will be interviewed at a local television station with a blue bedsheet hanging behind you for background. You will talk about the new housing complex and the economic boon that it will be for your district. You will talk about your commitment to your constituents.

You will be forthright.

The reporter waddles up from behind you and says, "How much longer are we staying?"

On your other side, the contractor is still talking about his building plans. He does not seem to notice the interruption.

You give the reporter the medium smile with just a hint of teeth and incline your head toward him for increased intimacy and say, "Until you have what you need."

He snorts. "You think I need to walk around a goddamn parking lot to write this shit? I could have written it sitting on the toilet."

Your smile widens just a bit and you chuckle and give the reporter a look that tells him that you acknowledge the ridiculousness of the situation and that you regret any inconvenience it has caused him—you feel his *pain*—but that *simultaneously* you feel the grave burden of your responsibility to the people you represent. You are a servant of the people. You are the voice of the people.

You could tell him about Betty Friedkin, who is seventy-eight years old (a proud American senior, you would call her) and living on her Social Security and who has trusted you to stand up for her against those Washington fat cats; you could tell him about Jamir Winslow, twenty-nine-year-old African American father of four (*proud* African American father), who is worried about his recent trouble with the state police and wants you to get behind the new federal civil rights bill, which contains strong language against racial profiling, that the fat cats are trying to block; you could tell him about Angela Martinez (proud Latin American—no, you think, that's not quite right, but you don't like the sound of "Hispanic American" and you don't think you've ever heard "Latin American American," although it would seem to make sense—mother of an indeterminate number of children), who wants you to clean up the water and the air and the streets and television—also, you think she wants you to stand up to the fat cats in Washington, but you can't be sure because you've never actually met her. You haven't actually met *any* of these people, but you have been *fully* briefed. You've got your hand on the pulse. You are willing to go the extra mile.

You give one hundred and ten percent.

Wes has been talking to the longhaired photographer, but when he saw the reporter come up alongside you he crept forward so that now he is hovering just over your left shoulder. He says to the reporter, "All I'm thinking about is the single-malt I left in the car. I'm hoping we can kill it on the ride back."

The reporter smiles at him and fades back to walk beside the photographer.

You lean close to Wes and say, "Why aren't you wearing a hard hat?"

"They're just for the pictures," he whispers. He looks at the sky. You follow his eyes. He says, "They haven't started building. There's nothing to fall on you."

Wes is not a bodyguard, but he has a big semiautomatic pistol slung under his left arm. You are not sure that he would be able to use it if the moment arose. Still, you are comforted knowing it's there. Although you very rarely think about the possibility of assassination.

Theo, your security man, trails the group, not smiling. He looks like he could be distantly related to you.

You pass a drugstore on the way to the car. You shake hands with a few people who are wandering in or out. You clap some shoulders. A gray-haired man in a plaid shirt tells you that he met your father once.

"They don't make them like that anymore," the man says. "He'd always shoot you straight."

"Yes," you say.

The car is a black Lincoln Navigator. You have had a row of seats added where the trunk used to be. You have had the original backseat turned around so that the two rows face each other. You sit next to the reporter while the photographer sits across from you snapping pictures. Theo drives. Wes sits beside him, half turned, leaning on the back of his seat, listening to everything you say.

Today is Wednesday (you saw the front page of a newspaper on the rack outside the drugstore before you got into the car). In two weeks, you will be thirty years old. You have not slept in six days.

After the television interview, you lock yourself in a canary-yellow stall in the station's men's room and chew a small handful of pearl-colored Benzedrine tablets. You sit on the closed lid of the toilet and press your palms against your forehead. Your throat is raw.

You hear footsteps in the hallway. You hear the sigh of the air spring on top of the bathroom door and then the footsteps are inside the room. They scrape along the tiles. A shadow appears outside the door of your stall.

Wes's voice says, "You all right?"

You are silent.

Wes says, "Maybe you ought to lie down for a while."

You look up at the closed door. You listen to Wes breathing.

He says, "I have something for you."

The outlines of the door are very clear.

You say, "Any good?"

"Do I ever let you down?"

You smile slightly. "Where is she?"

"In the hallway."

You groan. "I don't know if I can stand up."

"Don't worry," Wes says. "I'll bring her."

The shadow disappears and you hear the footsteps again and the sigh of the door and then the footsteps are in the hallway, getting softer. The footsteps stop and after a few seconds they are replaced by the harsh clacking of high heels. You reach out and unlock the stall door and listen to the high heels clattering into the room.

The girl who pushes open the door of your stall is dirty-blond and smooth-faced. She has wide hips and a narrow waist. She is wearing a gray skirt.

She says, "You were great."

You blink at her. "I haven't touched you."

"The interview."

"You saw it?"

"You were on after my weather report."

You frown. "I thought I knew the . . . ah . . . the meteorologist here."

She nods. "Veronica. She's in Peoria now. And I'm a weather girl."

"What?"

"I'm not a meteorologist."

"Right. Sorry about that."

"It doesn't matter." She smiles. "You know, since I got here I've wanted to meet you."

"I'm a rookie congressman. How do you even know who I am?"

"I like politics. Also, I've always been interested in your father."

"Oh."

She steps into the stall and closes the door behind her.

"What's your name?" you say. Your voice is hoarse.

"Annie."

She reaches behind her and slides the bolt.

You say, "It's good to meet you, Annie." You have to stop yourself from moving to shake her hand.

She says, "Just relax."

She kneels in front of you and smooths her skirt over her thighs and you lean your head back against the wall over the toilet. She is unzipping your fly and you think about speaking on the Senate floor and the way you'll thunder and the way you'll look on television (although it'll mostly be C-Span). You try to imagine what it is you'll be thundering about, but Annie has pulled your pants down low on your hips. She is unbuttoning the fly of your boxer shorts and now you can see yourself in the Rose Garden and you can see yourself in the White House press room, looking stern (the commentators will say that you have gravitas), and you can see yourself during the State of the Union getting a standing ovation from the *entire* audience (*both sides* of the aisle, *across* party lines—you are a *uniter*). You can see a black-and-white photograph of yourself as you stare out the window of the Oval Office, dressed in your shirtsleeves, contemplative, concerned, stoic. Annie has opened the fly of your boxer shorts and reached in and pulled you out and you watch her head begin to bob up and down. And then you don't think about anything at all.

You are at a horseshoe-shaped booth at the back of the diner and Wes is funneling people toward you a few at a time. You are using the medium smile with open mouth. You had your teeth whitened at the beginning of the campaign season.

Every time you shake, you grip the top of the other person's forearm with your left hand. You are giving casual intimacy. You are jovial. You have seven jokes that you are telling in sequence. Three of them are self-deprecating. (These show that your power has not gone to your head.) Four of them are about the president. (These show that you cannot be intimidated.) You have two dirty jokes that you do not tell as part of the sequence. You tell these only to old white men. You lean close to them and whisper. Sometimes, after the punch line, you slap the men lightly on the chest with the back of your hand.

You say, "I'm running for reelection as your representative in Congress. I want to go on fighting for you against the special interests and the Washington fat cats. I sure would appreciate your support."

You like this last sentence. It sounds like something your father would say.

The Benzedrine is washing over you in waves. Your eyes are wide open. You imagine that you can hear lobster-shaped microbes crawling through the fluid in your brain.

You watch the pink glow of the sunset through the long windows at the front of the room.

Wes comes over to the booth and says, "That's enough."

"Are we leaving?"

He nods. "We're taking the act out into the street. We'll catch some of the rush-hour crowd."

Wes nods to Theo, who has been standing in the corner watching your table. Theo pulls himself off the wall and leads you out. You wave at everyone who looks at you as you walk to the door. You shake hands with the people who are close enough.

Wes whispers, "Harrison."

You say loudly to the man behind the counter, "Mr. Harrison, I wish you'd give me the recipe for that apple pie. The wife keeps asking for it."

Harrison, who has a pasty-white bald head dotted with liver spots, smiles and shakes his head. "Trade secret."

You look at the people around you and say, "Looks like I'm sleeping on the couch tonight."

There is laughter. At the door, you turn back toward the room and give thumbs-up with your right hand held high above your head (thumbs-up with your hand held low is a cliché). You keep your arm slightly bent to make the gesture less formal.

On the street, you use the high-intensity smile. You do a lot of waving. People stream past you. Wes talks to the people who are waiting to talk to you. Wes is also using the high-intensity smile.

A woman with deep wrinkles creasing her cheeks, hair bleached blond, says that she never heard your father tell a lie.

"He was genuine," she says.

"Yes," you say.

"He could charm the panties off a nun." She laughs. It sounds like choking. "He was honest, though. An honest man."

She moves past you down the street.

During a lull, when the three of you are alone, Theo says, "Green jacket."

"What about him?" Wes says.

"He hasn't moved since we came out here. He keeps trying not to let me catch him looking at us."

"What do you think?"

"Don't know yet."

You glance at the man they're talking about. He is dressed in a fatigue jacket. He is probably in his mid-forties (proud forty-year-old American veteran). He is leaning against the side of a Laundromat on the opposite sidewalk. While you are watching, a girl in a tight gray skirt suit passes the Laundromat. Her hair is brown and flows around her face. You watch her as she moves down the street.

"You see that?" Theo says.

"The girl?" Wes says.

"He didn't look at her."

"Maybe he's a fag."

"Homosexual," you say automatically.

Theo nods, not looking away from the man in the green jacket. "Maybe."

"Homosexual American," you mutter. "*Proud* homosexual American veteran."

Theo says, "Start going for the car. Don't rush."

Wes puts a hand on your back to guide you. Theo keeps his body between you and the man across the street. You are still waving. Your smile does not falter.

Green Jacket is moving. He is walking parallel to you on the opposite sidewalk.

Wes says, "Can we make the car?"

"Maybe," Theo says.

When Green Jacket begins to cross the street, you are not more than fifty feet from the Navigator.

Theo says, "Go."

Wes takes hold of the back of your suit and starts running, pushing you in front of him. You look over your shoulder and watch Theo move to intercept Green Jacket. They come together in the center of the street. Theo grabs the man's wrist and spins him around. Theo kicks out Green Jacket's legs and knocks him facedown onto the pavement and falls on top of him. People on the sidewalk have stopped to

observe the action. Some of them watch Wes hustle you past
them.

As Wes opens the sliding door of the Navigator and shoves
you in, you give the bent-arm thumbs-up. The sky is dark.

Through the tinted back window, you watch Theo stand
and pick Green Jacket up from the asphalt. Green Jacket
looks angry. He is yelling. Theo says something to him. He
stops yelling and turns to walk away. The onlookers begin
moving again.

"Shit," Wes says.

"You'd rather it was a hit?"

He shrugs. "It would have gotten us some press."

Theo opens the driver's door and slips in behind the wheel.
He starts the engine and pulls away from the curb. He says,
"Guy was planning to spit on you."

Wes says, "You frisk him?"

Theo glances at him. "Of course." He turns back to the
road. "He was clean."

"He gonna sue us?" Wes says.

"Doubtful."

"Why doubtful?"

Theo shrugs. "He doesn't even know who we are."

"What the fuck are you *talking* about? You just said he
was ready to spit on us."

"On *him*," Theo says, jerking his head back at you. "But
he doesn't know who he is. Just figures he's *somebody*."

"Jesus Christ."

"Guy's a fuckin' loony tune, you ask me. Plus he was shit-
faced. At *least*. Probably won't even remember it in the
morning."

"Homeless?"

"We didn't get that far, but it wouldn't surprise me."

Wes shakes his head. "Sooner or later, every wack job
wants to be Oswald."

You say, "Doesn't he know about my antipoverty
program?"

"He didn't seem too enfranchised."

You shrug. "At least we won't be losing his vote."

Wes says, "We need to get you some sleep."

You imagine tiny decomposers devouring the old skin cells on Wes's face. If you watch him long enough without looking away, you can see him gradually dying.

Y our wife is sitting on the sofa in the living room when you get home. She is reading a newspaper. She does not look up at you. You cross the room and lean down and kiss the cold skin of her cheek.

She says, "Your father's coming over."

"Jesus," you say. "Tonight?"

She nods. "He called an hour ago."

"Why didn't you call the cell phone?"

"I didn't want to interrupt. Besides, I was getting the house picked up."

"Where's Ashley?"

"In her room. Maria's getting her ready." She looks up at you now. "How was it?" She has her hair tucked behind her ears. She is wearing a green skirt and a white V-neck sweater. She looks like she has no pores in her face. She photographs extremely well.

You take a deep breath. Then you give her the medium smile with the left corner of your mouth curled up, which she finds charming. She smiles back at you. You bend down and kiss her on the mouth. You give her the open-lipped kiss with no tongue.

She says, "You look tired. I thought you only had to go this hard the first time. Doesn't the incumbent get to rest?"

You say, "The more I win by this time, the more attractive it makes me as a Senate candidate two years from now. That's what we're campaigning for."

"Is it really going to happen?"

"Yes. Are you ready for it?"

"I was born for it."

"That's true."

She folds the newspaper and lays it down next to her and stands up. "I'm going to put on some perfume." She walks out of the room. Her walk is graceful and elegant and sexy enough to be feminine but gives no hint of her ever taking her clothes off or of there being anything between her legs or of the sounds she makes when you run your tongue around her nipples.

The Benzedrine is wearing off. The speed crash is making your body feel unbearably heavy. You walk as though you're underwater.

You call the cell phone from the phone in the hallway. Wes picks up on the second ring.

"My father's on his way over here," you say.

"He going to endorse us?"

"I don't know. I didn't talk to him."

Wes pauses. "Is something wrong?"

You hold the receiver in your right hand and use the index and middle fingers of your left hand to pinch the bridge of your nose. "I'm just a little worn out."

He says, "I'll be back there in two minutes."

"No," you say. "It's better if it's just the two of us."

Your father says, "You look like shit."

"Thanks, Pop."

"Are you sleeping?"

You shrug.

You are standing in the oak-doored vestibule of your house. Your father is on the stone porch at the top of the stone steps. His bodyguards are standing at the bottom of the steps next to a black Mercedes sedan.

Your father is thick-lipped and taller than you. His shoulders are very wide. He is wearing a tan raincoat and a brown fedora that covers his bald spot.

You say, "Aren't you going to come in?"

He slides past you into the house. In the entrance hall, your wife is standing with your daughter, Ashley, both of them facing the door and giving the high-medium smile with teeth.

You lock the door. You close your eyes and wait for the dizziness to pass.

When you come into the entrance hall, your father is leaning down toward Ashley.

"Put your hand out," he is saying.

She does.

He reaches into his coat and brings out his key ring and hands it to her. "There you go," he says.

Ashley giggles. She is wearing a flowered dress and white stockings and black shoes with gold buckles. She has blond hair and brown eyes.

He frowns. "Isn't that what you wanted?"

Ashley shakes her head.

He takes the keys back from her. He straightens up and makes a big show of patting his various pockets. "I don't know what else I can give you." He reaches into his coat again. "The only other things I have are these." He brings out a handful of caramels wrapped in gold paper.

Ashley claps.

"You want *these*?"

She nods.

"How old are you now?" your father asks her.

"Almost five."

"How close?"

She stares at her hands for a few seconds, her mouth moving. Then she turns and whispers loudly to your wife, "Mommy, how long until I'm five?"

"Two months," your wife says.

Ashley turns back to your father. "Two months."

He scowls. "Well, I guess we'll give it to you. Put your hand out."

He crouches down again and counts five caramels into her hand and puts the rest into his pocket.

"What do you say?" your wife says.

"Thank you, Grampa," Ashley says. "I love you." She kisses him on the cheek. He hugs her.

He stands up and hugs your wife. He kisses her on the cheek.

"I'm glad to see you," she says. She looks down at Ashley. "Time to say good night."

Ashley shakes her head. The high-medium smile has disappeared.

Your wife says, "Don't make your grandfather think you don't have any manners."

Ashley shakes her head again.

You say, "Getting enough sleep is important, especially for little girls. I knew a girl in high school named Emily Thomas who never slept more than four hours a night. She had to drop out. Now she's got three kids and no husband. She's a drain on our country's overextended welfare system. With these new fat-cat welfare-reform bills she may lose her only source of income."

They are all staring at you.

You say, "We don't need any more Emily Thomases."

Your father turns back to Ashley and says, "I thought you were almost five. Five-year-olds don't throw tantrums when it's time for bed."

She nods.

"Maria," your wife calls over her shoulder.

Maria appears wearing blue jeans and a gray sweater.

Your wife says, "Bedtime."

Your father says, "Good to see you again, Maria."

Maria says, "It's good to see you again, Governor."

"I'm not the governor anymore."

She frowns. "I thought you kept the title for life."

"You do, but it's a little embarrassing. It's like a woman keeping her husband's name after they're divorced."

Maria smiles. She takes hold of Ashley's hand and they walk to the stairs.

Your wife says, "I'm going to bed also."

She kisses your father again.

"They're dropping like flies," he says.

When the two of you are alone, you say, "Should we sit down?"

He shakes his head. "I'm not staying."

You give him the medium smile. "All business."

"Shouldn't I be?"

You shrug. "I am."

He nods. "Why didn't you ask for my endorsement last time?"

"I wanted to break in on my own."

"And now that you're in, all the pride is gone?"

Your eyelids are sagging. "It seems more expedient this way."

He says, "I liked that you wanted to do it by yourself. I respected your not wanting me to campaign for you. I respected your not wanting me to pay for your school."

"I don't care about respect anymore."

"What's happening to you?"

You look into his eyes. You are earnest and determined. Your head feels packed in cotton. You say, "My dreams are coming true."

Your father looks at you for a long moment. "I'm sorry," he says.

When he's gone, you sit on the bright white tile floor of your bathroom feeling your stomach churn. You listen to the buzzing of the fluorescent light over the sink. You wonder whether you should have spent some time in the army.

You kneel in front of the toilet and feel the nausea all over you, but you do not vomit. You grip the black porcelain sides of the bowl and stare at your reflection in the water. Your face is blurred by tiny ripples. You have dark purple fatigue bruises under your eyes. Your skin is pale. Still, you recognize the face. This surprises you somehow.

Behind you, in the hallway outside the bathroom, the wooden floor is creaking. The creaking comes closer and closer and then stops and you hear the muted slaps of bare feet on the bathroom tile. Then the footsteps stop and there is only the hum of the lightbulb.

Your wife says, "Aren't you coming to bed?"

You can imagine her face—mouth closed, eyebrows drawn together with concern, eyes wide with urgency and love. In the outside corner of one of her eyes, there might even be the beginnings of a tear.

You do not turn around. "Soon," you say.

"Please come with me."

You can imagine her eyes closing with sadness.

"Soon," you say again.

"At least look at me," she says. She is using the loving tone with a hint of pleading.

You close the lid of the toilet in front of you. You take a deep breath and push yourself up with your arms and turn around and sit on the closed lid.

Your wife is dressed in her white nightgown. The curves of her body make gray shadows in the fabric. Her face is almost as you pictured it, although she is using sadder eyes than you imagined. As soon as you are looking at her, she allows one of the tears to trickle out and along her cheekbone and past the corner of her mouth.

"I love you," she says. She sighs. Her cheeks draw up toward her forehead and she makes more tears that collect at the bottoms of her eyes, ready to spill.

You frown. You say, "Careful not to give too much too soon. Always try for the slow build. Also, it's better to err on the side of understatement."

She sniffs. "What?"

"Real emotion makes people nervous. It's important to reflect quiet calm. Ideally, you should be sitting down behind a big desk. It makes you look powerful but stable. It's vital to stay placid. Passion is too Mussolini."

She is silent.

"We've talked about this," you say.

"I know," she says. She pushes out a few more tears that leave wet streaks on her face.

"If you weren't ready for this, you should have said something earlier."

She is really pouring on the tears now. "But I thought things would still be the same between *us.*"

You spread your arms wide and give her the welcoming smile. "They are," you say.

BLUE
YONDER

The girl sat at one of the outdoor tables with a much younger girl who looked like her in miniature. They both had blond hair and enormous round eyes. The little girl wore a flowered sundress and sat as tall as she could, straining upward, her chin barely clearing the tabletop. The older girl wore a white blouse and high-heeled sandals and a black skirt that hung below her knees. She sat leaning forward, with her elbows on the table and one soft, smooth, tanned calf draped over the other. Her hair was gathered in back and held together with a silver clip. Her sunglasses had tortoise-shell frames and she wore them pushed back high on her forehead.

When the waiter brought my coffee, I motioned him close to me and said, "Do you know that girl?"

The waiter, whose name was Ricky and who spoke English with extreme care, said, "No, mister."

"She's never been here before?"

"No, mister," Ricky said. "I have not seen her."

I nodded. "Tell me your real name, Ricky."

"You don't want to know."

"Tell me anyway."

He told me.

"You're right," I said.

He smiled. "Will you eat?"

I shook my head and he took away my menu.

I did not want to be caught watching the girls, so I only glanced at them occasionally and the rest of the time I watched the people moving into the Public Garden. The sky was steel blue and cloudless. The street was all couples and families, and businessmen who walked side by side very fast. There was a group of boys trying to climb the statue of Washington. Washington sat rigid in his saddle while the boys grabbed at his boots and at the horse's neck.

The older girl was speaking on a cell phone now and I stared at her for a while and then I forced myself to turn back to the park and I noticed Lucien walking on the other side of the street. He was whistling in that nervous way he had and, although I couldn't hear it, I thought that the tune was probably from *Threepenny Opera* because that was almost always what he whistled. When he saw me, he stopped whistling and dashed across the lanes of traffic, between the speeding cars.

"Mr. Tolstoy, I presume," he said when he reached me, his chest heaving.

"Mr. De Quincey," I said.

He frowned. "No, no. All wrong. I haven't had any opium since I was seventeen and even then I could take it or leave it. Also, he was never a painter."

"Sorry," I said. "Short notice."

He flopped into the chair across from me.

"Mr. Basquiat would be better. Or perhaps Mr. Cézanne."

"They certainly would be."

Ricky appeared beside us. "It has been a long time, Mr. Lucien," he said.

Lucien smiled and spoke to him in French.

"Only English, please," Ricky said.

"You'll get rusty," Lucien warned him.

"No one speaks French back home," Ricky said. "Only the government."

Lucien shrugged. "I'll have an espresso then, Ricky—or is that too much Italian for you?"

"Don't be angry, Mr. Lucien. I'm only trying to improve myself."

"I know. I'm sorry, Ricky, I shouldn't be that way. Bring me an espresso, please."

Ricky walked back inside. Lucien said, "Are you working?"

"Some," I told him.

"I have been finding excuses to stay away from the studio. I despise it."

"The studio or finding the excuses?"

"Both."

Far down the street, a construction crew was repaving part of the sidewalk. The men in the crew wore orange vests. Their trucks poured gray exhaust. We could hear the faint, high-pitched beeps that the cement mixer made as it was backed into position, its cylinder turning lazily.

"In with the new," Lucien said.

Ricky brought Lucien's espresso and disappeared again.

"When did you leave the hospital?"

He smiled. "You've been thinking about how to ask me."

"Yes."

"You shouldn't worry so much. It ages you."

"You were released?"

"It's voluntary, anyway," he said.

"I thought it was only voluntary checking in."

"If your money's the right color, anything you do is voluntary."

"That's bullshit," I said.

He waved his hand dismissively. "Whatever it is, there's no point talking about it."

I looked at him for a while, not saying anything, and then he reached into his shirt and brought out a long, cream-colored cigarette.

I shook my head. "Can't do that here."

"I forgot," he said, and put the cigarette back inside his shirt. He sighed. "This really is a terrible city."

"Why are you here?" I asked him.

"Are we philosophers now?" he said.

I stared at him.

He shook his head. "So serious," he said. "You mean, why am I here and not in New York?"

"I mean, if you're leaving the hospital why come back *here*?"

"Too much New York. Even a month is too much. Also, there are no artists here."

"There are some."

"Some," he agreed. "But you can avoid them." He sipped at his espresso. "Why are *you* here?"

"Where would I go?" I took a deep breath. "So why no artists?"

He shrugged. "It seems lately as though the world is full of talentless men who suffer all the responsibility of possessing a really major talent."

"Why do you care about the deluded?"

"Because there is no difference between the way they think about what they do and the way I think about what I do."

"So?"

"So what is there to separate me from them?"

"The work."

He smiled without meaning it. "But I am judging my work and they are judging theirs and we are coming to the same conclusions and what if I am one of the deluded and everyone is laughing behind my back."

"No one's laughing."

"I used to think that if you knew when you woke up every morning that you were supposed to do a certain thing and you thought that you could be great at it then you *could* be great at it. But it isn't true."

"No," I agreed.

"Well, I don't want to wake up one day when I'm fifty and realize that I'm only a decent painter."

"There are worse things to be than a decent painter."

"Not if you are a decent painter who thought he was going to be a great painter." He looked at the sky. "I won't be a failure."

He lowered his eyes. "I had to agree to work with a doctor here," he said. "I mean, for them to let me leave I had to let them palm me off on somebody."

"You don't have to talk about it."

He put up his hand to stop me. "I gave you as my emergency contact. I hope that's all right. You're the only person I know who's still here."

"You know plenty of people."

"I am *acquainted* with plenty of people. I barely *know* anyone."

"Of course it's all right," I said.

"Jack," he said, "tell me I'm going to be a great painter."

"You will."

He grinned. "I wonder whether you would lie to me if we were talking about writing."

I drank some of my coffee, which was cool now, and looked at Washington. Lucien sipped at his espresso again and put it down and looked around and that was when he noticed the girls for the first time. He looked back at me.

"You see this?" he said.

"Since before you got here."

"What have you been doing about it?"

I shrugged. "I get too nervous talking to women I don't know. Especially when they look like that."

"My God," he said. "How old are you now?"

"Twenty-four."

He sighed. "You're squandering your youth."

"I don't think you have the right to talk about my youth. You're not even six months older than me."

He smiled. "But I am an old man."

"Well, why don't you gather yourself then—while you still may—and go over?"

"No," he said. "Why don't *we* go over?"

The girls were more beautiful the closer we got. When we reached their table, they looked up at us with their immense eyes and for a moment I could see nothing but the eyes of the older one and the way a few loose strands of her hair hung forward into her face. My heart was beating fast, as I had known it would, and I was afraid to speak because I wasn't sure whether I could catch my breath.

Then Lucien said, to the little girl, "Excuse me, madam, but you appear to have something in your ear."

The girls stared at him.

"Allow me," he said and reached behind the little one's head and when he pulled his hand back he was holding a quarter.

"I believe this is yours," he said to her.

She held out her palm and he dropped the coin into it.

"Very nice," the older girl said.

Lucien shook his head. "That's nothing. Now, if you want to see *real* talent—" He reached behind the little girl's head again and again brought out a quarter, but this time he put it in his mouth and bit down on it and then he was holding half a quarter with jagged teeth marks along its edge. The girls looked on, openmouthed. Lucien blew hard on the torn quarter in his hand and then suddenly it was whole again. The little girl gasped. The older girl applauded.

"Will you sit down?" she said.

I pulled over two chairs from the neighboring table and we sat. We introduced ourselves.

Kate, the older girl, said, "Where did you learn that?"

Lucien shrugged. "Around."

The little girl, whose name was Nina, looked at Lucien and said, "Where are you from?"

He smiled. "Where do you think I'm from?"

She frowned. "England?"

"Close," he said. "I'm from Denmark. Do you know where that is?"

She shook her head.

"Why aren't you tall and blond and pale?" Kate asked him.

"Good genes."

"You don't have much of an accent."

"I have enough," he said.

"So, how do you know each other?"

"We went to school together."

"Where?"

He told her.

"So," she said, "are you bankers or lawyers or trying to rule the world?"

"Trying to *make* the world."

"Lucien's a painter," I said.

"Is he good?" she asked me.

"He is good," I said.

"Jack is a writer," Lucien told her, "and even if you never see him again, you'll tell your grandchildren about the day you met him."

She looked at me.

Ricky came over and we ordered another round. The girls were both drinking orange juice.

"So," Lucien said, "are you two sisters?"

"I'm her aunt," Kate said.

Lucien watched the cars as they passed and said, "Don't they sound like the ocean?"

"What do you mean?" Kate asked him.

"The tires," he said.

"I thought painters were supposed to *see* differently," I said, "not *hear* differently."

"It just occurred to me," he said.

"I think I see what you mean," Kate told him.

The crew was finished with the sidewalk and had moved into the street. The cement mixer had been pulled away and replaced by a dump truck that was pouring hot tar. The men were spreading the tar before the paving truck came through with its enormous roller.

Nina tugged at my shirt. "Are you strong?" she asked me.

"Why?" I said.

"You look strong."

"So do you."

She nodded vigorously. "I am. I can even beat most of the boys in my grade at arm wrestling."

"Well, then, I know who to call when somebody's giving me a hard time."

She giggled.

"So what have you been doing this afternoon?" I asked her.

"We were shopping with my mother but she was taking too long."

"Is she meeting you here?" Lucien asked.

"No," Kate said. "We're spending the afternoon together."

"We should all go somewhere."

She smiled. "Where should we go?"

"I don't know," he said. "Where do people go?"

"We could ride the swan boats," I said.

"Wonderful," Lucien said. "*That's* what people do. I just don't have a sense of them lately. I'm only doing abstracts and landscapes now; no more portraits."

Nina turned to her aunt and said, "Can we?"

"I suppose so," Kate said.

We signaled to Ricky for the check.

"If I *were* painting portraits," Lucien said to the girls, "I would use both of you as subjects." They smiled. "And Jack, too," he said, turning to me. "Of course, Jack. It should be against the law for someone to be so talented *and* look like that. God ought to choose one gift or the other."

"It doesn't bother *me*," Kate said.

Lucien smiled. His eyes were bright. "You know," he said, "maybe it would be better if just the three of you went. There are some things I really should get done."

He stood.

"Are you sure?" I said.

"Sure, sure." He ran two fingers around the tiny bald spot on the back of his head. "You know, when my hair starts really thinning I'm going to shave it all off. I hope I won't look like a cancer patient." He clapped a hand on my shoulder. "Value your youth, young Tolstoy."

He kissed each of the girls on the hand and saluted us and then walked down the street in the same direction he had been heading when he had first seen me. We were quiet as we watched him get smaller and smaller and pass the construction site where the new-poured tar was flat and steaming. He turned the corner and passed out of sight and that was the last time I saw him until the night I was called to identify him. And when the sheet was pulled back I could hardly recognize him because of what the pistol had done when he fired it inside his mouth.

We stayed at the table for a while before we went to the swan boats. We laughed about things I can't remember. Kate kept touching my forearm. We listened to cars that sounded like the ocean.

THE DEATH OF COOL

Any of the people you pass on the street could pretend to trip and stumble into you and sorry sorry my mistake pour a glass full of cyanide onto your bare forearm. They could push you into traffic. They could swerve their cars into you. They could pull out a nine-millimeter Browning automatic or a snub-nosed thirty-eight or a twelve-gauge Remington shotgun with the buttstock filed down and the barrel chopped to let it fit inside a holster and do you wild wild West. They could shoulder you inside the sliding door of a waiting van and take you blindfolded to an abandoned warehouse and lock you in a coffin full of rats.

From the roof of any skyscraper, someone could be sprinkling pennies that the acceleration during the drop will turn into bullets raining on the sidewalk. Someone could smash a jar of hantavirus on the tracks at one of the downtown subway stops and let the trains carry the death from station to station. Any of the people stepping onto the bus you're riding could have bricks of plastic explosive taped to their chest. They could have covered the explosive with nails and bolts for shrapnel.

You are at their mercy. You are alive because they want

you alive or because they do not care whether you live or because they do not notice you.

You walk with your eyes down. You try to stay under the radar.

You depend on the kindness of strangers.

I lock my door. I take a breath. I speed-walk along the hallway of my building and almost make the stairs before I have to turn around. Back outside my apartment, I check the door and then sprint away from it toward the stairway and this time I get as far as the second-floor landing. I go back and check the door again. I rattle the knob so that I hear the bolt clicking against the inside of the locking mechanism. I take another breath.

I say to the empty hallway, "It's locked."

I go through versions of this routine every morning. You can never be too careful.

I hit the street and start walking.

Any time you slide into the backseat of a taxi, the driver could seal the doors and windows with a button on the dash and trap you inside a Plexiglas cage. After that, you're his. He could pump in chlorine gas through vents in the floor. He could take you to a car compactor. He could point you at the harbor and use a rock to hold down the accelerator. He could let in thousands of inch-long driver ants that would take less than fifteen minutes to strip all your flesh and turn you into a pile of dry white bones.

Public transportation is even worse.

Three days ago, the man waiting next to me on the subway platform got pushed in front of the train. He ended up facing me. The side of the train had pinned him against the side of the platform. Most of his upper body was sticking out of the gap.

The train doors were still closed. Passengers were crammed against all the windows, trying to see what had happened. I thought how strange it was, given the nature of my work and how many dead bodies I'd seen, that I'd never actually watched anyone die.

Then the man blinked.

My mouth opened. No sound came out.

The man said, "It doesn't hurt."

I knelt down beside him.

"I know I'm dying," he said.

A wide-eyed transit cop appeared above us.

The man said, "There's so much to do."

The transit cop said, "Do you have any family we can call?"

The man was silent.

My eyes burned. I said, "You don't have anything to worry about. Obviously, they'll receive the accidental death and dismemberment bonus."

The transit cop said, "If you tell us how to reach them, we can bring them here to say good-bye."

My vision blurred. I said, "If they can show you were on your way to work, they may have a claim on the benefit for death due to homicide while the policyholder is actively engaged in his or her employment. Generally, it's intended for soldiers and policemen, but there's a case pending in Nevada that's trying to get the morning commute included under the legal definition of the workday. They'll want to watch for that decision."

The man was looking around frantically. Now all he kept saying was, "Did anyone see who pushed me?"

I said, "Of course, if they could get this classified as business travel they'd make out like bandits. I admit that's kind of a long shot."

Another cop appeared. He was taller than the transit cop. He had thick pink forearms.

The big cop said, "I have a couple witnesses who say they got a pretty good look at the guy."

The man's eyes widened. "What was he like? Was he tall?

Was he thin? What was he wearing? Did he have a mustache?" He lowered his voice. "Was he black?"

The cop sighed. "Seems like he was just some homeless guy. Some nobody."

"But he can't be," the man said. "He *can't* be."

The EMTs arrived. One of them gave the man a sedative and the cop motioned me away.

"Did you see anything?" he asked.

"I just felt him get shoved past me and then someone started screaming."

"Doesn't matter. I'm sure you wouldn't have recognized the guy." He shook his head. "Must be weird knowing you got killed by someone nobody knows."

"There's no chance he'll make it?"

He shook his head again. "He's all smashed up and twisted around under there. The train's holding his guts in. As soon as we pull it away, his organs will all whoosh out. I've seen it before. It happens sometimes with the push victims. They're trying to stop their momentum so they fall closer to the platform. Every so often they get stuck. The suicides usually jump out pretty far and the impact breaks them like an egg."

I grind my teeth against my tongue. "So if we just left the train there and closed the station we could keep him alive indefinitely. But we're going to let him die so as not to delay rush hour."

The cop stared at me. "He can't live like that for more than a few hours. And it's important to end it before the shock wears off."

My hands were shaking. I couldn't stop them. "So he's finished."

The cop nodded. "Whenever I ride the train, I make sure to stand against the wall while it pulls in. I don't let anybody get behind me." He frowned. "Of course, that doesn't protect you from a bomber or some loony who wants to stick an ice pick in your throat. But I guess you can't worry about *everything*."

• • •

My office is on the fifty-fifth floor and for the last few days, since that morning in the subway, I have been taking the stairs. There's no limit to what they could do to your elevator.

I step out of the stairwell, and after nine hundred seventy-two eight-inch risers I'm barely even sweating. Your best weapon is your physical condition. An army is only as good as its feet. Even before a few days ago, I would never have let myself go.

The receptionist smiles as I pass her. She has curly brown hair and enormous breasts that don't sag. A few years ago, when I was still in college, I would have taken her home and dripped maple syrup all over her and stroked her belly button with a feather. Now, before I did that I would have to perform a full background check—call the IRS, lift her fingerprints from the phone receiver and run them through the FBI database. If the only things you know about somebody are what they've told you, then you don't know anything.

My boss is half-sitting on my desk, sipping his coffee. I never drink coffee. An army marches on its stomach.

My phone is ringing. My boss picks it up. "Claims," he says.

He listens. Then he says, "You want Sales. It's three-five-eight-oh . . . Same exchange . . . That's right."

He puts the phone down and looks at me. "Did you walk up again?"

I don't say anything.

He sighs. "Didn't we have this conversation yesterday?"

"It's not like the stairs are so much better. Someone could always just block the fire doors and drop in a handful of nerve-gas pellets."

"I'm not sure I understand."

"Someone could place charges that would destroy the support structure and send you plummeting all the way down through parking levels and sub-basements until you melt against the damp cement floor at the bottom."

"But what are the *chances* of that?"

"Not too high," I say. "But they exist. Last year, triggered stairway collapses were responsible for fifty percent of homicides by indoor dropping."

"Those are just numbers."

"Life is numbers."

He nods. "But in order to get *through* life, you need to accept small possibilities of catastrophe. That's risk management."

"What about risk elimination?"

"There's no such thing." He frowns. "I suppose you could shut yourself in your apartment and have someone slide your food under the door."

"I've thought of that," I tell him. "You'd still have to worry about poison in the food and about rocket attacks or aerial bombardment. Besides, what's the point of living unless you can find a way to be in the world? I'm not going to let them close me out of my life."

"Who?" he says.

"But I'm also not a sap. I'm not going to ride their goddamn *elevator*." I move closer to him. "You know that old myth about jumping just before the thing hits? It's bullshit."

He stares at me.

"For one thing, how would you know the right moment to jump? Even if there were windows, the timing would be almost impossible. Also, in a frictionless system the elevator would be falling at exactly the same rate you are. You wouldn't be able to generate any force against the floor. And even if you managed to jump, you'd probably just smack against the ceiling and then ping-pong around while the whole thing collapses from the impact and crushes you. It wouldn't do you much good."

My boss stands up off of my desk. He shakes his head. "Have it your way," he says.

• • •

rina Christina Molesky, widow of recently deceased policyholder Alexander I. Molesky, sole beneficiary of a term-life package with an after-tax value approaching three and a half million dollars, does not offer me anything to eat. She doesn't have the Honduran housekeeper, who keeps flitting around us while we sit at the glass-topped kitchen table, brew me a cup of tea. She doesn't tell her to bring out a pitcher of ice water.

Instead she says, "I already told everything to police."

"I understand that," I say.

"Now I have to tell everything again."

"Your husband had an abnormal amount of insurance for a man of his age and medical history. That, coupled with the nature of his death, raises a red flag."

"I do not see red flag."

"A suspicion."

"What suspicion?"

Alexander Molesky, thirty-eight-year-old male nonsmoker with a benign preexisting respiratory condition caused by prolonged childhood exposure to coal dust while working in mines in the Ukraine, father of two, had been president and cofounder of the Mad Russians Car Repair and Limousine Service as well as co-owner of an electronics store, a road-paving company and two junk and demolition yards until Saturday night, when he was found facedown in a gravel parking lot with a plastic bag over his head and both his thumbs missing. The total of his annual life insurance premiums had been twenty-seven thousand dollars.

I'm keeping close track of the maid with my peripheral vision because as soon as I look away she might dash forward and hit me with a syringe full of Dilaudid. They would let me flail around for a while until I passed out. Then they would drag me over to the oven. They would remove the racks. They would wrestle me inside and lock the door and set the dial to Self-Clean.

I say, "It's a long-standing principle of common law that

no one will be permitted to take advantage of his or her own iniquity."

"I am not seeing you."

"It's my job to make sure no one benefits from doing wrong."

She is biting her lip. "Why you're telling me this?"

I take a breath. "Any potential beneficiary who intentionally causes the death of the decedent will be denied the insurance to which he or she might otherwise be entitled."

"You think I murder my husband?"

I shrug. "Twelve percent of male homicide victims in the United States last year were murdered by or at the behest of their wives or domestic partners."

She stares at me.

I say, "For women that number is more like seventy-eight percent."

Her eyes leak tiny tears.

"This isn't personal," I tell her. "Look at the numbers."

"Numbers say I kill my husband?"

"Not necessarily. But you *could* have."

It's not the dying that bothers me. Everybody does that and, mostly, it's not as bad as you think. Some people just drop dead. (This is usually attributed to SCF, sudden cardiac failure, which accounted for 48.7 percent of last year's heart-disease deaths.) But when you're murdered, another person has become your God. They have forced you to bow down to them. And you'll never get even.

Maybe your waitress has ground up glass into your orange juice. Maybe your roommate will toss a plugged-in toaster into the bath with you. Maybe your wife has pumped up the water pressure in your house so when you turn the knob the showerhead howitzers through your skull. She'll fuck your best friend on the floor of your living room, rolling around on piles of money from your annuity payments. She'll spread rumors about you and talk about how she loved you in spite of your shortcomings.

She'll laugh.

I meet Sadie in the lobby of the Four Seasons and, as far as I can tell, I wasn't followed. During the walk over, I doubled back on my route twice. I boarded a city bus and, just as the doors were about to close, I jumped back down to the sidewalk. I went inside a Japanese restaurant and then darted through the swinging door into the kitchen and past white-jacketed sushi chefs who didn't even have time to turn around before I was through the emergency exit and out into an alley.

Sadie is wearing a short gray skirt. She has her sunglasses pushed up on top of her head. She is talking into a cell phone. When I reach her, she gives me a silent kiss and keeps talking into the phone. She smells like honey.

The bellhops stare at Sadie as they move around us. Hotel guests in chinos and short-sleeved polo shirts sneak peeks at her when their wives aren't watching. When we move into the bar, young lawyers with loosened ties glance over and then laugh together.

Any of them who wants her badly enough could follow me into the men's room and slide a three-inch blade into the space between the top of my spine and the bottom of my skull. If he used the right implement, the wound would hardly bleed. He could arrange me on one of the toilets with my feet on the floor and my pants around my ankles. Then he could lock the stall door and slither out through the gap at the bottom. No one would find me for hours.

We sit at a table near the door.

I say, "Somewhere in this room there's probably a guy who can outfight me. He could make me beg for my life."

Sadie looks up at me. "Let me call you back," she says into the phone.

I sweep my eyes around the room. "I'm tired of letting the law protect me. I'm tired of hiding behind the skirts of some cop. I'm tired of trusting in the other guy's morality." I shake my head. "There's no guarantee in that, anyway."

She gives me big eyes. "Baby," she says, "I don't know what you're talking about."

"I'm talking about self-reliance. I'm talking about the State of Nature. I'm talking about, if some guy can own me like that, how can you want me more than him?"

"I'm nervous about what this job is doing to you."

"You're supposed to love me, forsaking all others."

She takes a deep breath. "I think maybe it's time for a change."

"Either you're lying to me, or you're going against the order of things."

"Why don't you think about going to work for your father?"

"We talked about that," I say.

"You know you'll end up there sooner or later."

I am silent.

"Or, forget about your father," she says. "I'm sure one of your college friends would be happy to get you in at Goldman or Bear Stearns or Morgan."

"This isn't about where I *work*."

She takes a breath. "Is this because you're nervous about moving in with me?"

"I just want to know I can protect you."

She smiles. "That's sweet."

"Also, what if you're not who you say you are?"

"What?"

"I mean, obviously I've met your parents and I've seen where you allegedly grew up, but what if it's all a show? What if you're all just acting? What if everybody's in on it but me?"

Sadie's eyes are wet. She says, "There's something wrong with you."

"I used to have a dream where I was walking on a street somewhere and suddenly everyone turned toward me and started stalking me like zombies. The entire world was zombies, except for me. They were pouring out from everywhere to join the chase. I ducked down alleys. I raced through backyards and even through houses. At night, I broke into this skyscraper and hid under a desk on one of the high floors while helicopters shined spotlights in the windows."

"I think you need to talk to somebody."

I nod. "I think you might be right."

A waiter materializes to take our drink orders.

Monroe Grady says, "I hope you're not here about the Molesky thing. It's a gangland killing. A fucking infant could read this one."

I shake my head.

"What, then?" he says.

I don't say anything.

He sighs. "How long have we known each other?"

"A while," I tell him. "Four years?"

"And haven't I always shot you straight?"

"I think so."

"And don't you trust me?"

"That's an awfully complicated question."

He chews his bottom lip.

After a long time, I say, "I'm interested in learning how to defend myself."

"Those self-defense classes are mostly for girls."

"I'm looking for something . . . a little more serious."

He steeples his hands in front of him and taps his index fingers together. "How serious?"

"All the way."

We are at Monroe's desk in the middle of the homicide

unit, surrounded by cops who might all turn on me at once and throw me inside one of the soundproofed interrogation rooms. They could line the doors and windows with watertight tape and then flood the place. They could watch through the two-way mirror as the water rises and I start to panic. They could turn on the hidden microphones and listen to me drowning.

Monroe says, "Are you sure this isn't about the Molesky thing?"

"What do you mean?"

"I mean, are you here because you're worried about getting mixed up with those people?"

"Everybody's mixed up with everybody."

"But these Russian guys are dangerous."

"Everyone's dangerous. Besides, they're Ukrainian."

He rolls his eyes. "Whatever. It's all ex-KGB hardcases. They're worse than the Colombians."

I shrug.

"That doesn't worry you?"

"No more than anything else."

"Then I don't understand what you're asking me."

"I guess I'm looking for general rules."

"Safety rules?" he says. "Well, for one thing, you're always safer in a public place."

"But not *completely* safe."

He spreads his hands. "I don't know if completely safe is possible. You piss off the wrong guy and he decides to grease you no matter what the consequences to himself, there's not a lot to do."

"But you can make it hard on him."

"Sometimes the most you can do is give yourself a chance." He takes a breath. "But that's the rare case. Mostly, with a few simple precautions you give yourself the upper hand." He leans toward me. "First," he says, "be certain you're seeing all the angles. Once you know where the danger might come from, you can take steps to protect yourself. Always have an emergency plan."

I nod. "Well," I say, "I suppose the key is not to let them get control of you in the first place. Once they have you locked in the room and they start pumping the water, it's already too late."

He leans back away from me. "The water?"

I nod again. "Obviously it would be tough to smuggle anything through the metal detectors. It would be better to lift a service revolver from inside somebody's desk."

"Wait," he says. "I'm not following."

"You'd need to be set to go as soon as the situation starts to deteriorate. You'd have to get through the room as quickly as possible. Once you stopped moving, they would call the SWAT team and then you'd be forced to take hostages. After that, it's only a matter of time."

He is staring at me. "I think you may have misunderstood."

"You'd talk to the negotiator for a while and you'd make demands and he would stall and they would talk you out or wait you out or they'd decide you weren't going to crack and they'd roll flash-bang grenades in through the air vents and they'd make a three-point entry with assault-team members dressed in black jumpsuits. When they have resources like that," I say, "you can't afford to let them get coordinated."

Monroe is shaking his head. "You came here for my advice. My advice is just make sure you're aware of your surroundings. Be ready for anything."

"Don't be a victim," I murmur.

I used to sleep with an aluminum baseball bat beside my bed. Saturday afternoon, I replace it with a Smith & Wesson riot shotgun. I set the police lock on the front door. The police lock is an iron bar that sticks into a hole in the floor. To get past it, they'd need to take the door apart. They could use a sledgehammer. They could use a blowtorch. Either of those takes time. If they used a shaped charge to blow the door off its hinges, the lock might still hold.

Each of my windows is alarmed. I have installed motion detectors on the fire escape.

I will hear them coming.

In a perfect world, I would install security cameras in the hallways and the stairwell and in the street facing in every direction. I would have an antiaircraft battery on the roof. Every night, in a perfect world, I would booby-trap the living room windows with white phosphorous grenades. I couldn't do this to the windows in my bedroom because I would be too close to the blast area and a detonation would incinerate me.

Late Saturday afternoon, someone pushes my buzzer. I stare at the intercom for a long time before I press the Talk button and whisper, "Who is it?"

I press the Listen button.

Sadie's voice says, "It's me."

I buzz her in and wait with my eye against the peephole. I watch her appear at the top of the stairs and come toward me. I look for any sign of movement behind her. She reaches my door and knocks. I keep watching the stairway. She knocks again.

"Let me in," she says.

I undo the police lock and open the door and pull her inside and slam the door closed and reset the police lock and jam my eye back against the peephole. The hallway is still empty. I turn around. Today Sadie smells like gardenias.

"We need to talk," she says.

I say, "Every time I have to talk into the intercom, it gives away my position."

"I think we should see about getting you some help."

"How would you know you could trust them?"

"I've gotten some recommendations."

"I looked into it myself. I'm afraid it's hopeless."

Her face relaxes. "That's great that you've been looking. I thought you were going to say there wasn't a problem."

"Of *course*, I understand there's a problem." I shake my head. "Most of the available guys are Africans or South Americans who just drift from revolution to revolution and pretty much sell themselves to the highest bidder or attach themselves to the side that happens to be winning at any given moment. They have substandard training and suspect loyalty."

Past my window over Sadie's shoulder, the sun is setting. The sky burns pink and orange. Beside her, the television flashes and hums.

I say, "The English guys are mostly ex-SAS, so they obviously have the training, but they're prohibitively expensive. Also, they might have their own agendas. Same goes for the Americans. The fact is, it's a disreputable business that sometimes attracts disreputable people. You could get some crazed Nazi who's waiting for you to fall asleep so he can go to work on you with a chain saw. It's not worth the risk. There's too many freaks out there."

Sadie is silent.

Beside her, the anchorman shuffles his papers. He looks up from his desk. Normally, he says, a particle accelerator is built in a straight line.

Sadie steps toward me and touches my cheek. She is crying.

Speeding up the particle to any substantial velocity requires a great distance.

She pulls herself close to me and gazes up with wet eyes. "I love you," she says.

Because the largest particle accelerators are not even two miles long, their maximum velocity is low.

She says, "I want you to know that I'm not going to abandon you."

A cyclotron or synchrotron solves the distance problem by

moving the particle around in a circle over and over. This may one day allow a particle to achieve velocities approaching the speed of light.

She strokes my face. "I wish you could tell me that you'll snap out of it soon and everything will be all right."

But some theorists predict that accelerating a particle to such an extent will produce enough energy to create a small black hole.

Sadie says, "I'm so worried."

The anchorman pauses. He sets his jaw and looks stoic. The prospect of such an outcome, he says, would give the experiment a tiny but real possibility of destroying the Earth.

Monday morning, I bring a gun to the office because I'm ready. I'm ready if one of my former coworkers bursts in with an automatic rifle and starts executing secretaries. I'm ready if one of the custodians comes after me with the ax from the wall-mounted fire safety kit. I'm ready if the lobby explodes and flames shoot through the elevator shafts and the stairwells fill with black smoke. In that case I would go out the window.

Velcroed to the underside of my desk is a LALO, fast-open, base-jumping parachute rig. In thirty seconds, I can be strapped in and running full-out toward the floor-to-ceiling glass of the north wall. While I run, I will put a few slugs through the center pane to weaken it and then I will cover my face with my forearms and smash through into the sky.

My boss is sitting in my chair when I come back from the men's room. As I approach, I start fiddling with the zipper on my pants. It doesn't fool him. He says, "How many times have you washed your hands today?"

"I'm not sure."

"Try to understand my position."

I nod.

"I need you to be able to take care of yourself. I need to know that I can rely on you."

I nod again.

He leans back in my chair. "Do you remember what I said to you when I offered you this job?"

"You said you were worried I would be bored."

"Is that what's happening?"

"No."

"Do you feel you're having some sort of breakdown?"

"I'm questioning my assumptions."

If he makes a move, I can use my first shot to shatter his kneecap. Even the worst tough guy can't take that smiling. Probably my boss would drop his coffee and crumple to the floor. I would stand and walk around my desk and put the next shot straight into the top of his head.

"How's the Molesky thing?"

"Not bad. I'm meeting with his partners this afternoon."

"You think that's necessary?"

"They called me. They want to meet in some park down by the waterfront."

"And you think that's safe?"

"I'll be careful."

He nods. "I suppose you're right. It's just, they seem so unsavory. Why have contact with them if you don't have to?"

"I won't live in fear," I tell him.

One of them has a pasty-white chemotherapy complexion and steel-wool chest hair. The other is young and dark. They wear thick gold chains and silk shirts with the necks wide open.

They are sitting together on a green bench with cement feet. They are surrounded by trees. Looming behind them over the trees is the Mad Russians Car Repair and Limousine Service garage. It is the only building I can see.

The paler one stands to meet me. He slaps his hand against one of the trees. "To protect from parabolic microphone," he says. He puts out his hand. "I am Victor." We shake. "This is Michael." Victor leans toward me. "Michael, he don't speak English so good like me." Victor sucks on his teeth. "They frisk you already, yes?"

"Yes."

"I know they did. Otherwise you would have not get through. We own this park. They use metal detector, too?"

"Yes."

"Maybe you think we too careful?"

"No."

"Well," he says, "everybody is careful about something. Some man want to know all the time where is their woman. Some people afraid to drive car. I have a friend he don't like to fly because he don't understand how plane stay up. He is all the time waiting to fall, waiting to fall." He shrugs. "Me, I like fly."

"Me, too."

"Please sit down," he says.

I sit.

"Look down at your chest."

On my chest is a small dot of red light, the size of a pencil eraser.

"You know what this is?" he says.

"Yes," I tell him.

"You not scared?"

"Not really."

"How come you not scared? Because you know I am businessman so probably I don't kill you?"

I shake my head.

He smiles. "Because maybe you think you are like Superman?" He beats a fist against his chest. "You think bullet no hurt if it hit you?"

"No," I say. "It would hurt."

"So why you not scared?"

"Because there could always be a rifle pointed at me. Why should it be scarier just because I can see it?"

He says something in Russian. Michael says something back.

Victor turns back to me. "We think you are maybe very brave man."

I shrug.

He says, "I hope you not offended by rifle. Is necessary these days. These days, you frisk somebody, he still have bomb in his shoe and he blow himself up with you. Is crazy."

"Maybe he has packets of Sarin gas in his tooth fillings."

Victor holds up his hand. "So please you don't make sudden move because rifle always there. Because I don't know if you crazy."

"I'm not crazy," I say.

He takes a breath. "Is difficult way to live. People think is difficult in Russia, but in Russia you don't have to be scared of badman because you know why? Because is businessman. He want something. You give him, then probably you okay. But you find man who say I kill you because I enjoy or because God tell me, then you have crazy man and you can't say what he do and what he don't do."

At night it is completely dark in this spot. You can see stars that you never see from anywhere else in the city. They look like glowing powder. I know this because I was gazing at the sky last night while I duct-taped handguns to the underside of each of these benches. I had to put one on each because I didn't know where I'd be sitting.

Victor says, "And these crazy man is everywhere now. Okay, maybe not so much here. A few, but maybe not so much. Yes. Okay. But we has business all over the world. We go Africa. We go Uzbekistan. Sometimes Pakistan."

Packed into the dirt around the cement feet of each bench is enough C-4 to take the thing out of the ground and send pieces of its occupants flying all over. I have radio detonators hidden in the heels of my boots.

"Okay," Victor says, "so maybe we decide don't go, is too dangerous. You need protect yourself. But also you need take advantage of opportunity. Maybe everybody else scared to go so you go and you beat competitors and nothing bad happen. So maybe is good thing world is dangerous place because is easy to get success if you know how to be brave."

Somewhere on the ground behind me, covered with leaves, I have a 7.62 mm Dragunov SVD rifle with a forty-magnification starlight night scope. The rifle is fully assembled and wrapped in an oilcloth.

Victor is looking at me. "You are afraid of these man I mention?"

I shrug.

"You should be," he says. "If you Russian, if you American, they want kill you. I go Afghanistan when I am young man and I see these people crazy. And now they kill you when you go in restaurant or when you fly on plane or when you at work. But sometimes, you so worried about people like this you can't see how dangerous is the people right in front of you."

If it starts to break down, I will roll over the back of my bench and crouch behind its cement foundation. I will have to move very quickly and roll at an angle so as to ruin the sniper's aim. In the same motion, I will cover my ears and touch off the C-4 under Victor and Michael's bench. The cement will shield me from the concussion. The smoke from the explosion will blind the sniper. I will grab the pistol from under my bench to use against the bodyguards who will converge on me. I will pull the rifle out of the leaves and sling it across my chest in case, at some point, I have to take out the sniper.

I will have to remember to keep moving. If I hole up, they might send in dogs to find me.

"Is this why you asked me here?" I say.

"You know why I ask you here. I ask you here to talk about Sasha's murder."

"What about it?"

Victor smiles. "You meet Irina? She is very beautiful, no?"

"She's all right."

"And you meet also her maid? So, on night that Sasha disappear, this maid see him leave house with a man she know is old friend of Mrs. Molesky. She say she seen this man many times. He come to house, sometimes to see Sasha and they drink tea together and they make chess and they friends. So, okay. But also, she say, this man come sometimes when Sasha away. He come to see Mrs. Molesky, but she don't know what they do together. Maybe they also drink tea. Okay, so, but this maid she don't like go to police because maybe they make trouble for her because maybe she is not really citizen. So, I wasn't always citizen, but I take test and I say she could do same thing and then she don't have to be scared. But for now, I tell her, we wait to tell police and first I go find this man and I ask him if maybe he know something about what happen to Sasha."

He clears his throat. "So, we find him and we ask and he say he don't know nothing. And I say but you was with him on the night he get killed and maybe you see something and then he don't want to say. So we ask him again and he still don't want to say."

He says something in Russian. Michael smiles.

"So, we ask again and this time we really ask and this time he tell us. He say, he love Irina and she decide she want him to kill Sasha and pretend is some kind of gangster who kill him. Some kind of Marlon Brando. Okay, so he find this other man to help him and they take Sasha and they kill him and then they cut off thumbs and they put him in parking lot and they wait for police to find and say, Marlon Brando do this."

He spreads his hands. "So, we go and find other man and we tell him say if it's true and he don't want to say either. But then we ask him until he do say and it's true."

When he finishes, we are silent for a while.

"Why did you want to tell me this?"

He nods. "Here we come to this part: I want to know who get this money if Irina do not."

"Probably it would be split evenly among the children."

He nods.

"Of course, before I make that determination, I'll have to talk to Mrs. Molesky again."

He smiles. "Maybe she no be there when you go."

I don't say anything.

He says, "I like you. You are brave man. You are young. I hope you don't have to tell police what I just say about Mrs. Molesky."

"I like you, too. I'm glad you didn't push things too far."

He frowns. "I think maybe I don't follow you. I just want to make sure everything okay about Irina."

I sigh. "Are you the beneficiary of her life insurance?"

He narrows his eyes. "I don't think so."

I nod. "Then it's really not my business."

There is a tiny but real possibility that tomorrow will be the beginning of the revolution. If the system collapses, you will be ready to fill the void and prevent the slide into anarchy. You will assign jobs and ration food and gasoline and establish a command-and-control structure. You will provide for basic needs. You will build the whole world from the ground up. You will be king.

Of course, you hope none of this will be necessary.

Of course you hope that.

HIGHWAY

Eddie would not stop staring at the radio. He said that the V of the metal antennae reminded him of a girl with her legs spread. The radio sat on a narrow shelf above the grill. The man working the grill was so big that he was blocking Eddie's view. Eddie leaned forward in his chair and stretched his neck, trying to get a better angle. Carl reached across the table and snapped his fingers next to Eddie's face.

Eddie drew himself upright, startled. "Hey," he said. "What'd you do that for?"

"You're embarrassing me," Carl said.

"I was just having fun."

"You were acting like a goddamn retard."

Eddie's eyes narrowed. "I ain't no retard."

"Well, that's what everybody in here thinks now, watching you carry on like that."

"They don't think that," Eddie said.

"Have it your way. I thought you wanted to be normal."

"I do."

"Well, I'm just trying to help you."

"I know. I just forgot."

Carl shook his head. "Sometimes I don't know why I bother. Maybe I should leave it alone."

"No, please."

"Some people just don't want to change. I don't have to stay where I'm not appreciated."

"Please," Eddie said, reaching out to touch Carl's forearm. "Please, I'll be better."

Eddie and Carl sat by the door at a blue Formica table. Beside them was the high window that ran the length of the front wall of the diner. On the other side of the window was the parking lot and the white sun and the black line of the highway that disappeared, flat and uncurving, into the distance in both directions.

The waitresses wore blue dresses and white aprons. The three of them sat together at the far end of the room. They were the only other people in the diner. One of the waitresses was thin and old and hard. One of them was fat and old and hard. The third had smooth skin and dark blond hair that fell to her shoulders. When Carl put down his menu, the third waitress slid out of her chair. She swayed her hips slightly as she walked.

She stood beside the table and smiled at Carl. "What can I get you?" she asked him.

"What's good here?" Carl asked.

She shrugged. "It's all good."

He grunted. "That's quite a boy you have behind the counter."

"Luther?" the waitress said. "He's just like a big teddy bear."

"That so?" Carl said.

"He's the best cook we've had since I got here."

"When was that?"

"Two years ago."

He nodded. "And before that you were captain of the second-best cheer squad in the state."

"Third-best." She stared at him. "How'd you know that?"

Carl said, "We'll both have orange juice and coffee with cream—sugar in one—and I'll have the Denver omelet and he'll have the scrambled eggs and sausage and a side of French toast."

The waitress said, "How'd you know about the cheerleading?"

"His eye-cue is one sixty-three," Eddie told her. "That means he's a genius."

She smiled at Eddie. "Where'd they test you?" she asked Carl. "Army?"

"Something like that," he said.

"Where were you stationed?"

Carl frowned. "All over."

"My brother's at Fort Leavenworth. You ever get up there?"

"Time to time."

"What were you doing you had to move around so much?"

"I'm not really supposed to talk about it," he told her.

"Mysterious," she said.

He stared at her.

"My name is Celia."

"That's beautiful."

"Thank you." She stared at him again. "Don't you have a name?"

Eddie glanced at him.

"My name is George," Carl said.

"And your friend?"

"Steve," he said before Eddie could answer.

"Nice to meet you both," she said.

When the waitress was gone, Eddie said, "I don't even *like* the name Steve."

Carl said, "I almost called you Lenny."

"I don't understand. Why's that funny?"

"Never mind."

Eddie scowled. "Hey, I didn't know you was in the army."

Carl ignored him. He was remembering the way it felt to run over the groundhogs or rabbits or even the occasional coyotes that tried to dash across the road in front of his car. He would swerve toward them, leading them slightly, hoping to get them just at the bottom of the spine. If he hit them right, he would crush their back legs and then he could watch in the rearview mirror as they poured blood, scrambling to stand. Sometimes, if the road was empty, he would pull to the side and sit on the hood and listen to the sounds the animal made as it tried to drag itself away. Sometimes he would stand over it on the hot black asphalt and spit in its fear-widened eyes or grind his heel on its mangled legs. But none of that was as good as the feeling just before the hit when he saw the thing disappear under the bumper and waited for the thump of the tire going over and maybe the ringing of the head against the underside of the car.

He watched Celia as she moved behind the counter and gave their orders to the enormous cook.

"You think she liked you?" Eddie said.

"Sure."

"You going to try her?"

"I don't know."

Celia brought the orange juice and coffee. Carl watched the muscles in her legs. When she was next to him again, he examined her soft, hairless arms.

"Who gets the sugar?" she asked.

Carl pointed at Eddie. Celia set down their drinks.

"You must like it here," Carl said to her.

"Why do you say that?"

"Just a sense I get."

She nodded. "I love that everybody who comes in here is going somewhere."

"Makes you feel full of possibilities."

"It makes me feel like there are all these worlds around me that I'm not a part of."

"Makes you feel bigger and smaller at the same time."

She looked at him and did not say anything.

"Why don't *you* ever go?" Carl asked her.

"Where would I go?"

"Anywhere."

"You can't just go *any*where."

"We are," Carl said.

"You don't know where you're going?"

He shook his head. "We're just going."

Eddie was shifting restlessly in his chair.

Carl said, "You got a jukebox in here?"

Celia shook her head. "Just Luther's radio."

Eddie frowned. "It ain't even turned *on*."

Celia said, "I'll see if he can find some music for you."

She walked away from them and spoke to the cook. He nodded at her and turned on the radio. It was tuned to a blues station.

"That all right?" the cook said.

"It's all right," Eddie told him.

Eddie closed his eyes. His shoulders slumped forward slightly and he did not look quite so big.

The song ended and the station went to a newsbreak. When the lead story began, Eddie's eyes popped open and he said, "Turn that up."

Carl looked at him quickly. Luther glanced over his shoulder at them and turned up the volume on the radio. The announcer said what he had been saying all morning.

One of the old waitresses said, "I read where the cops think it might be the same fellas who set that girl on fire in Pennsylvania."

The other said, "I heard they raped the girls after they was dead."

"I heard they made the boy watch them do it."

"I heard he was still alive when they cut his thing off."

"Hell in a handbasket," the first one said.

Luther said, "Order up, Celia."

Celia brought their food on three plates. She had Eddie's

French toast balanced in the crook of her left arm. When she had put down the plates, she said, "I always told my mother I wanted it to make the news when I died."

Eddie looked up at her.

Carl said, "By the time that happens it won't do you much good."

"But it's how you know you were important," she said.

"But you don't want it like that," he said. He nodded at the radio.

"No," she said, "not like that."

She pulled a ketchup bottle from inside her apron and set it on the table. "I just want to be remembered."

"Those folks will be remembered." He nodded at the radio again. "Their names are on the front page of half the papers in the country."

She shuddered. "I don't think it's worth it."

Carl thought he saw Luther glance at him again. The newsbreak ended. Eddie poured a lake of ketchup in the center of his eggs and laid down neat lines of maple syrup on his French toast and began to eat.

When Celia was sitting at her table again, Carl stood and walked to the counter. Eddie was so concentrated on his food that he did not look up. Carl climbed onto one of the red swivel-top stools. Luther was spooning lard onto the grill from a white bucket.

Carl looked both ways to make sure there was no one near him. "You ever do any Lewisburg time?" he said quietly.

Luther did not turn around. "What makes you think I done time?" His voice was very soft.

Carl snorted.

Luther spread the lard with his spatula. He nodded. "No," he said. "Never Lewisburg."

"These people know?"

Luther glanced at the waitresses. "These people don't know nothing," he said.

"Luther your real name?"

Luther did not say anything.

"You know why I want to talk to you?" Carl asked him.

"I suppose I do."

"Eddie give it away with the radio?"

Luther shrugged. "A lot of things give it away."

"Yeah," Carl said. "Anyway, it appears we have a problem."

"Maybe."

"You know how to play Helen Keller?"

Luther nodded.

"So maybe we finish here and get back on the road and keep driving and you keep flipping your pancakes and the people here keep knowing nothing about nothing."

"I can live with that," Luther said. "But you have to leave the girl."

"What do you care about her?"

Luther shook his head. "She don't deserve that."

Carl glanced at Celia, who was pretending not to look at him. "What if I say no?" he said.

Luther turned around, the spatula still in his hand. He looked even bigger from the front. "Then you're right. We do have a problem."

"You think you can put us both down?"

"I think we can find out."

Carl stood up and walked back to the table. Eddie was still working through his eggs. Carl sat down across from him and poured ketchup beside his omelet. They ate in silence for a while.

When the state police car rolled off the highway and into the parking lot, Carl reached across the table and touched Eddie's hand. Eddie looked up and saw the car. He continued to eat, but more slowly.

Carl leaned back and unzipped his jacket and let his right hand fall into his lap.

The cops wore campaign hats with wide brims and powder-blue shirts with short sleeves. The first one in was short and thick with blond hair cut very close on the sides of his head. His partner was almost as tall as Eddie. The partner had brown hair and dimples.

The cops walked to the counter and did not sit. The short one said, "How you doing, Big Luther?"

Luther said, "Yourself?"

"Can't complain," the cop said. "I'll have an egg sandwich."

The tall cop said, "Make it two."

Luther went back to the grill.

The short cop swaggered toward the waitresses. The tall one leaned against the counter and looked at Carl and Eddie. Carl was picking at his omelet with his left hand so he could keep the right one in his lap.

"How you boys doing?" the cop said.

Carl smiled at him.

The cop said, "You from around here?"

Carl shook his head. "San Diego."

The cop frowned. "You don't look too San Diego."

Carl said, "What do you want me to do?"

The short cop was looking at them now.

"Where you fellas going?" the tall cop said.

Eddie put down his fork.

Carl said, "There some kind of problem?"

The tall cop said, "You been watching the news?"

"We've been on the road."

"From San Diego."

"That's right."

"That your Ford in the parking lot?"

"Yeah."

"How come you don't got California plates?"

"My sister's car."

The tall cop smiled. "You got all the right answers, don't you?"

Carl said, "We do something wrong?"

"I don't know," the tall cop said. "Did you?"

Eddie's hand was under the table.

Carl could feel the muscles tightening in his stomach.

Luther said, "Two egg sandwiches." He was holding a brown paper bag dotted with dark blotches of grease.

The tall cop paid him and took the bag without looking away from Carl and Eddie.

Luther said, "These boys been in here last night, too. I think they stayed at the Super 8. No way they could be the ones done them folks up north. They wouldn't have time for the drive."

"That's true," the cop said. He stood up from the counter. "You got a kind of a smart mouth," he said to Carl.

The short cop fell in behind him, looking mean.

Carl watched them through the window as they got back into the cruiser.

"Will they run the license?" Eddie asked him.

"They might. If they do, they'll probably wait until they're out of sight."

"Should we go?"

Carl waved to Celia. She came over.

"Are you done?" she asked.

He nodded. She took the check pad from the pocket of her apron and tore off the top slip. She put it on the table and kept her hand on top of it. She was smiling. She said, "I didn't know you were in here last night."

Carl was looking at Luther, but he was bent over the grill again with his back turned. Carl took a long breath and shifted his look to Celia. "I think you might make the news tonight."

Her smile wavered. "Why do you think that?"

"Because you've been talking to me."

The smile returned. "A girl talking to you isn't news."

Carl said, "Sometimes you make the news for being dead; sometimes you make the news for being alive."

She waited but he did not say anything more and she turned and took the dishes behind the counter.

In the parking lot Carl knelt in front of the Ford, holding his screwdriver. Eddie stood behind him, blocking the view from inside the diner. Carl removed the license plate and replaced it with one from the set he had stolen at the last rest stop. Then he and Eddie walked around to the back of the car and did the same with the rear license.

Carl pulled out of the parking lot and onto the on-ramp and merged with the traffic, which was heavier now than it had been when they pulled off. There were cars all around them. In the Ford, with the new plates, they looked just like everybody else.

THE ROPES

For the first day or so, even when I had visitors the doctors kept my room in velvet darkness and sometimes I couldn't tell whether I was awake. When I was sure I was awake, I wouldn't remember ever having slept. There were no clocks in my room. I had tried once to check the time on the digital watch one of the nurses had left on my bedside table, but the green light from the watch's face burned like a welding torch in the center of my brain.

It hurt to talk. Most of the time it hurt to open my eyes. I lay on my back and watched the glowing shapes that floated through my vision.

I couldn't remember the fight. The last thing I remembered was walking along the concrete aisle with the crowd screaming all around me. Spotlights made the ring rise up in front of me like a blue island in a sea of black. I wasn't sure how much to trust my memory, because the scene would always end just before I started up the stairs to the apron and it would always be followed by the same dream. In the dream, I was lashed to cliffs that overlooked the ocean. The dream was just as vivid as the memory. I could feel the waves crashing below me while gulls pecked at my heart.

I remembered bits and pieces of the day that led up to the fight. It had started out well for me. In the early morning, I had made love to a pretty green-eyed girl whose grandfather's great-grandfather had, indirectly, given orders to mine. Hers was Ulysses Grant. Mine, Thomas J. Folsom, had been with the Irish Brigade at Fredericksburg. It would have been more fiendish—or at least more interesting—if her grandfather's great-grandfather had (indirectly) killed mine. But Thomas Folsom was not even scratched at Fredericksburg. The Irish Brigade, however, took almost fifty percent casualties in a charge on the stone wall at Marye's Heights. The Union Army came at the wall in waves all afternoon. Before each charge the men would draw up wills and leave them with Headquarters Company. By the end of the day, they had lost more than seven thousand men in front of that wall. They never took it. I took Christina Grant-Stevenson at her parents' house in her childhood bedroom under a thumbnail moon.

After three days I could keep my eyes open most of the time and one of the nurses cracked the blinds in front of my window to let in a gray trickle of sunlight. The headache was constant. My eyes leaked. Everything I could see was blurred and doubled and squashed together. I had jumbled pictures of my mother sitting beside my bed and sometimes of my father sitting with her, but those scenes could have taken place fifteen minutes ago or fifteen years ago and I wouldn't have known the difference.

· · ·

Toward the end of the week, the headache would go away for long stretches and I would feel almost clear again. I could eat a little. I could lift myself out of bed. I could walk some, but my balance still hadn't come back and when I went anywhere I had to hold myself up with my hands against the wall.

I was sitting up in bed when Connelly came in. He wore a white track suit with green trim. He was holding a tweed watch cap in his hands and mashing it nervously. My mother closed the book she was reading and stood. She looked too long at Pete Connelly. Then she turned to me.

"I'm going to the cafeteria to find your stepfather," she said.

Connelly nodded to her as she passed him. She didn't acknowledge it.

He chewed his lip.

"You want to sit?" I said.

He sat in the chair my mother had left.

"Congratulations," I said. "I hear you took the whole thing."

He shrugged.

"You trying for the Olympics next?"

He shook his head. "Turning pro." He squinted at me. "Your face don't look too bad."

"I guess not," I said.

"They have to pack your nose?"

"No."

"That's good. You ever have that?"

I shook my head.

"I've had my nose broke three times," Connelly said, "and it never hurts getting broke like it does when they pack it. They cram the gauze in so tight it makes your eyes swell up like a frog's. You feel like your head's gonna pop."

"Glad I missed it."

He nodded and then swiveled his head to look around the room. "You're a college boy, right?"

"That's right."

"Don't see too many college boys in Open class. Not at the finals, anyway."

"I won the Novice two years ago."

He stopped examining the room and looked back at me. "Novice ain't Open," he said. "Ain't even hardly the same sport." He took a breath. "You good in college?"

"Yeah."

"That ain't the same sport, either."

"No," I agreed.

"How many years you have left?"

"I graduated a month ago."

"Congratulations," he said.

"Thank you."

"You fight light-heavy there, too?"

"The last three years. As a freshman I fought middle."

"That musta been tough for you to make. You ain't built like a middle." He took a breath. "But you ain't really tall enough for light-heavy, either. You got kind of a tweener build. What's your walk-around?"

"One-eighty, one-eighty-one."

He gave a little whistle. "Goddamn. I'm walking around at one-eighty-eight before breakfast and buck-ass naked. Guy I beat in the local finals in Houston said he dropped down from one-ninety-four. I can't believe you made it past regionals."

"Thanks."

"I didn't mean it like that."

"Never mind," I said. "I know how you meant it."

We were silent for a while.

Then Connelly said, "When they carried you out, I thought you was dead for sure. You wasn't moving or anything. They put one of those orange boards under your head. Your arms was all floppy."

"I'm not dead," I said. I didn't know what else to say.

Connelly said, "If you really had been dead, I don't know if I woulda been able to fight anymore. I was in a neutral corner when they started working on you, so I was by myself, and I felt alone like I never felt before. I felt like the worst person in the world."

"It wasn't your fault."

He narrowed his eyes. "They told me you didn't remember what happened."

"My mother told me about it. Someone has a video."

"You gonna watch it?"

"I don't know."

He nodded. "Anyway, it don't matter if it was my fault. It still woulda been me that killed you." He took a breath. "For a couple hours, I tried to blame you. I said you was just a fool college boy and you had no business here if you wasn't prepared and you couldn't protect yourself. But the truth is if you're here you had to earn your way here and anybody can get hit wrong and so maybe it's nobody's fault. But it's hard to make yourself believe that."

"No one would have blamed you if I'd died."

"Your mother blames me anyway."

"She's my mother."

Connelly looked through the open blinds at the parking lot below my window. "What do the doctors say?"

"They don't understand this stuff too well. They say once the swelling goes down in my brain, I'll probably get everything back all the way. Motor skills, memory, stuff like that. But now that I've had one like this, I'm much more likely to have another. Or even one of the kind that you never come all the way back from. So I have to take it easy for a while and after that I can live a normal life. But no more boxing."

He looked away from the window and stared at me. "I'm sorry," he said.

"I was pretty much done anyway. I would've liked to take

a shot at the Olympics, but that was probably just college-boy fantasy." I took a breath. "I couldn't beat those guys," I said.

He didn't say anything.

My mother sat next to my bed, reading one of her mysteries. I watched her with my eyes slitted, keeping my breathing slow and regular, careful not to move. After a while, without looking up, she said, "Some girl named Christina came to see you a few times while you were coming out of it. Do you remember?"

"No."

"She seems sweet."

"They all seem that way. It doesn't mean much."

"You don't really believe that. You're just saying it because you like the way it sounds."

"How does it sound?" I said.

"Like your father."

She still wasn't looking at me. She kept turning the pages of her book.

"Have you heard from him?" I said finally.

Now she looked at me. "He called when he read about it in the paper."

"What did he say?"

"He asked how you were."

"What did you tell him?"

"I told him how you were."

"Did you tell Hal he called?" Hal was my stepfather.

She smiled. "Don't change the subject."

"You still want to talk about Christina? I went to school with her. She's from around here."

"You know her well?"

"Not really."

My mother sighed. "That's not an awfully safe way to behave these days."

"I'm careful."

"Apparently not."

"I meant . . . during."

She made a face. "I knew what you meant. Are you going to call her to tell her you're all right?"

"Can we not talk about this?" I said.

"Fine."

She went back to her book. I closed my eyes. We didn't say anything else until my stepfather came into the room much later.

"Hal," I said.

"Alex," he said.

He moved to shake my hand and then reconsidered and stood uncertainly next to my bed. My mother stood and kissed him on the cheek.

"I spoke to the doctor," he said. "They're a little concerned about you flying. Something about the pressure change."

"So, where does that leave us?" I said.

"Well, I was thinking maybe we should just drive."

"To New York? That's two thousand miles."

"I know that." He glanced at my mother. "We could make an adventure out of it. We'd stay in some fun hotel each night. It shouldn't take us more than four days."

"I'm fine to fly."

"Alex," my mother said, "if it's not safe it's not safe."

"What's the danger? A little headache? I can make my own decisions. I'm twenty-one years old."

"Not quite."

I sent them back to their hotel. Then I packed my suitcase and stood it against the wall. A young dark-haired nurse brought my dinner. When she was gone, I called Christina at her parents' house to tell her I was leaving. She didn't seem surprised.

· · ·

After a week in New York, I still wasn't sleeping. My appetite came and went. Car-horn blasts made my heart flip-flop and set off fireworks in my head.

Some nights I would leave Hal's apartment after dinner and walk to Madison Avenue and watch all the people hurrying out together or, if it was late, watch the couples hurrying home together. I would walk into the park, which would be almost deserted, and then walk across to the West Side, praying for someone to jump out in front of me and put up his fists and dare me forward. There would be no neutral corners. There would be no mandatory eight counts. I would put this man on the ground and then stomp him until my bootprints showed on his chest. Thick blood would ooze from his ears. If I were still angry enough, I might lift him up by his hair and smack his face again and again into the pavement until his skull opened and poured gray-yellow brains.

One night, on Amsterdam in the high seventies, I watched a homeless man steal a pair of shoes from an outdoor display. I could have taken two steps to my left and gotten in front of him, but he was mean drunk or mean crazy, or both, and as he passed I could smell his antiseptic, old-sweat, hospital smell, which made me very sad. I didn't move. He jogged away with the shoes clutched against his stomach like a baby.

Walker, my stepbrother, came over from his mother's place in the West Village to take me to a movie.

We sat on the aisle. I used a sip of Walker's soda to wash down one of the codeine-laced Tylenols the doctor had prescribed because the tiniest sounds were like hammers beating against my eardrums. My senses had become so acute that I imagined my blood had been replaced with liquid amphetamines. I was very aware of the warm bodies around me and the way the whole theater smelled like hot butter. I could feel armies of microbes covering all of us and scuttling in huge columns along the cement floor. Walker, who was tall and handsome like his father, slouched in his seat and told me about the end of his sophomore year and how drunk he had gotten. He told me about the summer internship he had just begun at his father's law firm.

He said, "After I graduate, I'll probably put in a couple years as a trader. Your quality of life is really a lot better there than it is as an analyst. The danger is that you get tracked differently and you might not be able to move up as high. But after those two years I'll go to law school. Definitely on the West Coast. Probably Stanford. Again, it's a quality-of-life decision. After that I'll make a determination about which firm to work for, based on opportunity for advancement as well as quality-of-life considerations. Also, I've already started paying into a retirement fund. If you start paying when you're eighteen, by the time you're sixty-five it's like winning the lottery."

"What about the writing?"

He nodded. "I almost forgot. Being a trader will also leave me some time to write on the side. I mean, you only really need to be in the office while the market's open. You also have to entertain clients in the evenings, but I'm sure I'll still find some time. Anyway, I'll give myself those two years to make it with the writing and if that doesn't pan out I'll still have done some serious résumé building." He shook a few M&Ms into his hand and tossed them into his open mouth. "I'm pretty sure it'll work out. I mean, sometimes I take passages from *Gatsby* and make little corrections that any editor in the world would tell you are improvements. I'm not saying it's not a great book, I'm just saying there are some things I do differently that are just objectively better. I've been wanting to talk to you about that." He sipped his soda. "What about you? Do you know what you're gonna do now?"

"No," I said.

During the movie, whenever I felt the nausea coming I just closed my eyes and pressed my palms against my ears and mostly I was all right. Afterward, Walker took me to a party at his girlfriend's parents' duplex on Park Avenue. Bass from the stereo shook the floor. The air tasted like beer and sweat. I sat in an armchair and talked to a girl who had just finished her junior year at Dartmouth. We had to shout to hear each other over the music.

She was saying, "I just don't know if people realize how fucking good *The Waste Land* is. I mean, they say they know, but it's just so fucking good."

"Yes," I yelled at her, "it's very good."

"It's like Picasso. Or *Middlemarch*. Everybody always tells you how good they are. But they're really, *really* good. It's amazing."

"Are you studying English?"

She nodded. "I think maybe I'd like to be a writer. I keep meaning to be disciplined about it."

"That sounds like a good idea."

"I'm going to Tahiti this summer. I'm going to see some of the places Gauguin painted. I spent last semester in France. I visited his house. He's another one. Do you realize how good he was? How fucking *good*?"

"I think so," I told her.

When I came home, my mother was reading in the living room. I sat down next to her and turned on the television. The television was showing baseball highlights.

"Did you have fun?" my mother asked.

I shrugged.

"It was nice of Walker to want to take you out. It was his idea, you know?"

I took a breath. "I've been thinking I might go visit Dad for a while."

She was silent for a long time. Then she said, "Fine."

"Do you want to talk about it?"

"I told you it's fine. I think it's a good idea."

"I'm happy to talk about it if you want to."

"I'm trying to read," she said.

The bus went along Central Park West past buildings that looked like stretched-out Renaissance palaces—the Dakota, the San Remo, the Beresford—until the park ended and then across and uptown through East Harlem and then onto the raised highway into the Bronx. We passed over dull garages and bodegas with bright signs and the bombed-out skeletons of old warehouses. We passed boarded-up apartment houses and enormous political campaign banners and billboards that carried advertisements for the state lottery and for an amusement park and for a newsmagazine show.

The man next to me had his clothes packed into gray garbage bags that he had stuffed into the roof racks. Two rows in front of us, a baby was crying. When we got out onto the highway, the driver started the movie, which played on tiny screens mounted on the ceiling. I pressed my face against the air-conditioned glass of the window and tried to sleep.

During the layover in Boston, I went into the station men's room and splashed water in my eyes and rubbed at the sleep creases in my face.

In Boston, the baby and the man with the garbage bags got off and were replaced by young couples with straight teeth and matching luggage sets. We drove out of Boston and into the country for a while and then across the bridge to the Cape. We drove through narrow streets between clapboard houses and down to the dock, where the bus sighed to a stop.

The ferry was already docked when I stepped down off the bus. I went inside the Steamship Authority building and bought my ticket. I walked through the back door and up the ramp to the gangplank, which creaked in the wind, and across onto the ferry.

I sat outside on one of the white benches near the bow and waited for the cars to load. Some of the cars were delivery trucks. Some were old and dented. But mostly they were Mercedes and BMWs with new finishes that gleamed in the sun. When the cars were loaded, their passengers pulled themselves up the metal stairs to the deck. Most of them were families dressed in white polo shirts and no socks. As we pulled away, I looked over my shoulder and watched the low wooden houses of Woods Hole shrink into the shoreline and then watched the shoreline shrink into the ocean. Then I turned around and watched the water rushing past.

Gulls flew with the ferry. Sometimes one would land on one of the masts. He would sit for a while and then fly away and start circling again and another gull would take his place.

Two of the truck drivers stepped out of the snack bar in the middle of the upper deck and stood together by the railing. They spoke to each other quietly and laughed and spit into the water.

My father was waiting in the parking lot at Vineyard Haven. He was standing beside his truck, talking to the men who would direct the unloading of the cars. They were all smiling. Behind them the sun was setting. When he saw me, my father stopped smiling and nodded. He said something to the men. They glanced in my direction.

My father came toward me. He was wearing old blue jeans and a short-sleeved khaki dress shirt. He hugged me and I stood holding my bags, not sure whether to put them down.

He stepped back. "You feel all right?" he said.

"Sure."

"How was the trip?"

"Long."

He nodded. He took the bags out of my hands and walked back toward the car.

The night my father had his retina detached by Earnie Shavers in front of a full house at Madison Square Garden, he weighed one hundred ninety-seven pounds. Now he was at least twenty pounds over that. But he carried it well.

"He caught me with a lucky right hand at the end of the fourth," my father would say when he told the story. "The doctor stopped it between rounds. Shavers had dynamite in both hands. I once heard an old fighter say every time Joe Louis hit him with a jab it felt like he was smashing a light-bulb against his face. Well, Shavers didn't have Louis's jab, but when he landed that steam-shovel right it felt like all the lights in Yankee Stadium just got cracked against my skull. It was like a fire alarm going off inside my head. He had the best straight right I ever saw. Foreman had thunder in his right, but he didn't really throw it straight. Besides, I was never in with Foreman. I would put Shavers's right up there with Dempsey's or Louis's or Marciano's. Of course, I was never in with them, either. Anyway, Shavers had big-league power. But he had kind of a soft chin. If he hadn't caught me with that lucky right, who knows?" My father would pause here and look around at his audience long enough for them to take in his ruined nose and the drooping muscles around his left eye. "If the fight had gone on, maybe I would've been able to hurt him." He would smile. "If I'd done that, he would've killed me."

He slid my bags behind the backseat and hopped up into the truck. I climbed into the passenger seat. My father started the engine. As we pulled out of the parking lot, he gave the men on the dock a little mock salute.

"How long you planning to stay?" my father said.

"I'm not really sure." I looked at him. "That okay?"

"Of course it's okay," he said.

We were driving along the two-way road that curved

through the middle of the island. The houses were all set back in the trees. They were invisible from the road.

"How you fixed for money?" my father said. "You want me to get you on with Dave Mayhew? Or Billy Sanders's crew?"

"Maybe. See if Billy can use another roofer."

My father frowned. "You sure? I could ask Billy to let you drive one of the trucks and do some light carpentry or something."

"I'll make a lot more roofing. Plus I'll get a tan."

"We can talk about it later. Maybe you'll take it easy for a couple weeks just to humor the old man."

"I've *been* taking it easy."

He made the turn onto North Road. "How's your mother?"

"She's fine."

"She say anything when you told her you were leaving?"

"Not really."

He chuckled. "I'll bet she can't understand why you'd ever want to come back here. She couldn't stand it. When we moved out here, she thought I was a big shot just 'cause I'd seen some money. She thought we were gonna get invited to cocktail parties. Thought she was gonna be chairwoman of the Chilmark sewing circle. But you can't buy your way into that."

"I guess not."

He nodded. "It ain't like as soon as you put a little cash together you get invited down the Cape with Ethel Kennedy. It don't work that way."

"No," I agreed.

"It don't really bother me, you understand. I mean, at the beginning I felt bad for your mother." He grunted. "But she wised up quick, boy. You better believe she wised up."

"Maybe we shouldn't talk about her."

He shrugged. "Whatever you want."

"You tell anybody I was coming in?"

"I told Charlie McClure. He'll tell Tommy."

"Tommy still living at home?"

He nodded. "So's Luke Hanlan. Tommy and Luke're working for Billy these days."

We turned off the main road onto one of the dirt roads into the woods. The truck bounced over the ruts, just clearing the trees on both sides. We took a few turns and then suddenly the trees opened up into a clearing and there was my father's house. We parked on the gravel in front. Behind the house was a huge yard with a swimming pool and a hot tub. Past that, the trees closed in again like a wall.

"The truck looks funny parked in front of this place," I said.

My father smiled. "I know," he said. "It looks like the caretaker's truck."

In his sweltering office outside Oak Bluffs, Billy Sanders said, "I'd pay you just like I pay all the other carpenters. Obviously it's not like the roofers, but your old man says you might still be having some problems with your balance and I can't be responsible for that. Also, there's a few things we have to get straight. For one, you wear long pants and steel-toes on my jobs. I know some of the other guys are lax about that but that's not my problem. Also, I ever catch you stoned, you're gone right there. That kind of shit puts everyone at risk. If I have to, I'll start piss-testing everybody twice a month."

"I can live with that," I told him.

"I'll bet you can."

He started me at a tiny reshingling job in Oak Bluffs. In the course of that first morning, I discovered that the shock that traveled up my arm every time I swung my hammer made me feel like my eyes were bleeding. The second time I puked, Billy sent me home.

The rest of the day I lay on my father's couch, popping codeines and watching television. I imagined what it might be like to unscrew my head and crack open my skull and use steel wool to scrape the bruises off of my steaming brains.

The next day Billy sent me to Boston with Tommy McClure to pick up a load of Italian marble. On the ferry on the way back to the island, we ran into a pair of Sun Transport drivers. They sat with us at one of the indoor tables.

"How come Sanders didn't get us to move that stuff around for you?" one of them said. "He doesn't like his jobs done right?"

"He didn't want it to end up on the floor of some bath-house," Tommy said.

"There you go," the other one said.

"There I do go," Tommy said.

"Who's your friend?" the first driver said. "I ain't seen him around."

"He's Galahad Kincaid, the famous race-car driver. He's here on his honeymoon."

"I'm the man who shot Liberty Valance," I said.

The first driver sighed. "You gonna tell us who he is?"

"Sure," Tommy said. "He's Alexander Folsom, the famous prizefighter."

The driver rolled his eyes.

"No, really. He's the kid who almost got killed at the Golden Gloves. It was on the news. You musta seen it."

The first driver stared at me. "That really you?"

I shrugged.

He said, "Didn't your father go the distance with Jerry Cooney?"

"Quarry," I said.

"What?"

"It was Jerry Quarry."

He nodded. Then he glanced at his friend. "Must be tough," he said, "being Ron Jeremy when your old man's Johnny Wad."

I shrugged again. "I don't really think about it much. Besides," I said, "your wife doesn't seem to feel the difference." All four of us laughed at that. The first driver pounded me on the shoulder. The other passengers didn't look at us.

When the announcement came over the loudspeaker, we walked down inside the cargo bay and sat in the truck while the ferry was brought into its slip. The cars were unloaded one row at a time. When it was our turn, I drove across the ramp and out of the parking lot and through the intersection at Five Corners.

When we got to Edgartown, Tommy said, "Slow, now. I sometimes miss the driveway."

I slowed the truck. We passed a deer-crossing sign.

"On the left," Tommy said.

I eased the truck onto the dirt path through the woods and drove straight until the trees opened onto an overgrown field. The road curved around to an iron gate in the middle of a tall hedge. I stopped in front of the gate and Tommy jumped down and unlatched the gate and swung it open. I drove through. He closed the gate and jumped back up beside me. We were on a cement driveway in the middle of an enormous lawn. The lawn slanted up gradually to the edge of a cliff and behind that was the ocean. Just in front of the edge of the cliff was the biggest house I had ever seen. A few hundred feet away from the house was another house maybe half its size. Scaffolding covered the smaller house like vines.

Tommy said, "You're not gonna believe this place, kid."

The big house was five stories tall and had a huge deck in back facing the ocean. From the front of the house, you could see an immense piece of the island. You could see other houses built into the cliffs and long empty private beaches and huge fields filled with grazing cows. But you couldn't see any of the cars passing on the road below. The view of the road was blocked by the hedge and the trees.

Billy waved us over and we began unloading the boxes of eighteen-by-eighteen-inch filled-travertine tiles and straining to lay them softly on the dolly. When the dolly was full, we rolled it up the ramp and into the foyer of the smaller house. The walls of the foyer had already been painted linen white. We rolled the dolly across the plywood subfloor of the foyer and into the living room and stacked the boxes against the wall.

As we were loading another set of boxes onto the dolly, a new-looking Lexus SUV came through the iron gate and along the driveway and pulled up in front of the big house, spraying gravel. I used my forearm to wipe the dust and sweat out of my eyes.

Tommy glanced at me and didn't say anything.

The girl who got out of the SUV had dark brown hair that fell to her shoulders. She wore sunglasses and gray knit shorts and a yellow tank top. Her legs were tan all the way down past her ankles.

The hammering on the roof stopped. Billy Sanders was standing near the entrance to the smaller house, by the base of the scaffold. He pretended not to notice any of it. The girl walked up the stone steps and into the house. The hammering started again.

"Jesus Christ," Tommy murmured. "Jesus, my good Christ."

I shrugged. "Plenty around like her."

He snorted. "Not around me."

"She's too short for you. Also, girls like that don't age well. They shrivel up like raisins. They end up having to buy new faces every few years."

"Just once I want to know what it's like to be with a girl like that."

"It's like being with any girl."

He shook his head. "I'll bet her pussy tastes like peaches and cream."

"Vinegar," I said.

"You're a cynic," Tommy told me.

Billy Sanders shuffled over to us. "How's your head?" he asked me.

"Fine as long as I stay out of the sun."

"What do you think happened yesterday?"

"I'm not sure. Good days and bad days."

He nodded. "Any time you need a break, just say so." He scratched his chin. "No need to be a hero."

There were never fights on the island. It did not have the seamy side of Gloucester or Province-town, where every so often two fishermen would carve each other into jigsaw puzzles outside some waterfront bar. In those places, especially during the off-season, there would be times when one of the fishing boats would chug back into the harbor one man short. The crew would tell stories of freak squalls and rogue waves taller than the mast. As far as they could figure, the lost man must have been washed overboard in the dark. It was impossible to investigate cases like that. As long as the crew kept telling the same story, the event joined the legend of the place and the name of the vanished man joined a list on a monument in the town square built to honor locals lost at sea. Most of the time, of course, the story was true. But once in a while the thing would smell wrong and everyone would know it and nothing would ever be done about it but the feeling of it would hang over everything like a fog. In a place like that, you could feel the violence in your sweat.

The island was not that way. There was alcoholism in the local population and there were lean winters as in any summer town, but the place was not threatening. This was a source of disappointment for me during the days I spent imagining how I would meet the girl from the big house in Edgartown. I wanted to pull her out from the middle of a brawl between Portuguese fishermen. I wanted to save her from a mob of drunken sailors. I wanted to discover her being harassed by a giant longshoreman and step between them and push her behind me.

The longshoreman would grin like a crocodile. He would swing at me with a fist the size of a cinder block. I would step to the side and let him stumble past me and hit him on the ear with the heel of my hand, which was what my father had taught me to do if I ever had to fight without gloves. He would come at me again and I would step inside his next punch and bring my elbow straight down on the bridge of his nose. Blood would pour like a dam had broken. Then his knife would be out. I would keep my eyes locked on the knife hand. When he slashed, I would suck myself up away from the blade. We would circle for a while. He would be tired by now because he was so big. Eventually, he would move too slowly with the knife and I would grab his wrist and pull myself toward him and thumb him hard in the Adam's apple. That would be the end of it. The knife would clatter to the pavement and he would sink to his knees. I would take the girl's hand and walk down the street with her, leaving the enormous longshoreman on the ground behind us, holding his neck with both hands, trying to grunt the pain away.

It didn't happen like that. What happened was that I ran into Thatcher Harrison at the supermarket in Vineyard Haven.

I was with my father. He was leaning forward on the handlebars of his shopping cart, pushing it absently in front of him. We were in the freezer section.

My father was saying, "Get a couple of the family-size lasagnas. We're almost out. Also, get the big pack of chicken cutlets and that ice cream you like."

Thatcher came around the corner at the far end of the

aisle. He didn't notice me. He was talking to a young girl who kept trying to climb into his cart. When he came close, I said his name and he jerked his head toward me. Then he smiled. "Alex," he said.

We shook hands. I introduced him to my father. He introduced the girl, who turned out to be his sister.

"How long are you here?" he asked me.

"Not sure."

"Don't you have to get back to start your job?"

"No job," I said.

He gave me the phone number at his parents' house on the island. I gave him my father's number. We said good-bye and they moved past us down the aisle.

"He lived on the floor below me," I told my father.

"Looks like a frat boy," he said.

"Not his fault."

"Also, what kind of name is Thatcher?"

"He's all right," I said.

My father shrugged. "Have it your way."

That night, while my father and I were eating canned beef stew and instant biscuits, sitting on the couch in the living room so that we could watch the baseball game, Thatcher called to invite me to a party.

Two-tenths of a mile after the sign for East Chop, I passed the stone wall and the cluster of mailboxes that Thatcher had used as landmarks in his directions. At the light blue mailbox, I turned onto the dirt road into the woods. The road curved around to the right and then I could hear the music. When the trees opened, I saw the ocean and the glow from the fire. The flat stretch of sand in front of the dunes was filled with cars. I parked my father's truck off the road next to a green Land Rover. I walked between the parked cars toward the fire.

Open coolers full of ice and beer rested on the sand at the

foot of the dunes. The big stereo sat next to them on a lawn chair. In front of the stereo, down toward the water, was the bonfire. People were strewn all over, dancing or lying on blankets in the sand or drinking and talking in tight circles.

I walked down one of the dunes and took a beer from the cooler. The flickering of the fire made my stomach churn. My vision blurred. I felt as though I was on the pitching deck of a ship. I sat down in the sand and held the cold, sweating beer can against my forehead.

Thatcher sat down next to me. He was wearing jeans and a blue dress shirt with the sleeves rolled up. He had a navy sweater tied around his shoulders. "I was hoping you'd come," he said.

"This your party?"

"Not really. Some friends of mine own this beach."

"How nice for them."

"Isn't it?" He smiled. "You want to come let me introduce you around?"

"Give me a second."

"You still recovering from that thing?"

"I hope so. I'm still feeling it, anyway."

"Must be rough."

I shrugged. "I'm used to it now. It's part of my day-to-day. If it went away, I think I might actually miss it."

He looked at me. "You really believe that?"

"I don't know. Maybe I just said it."

We sat and drank together. The light from the fire played tricks with my vision and when I first saw her I thought it was my imagination. It would have been easy, through the heat shimmer, to have seen her face on another girl. I stared for a while. The face didn't change.

"Who's that?" I said.

Thatcher squinted into the firelight. "Which one?"

"In the white sweater. Talking now. Just touched the elbow of the girl next to her."

"Jamie Mitchell."

"What's funny?"

He shook his head. "Nothing."

"That bad?"

"You up to another beating?"

"For her?"

He shrugged. "I'll take you over."

We stood. I brushed the sand off my jeans.

Jamie Mitchell was standing with several other people. They were close enough to the fire that I could feel the heat on my skin as we walked toward her. When we arrived, the group stopped talking and looked at us.

"This is Alex," Thatcher said. "We went to college together."

The people in the circle introduced themselves. A kid with curly hair and a shell necklace said, "Where are you staying on the island?"

"My father has a house near Menemsha," I told him.

"What does he do?"

"As little as possible."

I looked around the circle and paused too long when I came to Jamie. I lowered my eyes. My heart was beating so hard I thought it might choke me.

"I love your sweater," she said.

I was wearing an old gray cable-knit sweater of my father's. "I think it's called a fisherman's sweater," I said.

She nodded. "I've never seen one like it."

The curly-haired kid said, "It's like the kind Picasso used to wear."

"Those were striped," someone said.

"I mean the *style*," the kid said.

"Also, Picasso's were more jerseys than sweaters. I think they were Cuban or something."

"I don't know about Cuban," someone else said and then the conversation was away from me.

Jamie moved over so that she was standing next to me. "I know you," she said.

"That's not impossible."

"You're working on my fiancé's house."

"Your fiancé," I said.

"Well, it's not really *his*. It's his family's."

I didn't say anything.

"You look like an athlete," she said.

"So do lots of people," I said.

"He's a boxer," Thatcher said.

"Not anymore," I said.

Thatcher turned to me. "You didn't tell me that."

I shrugged.

"What happened?" Jamie asked me.

"I got hurt."

"Were you a good boxer?"

"Yes."

"Could you have been a professional?" she said.

"Anyone can be a professional. All you have to do is pass the physical."

"Could you have been a champion?"

"No."

"Could you have come close?"

"No."

"I thought you were good."

"I am."

"I don't think I could ever hit anybody," she said.

"Almost everybody thinks that before they do it." I took a breath. "When I was five years old, my father brought me home a tiny pair of gloves. He showed me how to put them on and lace them up and make sure they were tight enough. Then he got down on his knees in front of me and told me to hit him."

Jamie's eyes were wide. "Did you?"

"Not at first. I just stared at him. Then he said, 'Hit me. You won't kill me.' "

"So you hit him."

I nodded. "All you need to learn is that you can hit him

and he can hit you and that it might hurt but you're not going to kill each other."

"Except sometimes," she said.

I nodded again. "Except sometimes."

The next day was Sunday and the hours stretched out like a desert. I went down into my father's basement and lifted his weights for a while. When I was done, I went running. I ran through the headache. The sun was heavy on my shoulders. My breath came in gasps and moans. Cramps seared my chest. When I got back, I walked back and forth along the porch with my hands on my hips. My throat felt raw. I coughed a few times and spit into the bushes.

I sat on the couch and thought about how I didn't have anything. The thought didn't give me any of the delicious self-pity thrill I was expecting. My father wandered downstairs from his bedroom. He flopped down across from me in his armchair.

"Why wasn't I a better fighter?" I said after a while.

He stared at me. "I didn't think you cared too much about that."

"Sometimes I wanted it so badly I thought I'd go crazy."

"Maybe you just want it now that you can't do it anymore."

"Why didn't you ever come watch me?"

He shrugged. "Who needs to watch two middle-class college boys fight? Fighting's what you do when you can't think what else to do. Middle-class boys always have something else. They don't need it enough to be good at it."

"What about Ali?"

"Ali's *black* middle class."

"That makes no difference to me."

"I'll bet it makes a difference to him."

I chewed my lip. "Anyway," I said, "why didn't you come watch me just because I was your son?"

He shifted his weight, which made the chair creak. "I don't need to watch my son try to be a thug."

"Then why did you teach me at all?"

"I also didn't want you to be one of those lily rich boys who doesn't know how to take care of himself. But there's a long way between that and being able to handle the real bangers."

"The guys I saw at the Gloves weren't bunnies."

He nodded. "Look what they did to you," he said.

I didn't call Thatcher Harrison for her phone number or to ask him to arrange another meeting. I didn't go to work every day at the house in Edgartown praying for her to show up. I was happy not to be seeing her again. I was happy during the bright mornings and the hot, lazy afternoons and I was very happy at night when I would lie in bed and dream I had been washed overboard and dragged away by the tide.

Thursday evening, my father and I met Billy Sanders and Dave Mayhew at the bar in Oak Bluffs. We sat at a table by the window. We all ordered beer.

The waitress squinted at my driver's license when I gave it to her. "Happy birthday," she said. She gave the license back to me.

"I remember my twenty-one," Dave Mayhew said when the waitress had gone.

"I don't," Billy Sanders said.

"I was with two girls at once," Dave said. "It was the only time."

"How much that cost you?" Billy said.

"Didn't cost me nothing."

"Like hell. You're not Sinatra."

Dave smiled. "My old man paid."

"Nice of him," my father said.

"I thought so."

"That the plan for tonight?" Billy said. "I could give him tomorrow off if he's having trouble walking."

"Having trouble walking anyway," I said.

"That's true. Good thing your father's got friends in high places."

"Like who?" Dave said.

Billy ignored him. "Otherwise you'd be out of luck. We don't really need a gimp on the job. Especially not one who can only work every other day." Billy had been drinking before he came to meet us. I hadn't noticed it until now.

"Go a little easy," my father told him.

"It's his birthday. Didn't you always take some on your birthday?"

"Sometimes. But that doesn't mean he has to."

This time when I saw her I was sure I was imagining it. We were on our third round of beers. I was looking across the street through the fading light and really it could have been almost anybody with the right body. She was with another girl. They were waiting in line outside the old wooden building that held the carousel. I watched them until they were out of sight inside the building.

When I turned back to the table, Dave Mayhew was smiling. So was my father.

Billy said, "That wouldn't be the girl who's marrying Greg Cunningham, would it?"

"How do you know I wasn't looking at the other one?"

He stared at me. "It *was* her, wasn't it?"

"It might have been," I admitted.

He shook his head.

"Your problem," I said, "is you've got no imagination."

He frowned.

My father said, "I spent my twenty-first birthday in jail."

We looked at him. He wasn't smiling anymore.

Dave said, "You never told me that."

My father shrugged. "It's not much of a story."

"Was it about a girl?"

"Why would you ask that?"

"I don't know. It seems as likely as anything else."

My father nodded. "But it wasn't jailbait and it wasn't any kind of restraining-order business."

"No," Dave said, "it wouldn't be that."

"As far as the cops were concerned, it wasn't about her at all. For them it was about her husband and whether he was gonna die."

"He come close?"

"Pretty close. He stayed in the coma almost three days."

"Rich man?"

"Rich man's son."

"He hit you first?"

"He didn't hit me at all. But he *swung* first."

"I suppose you told them that."

"Sure. But I had turned pro by then. My lawyer said it was the same as if he'd thrown a punch at me and I had pulled out a gun and shot him."

"What'd they want you to do?"

"Not use my hands, I guess. Maybe if I'd have just kicked him I would have been all right."

"You would have had to take off your shoes," Billy said. "Otherwise, the legal issue is still the same."

"I'm not sure he would have been willing to wait for that. He seemed quite anxious to get at me. Anyway, it wasn't really my hands that did the damage. It was the curb that got him on the way down. The cops didn't think too much of that distinction."

"Hard to blame the curb," Dave said. "It was just standing there."

"So was I," my father said. He sighed. "To be honest, I probably should have thought about the curb, but I hadn't fought outside a ring since I was fifteen. I forgot that on the street when they go down they don't just hit the canvas."

"Canvas can still hurt them if they hit wrong."

"Not like pavement." My father sipped his beer. "I was pretty dumb back then. You know, the thing that bothered me most in the lockup wasn't wondering how long I might be there or how I was gonna feel if he died. What really got under my skin was that the other prisoners didn't know who I was."

"You mean because if they'd known who you were they'd have left you alone?"

"They left me alone anyway. Everybody there was pretrial. They were all on best behavior. I just wanted them to know who I was. I wanted them to know we might have come from the same kind of place but I was somebody now. I wasn't like them."

Dave frowned. "You were young."

"Yeah."

"If you went to jail now, they'd know you," I said.

My father shook his head. "No, they still wouldn't. But it wouldn't matter to me so much."

"Smart man," Billy said.

My father took a deep breath. Then he smiled. "Handsome, too," he said. "Rare for a white pug these days."

Dave smiled back at him and nodded. "After the fifties, the white guys got pretty unfortunate. Faces like chew toys and clumsy and no class."

"There were still some," I said. I was happy to be talking about something else.

"Some," Dave said. "But mostly they were like that Chuck what'shisname that knocked down Ali."

"Wepner," my father said.

Dave nodded again. "Wepner."

Billy said, "Why haven't I heard of him if he knocked down Ali?"

"Ali didn't stay down," Dave told him.

"Sometimes they won't," my father said. "It can be awfully discouraging."

"Right after the knockdown, Wepner was in the neutral corner and he leaned out and said to his manager, 'Start the car. We're going to the bank. We're millionaires.' "

"Premature," my father said.

Dave grinned. "The manager said, 'You might want to turn around before we start counting our money, 'cause he just got up. And he looks pissed.' "

"He was, too. He knocked Wepner out of the ring."

"Not all the way. But he took him apart. After the ref called it, Wepner almost couldn't make it back to his corner."

"At least he didn't make any excuses."

"Like Liston did. Neither of them could stay in with Ali, though."

My father shrugged. "Neither could most people."

We drank. I watched the carousel building. When Jamie and the girl with her appeared in the doorway, I pushed my chair back and said, "I have to go."

My father looked at me. "Where?"

I stood. "Thanks for the beers. I'll find my own way back."

"What should I tell your mother when she calls to say happy birthday?"

"Tell her I'll call her when I get back if it's not too late."

He waved his hand. "I'll let the machine answer," he said.

I was across the street and standing in front of her before I realized I didn't have anything to say. The other girl was staring at me.

Jamie smiled. "Hello," she said.

I felt her voice in my stomach. "I don't know if you remember me."

"Don't be silly."

I gestured toward the bar. "I was having a drink with my father," I explained. "I saw you out the window."

"Is that him on the left?"

"That's right."

She nodded. She turned to the other girl. "Stephanie
Durham. Alex"—she turned back to me—"I forget your last
name."
"Folsom."
I shook Stephanie's hand.
"I'm about to take Stephanie home," Jamie said. "You
probably need to get back."
"Not really. I was feeling a little strange in there. Like my
head was full of paint."
"Alex was injured in the ring," she told Stephanie. "He's a
boxer."
"Really?" Stephanie said.
"No," I said, "but I used to be."
"Well," Jamie said, "would you want to take a ride?
Stephanie lives in Chilmark."
"Maybe."
"The air might be good for you. If I stop in Menemsha,
would you walk out on the jetty with me?"
"I don't see why not. It's down the road from my father's
house."
She smiled. "It's my favorite place in the world."
We drove on the road that twisted along the north side of
the island. There were forests on both sides and the road had
been cut in between. It was easy to imagine the island before
the road was here. It was easy to imagine the time when the
seas were frozen and the island was lifted by glaciers the size
of countries and laid down again and lifted again and laid
down until the ice melted. It was easy to imagine the time
before that when dinosaurs grazed over the ground where the
yacht club now stands and stomped giant footprints into the
private beaches.
We dropped Stephanie and got back on the road into Menemsha. We parked at my father's house and walked down
toward the water. The sky was dark now. The air was full of
mosquitoes.
"Your father was a boxer, too?" Jamie asked.

"You mean, because of his face?"

"Yes."

I nodded. "He was a boxer."

"Was he born here?"

I shook my head. "East Boston."

"When did he come?"

"When he stopped boxing."

"He brought your mother?"

"And me, but I was just a baby."

"And you lived here year-round?"

"Until she left him."

We walked along a fence past a yard with several dogs tied up inside it. The dogs turned their heads with us as we passed them.

Jamie said, "You graduated with Thatcher?"

"That's right."

"Do you know what you're going to do now?"

"I don't like to talk about it."

"What do you mean?"

"I don't like a lot of talk about plans. Most things you either do or you don't do. It doesn't help much either way to talk about it."

"I agree. Let's not talk about it."

"It doesn't leave much to talk about."

We passed Larsen's, the fish market, which was dark inside. The air tasted like salt. This close to the beach, there were no more mosquitoes. We walked through the parking lot beside the dock. We walked onto the sandy part of the parking lot and then up onto the sand and then onto the huge square stones that had been crammed together to make the jetty. We walked all the way out to the rusted light tower. In front of us we could see the blue light of the buoy and hear its bell ringing as the waves jostled it. In the darkness the water was like the top sheet on an enormous bed.

"I used to come here when I was a little girl," Jamie said.

"Pretty far from Edgartown."

"My family's house is out near Gay Head. I go to Edgartown to visit Gregory."

"I haven't seen you there lately."

"He usually only comes up on the weekends. He works during the week."

"Doing what?"

"Banking."

"Where?"

"New York."

"I meant, which bank?"

"Oh. Does it matter?"

I smiled. "Probably not. How did you meet him?"

"Our parents are friends. I've known him forever."

"How long have you been engaged?"

"A year."

I scraped my teeth against my lip. "I've never known anyone my age who was getting married."

"It's not so rare."

"I was shocked when you told me."

"Didn't you see my ring?" she said. "It's as big as the Ritz."

"I don't usually notice things like that."

We were silent for a while.

"We could talk about boxing. I've always wanted to know about it."

I shook my head. "No good."

"You shouldn't look at me that way," she said.

"What way?"

"You know."

"It's too dark for you to see how I'm looking at anything."

"There's a moon," she said.

"So you drove me all the way out here just because you felt sorry about my poor head?"

"Don't be mean. I'd like to be your friend."

"A girl like you is drowning in friends. What's one more or less?"

The air was cold off the ocean. Jamie was hugging herself to stay warm. "I like you," she said. "You're more interesting than most of the people I know."

I wanted to lean over and kiss her and smell her hair and carry her back to the house and lay her down on my bed and feel how warm she was. But I didn't know how to do any of that.

Some time later, I walked her back to her car and watched her drive away.

When the phone rang the next evening, I knew it wouldn't be her. Still, I wasn't surprised when I lifted the receiver and heard her voice.

"Thatcher gave me your number."

"Yes," I said.

"Can I come see you?"

"Of course."

"Right now?"

"If you want."

"You don't want me to?"

I listened to the ticking silence.

"I really do want to be your friend. I think maybe you got the wrong idea last night."

"Did I?" I said.

I strained to hear her breathing.

"I'm used to getting everything I want," she said after a long time. "I've never had to resist my impulses."

I didn't know what to feel. Until then, I had never quite believed any of it was true. "So why not just never see me again? Why make it hard on yourself?"

"Exposure is the only cure, I think. Anyway, it's a good test. Resisting temptation is part of what it means to be an adult."

"I don't know what it means to be an adult."

"Can I come over there?"

"Yes," I said.

I went into the living room to wait. I couldn't sit still. I paced in front of the window. Every time I heard a car engine I held my breath. My father sat in his armchair and shook his head.

When Jamie's SUV pulled into the driveway, my father said, "You're on your own." He dragged himself out of his chair and shuffled up the stairs to his bedroom.

She walked quickly toward the house with the light fading behind her. She was wearing a flowered sundress and white canvas sneakers. I met her at the door.

"Do you want to come in?"

"Come out," she said. "It's so beautiful."

We walked to the far end of my father's lawn without speaking. Next to us, the pool was steaming.

"Do you want to go swimming?" I said.

"It's a little cold for that."

"It's heated."

"Even so."

I imagined for a moment that the sound of the crickets was really the sound of the trees' breathing.

"Doesn't your fiancé usually come in on the weekends?"

"They were having weather problems in New York."

"He flies," I said.

"Of course."

"Of course."

She looked away from me. "I want you to teach me to fight."

"You know, sometimes I feel like that's all anybody ever wants to talk to me about."

"It's interesting," she said. "It's also safe. Anyway, I don't want to talk about it, I want you to teach me."

"Now?"

"Why not?"

I took a breath. "I haven't really been practicing."

"But you didn't forget how." She sighed. "You can't live your whole life treating yourself like you're made of china."

I ran my tongue over my bottom lip. "Make a fist," I said. She smiled.

"Keep your thumb bent and down to the side. If you keep it straight out like that you'll break it." I walked around behind her. "Now, keep your right hand locked against your jaw. Keep the left up too, but out in front of you and turned out a little. Keep your elbows in tight to your body. When you punch, you start and end in this position. Don't pull your hands back or drop them down before you throw and don't leave them stuck out for show after they land. You get back to this position as quick as you can. Make sure you're off balance as little as possible. Make sure your legs never cross. Keep your chin down. Always be ready. When you punch, explode from your legs and through your shoulder and throw your fist straight out like a bullet out of a gun."

She tried that a few times.

"You have to step into your punches," I said.

"That feels unnatural."

"As you get better, the step gets smaller. When you're good, the step is so small you almost can't see it."

"So why learn it this way?"

"At the beginning you have to take a real step to learn how to throw with your weight behind it."

She frowned.

"My father used to say imagine there's a ditch in front of you filled with alligators. Every time you punch, you have to think about stepping over the ditch."

She sighed. "When do I get to fight *you*?"

"I'm not sure you're ready for that."

"I thought you said you'd teach me."

"Not in one night. Where's your patience?"

"I don't have much." She turned toward me. "Come on. Tell me how you'd fight you. If you were me."

I looked at her. Then I said, "You'll want to stay inside to take away my reach advantage."

"What's 'inside'?" she asked.

"Inside just means close to me."

"So I have to stay close to you."

I felt the tingle along my spine. "Right," I said. "But first you have to *get* inside."

"How?"

I shrugged. "There's no one way. Mostly, you have to be willing to pay the price. I'll be trying to keep you off me by jabbing, which holds you at the proper range for my overhand right. Some people say jab a jabber, which means your job would be to counter with your own jab and use that to cover you so you can get close to me. Another way would be to just bull in under my jab. You'd have to eat a few if you did that, but probably you'd have to eat a few no matter what. Anyway, once you're inside you'll have to crowd me so I can't create enough distance between us to use my right hand and so you can keep us fighting inside where the shorter fighter has an advantage because it's easier for him to work to his opponent's body."

"Her," she said.

"What?"

"Easier for *her*."

I smiled. "If you can stay inside against a tall opponent, there's a chance he'll just fold, because the really tall guys usually aren't effective close in."

"You're not all that tall. You're not even six feet."

"Tall enough. Taller than you, anyway. But, unfortunately for you, my left hook is my best punch, which means I'm more dangerous inside than out. The only way to give yourself a chance is to try to beat me to the punch and throw your own left hook inside mine. If yours lands first and hits me as I'm putting my body into mine, then you'll be using my own power against me."

"Kind of like jab a jabber."

"Kind of," I said.

We walked back to the house with our bodies very close to each other but not touching. When we hugged good-bye at the door, she wouldn't let go. I looked at her.

"One of your eyes is smaller than the other," she said.

"I realize that."

"It's not noticeable unless you're really close and really looking."

"Yes."

She was looking up at me with big eyes.

Much later, when my headaches were gone and the summer had ended and Jamie's wedding was coming like a train, my days would blend together. I woke up. I ate. I worked. I lay in bed with Jamie and pulled the covers over us and the hours didn't pass and the world disappeared. I slept. At the end of every day there would be a moment when I thought I couldn't take it.

"You can't marry him," I would say then. "I love you."

"It's not that easy," Jamie would say.

"It should be," I would tell her.

But that night, in my father's living room, I didn't know about any of that. I said, "I'm going to kiss you."

"All right," Jamie said.

"Unless you tell me not to, I'm going to kiss you."

"Yes."

"Do you want me to?"

"Yes. You know I do."

I kissed her with my hands around her waist. She had one hand on the back of my neck. When we took a breath, I leaned back and looked at her face. I moved in again and kissed her again and then we were tearing at each other like animals. I was happy and desperate and delirious and frustrated all at once. Still, some part of me was very calm.

I took her to bed.

"Talk to me," she whispered after a while.

I pressed my lips against her ear, burying my face in her hair. "It's mine," I growled.

She gasped and pulled herself toward me even harder.

"It's mine," I told her.

"It's yours," she said between breaths.

My teeth were clenched. "It's always mine."

She held herself against me so that her back wasn't touching the bed. "Oh, my God," she said.

I licked her ear.

"Oh, my God," she said. "I'm coming."

She moved her hips against me. I felt the wave rising inside me, so I closed my eyes and thought about pain. Jamie's arms tightened around my neck.

"I'm coming," she said.

I felt the wave rising again. I imagined smoldering cities that bled rivers of refugees with burnt-paper skin hanging off them like rags. I pulled my head back out of Jamie's hair and opened my eyes to make sure she was still there. Her eyes were shut. Her lips shook like she was about to cry.

"I'm coming," she said. "I'm still coming."

This is real, I thought. But, really, it didn't matter.

A NOTE ABOUT THE AUTHOR

Benjamin Cavell attended Harvard College, where he was a boxer and an editor for The Harvard Crimson. Rumble, Young Man, Rumble *is his first book.*

A NOTE ON THE TYPE

The text of this book was composed in Trump Mediæval.
Designed by Professor Georg Trump (1896–1985) in the mid-
1950s, Trump Mediæval was cut and cast by the C. E. Weber
Type Foundry of Stuttgart, Germany. The roman letter forms
are based on classical prototypes, but Professor Trump has
imbued them with his own unmistakable style. The italic
letter forms, unlike those of so many other typefaces, are
closely related to their roman counterparts. The result is
a truly contemporary type, notable for both its
legibility and its versatility.

Composed by Creative Graphics, Allentown, Pennsylvania

Printed and bound by R. R. Donnelley & Sons, Harrisonburg, Virginia

Designed by Iris Weinstein